LYLE

CASHING IN ON COLLECTING AMERICANA

Anthony Curtis

A PERIGEE BOOK

While every care has been taken in the compiling of information contained in this volume, the publisher cannot accept liability for loss, financial or otherwise, incurred by reliance placed on the information herein.

All prices quoted in this book are obtained from a variety of auctions in various countries during the twelve months prior to publication and are converted to dollars at the rate of exchange prevalent at the time of sale.

The publishers wish to express their sincere thanks to the following for their involvement and assistance in the production of this volume:

Eelin McIvor (*Sub Editor*)	Frank Burrell (*Graphics*)
Nicky Fairburn (*Art Director*)	James Brown (*Graphics*)
Annette Curtis (*Editorial*)	Donna Rutherford
Catriona Day (*Art Production*)	Jacqueline Leddy
Donna Cruickshank (*Art Production*)	Eileen Burrell
Angie Demarco (*Art Production*)	

Perigee Books
are published by
The Berkley Publishing Group
200 Madison Avenue
New York, NY 10016

Library of Congress Cataloging-in-Publication Data

Curtis, Tony, date.
Cashing in on collecting Americana / Anthony Curtis.
p.   cm.
Includes index.
ISBN 0-399-51809-6
1. Americana—Collectors and collecting—Catalogs.   I. Title.
NK805.C88   1993   93-2841   CIP
973'.075—dc20

Cover design by Pat Smythe

Printed in the United States of America
7   8   9   10

This book is printed on acid-free paper.
∞

Trash or Treasure?

T he urge to collect starts very early in life – look at the stamp collections and scrap books which have entranced countless numbers of boys and girls over the last hundred years or so, to say nothing of the cards, stickers or whatever which are 'swapped' daily in schoolyards the world over.

And it's getting more and more difficult to assess just what collectibles are going to fetch big money in the future, given that, as the purists lament, the market appears to be becoming wackier by the moment.

In the past year, the major auction houses have offered collections of such items as Vintage Jeans, Baseball Cards, cells. from Walt Disney cartoons, Coca Cola signs, gas stoves, Hollywood posters and 'personality' items by the score.

Nostalgia has got to be the moving force here, which means that, more than ever, these old, fondly kept souvenirs in the attic have a real chance of fetching big money. If you can bring yourself to part with them that is.

With the 'personality cult' syndrome running at an all time high, the art is to spot who are the men and women of the moment, and which of them will pass into the realms of immortality alongside Shakespeare, George Washington, Lincoln, etc. At Christie's in New York recently, bidders gambled that Muhammed Ali belonged to the latter category, when they took a pair of his autographed fight trunks to $13,200. Then, too, baseball stars are always a good bet, now that the early years of this century have become established as a kind of

The 1907 Honus Wagner NL Champion Batter presentation Medal in the form of a yellow eagle above crossed baseball bats and pendant plaque set with flags and baseball player.
(Christie's) $77,000

golden age of the game, featuring such immortal names as Honus Wagner, Eddie Plank and Sherwood Magee. A Sherwood Magee cigarette card with a spelling error fetched $26,000 while Honus Wagner's NL Champion Batter's Presentation Medal of 1907 went all the way to $77,000. Nor must we forget that Sotheby's in New York achieved the all time record of $451,000 for the Honus Wagner T206 cigarette card.

Away from such heady and volatile heights (though the popularity of such items shows no signs of waning) there is the rich mainstream of traditional Americana collecting, which continues to increase in popularity.

The T206 Sherwood Magee 'Magie' error card, the reverse featuring an advertisement for Piedmont cigarettes, near mint condition, 1909–11.
(Christie's) $26,000

Muhammed Ali World Championship autographed fight trunks, black and white satin trunks worn during Ali's bout with George Foreman in Zaire in 1974, and presented to Daniel Ray, who was in Ali's corner. (Christie's) $13,200

In this wide field there are collecting themes to suit all tastes and pockets, and in this book examples will be found of just about all of them. Its aim is to help you recognise potentially valuable items when you see them, and tells you what similar examples have fetched at auction recently. Remember, however, that condition plays a vital part in determining the value of any item. Prices quoted here are for pieces in fair and average condition. Remember, too that the popularity of the collecting field can play almost as important a part as the rarity of the object.

Collecting is a world full of surprises and amazing opportunities. We hope that the information contained in this book will help you to enjoy it even more.

Anthony Curtis

Acknowledgements

AB Stockholms Auktionsverk, Box 16256, 103 25 Stockholm, Sweden
Abbotts Auction Rooms, The Auction Rooms, Campsea Ash, Woodbridge, Suffolk
Abridge Auction Rooms, Market Place, Abridge, Essex RM4 1UA
Allen & Harris, St Johns Place, Whiteladies Road, Clifton, Bristol BS8 2ST
Jean Claude Anaf, Lyon Brotteaux, 13 bis place Jules Ferry, 69456 Lyon, France
Anderson & Garland, Marlborough House, Marlborough Crescent, Newcastle upon Tyne NE1 4EE
Antique Collectors Club & Co. Ltd, 5 Church Street, Woodbridge, Suffolk IP 12 1DS
Auction Team Köln, Postfach 50 11 68, D-5000 Köln 50 Germany
Auktionshaus Arnold, Bleichstr. 42, 6000 Frankfurt a/M, Germany
Barber's Auctions, Woking, Surrey
Brian Bates, Fairview, Maer, Newcastle, Staffs
Bearnes, Rainbow, Avenue Road, Torquay TQ2 5TG
Biddle & Webb, Ladywood Middleway, Birmingham B16 0PP
Bigwood, The Old School, Tiddington, Stratford upon Avon
Black Horse Agencies, Locke & England, 18 Guy Street, Leamington Spa
Boardman Fine Art Auctioneers, Station Road Corner, Haverhill, Suffolk CB9 0EY
Bonhams, Montpelier Street, Knightsbridge, London SW7 1HH
Bonhams Chelsea, 65–69 Lots Road, London SW10 0RN
Bonhams West Country, Dowell Street, Honiton, Devon
British Antique Exporters, School Close, Queen Elizabeth Avenue, Burgess Hill, Sussex
William H Brown, The Warner Auction Rooms, 16–18, Halford Street, Leicester LE1 1JB
Butterfield & Butterfield, 220 San Bruno Avenue, San Francisco CA 94103, USA
Butterfield & Butterfield, 7601 Sunset Boulevard, Los Angeles CA 90046, USA
Central Motor Auctions, Barfield House, Britannia Road, Morley, Leeds, LS27 0HN
H.C. Chapman & Son, The Auction Mart, North Street, Scarborough.
Christie's (International) SA, 8 place de la Taconnerie, 1204 Genève, Switzerland
Christie's Monaco, S.A.M, Park Palace 98000 Monte Carlo, Monaco
Christie's Scotland, 164–166 Bath Street Glasgow G2 4TG
Christie's South Kensington Ltd., 85 Old Brompton Road, London SW7 3LD
Christie's, 8 King Street, London SW1Y 6QT
Christie's East, 219 East 67th Street, New York, NY 10021, USA`
Christie's, 502 Park Avenue, New York, NY 10022, USA
Christie's, Cornelis Schuytstraat 57, 1071 JG Amsterdam, Netherlands
Christie's SA Roma, 114 Piazza Navona, 00186 Rome, Italy
Christie's Swire, 1202 Alexandra House, 16–20 Chater Road, Hong Kong
Christie's Australia Pty Ltd., 1 Darling Street, South Yarra, Melbourne, Victoria 3141, Australia
A J Cobern, The Grosvenor Sales Rooms, 93b Eastbank Street, Southport PR8 1DG
Cooper Hirst Auctions, The Granary Saleroom, Victoria Road, Chelmsford, Essex CM2 6LH
Nic Costa, 166 Camden Street, London, NW1 9PT
The Crested China Co., Station House, Driffield, E. Yorks YO25 7PY
Clifford Dann, 20/21 High Street, Lewes, Sussex
Julian Dawson, Lewes Auction Rooms, 56 High Street, Lewes BN7 1XE
Dee & Atkinson, The Exchange Saleroom, Driffield, Nth Humberside YO25 7LJ
Garth Denham & Assocs. Horsham Auction Galleries, Warnsham, Nr. Horsham, Sussex
Diamond Mills & Co., 117 Hamilton Road, Felixstowe, Suffolk
David Dockree Fine Art, 224 Moss Lane, Bramhall, Stockport SK7 1BD
Dowell Lloyd & Co. Ltd, 118 Putney Bridge Road, London SW15 2NQ
Downer Ross, Charter House, 42 Avebury Boulevard, Central Milton Keynes MK9 2HS
Hy. Duke & Son, 40 South Street, Dorchester, Dorset
Du Mouchelles Art Galleries Co., 409 E. Jefferson Avenue, Detroit, Michigan 48226, USA
Duncan Vincent, 105 London Street, Reading RG1 4LF
Sala de Artes y Subastas Durán, Serrano 12, 28001 Madrid, Spain
Eldred's, Box 796, E. Dennis, MA 02641, USA
R H Ellis & Sons, 44/46 High St., Worthing, BN11 1LL
Ewbanks, Welbeck House, High Street, Guildford, Surrey, GU1 3JF
Fellows & Son, Augusta House, 19 Augusta Street, Hockley, Birmingham
Finarte, 20121 Milano, Piazzetta Bossi 4, Italy
John D Fleming & Co., 8 Fore Street, Dulverton, Somerset
G A Property Services, Canterbury Auction Galleries, Canterbury, Kent
Galerie Koller, Rämistr. 8, CH 8024 Zürich, Switzerland
Galerie Moderne, 3 rue du Parnasse, 1040 Bruxelles, Belgium
Geering & Colyer (Black Horse Agencies) Highgate, Hawkhurst, Kent
Glerum Auctioneers, Westeinde 12, 2512 HD's Gravenhage, Netherlands
The Goss and Crested China Co., 62 Murray Road, Horndean, Hants PO8 9JL
Graves Son & Pilcher, 71 Church Road, Hove, East Sussex, BN3 2GL
Greenslade Hunt, 13 Hammet Street, Taunton, Somerset, TA1 1RN
Peter Günnemann, Ehrenberg Str. 57, 2000 Hamburg 50, Germany
Halifax Property Services, 53 High Street, Tenterden, Kent
Halifax Property Services, 15 Cattle Market, Sandwich, Kent CT13 9AW
Hampton's Fine Art, 93 High Street, Godalming, Surrey
Hanseatisches Auktionshaus für Historica, Neuer Wall 57, 2000 Hamburg 36, Germany
Andrew Hartley Fine Arts, Victoria Hall, Little Lane, Ilkely
Hauswedell & Nolte, D-2000 Hamburg 13, Pöseldorfer Weg 1, Germany
Giles Haywood, The Auction House, St John's Road, Stourbridge, West Midlands, DY8 1EW

7

Heatheringtons Nationwide Anglia, The Amersham Auction Rooms, 125 Station Road, Amersham, Bucks
Muir Hewitt, Halifax Antiques Centre, Queens Road/Gibbet Street, Halifax HX1 4LR
Hobbs & Chambers, 'At the Sign of the Bell', Market Place, Cirencester, Glos
Hobbs Parker, Romney House, Ashford, Ashford, Kent
Hotel de Ventes Horta, 390 Chaussée de Waterloo (Ma Campagne), 1060 Bruxelles, Belgium
Jacobs & Hunt, Lavant Street, Petersfield, Hants. GU33 3EF
James of Norwich, 33 Timberhill, Norwich NR1 3LA
P Herholdt Jensens Auktioner, Rundforbivej 188, 2850 Nerum, Denmark
Kennedy & Wolfenden, 218 Lisburn Rd, Belfast BT9 6GD
G A Key, Aylsham Saleroom, Palmers Lane, Aylsham, Norfolk, NR11 6EH
Kunsthaus am Museum, Drususgasse 1–5, 5000 Köln 1, Germany
Kunsthaus Lempertz, Neumarkt 3, 5000 Köln 1, Germany
Lambert & Foster (County Group), The Auction Sales Room, 102 High Street, Tenterden, Kent
W.H. Lane & Son, 64 Morrab Road, Penzance, Cornwall, TR18 2QT
Langlois Ltd., Westway Rooms, Don Street, St Helier, Channel Islands
Lawrence Butler Fine Art Salerooms, Marine Walk, Hythe, Kent, CT21 5AJ
Lawrence Fine Art, South Street, Crewkerne, Somerset TA18 8AB
Lawrence's Fine Art Auctioneers, Norfolk House, 80 High Street, Bletchingley, Surrey
David Lay, The Penzance Auction House, Alverton, Penzance, Cornwall TA18 4KE
Brian Loomes, Calf Haugh Farm, Pateley Bridge, North Yorks
Lots Road Chelsea Auction Galleries, 71 Lots Road, Chelsea, London SW10 0RN
R K Lucas & Son, Tithe Exchange, 9 Victoria Place, Haverfordwest, SA61 2JX
Duncan McAlpine, Stateside Comics plc, 125 East Barnet Road, London EN4 8RF
John Maxwell, 75 Hawthorn Street, Wilmslow, Cheshire
May & Son, 18 Bridge Street, Andover, Hants
Morphets, 4–6 Albert Street, Harrogate, North Yorks HG1 1JL
D M Nesbit & Co, 7 Clarendon Road, Southsea, Hants PO5 2ED
Onslow's, Metrostore, Townmead Road, London SW6 2RZ
Outhwaite & Litherland, Kingsley Galleries, Fontenoy Street, Liverpool, Merseyside L3 2BE
J R Parkinson Son & Hamer Auctions, The Auction Rooms, Rochdale, Bury, Lancs
Phillips Manchester, Trinity House, 114 Northenden Road, Sale, Manchester M33 3HD
Phillips Son & Neale SA, 10 rue des Chaudronniers, 1204 Genève, Switzerland
Phillips West Two, 10 Salem Road, London W2 4BL
Phillips, 11 Bayle Parade, Folkestone, Kent CT20 1SQ
Phillips, 49 London Road, Sevenoaks, Kent TN13 1UU
Phillips, 65 George Street, Edinburgh EH2 2JL
Phillips, Blenstock House, 7 Blenheim Street, New Bond Street, London W1Y 0AS
Phillips Marylebone, Hayes Place, Lisson Grove, London NW1 6UA
Phillips, New House, 150 Christleton Road, Chester CH3 5TD
Pinney's, 5627 Ferrier, Montreal, Quebec, Canada H4P 2M4
Pooley & Rogers, Regent Auction Rooms, Abbey Street, Penzance
Harry Ray & Co, Lloyds Bank Chambers, Welshpool, Montgomery SY21 7RR
Rennie's, 1 Agincourt Street, Monmouth
Riddetts, Richmond Hill, Bournemouth
Ritchie's, 429 Richmond Street East, Toronto, Canada M5A 1R1
Derek Roberts Antiques, 24–25 Shipbourne Road, Tonbridge, Kent TN10 3DN
Rogers de Rin, 79 Royal Hospital Road, London SW3 4HN
Russell, Baldwin & Bright, The Fine Art Saleroom, Ryelands Road, Leominster HR6 8JG
Sandoes Nationwide Anglia, Tabernacle Road, Wotton under Edge, Glos GL12 7EB
Selkirk's, 4166 Olive Street, St Louis, Missouri 63108, USA
Skinner Inc., Bolton Gallery, Route 117, Bolton MA, USA
Southgate Auction Rooms, 55 High St, Southgate, London N14 6LD
Henry Spencer, 40 The Square, Retford, Notts. DN22 6DJ
Spink & Son Ltd, 5-7 King St., St James's, London SW1Y 6QS
Street Jewellery, 16 Eastcliffe Avenue, Newcastle upon Tyne NE3 4SN
Stride & Son, Southdown House, St John's St., Chichester, Sussex
G E Sworder & Son, Northgate End Salerooms, 15 Northgate End, Bishop Stortford, Herts
Taviner's of Bristol, Prewett Street, Redcliffe, Bristol BS1 6PB
Tennants, 27 Market Place, Leyburn, Yorkshire
Thomson Roddick & Laurie, 24 Lowther Street, Carlisle
Thomson Roddick & Laurie, 60 Whitesands, Dumfries
Timbleby & Shorland, 31 Gt Knollys St, Reading RG1 7HU
Venator & Hanstein, Cäcilienstr. 48, 5000 Köln 1, Germany
T Vennett Smith, 11 Nottingham Road, Gotham, Nottingham NG11 0HE
Duncan Vincent, 105 London Road, Reading RG1 4LF
Wallis & Wallis, West Street Auction Galleries, West Street, Lewes, E. Sussex BN7 2NJ
Ward & Morris, Stuart House, 18 Gloucester Road, Ross on Wye HR9 5BN
Warren & Wignall Ltd, The Mill, Earnshaw Bridge, Leyland Lane, Leyland PR5 3PH
Dominique Watine-Arnault, 11 rue François 1er, 75008 Paris, France
Wells Cundall Nationwide Anglia, Staffordshire House, 27 Flowergate, Whitby YO21 3AX
Woltons, 6 Whiting Street, Bury St Edmunds, Suffolk IP33 1LH
Peter Wilson, Victoria Gallery, Market Street, Nantwich, Cheshire CW5 5DG
Woolley & Wallis, The Castle Auction Mart, Salisbury, Wilts SP1 3SU
Austin Wyatt Nationwide Anglia, Emsworth Road, Lymington, Hants SO41 9BL

CONTENTS

Early 20th century drug store. Moxie sign, 23½ x 31¾in. $1,250

American 19th century sheet metal hatter's sign, 14in. high. $2,000

Duke's tobacco advertising sign, America, 18½in. wide. $500

Painted and decorated rubber trade sign, Ales Goodyear Shoe Co., Nagatuck, Connecticut, late 19th century, painted red and enhanced with white and blue, 35¼in. high. (Skinner Inc.) $935

'New England Organ Company' advertising sign, 24 x 34in. $1,000

Lithographed sheet metal trade sign, National Carbon Company, Cleveland, Ohio, early 20th century, 26¼in. high. (Skinner Inc.) $425

Dr. Fitler's Rheumatic Syrup sign, circa 1880, 19½ x 13½in. $3,000

'Coca Cola' advertising tip tray, oval, America, circa 1907. $400

Lithographed advertisement for Egyptienne 'Straights' cigarettes, 31in. high. $200

A painted and stenciled wooden trade sign, American, early 20th century, bearing an oil rig and motor-driven transport truck on a mustard ground within a green-painted and gold-stenciled frame, 35¼in. long. (Christie's) $3,520

'Dr. Harter's little liver pills' advertising pitcher, silver plate, 13in. high, *Dr. Harter's Iron Tonic* on reverse. (Skinner Inc.) $270

A 1920's metal-body hanging advertising sign in the shape of a film box with hanging panel and mounted bracket. (Christie's) $285

Henry Raleigh, 'Halt The Hun! Buy US Government Bonds Third Liberty Loan', double crown. (Onslow's) $30

Painted and decorated painter's sign, America, late 19th century, painted red and embellished with white, yellow and blue flourishes, 32¼ x 28½in. (Skinner Inc.) $1,320

A metal Rose & Co. lithograph sign, and advertisement for 'Merchant Tailors', circa 1900, 26½in. high. $450

Poster for George Humphrey's bookstore, by M. Louise Stowell, 1896, 11 x 15½in. (Robt. W. Skinner Inc.) $300

A photographic electric advertising lamp with decorated shade *Travel with a Kodak* and *Remember with a Kodak*, 13½in. high, mid 1920s. (Christie's S. Ken) $400

'8 Bells' comedy poster, by Strobridge Lithograph Co., Ohio, circa 1910, 40 x 30in. $150

'Star Wind Mill' advertising poster, 20th century, depicting a windmill inscribed *FLINT AND WALLING M.F.G. CO., KENDALLVILLE, IND.*, 14 x 11in.
(Butterfield & Butterfield)
$550

Antique advertising sign in the form of a boot, painted black and inscribed *J.W. Bilodeau*, 27in. high.
(Eldred's) $66

Important carved wood trade sign, in the form of a bull's head with antique swirl glass marble eyes, carved by John Bent, Edgartown, Massachusetts, 35³/₄in. x 40in.
(Eldred's) $4,675

A leaded glass pharmacy sign, America, 64½in. wide. (Robt. W. Skinner Inc.)
$1,000

'Flea Circus' stained glass window, circa 1900, 5ft. long. (Robt. W. Skinner Inc.)
$750

Edward Henry Potthast (American, 1857–1927), *The July Number – The Century*/ An advertising poster for the July 1896 issue, 21¹/₄ x 16in.
(Skinner Inc.) $275

A carved and painted cigar store Indian, American, late 19th century, carved in the form of an Indian princess with a gold feather headdress above long groove-carved black hair and carved gold earrings, 72¹/₂in. high.
(Christie's) $13,200

Tin advertising sign for 'Murphy Da-Cote Enamel', lithograph by H. D. Beach, Co., Ohio, circa 1925, 27 x 19in. (Robt. W. Skinner Inc.)
$1,250

A metal Kodak store sign, triangular with heavy metal bracket, 'Developing Printing Enlarging'. $200

Crown, American petrol pump globe, made of glass. (Onslow's) $700

A shaving advertising sign, advertising 'Antiseptic Cup, Brush and Soap', circa 1910, 18¼ x 14in. $700

A 19th century roll down wall cigar advertisement, chromolithographed on canvas backed paper, 54 x 39½in. $250

Late 19th century Clock Shop trade sign, iron and zinc painted, 23in. wide. $350

Painted and decorated trade sign, signed 'T. M. Woodward', Worcester, Massachusetts, circa 1873, the rectangular bowed metal panel painted dark green and decorated in polychrome, 48in. high. (Robt. W. Skinner Inc.) $40,000

Late 19th century Elgin watch advertising sign, entitled 'My Elgin's All Right', 22 x 15in. $300

Walnut cabinet used for the display and storage of fabric dyes, the polychrome decorated door inscribed *It's easy to dye with Diamond Dyes*, 23in. wide. (Eldred's) $385

A metal 'El Roi-Tan' chromo-lithograph advertising sign, 24¼ x 20in. $200

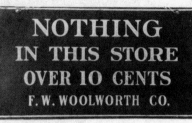

'White Rock' advertising tip tray, copy reads 'White Rock, The World's Best Table Water.' $75

Reverse on glass Woolworth's sign, circa 1900, 20 x 36in. $1,000

'Reliance' cigar display, manufactured by Nosch & Co., circa 1880, 17½in. high. $2,500

'Buckeye' Farm Equipment sign, by The Winters Print & Litho Co., Springfield, Ohio', 1880-1890, 30 x 21¾in. $750

The Spalding Co. Iron Advertising trade sign, the cast-iron pocket watch frame with zinc painted face, 22¼in. high, circa 1890. $750

Tobacco advertising sign, 'Red Indian', chromolithographed on thin cardboard, circa 1900, 28 x 22in. $550

None Such Mince Meat sign, head of an Onondaga Indian chief, circa 1890, 28 x 20in. $2,500

A polychrome zinc trade sign, America, early 20th century, in form of a hip-roofed house with projecting porch, 32in. high. $800

Large lithographed tin sign advertising Harvard Beer, circa 1910, 26¾in. wide. $1,000

Rare pair of Southeast American Indian moccasins, probably Delaware, circa 1880s, pink, turquoise and dark blue beaded decoration, 10in. long. (Eldred's) $990

Acoma polychrome pottery jar, with wide flaring sides and tapering rim, a geometric band at top, 10¼in. high. (Butterfield & Butterfield) $1,980

Pair of Athabaskan boots, circa 1910, with beadwork decoration. (Eldred's) $193

Hopi Kachina doll representing Heheya, shown with arms pressed to the midriff, the red and yellow torso supporting a pale blue casemask, 9¾in. high. (Butterfield & Butterfield) $715

Pair of Crow beaded gauntlets, partially beaded on hide, with stars on the hands, the cuffs filled by an elaborate floral configuration in polychrome beads, 16in. long. (Butterfield & Butterfield) $660

Sioux beaded panel from the Battle at Little Big Horn, consisting of a trapezoidal hide panel taken from a cradle cover, fully beaded with stepped triangles, diamonds and a roll-beaded edge, 16in. long. (Butterfield & Butterfield) $6,600

Northern Plains beaded yoke, fully beaded on buffalo hide, depicting a four-directional diamond medallion flanked by two corner stars, 16½in. long. (Butterfield & Butterfield) $935

Ojibwa beaded bandolier bag, consisting of a loom-beaded geometric panel with tab and tassel suspensions, fastened to a cloth background, 46in. long. (Butterfield & Butterfield) $1,980

Rare Navajo Germantown sampler, mixed recarded background with blue, white and yellow geometric decoration, 21in. square. (Eldred's) $605

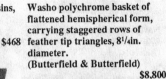

Pair of Santee Sioux moccasins, circa 1870s, with floral decoration, 7in. long. (Eldred's) $468

Washo polychrome basket of flattened hemispherical form, carrying staggered rows of feather tip triangles, 8¼in. diameter. (Butterfield & Butterfield) $8,800

Makah wood wolf headdress, having allover relief-carved ovals and characteristic motifs, 22in. long. (Butterfield & Butterfield) $770

Northwest Coast bentwood box, the square container painted on opposing sides with elaborate traditional renditions of supernatural beings or animals, 25¼in. high. (Butterfield & Butterfield) $4,950

Apache basket, with central solid four-petal device, surrounded by double-banded and solid zig-zags in a diamond lattice pattern, 18¼in. diameter. (Butterfield & Butterfield) $1,540

Woodlands Indian mittens, circa 1890, with floral beadwork decoration, 11in. long. (Eldred's) $770

Zuni polychrome pottery bowl, the interior with linear rim band, solid colored parrots in contrasting tones, 11¼in. diameter. (Butterfield & Butterfield) $8,800

Hopi Kachina doll representing Hututu, standing with arms close to the body, the case mask with domed top, semi-circle ear and one long horn, 14¼in. high. (Butterfield & Butterfield) $3,025

Pima miniature basket, very finely woven, the slightly flaring sides drawn with concentric angular box meanders, 5¼in. diameter. (Butterfield & Butterfield) $825

Northwest coast polychrome wood face mask, carved and incised cedar, 9½in. high. $3,000

Navajo Gray Hills rug, circa 1920, 48 x 84in. (Eldred's) $880

Woodlands wood face mask, Seneca False Face Soc., 14in. high. $650

A classic Navajo chief's blanket, woven in single strand homespun and raveled yarn, 82 x 62in. (Skinner Inc) $35,000

A Verneh horse blanket, the blue field with rows of stylized animals, 5ft.5in. x 4ft.7in. $1,500

Navajo Yei rug, woven with two rows of opposing skirted Yeibachi figures in red, white and black on a natural gray ground, 66 x 96in. $1,500

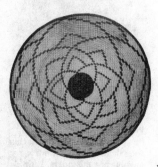

Southwestern coiled basketry tray, Apache, 22½in. diam. $1,500

Navajo pictorial Germantown weaving with full yarn tassels on corners, 58 x 92in. $350

Southwestern polychromed jar, Acoma, 13¼in. diam. $1,500

Woodlands husk face mask, composed of bands of braided cornhusks, 11½in. high. $1,500

Pacific Northwest Coast Attu circular basket with cover, 4in. high. (Christie's) $1,980

Cherokee polychrome wood face mask, Boogerman Dance Mask, made by Will West Long, 16in. high. $750

Plains beaded hide blanket strip, Sioux, sinew sewn, 66in. long. $1,500

Quilled tanned skin shirt, circa 1840. (Christie's) $52,700

Early 19th century Northern Plains pipe tomahawk, 18in. long. $5,000

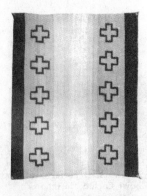

Navajo woman's manta, home-spun, 33½ x 42in. $3,000

A Southwestern polychrome basketry tray, Yavapai, woven in red and dark brown designs on a golden field, 14½in. diam. $1,250

Navajo pictorial weaving, woven on a natural gray ground with geometric design motifs, 47 x 76in. $1,000

Woodlands wood bowl
of oval form with handle
in form of a human head,
13in. long. $7,100

A Navajo silver Concho belt,
comprised of nine open-
center conchos and a
buckle. $1,000

Southwest Indian black
circular pot, signed Maria,
8in. diameter. $1,500

Northwest coast wood
polychromed ladle,
'1907', 21in. long.
          $750

Northwest Coast polychrome
wood rattle, cedar, carved in
two sections and joined with
square metal nails, 11¼in.
long. $500

Plains beaded and fringed
hide pipebag, Sioux/Arapaho,
1880's, 23½in. long. $1,750

Antique American Indian
basket from Oregon, 9 x 7in.,
circa 1890. (Du Mouchelles)
          $100

Eskimo painted hide, ink
gouache on native tanned
sealskin, signed Wilber
Walluk, 42 x 48in.
          $1,500

Southern Plains painted
buffalo fur robe, 92in. long,
67in. wide. $750

Zia Olla, white slipped
olla decorated on black
and red, 12in. diam.
          $800

20th century Tlingit carved
wooden rattle, 12in. long.
          $2,000

Southwestern pottery dough
bowl, Cochiti, the interior
painted over a cream slip in
black foliate motifs, 14in.
diam. $1,750

California coiled basketry bowl, oval, 10½in. long, 4in. high. $1,500

Northwest coast bone and horn spoon in two sections, 8½in. long. $1,250

Apache basketry bowl with radiating rows of triangles, 13in. diameter. $600

Haida carved wooden feast dish with flat elongated ends, 17½in. long. $2,500

North-west Coast wooden raven rattle, early 19th century, 14¾in. long. (Christie's) $35,200

Northwest coast wood model canoe, the sides painted with stylized totemic designs, 26in. long. $3,000

A Navajo pictorial rug, 9ft.11½in. x 5ft.5½in. (Robt. W. Skinner Inc.) $2,500

A Southwestern basketry tray, Apache, woven in devil's claw on a dark golden field, 19in. diam. $2,000

A Cascades/Plateau imbricated coiled basket, Klikitat, 19th century, 7¼in. high. $750

Eastern Sioux beaded buckskin trousers, 40in. long. $1,000

Yokut polychrome pictorial friendship basket. (Butterfield & Butterfield) $24,200

A North American Plains Indian leather drawstring purse with blue and white bead decoration. $250

Plateau American Indian beaded flatbag, white ground, red and blue abstract floral design, circa 1940-1950, 12 x 13in. (Du Mouchelles) $150

American South West Indian figural rug, white ground depicting Indian hunter with a deer, a monkey and a squirrel, 6ft.4in. x 4ft.8in. (Du Mouchelles) $700

Plateau American Indian beaded flatbag, blue ground, one side with crossing American flags, the verso with flower and bird, beaded strap, circa 1930, 7 x 9in. (Du Mouchelles) $400

American South West Indian runner, red ground having square and triangular medallions linked in barber pole fashion, 5ft. x 2ft. (Du Mouchelles) $300

Arapaho American Indian wood quirt with brass tacks, horsehair and beaded suspension, leather suspension at opposite end, circa 1910. (Du Mouchelles) $200

American Indian contemporary San Carlos design Apache vase by Manna, 17in. high. (Du Mouchelles) $300

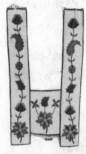

American Indian Flathead tribe elk hide dress, circa 1930-40, red and black beadwork at top, with fringe, 49in. high. (Du Mouchelles) $400

Navajo striped Indian rug, circa 1900, vibrantly colored stripes of brick red, gray, bittersweet and black, 3ft.2in. x 4ft.6in. (Du Mouchelles) $550

An American Indian beaded martingale from the Nez Perce tribe, with white ground, floral design and bells at bottom, circa 1910, 33in. high.(Christie's) $900

Nez Perce American Indian beaded stroud cradle hood cover, blue ground with colorful beaded sprays, red yarn fringe, demi-lune shape, 12 x 14in. (Du Mouchelles) $325

American South West Indian figural blanket, eagle attacking a serpent design in orange, black, brown, and yellow against white, 4ft. x 6ft.6in. (Du Mouchelles) $700

North Eastern American Indian water drum, wood with hide, black band decoration, circa 1900, 9in. high, 11in. diam. (Du Mouchelles) $95

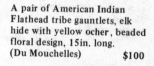

Plains Indian elk hide beaded lady's moccasins, circa 1900, 9½in. long. (Du Mouchelles) $85

Nez Perce American Indian lady's beaded leather belt, turquoise ground with geometric designs, 2in. wide, 34in. long. (Du Mouchelles) $175

A pair of American Indian Flathead tribe gauntlets, elk hide with yellow ocher, beaded floral design, 15in. long. (Du Mouchelles) $100

American South West Indian blanket, ivory ground having red, blue, green, wine, orange, yellow and black geometric clusters, 3ft.10in. x 6ft.4in. (Du Mouchelles) $200

American South West Indian rug, red ground with diamond design in center, 6ft. x 3ft2in. (Du Mouchelles) $700

Navajo blanket with a chocolate ground, lightning and zigzag designs in peach, ruby, tan and gray, 6ft.9in x 4ft. (Du Mouchelles) $1,000

Maidu basket, with concentric serrated and stepped triangle devices flanked by a variety of eccentric floating motifs, 10¼in. diameter.
(Butterfield & Butterfield)
$550

Apache olla, woven with vertical rows of connected outlined diamonds, zig-zags and stripes, 13in. high.
(Butterfield & Butterfield)
$1,100

American Indian woven basket, circa 1900, black motif in stepped block configuration, 18in. diameter.
(Du Mouchelles)
$3,500

Large Acoma pottery jar, painted overall in a fine-line repeat compartment pattern, 19in. high.
(Butterfield & Butterfield)
$770

Navajo Germantown rug, the field divided into two panels, showing various diamond, plant life and lightning bolts, 3ft. 2in. x 2ft. 3in.
(Butterfield & Butterfield)
$1,540

Anasazi cradle, Four Mile culture, circa 1375–1450 A.D., consisting of two parallel flat wood slats, supporting a slightly concave and rounded seat of plaited fibers, 30in. long.
(Butterfield & Butterfield)
$4,675

Navajo chief's style rug, in a nine-spot box pattern, each compartment centering concentric crosses, 4ft. 11in. x 7ft.
(Butterfield & Butterfield)
$4,125

Apache polychrome basket, the solid and checkered center ringed by multi-banded zig-zags, 19in. diameter.
(Butterfield & Butterfield)
$2,475

Navajo Germantown blanket, the banded pattern alternating panels of connected stepped diamonds, diamond halves, zig-zags and stripes, 6ft. 7in. x 4ft. 9in.
(Butterfield & Butterfield)
$11,000

Mesa Verde black on white pottery mug, the loop handle painted with a diamond lattice and pierced to resemble a keyhole, 4¹/₂in. diameter. (Butterfield & Butterfield)

$770

Navajo pictorial rug depicting three human figures, each wearing striped conical hats and jewelry , within a reciprocal stepped zig-zag border, 4ft. 2in. x 6ft. 2in. (Butterfield & Butterfield)

$3,300

Panamint polychrome pictorial bottleneck basket, of characteristic form, deer and appended hourglass devices on the sloping shoulder, 4¹/₄in. high. (Butterfield & Butterfield)

$5,225

Zia polychrome pottery jar, painted in two panels of scalloped bands, stylized floriforms and geometrics, 10¹/₄in. high. (Butterfield & Butterfield)

$2,420

Northeast California polychrome basketry pitcher, the globular body drawn with zig-zag bands of quail topknot motifs and floating diamonds, 14¹/₂in. high. (Butterfield & Butterfield)

$1,100

Pima polychrome olla with straight flaring sides, drawn allover in a diamond lattice pattern, each compartment with smaller diamonds, 12in. high. (Butterfield & Butterfield)

$1,650

Zuni polychrome pottery jar, painted with volutes, rosettes and a narrow band of scrolls over traditional deer with heart lines, 10¹/₂in. high. (Butterfield & Butterfield)

$4,950

Navajo Germantown rug with a central row of concentric solid and serrated diamond lozenges and complementary diamond halves, 5ft. 4in. x 3ft. 3in. (Butterfield & Butterfield)

$4,125

Hopi polychrome pottery bowl, painted on the interior with an asymmetrical arrangement of swimming tadpoles below stepped panels, 13³/₄in. diameter. (Butterfield & Butterfield)

$495

Oval Micmac quillwork and birch bark box, late 19th century, wooden bottom, 8½in. wide. (Eldred's) $743

An Indian-style covered woven basket, 1916, 8¼in. high, 10½in. diam. (Robt. W. Skinner Inc.) $450

California coiled basketry tray, Pomo gift basket, with cotton twine and shell disk handle. (Robt. W. Skinner Inc.) $1,200

Southern Ojibwa engraved birchbark instruction scroll, Mide Ghost Lodge Menominee, 67in. long. (Robt. W. Skinner Inc.) $1,300

Hopi Kachina doll representing a Hemis, wearing stepped polychrome tableta, painted sash and moccasins, 13½in. high. (Butterfield & Butterfield) $1,210

Navajo fringed Germantown rug, woven on a bright red ground in navy-blue, dark red, pink, white and green, 76 x 83in. (Robt. W. Skinner Inc.) $7,750

Plains beaded and fringed hide cradleboard, Ute Reservation Period, 39in. high. (Robt. W. Skinner Inc.) $650

A four-color Chocktaw Indian plaited basket, 4½in. high, and a handled three- color Cherokee basket, 11½in. high. (Robt. W. Skinner Inc.) $275

Plains beaded hide boot moccasins, Southern Cheyenne/Arapaho, 1880's, 15in. high. (Robt. W. Skinner Inc.) $1,800

Southwestern pre-historic pottery bowl, late 13th/early 14th century, 16½in. diam. (Robt. W. Skinner Inc.) $3,300

Plains beaded and quilled hide 'Possible' bag, Sioux, late 19th century, 20¾in. long. (Robt. W. Skinner Inc.) $1,500

Late 19th century Plains carved red Catlinite pipehead, in the form of an eagle's claw clutching an ovoid-shaped bowl. (Robt. W. Skinner Inc.) $275

Plains pony beaded and fringed hide dress, 19th century, formed of two skins, 51in. long. (Robt. W. Skinner Inc.) $7,200

American Indian wood Kachina doll, Hopi of flattened form, probably 'Shalako Mana', 11in. high. (Robt. W. Skinner Inc.) $2,800

Navajo pictorial weaving, woven on a burgundy ground in white, green, brown, black and pink, 43 x 57in. (Robt. W. Skinner Inc.) $900

Eskimo/Northwest Coast polychrome wood mask, 19th century, cedar, 8½in. long. (Robt. W. Skinner Inc.) $2,200

Southern Ojibwa engraved birchbark document scroll, Mide-Wiwim Society, 61in. long. (Robt. W. Skinner Inc.) $1,700

Great Lakes loom beaded cloth bandolier bag, late 19th century, 36in. long. (Robt. W. Skinner Inc.) $850

Pair of Plains beaded moccasins, with green ground and orange chevrons. $550

Pair of Blackfoot beaded legging strips in chevron and geometric design, 25in. long. $850

Tlingit carved alderwood feast bowl, of shaped form, 14in. long. $2,500

Maidu coiled polychromed basket of globular shape, 11¾in. diam. £800

Northwest coast polychromed carved wood raven rattle, carved in two sections, 12¼in. long. (Robt. W. Skinner Inc.) $4,000

American painted, footed and plaited compote basket, 12in. diam. $500

Eastern Woodlands bandolier bag with beaded trim, 37in. long. $1,300

Plains quill child's vest with cloth lining, 10½in. wide. $1,500

Cheyenne beaded cradle with red, white and blue hood, and cloth skirt, 32in. long. $700

Acoma pottery ola with black and red stylized design, 12in. diameter. $1,500

Pair of Woodlands child's moccasins in green and orange quillwork. $800

Tlingit basketry bowl of tall cylindrical form, 9in. high. $1,250

Apache basketry bowl with radiating key design, 16½in. diameter. $550

Cheyenne quilled and beaded cradle with hide top, 16in. long. $1,500

Pair of Ojibwa beaded hide moccasins with canvas vamps and cuffs. $200

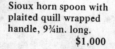

American painted rectangular plaited basket, 5½in. high. $800

Sioux horn spoon with plaited quill wrapped handle, 9¾in. long. $1,000

Kiowa cradleboard model, fully beaded on canvas over a fabric and rawhide foundation, 13in. long. $2,000

Hopi painted skin 'baby show' poster with fringed bottom, 36 x 32in. $600

Navajo child's blanket in gray and black stripes with geometric squares, 52in. long. $6,000

Woodlands beaded hide jacket with double collar. $4,000

Apache basketry ola with geometric dog and figural motif, 7½in. high. $550

Pair of Blackfoot man's leggings of tanned leather and canvas beadwork. $800

Ojibwa beaded bandolier bag with floral motif, 35in. long. $800

Plains beaded buckskin
tipi bag, 20 x 13in.
$1,500

Northwest coast mask,
Kwakiutl, with movable
eyes, 13½in. high.
$1,750

Plains beaded hide cradle
cover, Sioux, 1880's, 19in.
long. $1,750

A Navajo silver Concho belt,
comprised of seven oval
conchos, six butterflies and
open center buckle. $2,000

An unusual Naskape moose
skin pouch, decorated with
imprinted geometric designs
in red paint, 50 x 28cm.,
19th century.
(Phillips) $10,465

A Navajo silver and turquoise
Concho belt, hand-hammered
silver, comprised of seven
oval conchos and six butterflies. $2,000

'Long Hair Dancer', by Bruce
Timeche, tempera, signed,
10 x 13in. $500

Two Plains paint decorated
parfleche containers, Crow,
a shoulder bag, 12 x 13in.
and a case 12 x 23½in. $750

A Cascades/Plateau imbricated coiled basket, Klikitat,
19th century, 10¼in. high.
$1,000

Plateau beaded vest stitched with figures of horses, Indians and flowers, 21in. long. $800

Miniature decorated covered storage basket, North East American Indian, late 19th century, 3in. high. (Skinner Inc.) $2,800

Handled burl bowl, North American Indian, Plains, 19th century, with shaped ends and carved handles, 14¼in. long. (Skinner Inc.) $2,600

Painted two pocket splint wall basket, Northeast Woodland Indians, mid 19th century, the high back with hanging bracket, 26in. high. (Skinner Inc.) $2,000

A North American Indian beadwork boy's shirt, possibly Blackfeet, decorated with geometric designs in multicolored and metallic beads, 60 x 60cm. (Phillips London) $4,186

Three pocket wall basket, North East American Indian, 19th century, wooden hanging loop above four graduated pockets, traces of red stain, 30in. high. (Skinner Inc.) $2,100

A Woodlands buckskin bag, the surface covered with a geometric design in dark and light blue, red and white beads, 16cm. high. (Phillips London) $72

A Blackfeet blanket strip, comprising a broad band bordered in pink, linking four discs covered with concentric circles, 1.70cm. long. (Phillips London) $3,703

A Cree black stroud octopus bag, decorated in multicolored glass beads, with a tree bearing exotic flowers, fruits and leaves, 46.5cm. high. (Phillips London) $2,592

Paint decorated covered storage basket, Northeast American Indian, 19th century, of circular form, 13¼in. high. $400

California coiled basketry bowl, Pomo, diam. 12in., 5¾in. high. $600

Nez Perce twined cornhusk bag, 13½ x 18in. $575

Southwestern polychrome pottery jar, San Ildefonso, black on red, Powhoge Period, 12½in. diam. $1,250

Cheyenne beaded and quilled cradle cover with hide top. $800

Tlingit twined spruce root rattle top basket, 5¼in. diam. $600

Navajo blanket with red field and diamond and line motif, 75in. long. $6,000

Pair of Apache beaded moccasins with chequerboard and banded decoration. $450

Navajo Germantown woman's blanket with red field and line and diamond motif, 78½in. long. $7,500

Apache basketry bowl with vertical bands of rattlesnake design, 24in. diam. $3,000

Maidu twined burden basket of characteristic conical form, decorated with three serrated zig-zag bands, 18½in. high. $850

Eastern Woodlands cap with multi-coloured floral beaded decoration, 10½in. long. $750

Nez Perce twined cornhusk bag, false embroidered in homespun wool and natural grass, 19 x 24in. $500

Southwestern polychrome pottery jar, Zia, 14in. diam. $2,250

Nez Perce twined cornhusk bag, false embroidered in natural dyed cornhusk and grass, 19½ x 26in. $575

Apache beaded and fringed hide bag with drawstring top, 15in. long. $500

Plains painted hide, Shoshoni, depicting numerous scenes, 28 x 23in. $1,750

Great Lakes beaded cloth bandolier bag, early 20th century, 42in. long. $750

Southwestern pottery jar, Zia, painted over a pinky cream slip in black and red, 12¾in. diam. $1,500

'Untitled', by Gerda Christofferson, pastel portrait, signed and dated '57, 18½ x 24in. $425

A Hopi polychrome pottery canteen, painted over a creamy yellow slip in dark brown linear and 'Koshare' figural decoration, 3¼in. high. $350

'Owl Kachina', by Peter Shelton, acrylic on paper, signed 'Hoyewva '64', 14 x 21in. $750

'Deer Dancers', by Harry Fonseca, signed in interlocking initials, dated 1975 on back, acrylic on canvas board, 20 x 23in. $650

Navajo rug, woven on a natural shaded gray field, 108 x 144in. $3,000

Large Navajo pictorial weaving, woven on a red field in mustard, white and navy, 61 x 88in. $3,000

Northwest coast mask, Bella/Bella Coola, of polychrome cedar wood, 12.5/8in. high. $49,000

'King of the Herd', by Quincy Tahoma, tempera, signed and dated '53, 6½ x 10in. $800

A Southwestern polychrome canteen, Zia, 19th century, painted over a cream slip in black and red, 10¾in. deep. $1,800

'Sioux Maiden', by Gerda Christofferson, pastel portrait, signed and dated '57, 19 x 24in. $575

A Southwestern polychrome jar, Zia, with indented base, flaring sides and tapering rim, 12½in. diam. $1,500

Navajo Germantown weaving, woven on a red ground in black and white, 41 x 69in. $1,750

'Apache Mountain Spirit Dance', by Carl Nelson Gorman, signed 'Kin-Ya-Onny-Beyeh', oil on canvas, 19½ x 23½in. $1,250

'Warrior', by Velino Shije Herrera, signed 'Ma-Pe-Wi' '45', tempera on white paper, 9½ x 12½in. $1,000

Basket Maker, by Patrick Robt. Desjarlait, tempera, signed, 14 x 17in. $2,000

A Southwestern polychrome storage jar, San Ildefonso, of tall rounded form. 12½in. high. $1,000

Navajo Germantown serape, finely woven on a red ground, 47 x 68in. $3,000

An early 20th century oak cased 'Shooting Star' pinball machine, 92cm. high. (Spencer's) $424

'Twenty One' amusement machine made in the U.S.A., circa 1930. (Costa/Bates) $450

Columbus, Ball Chewing Gum Vendor, circa 1932, U.S.A. $175

'Rol-a-top' produced by Watling with twin jackpot, made in the U.S.A., circa 1936. $3,000

Mid 1930's, Mutoscope 'Adam & Eve', manufactured in the U.S.A. (Nic Costa) $1,000

Dutchboy, circa 1930, U.S.A. $750

Bursting Cherry, U.S.A., circa 1938. (Costa/Bates) $700

'Sneezy' dice shaker amusement machine made in the U.S.A., circa 1930. (Costa/Bates) $270

A 'Stars of the Silver Screen' machine, circa 1935, 27in. high. $600

Mills amusement machine, with Mystery Payout, made in the U.S.A., 1960's. (Costa/Bates) $450

Reel 21 gaming machine by Groetchen, U.S.A., 1930's. (Brian Bates) $350

American 'twenty-one' gambling machine, circa 1930, 13½in. wide. $225

Extraordinary, circa 1933, U.S.A. $750

Caillie Brothers grip-test amusement machine in green-painted case, circa 1910, 59in. high. $1,500

Try Your Grip, by the Mechanical Trading Company, circa 1895. $2,000

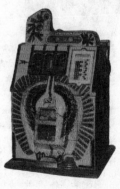

'Tommy', pin ball machine, made by Stoner Bros., U.S.A., circa 1938. $650

A 'Novelty Merchantman' crane by the Exhibit Supply Co. Chicago, the crane takes the form of the bow end of a merchant ship with the grab as a derrick, 71in. high. (Bonhams) $853

'War Eagle' produced by Mills in the U.S.A., circa 1932. $2,000

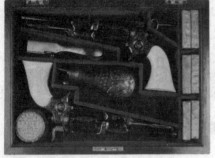

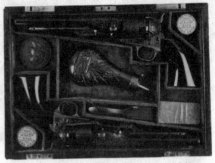

Outstanding cased pair of engraved presentation Colt Root model 1855 percussion revolvers, circa 1863, .31 caliber, 4¹/₂in. barrels marked *Address Col. Colt New York, U.S.A.*
(Butterfield & Butterfield) $220,000

Deluxe engraved cased pair Colt model 1860 army percussion revolvers, .44 caliber, serial numbers 151388 and 151389, 7¹/₂in. barrels, marked *Address Col. Saml. Colt New York, U.S. America.*
(Butterfield & Butterfield) $286,000

Rare Colt single action new army revolver, caliber 41, 6in. barrel marked Colt D.A. 41 on left side, produced in the 1890s.
(Butterfield & Butterfield) $8,800

A Colt 1851 model navy percussion revolver, No. 204033 for 1868, the octagonal sighted barrel with New York address, 13in. long.
(Christie's) $1,242

A rare Colt Hartford-English dragoon percussion revolver, No. 477 for 1853, the blued barrel with New York address, blued cylinder with traces of roll-engraved Texas Ranger and Indian scene, case-hardened frame and rammer, the lid with trade label of *I. Murcott, 68 Haymarket, London*, London proof marks, 14¹/₄in. long.
(Christie's) $11,869

A good rare 6 shot .44 inch 3rd Model, Hartford-English Colt Dragoon single action percussion revolver No. 635, 13½ inches, round barrel 7½ inches stamped on octagonal breech. "Address Saml Colt New York City", London proved, underlever rammer. Cylinder roll engraved with Indian attack scene, "Model U.S.M.R. Colt's Patent". (Wallis & Wallis) $8,650

A Colt 1849 model pocket percussion revolver, the blued sighted barrel engraved *Sam Colt* in gothic script on the top flat, in original American mahogany case lined in blued velvet with accessories including 'eagle and shield' flask, 9in. (Christie's S. Ken)

$4,519

Deluxe cased and engraved Colt model 1860 army percussion revolver with matching shoulder stock, .44 caliber, 8in. barrel marked *Address Col. Samuel Colt, New York, U.S. America.*
(Butterfield & Butterfield)

$308,000

A 6 shot .44in. Colt model 1860 single action army percussion revolver, 13½in. overall, barrel 8in., with New York address, replacement ivory grips.
(Wallis & Wallis)

$2,162

Cased Remington New Model police revolver, serial number 7168, factory converted to .38 rimfire caliber, 3½in. octagon barrel marked with Remington address, patent dates and *New Model.*
(Butterfield & Butterfield)

$8,800

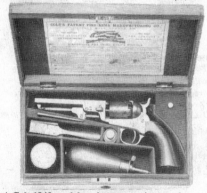

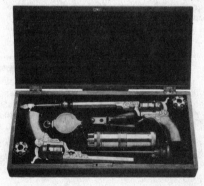

A Colt 1849 model pocket percussion revolver, with blued octagonal sighted barrel stamped with New York address, cylinder with roll engraved stagecoach hold-up scene, case-hardened frame and loading lever, silvered trigger-guard and back-strap, 9½in.
(Christie's)

$3,201

Pair of cased belt Model Paterson revolvers (No. 2), Patent Arms Manufacturing Company, circa 1837–40, serial No. 626 and 678, in untouched condition, engraved *Abraham Bininger*, barrel 5½in. long.
(Skinner Inc.)

$242,000

A 6 shot .44in. Colt Army single action percussion revolver, 14in., round blued barrel 8in. stamped *Address Col Saml Colt New York U.S. America* color hardened creeping rammer, blued rebated cylinder, one piece wooden grip.
(Wallis & Wallis)   **$1,890**

An American Volcanic lever-action (rim fire) target pistol, No. 527, with sighted octagonal barrel stamped *The Volcanic Repeating Arms Co. Patent Newhaven Conn. Feb. 14. 1854*, brass frame, 15in. long.
(Christie's)   **$3,848**

Historic Colt Whitneyville Walker model 1847 Dragoon percussion revolver, .44 calibre, 9in. half round octagon barrel marked *Address Sam'l Colt, New York City* and *U.S. 1847* over wedge.
(Butterfield & Butterfield)   **$275,000**

A Colt second model Hartford Dragoon percussion revolver, the barrel with New York address, cylinder with roll engraved Texas Ranger and Indian scene, brass square-back trigger-guard and back-strap, mid-19th century, 14¹⁄₂in.
(Christie's S. Ken)   **$4,453**

Rare and unique cased Colt Paterson belt model percussion revolver, engraved and silver banded, .34 caliber, 4⁵⁄₈in. barrel marked *Patent Arms M'g Co. Paterson N.J. Colts Pt.*
(Butterfield & Butterfield)   **$770,000**

A Colt 1860 model army percussion revolver of presentation quality, No. 151695E for 1864, with sighted barrel with New York address, rebated cylinder with naval engagement scene, wolf head engraved hammer, frame cut for a shoulder-stock, London proof marks, 14¹⁄₂in. long.
(Christie's)   **$6,646**

A good .38in. center fire Winchester model 1873 full tube magazine underlever sporting rifle, 41in. overall, round barrel 22in. with London proofs, deluxe walnut stock with finely checkered fore end and wrist.
(Wallis & Wallis) **$1,796**

Volcanic carbine, manufactured by New Haven Arms Company, calibre 38, 16½in. octagonal barrel, blued finish, unengraved brass frame and butt plate, walnut stock, case hardened hammer, blued lever, serial No. 86.
(Butterfield & Butterfield) **$23,100**

Rare historic engraved first model Colt Lightning saddle ring carbine, serial number 3543, .44 calibre, 20in. barrel with carbine sight and marked with early Hartford address, sliding safety lock in trigger guard bow, frame, tangs, trigger guard and butt plate scroll-panel engraved by Cuno Helfricht.
(Butterfield & Butterfield) **$52,250**

Rare Winchester 'One of One Hundred' model 1873 rifle, caliber 44–40, 24½in. octagonal barrel, first type with mortised dust cover, engraved and banded on breech and muzzle, top of barrel engraved *One of One Hundred*, deluxe checkered stock and forearm, made in 1876.
(Butterfield & Butterfield) **$60,500**

Rare Colt double rifle, calibre 45–70, 28in. round side by side barrels, double trigger and double hammer, case hardened frame, hammers and butt plate with brown damascus finish on barrels, oil stained checkered walnut stock and forearm, blued trigger guard, lever and rear and front sight.
(Butterfield & Butterfield) **$20,900**

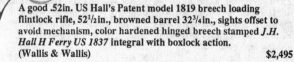

A good .52in. US Hall's Patent model 1819 breech loading flintlock rifle, 52½in., browned barrel 32¾in., sights offset to avoid mechanism, color hardened hinged breech stamped *J.H. Hall H Ferry US 1837* integral with boxlock action.
(Wallis & Wallis) **$2,495**

A half length publicity photograph of Nat King Cole signed and inscribed *To Lou Best of Luck, Nat King Cole,* 10 x 8in. (Christie's S. Ken) **$250**

Apollo 11, signed and inscribed color 8" x 10" by Neil Armstrong, Michael Collins and Buzz Aldrin, three quarter length in space mount. (T. Vennett-Smith) **$425**

A head and shoulders publicity portrait of Chet Baker, signed and inscribed *Hope to See You Soon Chet Baker,* 10 x 8in. (Christie's S. Ken) **$160**

Peter Lorre, signed piece, with attached newspaper photo. (T. Vennett-Smith) **$95**

Apollo 11, a good color signed 8" x 10" by Neil Armstrong, Buzz Aldrin and Michael Collins, showing Aldrin walking on the moon. (T. Vennett-Smith) **$600**

Tony Zale and Rocky Graziano, signed 8" x 10", in boxing pose. (T. Vennett-Smith) **$60**

Charles Lindbergh, signed 5" x 7.5" heavystock magazine photo, full length standing in front of the Spirit of St. Louis at Curtiss Field a few days prior to his historic airflight, 1927. (T. Vennett-Smith) **$1,250**

Louis Armstrong — One of two publicity photographs, signed and inscribed *My Best Wishes to E. H. Wilkinson From Louis Armstrong, 10/11/32,* (Christie's S. Ken) Two **$500**

Rita Hayworth, large signed album page, overmounted beneath 7" x 8" reproduction photo. (T. Vennett-Smith) **$115**

Raphael Semmes, Rear-Admiral and famous Confederate Captain of the 'Alabama', which destroyed 82 Union Ships before being sunk itself, signed piece.
(T. Vennett-Smith) $200

Errol Flynn — a rare collection of six autograph letters, signed, each written by South West London College schoolboy Errol Flynn to Mary White, the sister of a colleague, majority written by Flynn at the age of thirteen, various dates 8th—17th November 1922 and 24th January 1924.(Christie's S. Ken) $4,500

Dwight D. Eisenhower, signed 8" x 10", to lower white border, with typed inscription, 'For Margaret Montgomery Zogbaum'.
(T. Vennett-Smith) $200

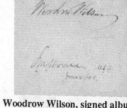

W.F. Cody, 'Buffalo Bill', autograph letter, on one side of a correspondence card, 4th November 1887,, to an unnamed correspondent, thanking him for a magazine which Cody prizes highly.
(T. Vennett-Smith) $650

Louis Armstrong, signed piece.
(T. Vennett-Smith) $105

Woodrow Wilson, signed album page, also signed by E.M. House, 21st June 1919.
(T. Vennett-Smith) $100

Mike Tyson, signed color 8" x 10", three quarter length in boxing pose.
(T. Vennett-Smith) $150

Harry Langdon, signed and inscribed album page, overmounted beneath 5" x 9" photo.
(T. Vennett-Smith) $75

Bogart and Bacall, a good pair of individual signed cards, overmounted beneath 8" x 10" reproduction photo.
(T. Vennett-Smith) $475

A page from an autograph book with manuscript inscription 'To Marilyn — Love and Kisses Marilyn Monroe'.
(Christie's)   £605

Fats Waller, signed postcard, in green ink, full length seated, playing piano.
(T. Vennett-Smith) $200

A good head and shoulders portrait photograph signed and inscribed, with a contract comprising a typescript agreement between Hal E. Roach studios and Marjorie Whiteis.
(Christie's)   £990

Montgomery Clift, boldly signed album page, overmounted beneath contemporary postcard, 7.25" x 12" overall.
(T. Vennett-Smith) $135

Andy Warhol, signed color postcard reproduction of 'Marilyn' from his 'Ten Marilyns'.
(T. Vennett-Smith) $325

Bela Lugosi, large signed album page, in red ink, overmounted beneath 6" x 7.5" photo.
(T. Vennett-Smith) $200

Ronald Reagan, signed 8" x 10", head and shoulders.
(T. Vennett-Smith) $175

Al Jolson, signed and inscribed album page, in pencil, overmounted beneath 7.75" x 8.5" photo.
(T. Vennett-Smith) $100

Neil Armstrong, signed and inscribed color 8" x 10", half length wearing spacesuit.
(T. Vennett-Smith) $250

Judy Garland, irregularly clipped signed piece laid down to modern plain postcard.
(T. Vennett-Smith) $135

A page from an autograph book with manuscript inscription 'Love and Kisses Marilyn Monroe'; with a collection of thirty-two clipped signatures and autographs.
(Christie's) $1,320

Marilyn Monroe signed autograph from an album page.
(Vennett Smith) $1,500

A good full-length portrait photograph of Charlie Chaplin in his famous tramp guise, signed and inscribed 'With best wishes, Sincerely Charlie Chaplin', 7 x 5¼in.; and a half-length publicity photograph. (Christie's)
Two $570

Andy Warhol, Marilyn, silkscreen, printed in colors, 1967, signed in pencil and stamp numbered *75/250* on reverse, published by Factory Addition, New York, 36in. x 35⁷/₈in.
(Phillips) $46,000

Gary Cooper, signed cover of Royal Performance Programme, at the Coliseum, Charing Cross, 9th November 1938.
(T. Vennett-Smith) $100

Charlie Chaplin autographed menu, for the 'Critics' Circle Film Section, Luncheon to Charles Chaplin Esq, Empress Club, W.1., 10.X.52', signed 'Charlie Chaplin'. (Christie's) $110

Errol Flynn, signed and inscribed album page, overmounted beneath 7" x 8" reproduction photo.
(T. Vennett-Smith) $125

Neil Armstrong, signed edition of the Tribune for Saturday, 2nd August 1969, featuring picture of Armstrong and captioned 'First to the Moon'.
(T. Vennett-Smith) $210

John Steinbeck, small signed card.
(T. Vennett-Smith) $175

Lon Chaney Snr., small signed piece, cut from
official document, rare, slight stain.
(T. Vennett-Smith) $420

Dwight D. Eisenhower, and Mamie Doud
Eisenhower, signed 9.75" x 10" color
Christmas Greetings plaque, 1957.
(T. Vennett-Smith) $175

Astronauts, Space Shuttle Discovery STS-29
crew, signed by Capt. Michael L. Coats, Col.
John E. Blaha, Col. James F. Buchli, Col.
Robert C. Springer and Dr. James P. Bagian,
postally canceled Cape Canaveral, 13th
March 1989.
(T. Vennett-Smith) $160

Astronauts, Space Shuttle Discovery STS-51-1
crew, signed by all five members of the crew,
including Joe Engle, James D. van Hoften and
three others, postally canceled Kennedy Space
Center, 27th August 1985.
(T. Vennett-Smith) $135

Sitting Bull, rare pencil signature on 5.25" x
2" photographers mount board, (the image
above removed at some stage of the signature's
life).
(T. Vennett-Smith) $1,450

Brigham Young, small signed piece.
(T. Vennett-Smith) $220

Three Abraham Lincoln autograph letters and
a gold handled cane, the letters dated Execut-
ive Mansion Washington, July 25, 1864.
(Skinner Inc.) $66,000

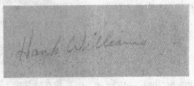

Hank Williams Snr., pencil signature on the
inside of a bar matchbook, 4" x 1.5", rare,
some creasing.
(T. Vennett-Smith) $385

Tyrus Cobb, Als, 5/16/1952, 5 pages content including Cobb's opinion of the lack of skills of current BB players, poor managing, greediness of current BB players.
(Du Mouchelles) $7,000

T206 Sherwood Magee "Magie" Error Card, 1909-11, reverse features advertisement for Piedmont cigarettes.
(Christie's N. York) $26,000

Hand-written letter signed 'Babe Ruth', dated 4/26/1923, letterhead reads 'Babe Ruth, New York', thank you note about an honor bestowed upon him by Mr. Harry Salsinger.
(Du Mouchelles) $3,500

Babe Ruth and Lou Gehrig autographed baseball, circa 1928, signed during spring training at the 'Al Lang Stadium', St. Petersburg, Florida.
(Du Mouchelles) $6,000

1952-3 Yankee signed Team Ball including 'Joe DiMaggio', 'Billy Martin', 'Phil Rizzuto', 'Ralph Houk', etc., official American League ball.
(Du Mouchelles) $600

Babe Ruth, 700th Home Run Ball, autographed by the team, dated July 13, 1934, with a King Gum colored baseball card, with display stand, letters of provenance.
(Du Mouchelles) $8,500

'T206 Honus Wagner' card, dating from around 1910, depicts Honus Wagner, reverse carries an advertisement for Piedmont cigarettes.
(Sotheby's) $451,000

Honus Wagner N.L. Champion Batter presentation medal, 1907, designed as a yellow gold eagle wearing a rose gold ribbon inscribed "Champion Batter" in red enamel block lettering.
(Christie's N. York) $77,000

Babe Ruth, irregularly trimmed 5.75" x 6.75" signed newspaper photo, full length seated by a long row of baseball bats.
(T. Vennett-Smith) $800

BASKETS

Nantucket basket, Massachusetts, early 20th century, on a turned wooden base inscribed with concentric circles, 4in. high. (Skinner Inc.) **$950**

Miniature melon basket, America, late 19th/early 20th century, 4¼in. high. (Skinner Inc.) **$935**

Nantucket basket, Massachusetts, second half 19th century, small bound oak rim above woven body, 4in. high. (Skinner Inc.) **$950**

Open-carved whalebone mahogany sewing basket, second half 19th century, 6½in. high. (Skinner Inc.) **$2,970**

Nantucket basket, Massachusetts, late 19th/early 20th century, bound oak rim above a deep sided circular woven rattan body, 6in. high. (Skinner Inc.) **$2,100**

A polychrome woven splint lunch basket, probably Maine, 12in. high, 15in. long, 7½in. wide. (Christie's) **$100**

A 19th century American large polychrome woven splint market basket, 19in. wide. (Christie's) **$175**

Small splint basket, 19th century, bent oak handle above the single bound oak rim, 8½in. high. (Skinner Inc.) **$80**

Oval Nantucket basket, Massachusetts, late 19th/early 20th century, double bound oak rim above a woven rattan body, 5in. high. (Skinner Inc.) **$300**

BASKETS

A woven splint storage basket, with sloped shoulders tapering to base, (some original paint) 8in. high. (Christie's) $100

Nantucket pocketbook basket, Jose Formoso Reyes, Nantucket Island, Massachusetts, circa 1949, deep sided oval form of woven splint on an oval base, 15.5 x 19cm. (Robt. W. Skinner Inc.) $1,400

A rye coil basket, with side handles released from overlay on circular base (some blue paint), 6½in. high. (Christie's) $100

Nantucket basket, Nantucket Island, Massachusetts, late 19th century, with shaped handle, brass ears, 6³/₈in. high. (Skinner Inc.) $660

Nantucket covered work basket, A.D. Williams, Nantucket Island, Massachusetts, 20th century, wooden base with partial paper label, 8¹/₂in. high. (Skinner Inc.) $1,210

Nantucket Basket, late 19th century, deep sides with turned base reinforced with four screws, 8½in. high. (Robt. W. Skinner Inc.) $650

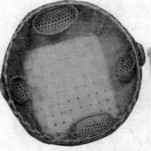

Oblong Nantucket basket, Nantucket Island, Massachusetts, late 19th century, bound oak rim above a woven rattan body, 11in. long. (Robt. W. Skinner Inc.) $1,500

A Shaker splint sewing basket, probably Enfield, Connecticut, 19th century, 15½in. diam. (Christie's) $880

Oblong Nantucket basket, Alfred D. Williams maker, Nantucket Island, Massachusetts, late 19th/early 20th century, 11in. long. (Robt. W. Skinner Inc.) $1,100

49

Rare miniature painted shaker box, Enfield, New Hampshire, dated *March 1836,* painted yellow, 7.3cm. (Skinner Inc.) $23,000

A painted maple lap desk, New York State, circa 1840, 19in. wide. (Christie's) $2,200

A knife box, America, 19th century, rectangular form with outward flaring sides and shaped ends. (Robt. W. Skinner Inc.) $700

A grain-painted document box, probably New Hampshire, circa 1831, 24½in. wide. (Christie's) $440

A painted and decorated 'Tree of Life' domed top box, American, circa 1840, 33in. long. (Robt. W. Skinner Inc.) $1,900

A Federal figured maple tray, New England, 1790–1810, with a flaring gallery and shaped divider pierced to form a handle, 13½in. wide. (Christie's) $4,620

A birch pipe box, America, late 18th/early 19th century, shaped back and single thumb-molded drawer, 14¼in. high. (Robt. W. Skinner Inc.) $550

A Chippendale inlaid walnut desk-box, Salem, Massachusetts, 1750–80, the hinged molded rectangular top decorated with stringing and centered by a compass star over a conforming case enclosing an elaborately fitted interior, 22½in. wide. (Christie's) $6,050

Four oval Shaker boxes, America, 19th century, each with fitted lid (minor imperfections). (Skinner Inc.) $3,100

A Federal inlaid ash and mahogany document box, probably Pennsylvania, 1790-1810, elaborately inlaid with bands of diagonal inlay centering a compass star and two fans in a shaped reserve, 20in. wide. (Christie's) $2,420

A painted and decorated clock repairer's box, America, 19th century, painted dark red and decorated with polychrome eagle in flight grasping an American flag, 20in. wide. (Robt. W. Skinner Inc.) $4,200

Painted and decorated dome top box, America, circa 1830, grain painted in brown over red and decorated with panels of leafage, 76.5cm. long. (Skinner Inc.) $850

Round baleen box, America, mid 19th century, sides engraved with patriotic devices, ship at sea, building and leafy vine borders, 8³/₈ in. diameter. (Skinner Inc.) $400

An inlaid and painted Masonic box, Lawrence, Massachusetts, dated 1858, the rectangular box decorated with Masonic symbols, 7¼ in. wide. (Robt. W. Skinner Inc.) $800

A smoke grained dome-top box, American, circa 1830, 18¼ in. long. (Robt. W. Skinner Inc.) $1,200

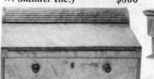

Shaker butternut sewing box, the drawers with ebonized diamond escutcheon and turned ivory pull, New England, circa 1820, 7½ in. wide. (Robt. W. Skinner Inc.) $7,750

A bird's-eye maple roll-top lap desk, America, circa 1820, tambour roll above fold-out writing leaf and single drawer, 9 x 14 in. (Robt. W. Skinner Inc.) $1,000

Joined oak and yellow pine box, Connecticut or Massachusetts, circa 1700, 27 in. wide. (Skinner Inc.) $12,100

Carved, turned, painted and gilded cenotaph, New England, 1800, decorated with green bannerole inscribed *Washington*, 35 in. high. (Skinner Inc.) $25,300

Rosewood cased surgical set, circa 1870, by G. Tiemann Co., 67 Chatham Street, N.Y., NY, containing approximately sixty-eight instruments in fitted velvet compartments. (Eldred's) $1,980

Six graduated oval Shaker boxes, America, 19th century, natural varnish finish, 2³/₄–5¹/₂ in. high. (Skinner Inc.) $2,000

Wallpaper covered wooden hat box, America, circa 1840, of oblong form, the fitted lid covered with Castles in Spain pattern, 11½ in. high. (Skinner Inc.) $3,500

Yellow painted oval Shaker carrier, probably Harvard, Massachusetts, late 19th century, three fingered box with carved handle. (Skinner Inc.) $6,600

A painted and decorated document box, attributed to Heinrich Bucher, Reading, Bucks County, Pennsylvania, 1770-1780, the hinged domed lid lifting to an open compartment, 13 in. wide. (Christie's) $6,600

A Daylight Kodak, circa 1891, small and rare roll film camera for daylight loading, twenty-four exposures, 2¼ x 3¼in. $1,750

A very rare 2¼ x 3¼ inch-rollfilm No. 2 Cone Pocket Kodak camera with black morocco leather covered body, collapsible optical finder and sighting arm.
(Christie's S. Ken) $6,477

Eastman Kodak Co., polished wood B Ordinary Kodak camera with string-set shutter and brass bound lens. $1,750

Eastman Kodak Co., Rochester, U.S.A., 120-rollfilm Boy Scout Brownie camera with green body covering, olive green paint and chrome styled front with Boy Scouts of America emblem.
(Christie's) $235

Eastman View No. 2, improved model of Century View and Empire State No. 2 with Scientific Lens Co. 6½ x 8½in. f16 wide angle lens. $500

No. 4-A Speed Kodak model A, serial 383, roll film camera for pictures 4¼ x 6½in., circa 1908. $500

A panoramic camera, the Eastman Kodak No. 4 Panoram-Kodak, model D, circa 1910, 10¼in. long. $100

Eastman Kodak Co., Rochester, NY, 5 x 4 in. No. 4 Folding Kodak camera No. 465 with a Bausch and Lomb pneumatic shutter. $750

The American Camera Co, 2¼ x 2¼ in. 'Demon' detective camera with lens, flap shutter, changing bag and unexposed plates all in maker's original box. $1,250

A good and rare autographic Vest Pocket Kodak camera no. 14265 with leather covered body and crackle finish front and side panels. $450

A Photoret Magazine Snap-Shot Watch camera by The Magic Introduction Co., New York. $500

A blue coloured Kodak Petite camera with cloth colored body and original blue colored bellows in maker's fitted styled case. $250

A 127-film blue Kodak Petite camera with cloth covered body, by Eastman Kodak Co., Rochester, NY, U.S.A. with 'flash' pattern baseboard and original blue bellows. $800

Eastman Kodak Co., Rochester, New York, a 120-rollfilm cardboard-body George Washington Kodak camera with blue star-patterned body covering, nickel fittings, the body with red window. (Christie's) $29,000

A cardboard-body novelty Kodak advertising camera with pop-up doll's head and opening drawer marked *Kodak*. (Christie's S. Ken) $845

A 16mm. Cine Kodak A camera no. 4091 with black and polished metal body, hand-crank and a Kodak Anastigmat f/1.8 25mm. lens. (Christie's S. Ken) $600

A Stereo Kodak model 1 camera with a pair of Kodak Anastigmat f 7.7 130mm. lenses, set into an EKC Ball Bearing shutter. (Christie's) $395

An Eastman Kodak Co. red Vanity Kodak camera No. 96456 with 'Vest Pocket Kodak Series III' on catch. (Christie's) $270

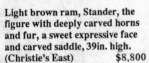  

Light brown ram, Stander, the figure with deeply carved horns and fur, a sweet expressive face and carved saddle, 39in. high. (Christie's East) $8,800

A carved wood dog, Jumper, the figure with deeply carved fur and sweet expression, carved collar, chains and saddle with tassels, 53in. long. (Christie's East) $14,300

A carved wood horse, Jumper, the figure with carved mane, saddle and flowing blanket, 49in. long. (Christie's East) $3,080

A carved wood horse, Prancer, the figure in skygazer pose with deeply carved flowing mane and jeweled trappings, 53in. long. (Christie's East) $20,900

A carved wood Uncle Sam chariot, with a deeply carved image of Uncle Sam and an American eagle above an American flag. (Christie's East) $7,150

A carved wood zebra, Jumper, Stargazer pose, the figure with rearing head and carved cropped mane, 42in. long. (Christie's East) $8,800

A carved wood stork, the figure in a striding pose with deeply carved feathers, saddle with a baby at cantle and blanket, 67in. high. (Christie's East) $25,300

Carved and painted jumper, Charles Marcus Illions, circa 1910, original paint, horsehair tail. (Skinner Inc.) $7,700

Multi colored giraffe, Stander, the figure with carved short cropped mane and sweet expressive face, 59in. high. (Christie's East) $9,350

An American carved wood horse, Jumper, the figure with a frightened expression and deeply carved mane, jeweled trappings and saddle with tulips at cantle, 55in. long.
(Christie's East) $1,870

A carved wood double-sided chariot, with deeply carved depictions of a woman riding a swan adorned with flowers, ribbons and sleeping lion, 54in. long.
(Christie's East) $2,860

A carved wood pig, Jumper, the figure with a corn cob in its mouth and corn stalk flowing from mouth to rear, 49in. long.
(Christie's East) $8,800

A carved wood leaping frog, the figure with whimsical expression and carved saddle, vest and bow tie, 38in. high.
(Christie's East) $17,600

A carved wood rocking chariot, with a deeply carved depiction of a woman holding onto stylized waves amongst carved flowers and jeweled trappings.
(Christie's East) $2,750

A carved wood zebra, Jumper, the figure with short carved mane and looped tail, 43in. long.
(Christie's East) $11,000

An American carved wood horse, Prancer, the figure with expressive face and deeply carved mane, saddle and blanket, 55in. long.
(Christie's East) $8,800

Carved inside row prancer, Dentzel, circa 1900, stripped and primed, 53in. high.
(Skinner Inc.) $7,700

A carved wood cat, the figure in a leaping pose, with a sweet expressive face and deeply carved bow at the neck, 49in. long.
(Christie's East) $19,800

A Roman key hanging chandelier, the whole overlaid with metal grid simulating leaded segments, 24in. diam. (Robt. W. Skinner Inc.) $1,000

Leaded glass hanging shade, attributed to Duffner & Kimberly, with green wreath and swag design incorporating red-amber flame designs, 24in. diameter. (Skinner Inc.) $500

Tiffany bronze and favrile swirling leaf hanging lamp, raised rim and shaped beaded apron on leaded glass dome, 22in. diameter. (Skinner Inc.) $9,350

Early 20th century hammered copper and bronze chandelier with seven Steuben shades, 20in. diam. (Robt. W. Skinner Inc.) $2,750

Tiffany bronze and favrile turtleback chandelier, half-round dome of amber and white striated ripple glass segments, 19in. diameter. (Skinner) $15,000

A hammered copper lantern with tinted amber glass, by Gustav Stickley, circa 1912, 22in. high. $4,000

Oak and slag glass chandelier, 20th century, square ceiling plate suspending five chains through oak cross brace with five shades pendant, 36in. diameter. (Skinner Inc.) $400

Leaded glass ceiling lamp, with red and green swag border, mounted with tricon gilt metal chain and central hooked socket, 15in. diameter. (Skinner Inc.) $400

Fine American Renaissance parcel-gilt and patinated bronze twenty-four-light chandelier and two matching sconces, circa 1872, 4ft. 7in. high. (Butterfield & Butterfield) $14,300

AMERICAN

Pottery has been a thriving American tradition from earliest times, and examples by native Americans are a prominent feature of every sale of Red Indian wares. Among the white settlers, the traditional pottery of the United States was redware, which was produced from the time of the earliest settlers in just about every town and village. It was only really supplanted by stoneware in the 19th century, due to persistent fears that the lead oxides which gave it its color could be poisonous.

During the 19th century such firms as Norton and Fenton and the United States Pottery Co at Bennington had been turning out commercial wares, but, with the exception of the Chelsea Keramic Art Works, founded in 1866, art pottery as such did not exist in the US before 1879. The Centennial Exhibition of 1876 may possibly have acted as a touchstone for the development of a decorative pottery industry. In any case Ohio became a principal center for the production of such wares, with six potteries opening in Cincinnati alone in the next ten years.

Anna pottery snake jug, with four snake heads and lower torso of man, with initials *A.M.A.B.* and *C2WK Anna ILL 1881*, 9in. high.
(Skinner Inc.) $2,750

A porcelain pitcher, by The Union Porcelain Works, Greenpoint, N.Y., designed by Karl Mueller, circa 1880, 9¼in. high. $3,000

A pair of plates from the Dewitt Clinton part dinner service, circa 1805, 8⅞in. diameter.
(Christie's) $1,750

Parian pitcher, America, 19th century, with figures of George Washington in relief, 10in. high.
(Skinner Inc.) $935

An Omega earthenware vase by Roger Fry, covered in a finely crackled white tin glaze with yellow ocher and blue abstract decoration, circa 1914, 16.5cm. high.
(Christie's) $1,674

San Ildefonso blackware pottery plate, Maria/Popovi, the shiny black surface with a repeat feather pattern within three encircling bands, 14in. diameter.
(Butterfield & Butterfield)
$5,500

Santa Clara Blackware pottery jar, Christina Naranjo, carved to depict an Avanyu below a rim band of parallel linear devices, 9¼in. high.
(Butterfield & Butterfield)
$1,100

Santo Domingo pottery olla, circa 1910, black and white geometric decoration, 11in. high. (Eldred's) $440

Important Union porcelain Liberty cup and saucer, Greenpoint, New York, circa 1880, white molded body with Justice on the one side and Hermes on the other, 4in. high. (Skinner Inc.) $2,250

Ernst Wahliss Art Nouveau pottery plaque, with portrait of an appealing young couple holding musical score, 21 x 18in. (Skinner Inc.) $2,420

A sepia Fitzhugh-pattern part dinner service, circa 1800, each piece painted at the center with a flower within radiating panels of animals and trellis pattern and surrounded by four clusters of fruit, flowers and scholar's utensils, all below a band of birds perched in branches and butterflies at the rim, 40 pieces. (Christie's) $7,500

San Ildefonso pottery jar of hemispherical form, painted on the body, lip and both sides of top, in black on red, 11¼in. high. (Butterfield & Butterfield) $9,900

A pair of late 19th century painted chalkware doves, American, 11½in. high. (Christie's) $528

San Ildefonso Blackware pottery plate, Maire, painted in a large-scale repeat feather pattern within a triple perimeter band, 11in. diameter. (Butterfield & Butterfield) $2,090

Porcelain pitcher, American China Manufactory, Philadelphia, circa 1830, each side decorated with floral bouquets, 9½in. high. (Skinner Inc.) $1,850

Rockingham glazed mantel ornament, possibly midwestern United States, 19th century, in the form of a recumbent lion, 15in. wide. (Skinner Inc.) $750

An Art Pottery matt green umbrella stand, early 20th century, the domed top with triangular cut-outs, unsigned, 26½in. high.   (Skinner Inc.) $375

Grotesque pottery jug, America, late 19th/early 20th century, carved into a devil-like mask, 19in. high. (Skinner Inc.) $400

A five-piece Picard China Co. porcelain breakfast set, decorated with the 'Aura Argenta Linear' design, artist signed by Adolph Richter, circa 1910-30. (Skinner Inc.) $500

A painted chalkware cat, Pennsylvania, mid 19th century, painted and decorated with red, yellow and black water color , 10¾in. high. (Christie s New York) $2,000

Important Union porcelain Heathen-Chinee pitcher, Greenpoint, New York, 1876, the relief of Bill Nye, knife in hand, attacking Ah Sin for cheating at cards, 9⅝in. high. (Skinner Inc.) $3,000

Vance faience vase with molded mermaid decoration, Ohio, circa 1905, with repeating figures and fish (some chips and roughness), 12½in. high. (Skinner Inc.) $275

Vance/Avon faience pottery water pitcher, Tiltonville, Ohio, circa 1902, molded relief decoration of hunt scene and grapes, 12½in. high. (Skinner Inc.) $200

BENNINGTON

Bennington is the name often, and erroneously, given to American Rockingham ware in general. The Vermont town had two potteries; the smaller was a stoneware factory belonging to the Norton family (operated 1793–1894) while the larger belonged to Christopher Fenton (called the US Pottery Co from 1853), who produced many different wares, from yellow and Flint Enamel, to parian ware and porcelain.

Flint enamel lion mantle ornament, Lyman Fenton and Co., Bennington, Vermont, circa 1849-1858, 9½in. high, 11in. long. (Skinner Inc.) $9,000

Cobalt decorated stoneware crock, J. & E. Norton, Bennington, Vermont, 10½in. high. (Robt. W. Skinner Inc.) $375

Four gallon Bennington jug with bird, Bennington, Vermont, 1859-1861, 18in. high. (Robt. W. Skinner Inc.) $600

'J. & E. Norton, Bennington, VT' two-gallon stoneware crock, 1850-59, 9¼in. high. (Robt. W. Skinner Inc.) $1,000

Large Toby pitcher, possibly Bennington, Vermont, 1849, seated gentleman with tricorn hat, 10¾in. high. (Robt. W. Skinner Inc.) $250

A four-gallon salt-glazed and decorated stoneware crock, 'J. Norton & Co., Bennington, VT,' 1859-1861, with everted neck above applied lug handles, 17in. high. (Christie's) $1,000

A flint glaze enamel poodle with basket of fruit, Bennington, Vermont, 1849-58, 8½in. high. (Robt. W. Skinner Inc.) $1,500

Two gallon Bennington stoneware jar, circa 1855, 13¾in. high. (Robt. W. Skinner Inc.) $1,250

CHELSEA KERAMIC ART WORKS

Alexander Robertson founded the Chelsea Keramic Art Works near Boston Mass. in 1872, in partnership with his brother Hugh and later his father James. They produced reproductions of Greek vases, ornamental plaques and tiles, often with decorations in high relief.

Shortly after 1876, Hugh introduced an earthenware with underglaze decoration in colored slip, which was marketed as 'Bourg la Reine' ware, and also turned to oriental glazes and designs. The firm failed in 1888, but a new company, the Chelsea Pottery, was reopened in 1891 and in 1896 moved to Dedham, where it became known as the Dedham Pottery.

Marks include an impressed *CKAW* or the name in full, with artist's marks also incised.

Late 19th century Chelsea Keramic Art Works square molded vase, 7½in. high, 4in. diam. $475

A Chelsea Keramic Art pottery vase with blue-green glossy glaze, circa 1885, 11¼in. high. $600

Chelsea Keramic Art Works slipper, Massachusetts, circa 1885, mottled olive green and brown glaze, 6in. long. (Skinner Inc.) $225

Chelsea Keramic Art Works double handled vase, Massachusetts, circa 1885, blue-green and brown glaze, 6¼in. high. (Skinner Inc.) $150

Late 19th century Chelsea Keramic Art Works oxblood vase, 8¼in. high. (Robt. W. Skinner Inc.) $675

Late 19th century Chelsea Keramics Art Works pottery vase, Mass., 10½in. high. (Robt. W. Skinner Inc.) $2,000

Late 19th century Chelsea Keramic Art Works pottery 'oxblood' vase, 8in. high. (Robt. W. Skinner Inc.) $1,750

DEDHAM

The Dedham Pottery was established in 1895, following the move of the Chelsea Keramic Art Works to Dedham Mass. under Hugh Robertson, who had succeeded his father as master potter at Chelsea. At Dedham, Robertson produced a crackle glaze on a heavy stoneware decorated with borders of bird and animal designs. Dedham Ware was made in forty eight patterns and proved very popular. Its mark is *Dedham Pottery* over a crouching rabbit.

Dedham Pottery day/night pitcher, early 20th century, blue decoration on white craquelure ground, 5in. high. (Skinner Inc.) $400

Early 20th century Dedham pottery rabbit figural flower frog, 6¼in. high. $700

Dedham pottery crackleware vase, Dedham, Massachusetts, late 19th century, initialed *HCR*, for Hugh Robertson, (repair to neck) 9in. high. (Skinner Inc.) $1,600

Eight Dedham pottery Birds in Potted Orange Tree plates, Massachusetts, early 20th century, 8in. diam. (Skinner Inc.) $1,600

Late 19th century Dedham pottery experimental drip vase, 6¼in. high. $650

Dedham Pottery Stein, Massachusetts, early 20th century, rabbit pattern, impressed and ink stamped marks, 5¼in. high. (Skinner Inc.) $175

Early 20th century Dedham pottery plate, stamped and dated 1931, 8¾in. diam. $2,000

Early 20th century Dedham pottery cylindrical pitcher in grape pattern, 4½in. high. $900

A Dedham pottery crackle-ware vase, 8in. high, circa 1900. $2,000

Dedham pottery cat plate, early 20th century, stamped, 9in. diameter.
(Skinner Inc.)   **$4,840**

Early 20th century Dedham pottery large milk pitcher, Rabbit pattern, 8½in. high. (Robt. W. Skinner Inc.) $325

Late 19th century Dedham pottery vase with oxblood and black glaze, 7¼in. high. $1,500

Late 19th century Dedham pottery experimental vase, pink star drip design on green, 10¼in. high. $6,000

Dedham Pottery experimental vase, Massachusetts, late 19th/ early 20th century, executed by Hugh C. Robertson, 6in. high. (Skinner Inc.)   **$275**

Late 19th century Dedham pottery volcanic oxblood vase, 7.1/8in. high. $7,250

Dedham pottery pomegranate plate, early 20th century, impressed mark, 10in. diameter. (Skinner Inc.)   **$2,475**

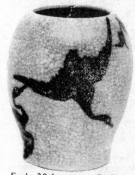

Early 20th century Dedham pottery decorated crackle-ware vase, 7½in. high. (Robt W. Skinner Inc.) $1,750

FULPER

The Fulper pottery was originally established in 1805 in Flemington New Jersey, to produce drain tiles from local clay. From 1860 onwards it also turned out a range of domestic wares but it was not until 1910 that it turned to art pottery. Early pieces showed much Chinese influence and used colors from the famille rose palette. Lamps with pierced pottery shades were also produced and vases which were characterized by their angular shape. The pottery used a number of glazes including a brownish black intended to resemble dark oak. In 1926 Fulper bought out a pottery in Trenton, NJ, and the operation moved there in 1929, though a showroom was retained in Flemington.

Fulper pottery copper dust vase with two handles, Flemington, New Jersey, circa 1915, 6in. diam. (Robt. W. Skinner Inc.) $175

Fulper pottery buttress vase, with glossy streaked glaze in muted green and metallic brown flambé, 8in. high. (Skinner Inc.) $385

A Fulper pottery centerpiece on pedestal base, hammered olive-green on paler green glaze, circa 1915, 10½in. high. (Robt. W. Skinner Inc.)$1,350

Fulper pottery double handled vase, Flemington, New Jersey, circa 1915–25, no. 575, glossy green and eggplant glaze, impressed vertical mark, 6¾in. high. (Skinner Inc.) $185

Fulper Pottery urn, Flemington, New Jersey, circa 1915, cucumber green crystalline glaze, vertical ink mark, 13in. high. (Skinner Inc.) $1,350

Early 20th century Fulper pottery candle lantern, 10½in. high. (Robt. W. Skinner Inc.) $500

A Fulper pottery and leaded glass table lamp, New Jersey, signed Vasekraft, stamped "Patents pending in United States and Canada, England, France and Germany", 20½in. high. (Robt. W. Skinner Inc.) $10,000

GRUEBY

The Grueby Faience Co was formed in 1897 by William H Grueby in East Boston, MA, initially manufacturing tiles, Della-Robbia style plaques and vases. From 1898 matt glazes of opaque enamel were used in shades of blue, brown, yellow and sometimes red. The most characteristic of these, however is dark green with a veined effect. Vases were hand thrown, some plain, others decorated with geometrical patterns or plant forms in low relief. From 1904 glazed paperweights were made in scarab form.

Grueby art pottery usually bears the artist's signature incised and often *Grueby Pottery Boston USA* impressed in a circle surrounding a lotus blossom motif. Grueby Faience was declared bankrupt in 1908 and though a new company was formed for architectural ware, vase production had ceased entirely by 1913. The tile manufacture was sold in 1919, and finally ceased operation around 1930.

Grueby pottery two tile scenic frieze, Boston, circa 1902, depicting four cows in various states of grazing and repose. (Skinner Inc.)
$6,000

Grueby Pottery wide-mouth vase, Boston, circa 1905, with molded leaf decoration, matte oatmeal glaze exterior, 3¹/₂in. high.
(Skinner Inc.) $300

A Grueby pottery vase, Boston, Mass., circa 1905, 13½in. high. (Robt. W. Skinner Inc.) $3,250

A Grueby Art pottery molded vase/lamp base, circa 1905, 12¾in. high. $3,250

Grueby Faience Co. vase, Boston, Massachusetts, circa 1902, with bulbous vase molded design, matte green glaze, 7in. high.
(Skinner Inc.) $500

A Grueby pottery experimental drip glaze vase, Boston, Massachusetts, circa 1905, with wide rolled rim and short neck, 11¼in. high. (Robt. W. Skinner Inc.) $3,500

A Grueby two-color pottery vase, circa 1905, 13in. high.
$5,750

Early 20th century Grueby pottery vase, Mass., 4¾in. high. (Robt. W. Skinner Inc.) $400

Grueby pottery Polar Bear tile, Boston, rectangular-form with molded decoration of polar bear, 5⅝in. x 7in. (Skinner Inc) $325

Navy blue Grueby pottery vase, Boston, circa 1910, impressed and artist initialled (glaze imperfection and bubble bursts), 5½in. high. (Skinner Inc.) $1,750

A Grueby pottery vase, signed with logo, circa 1905, 11.7/8in. high. (Robt. W. Skinner Inc.) $2,250

Late 19th century Grueby Faience Co. bust of 'Laughing Boy', based on a statue by Donatello, 11in. high. (Robt. W. Skinner Inc.) $1,500

Grueby pottery vase, Boston, Massachusetts, circa 1905, decorated with iris alternating with leaf blades, artist initialled by Ruth Ericson. (Robt. W. Skinner Inc.) $1,750

Grueby pottery monumental floor vase, Boston, Massachusetts, circa 1905, the body with repeating broad thumb molded and ribbed decoration, 21in. high. (Robt. W. Skinner Inc.) $3,500

Grueby pottery lamp base, Boston, c. 1905, having an elongated neck flaring towards bulbous base, artist signed 'A.L.' for Annie Lingley, 24¼in. high. (Skinner Inc) $3,000

Grueby pottery vase, Boston, circa 1905, partial paper label and artists monogram *JE* (minor nicks), 12in. high. (Skinner Inc.) $2,000

MARBLEHEAD

The Marblehead pottery was established in 1905 with the view of providing occupational therapy for patients in a local Massachusetts sanatorium. After a short while, however, it was operating as a separate commercial venture. The pottery produced earthenware vases and bowls, in simple, often straight-sided shapes, and covered in muted matt glazes. Characteristic decoration includes animal and flower motifs and also features of the Massachusetts coast such as seaweed, fish, ships etc. Its produce was sold from 1908 onwards. The Marblehead mark consists of an impressed *M* and the emblem of a sailing ship, with the potter's initials incised.

Decorated Marblehead pottery bowl, Massachusetts, circa 1905, squat shallow form, initialled *HT* for Hannah Tutt, 7½ in. diam. (Robt. W. Skinner Inc.) $600

Decorated Marblehead pottery vase, Massachusetts, circa 1905, stamped with logo and incised with early *MP* mark, 5¾ in. (Skinner Inc.) $1,500

Marblehead Pottery decorated vase, Massachusetts, early 20th century, with design of alternating elongated trees, 6³/₈ in. high. (Skinner Inc.) $1,000

Marblehead pottery experimental landscape vase, executed by Arthur E. Baggs, circa 1925, 7¼ in. high. (Skinner Inc.) $3,000

Marblehead Pottery decorated vase, Massachusetts, early 20th century, with repeating design of parrots on branches, 7 in. high. (Skinner Inc.) $1,250

Marblehead Pottery decorated vase, Marblehead, Massachusetts, early 20th century, with incised and painted repeating design of flowers, 3³/₄ in. high. (Skinner Inc.) $1,500

A decorated Marblehead pottery four-color vase, Mass., circa 1910, 6 in. high. $2,000

NEWCOMB POTTERY

This American pottery was set up in 1895 at Newcomb College, New Orleans, a women's section of Tulane University, Louisiana. Essentially, the work of professional potters was bought in to be decorated by the students and the emphasis was on local materials and decorative motifs, such as indigenous trees like magnolia or palms. The products were mainly low fired earthenware painted in underglaze colors, predominantly blue, green and yellow. These were given a glossy glaze at first, but after 1910 softer colors and matt glazes were brought in and decoration became more naturalistic, with some motifs being modeled. The pottery continued in existence until 1930.

A Newcomb College pottery high glaze mug, New Orleans, signed by Ada W. Lonnegan, circa 1901, 4¼in. high. $1,500

Early 20th century Newcomb College pottery vase, Louisiana, stamped and initialed KS. 5in. high. $650

A Newcomb pottery floral vase, New Orleans, circa 1928, initialed by Henrietta Bailey, 5¼in. high. (Robt. W. Skinner Inc.) $750

Newcomb College Pottery vase, New Orleans, Louisiana, circa 1905, the flaring cylindrical form with incised and painted decoration, 9³/₄in. high. .(Skinner Inc.) $2,000

Newcomb pottery vase, Louisiana, circa 1920, initialled 'AFS', 6.1/8in. high. $1,000

Newcomb pottery carved vase, New Orleans, Louisiana, circa 1931, impressed *NC SY 72*, 8½in. high. $2,600

Newcomb pottery cylindrical vase, Louisiana, circa 1897, 7½in. high. $1,500

OHR

George Ohr (1857–1918) was an American artist potter who was based in Missouri. His work was characterised by being of very thin porcelain, which was then distorted by being squeezed or folded into weird forms with handles then applied. His glazes were notable for their flowing colors, such as green and plum.

Most of his pieces are marked with *G E Ohr, Biloxi, Miss.*

A G. E. Ohr pottery vase, the concave-shaped mouth with elongated folded handles, circa 1900, 10in. high. $3,500

George E. Ohr Pottery vase, Biloxi, Mississippi, circa 1904, fluted top on cylindrical form, midnight blue over cobalt glossy glaze, 5in. high. (Skinner Inc.) $700

George E. Ohr Pottery vase, Biloxi, Mississippi, circa 1898, mottled olive green iridescent glaze, 4in. high. (Skinner Inc.) $300

A 20th century molded pottery 'steamboat' pitcher, cast after the original by George E. Ohr, 9in. high. $300

Late 19th/early 20th century George Ohr art pottery vase, Mississippi, 4in. high. $700

PAUL REVERE

The Paul Revere pottery was established in the early years of the 20th century in Boston, for the purpose of training girls from poor immigrant backgrounds, the profits to be used for their education in other subjects. It produced earthenware nursery and breakfast bowls and dishes etc. decorated with stylized floral motifs, mottoes etc, with the decoration often confined to the borders. Pieces were marked with initials or with *SEG* for Saturday Evening Girls (q.v.)

Paul Revere Pottery decorated tea tile, Boston, Massachusetts, early 20th century, with central decoration of a cottage, 5³/₄in. diameter. (Skinner Inc.) $300

Paul Revere Pottery decorated vase, Boston, Massachusetts, early 20th century, with incised and painted band of tree design, 8¹/₂in. high. (Skinner Inc.) $1,750

REDWARE

Redware is the original pottery of the American colonies. Its manufacture began in the early 1600s, lasting well into the 19th century, with a potshop in just about every village.

Redware was cheap and easy to make. Its basic color came from the presence of iron oxide in the clay, which, when fired produced various red tones. It could however be given various other colors by additions to the glaze. While imperfections in the clay often provided interesting natural decorations, the prevalent form of intentional decoration was the use of slip.

One of the earliest recorded potteries was at Jamestown, Virginia, which was operating in 1625. Carolina and Georgia were other states with a strong pottery tradition. Most important of all, however, was Pennsylvania, where the Amish carried slip decoration one stage further to make intricate sgraffito designs.

The disadvantages of redware are that is brittle, easily broken, and porous, making it unsuitable for a number of domestic uses.

A 19th century Redware deep platter, with squiggle decoration, 17½in. long. (Robt. W. Skinner Inc.) $1,250

Brown-glazed Redware mantel ornament, America, 19th century, 12in. high. (Skinner Inc.) $225

A 19th century Redware covered jar, Gonic pottery, New Hampshire, 11½in. high. (Robt. W. Skinner Inc.) $600

One of two 19th century slip-decorated Redware dishes, American, 9¼in. and 11¾in. diam. (Christie's) $300

A 19th century slip-decorated Redware dish, American, 10½in. diam., and a bowl 7½in. diam. (Christie's) $350

A manganese decorated Redware jar, by John W. Bell, 1880-95, 12½in. high. (Christie's) $525

A mid 19th century Moravian slip-decorated Redware bowl, probably Salem, N. Carolina Jacob Christ type, 13½in. diam. (Christie's) $275

ROOKWOOD

The foundation of the Rookwood pottery in 1880 received enormous publicity because it was established by a Cincinnati society lady, Maria Longworth Nichols. Its initial aim was to produce a better art pottery rather than commercial success, but in 1883 William Taylor, a friend of Mrs Nichols, was appointed manager, and he both extended the range of designs and organized a distribution network on sound commercial lines.

Though some utility wares were made in the early years, the emphasis was mainly on art pottery which was made using various techniques. The results were often characterized by carved, incised or impressed designs in high relief, often with gilt decoration and overglaze painting or slip painting under the glaze. This last, in which rich warm colors were airbrushed to give an evenly blended background, became known as 'Standard' Rookwood.

Tinted glazes and colored bodies were introduced and in 1884 an aventurine glaze was developed by accident, in which bright gold crystals appeared deep under the surface. This became known as 'Tiger Eye'.

When Mrs Nichols remarried in 1886, her interest in the pottery waned, and in 1889 she transferred the ownership to Taylor. Under his direction, floral decoration on rich brown, orange and yellow backgrounds and on pink and white 'Cameo' pieces predominates. He moved the business to larger premises at Mount Adams, Cincinnati in 1892, and 'Iris' 'Sea Green' and 'Aeriel blue' designs appeared.

Besides floral decoration, Rookwood pieces now were also adorned with portraits of

Rookwood pottery Spanish water jug, Cincinnati, Ohio, 1882, cobalt blue glaze on strap handled, double spout round pitcher, 10in. high. (Robt. W. Skinner Inc.) $400

Rookwood pottery scenic plaque, 'The End of Winter', Cincinnati, Ohio, 1918, original frame, 12¼in. x 9¼in. (Skinner Inc.) $2,500

A Rookwood pottery Indian squaw portrait vase, circa 1899, 11in. high. $700

A Rookwood pottery vase with sterling silver overlay, circa 1899, signed by J. Zettel, 8½in. high. $2,400

A Rookwood pottery vase with sterling silver overlay, initialed C.C.L., for Clara C. Linderman, 1906, 7¼in. high. (Robt. W. Skinner Inc.) $1,500

A Rookwood pottery decorated pitcher, artist's initials MLN for Maria Longworth Nichols, 1882, 6in. high. (Robt. W. Skinner Inc.) $700

ROOKWOOD

American Indians, Negroes, animals, and figures from Old Master paintings.

The pottery was outward looking in that it sent several of its leading designers to study in Europe. Among these was Artus van Briggle, who came back with the idea of a matt glaze, and this was incorporated into regular production from 1901. Following this, the production of architectural ware, tiles and medallions etc. began.

Taylor died in 1913, and the factory continued to live on its reputation for almost thirty years. Its earlier successes were never repeated, however, and it closed through bankruptcy in 1941.

Early Rookwood art pottery was confined to pieces individually decorated by the artist, and they commonly signed or initialed their works. Often, too these were dated. From 1886 a reversed *R-P* was officially adopted, with a flame point added for each year up to 1900. A Roman numeral was then added after the new century.

Rookwood iris glaze pansy vase, Cincinnati, Ohio, 1901, decorated with white pansies on lavender and blue ground, 6¾in. high. (Robt. W. Skinner Inc.) $325

One of a pair of Rookwood stoneware bookends, model- ed as sphinx holding books, light brown glaze, 18cm. high. $400

Three Rookwood pottery standard glaze mouse plates, Cincinnati, Ohio, circa 1893, each depicting a mischievous mouse, 7in. diam. (Robt. W. Skinner Inc.) $600

A Rookwood pottery wax- resist floral vase, Ohio, 1929, artist initialed LNL for Elizabeth N. Lincoln, 17in. high. (Robt. W. Skinner Inc.) $1,000

Rookwood pottery wax resist vase, Cincinnati, 1929, decorated with blue and green dogwood blossoms, 11¾in. high. (Skinner Inc.) $300

Rookwood pottery silver overlay mug, Cincinnati, Ohio, 1891, marked 'Gorham Mfg. Co.' 6¼ in. high. (Robt. W. Skinner. Inc.) $1,000

A Rookwood standard glaze pottery Indian portrait vase, decorated by Grace Young, date cypher for 1905, 30.5cm. high. $4,500

ROOKWOOD

Rookwood Pottery Vellum vase, Cincinnati, Ohio, 1907, executed by Elizabeth Neave Lingenfelter Lincoln (1892-1931), 8in. high. (Skinner Inc.) $175

Rookwood Pottery vase, Cincinnati, Ohio, 1887, executed by Kataro Shirayamadani in his first year with the pottery, 12in. long. (Skinner Inc.) $1,250

Rookwood Pottery vase, Cincinnati, Ohio, circa 1883, with silver glaze neck, three impressed gold bands over body, 10½in. high. (Skinner Inc.) $1,500

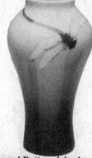

Rookwood decorated vellum vase, Cincinnati, Ohio, 1910, executed by Edward Diers (1896–1931), 8¾in. high. (Skinner Inc.) $300

Rookwood Pottery scenic vellum plaque, Cincinnati, Ohio, 1914, executed by Edward George Diers, (1896–1931), 10¾in. high. (Skinner Inc.) $1,250

Rookwood Pottery iris glaze vase, Cincinnati, Ohio, 1906, executed by Charles Schmidt (1896–1927), 9⅝in. high. (Skinner Inc.) $4,000

Rookwood Pottery wax resist vase, Cincinnati, Ohio, 1928, executed by Elizabeth Neave Lingenfelter Lincoln (1892–1931), 11in. high. (Skinner Inc.) $300

Two Rookwood Pottery tiger eye vases, Kataro Shirayamadani, Cincinnati, Ohio, (1887–1915 and 1925–1948), 14½in. high. (Skinner Inc.) $3,000

Rookwood Pottery porcelain vase, Cincinnati, Ohio, 1925, executed by Kataro Shirayamadani (1865–1948), 8in. high. (Skinner Inc.) $1,000

ROOKWOOD

Rookwood Pottery vase with sterling silver mesh, Ohio, 1893, 11¾in. high. $2,000

Rookwood standard glaze jug, with Palmer Cox figure, Ohio, 1891, artist's initials H.E.W., 6in. high. $1,100

A Rookwood Pottery iris glaze vase, initialed by Olga G. Reed, circa 1902, 7¼in. high. $450

Rookwood Pottery standard glaze pitcher, Cincinnati, Ohio, 1890, decorated with clover and grasses, 12¼in. high. (Robt. W. Skinner Inc.) $800

Rookwood Pottery scenic vellum plaque, signed C. Schmidt, 1921, 12½ x 8½in. $850

Rookwood Pottery scenic vellum vase, Cincinnati, 1913, decorated with landscape scene in gray-blue on shaded yellow to peach background, 13⁵/₈in. high. (Skinner Inc) $2,000

Rookwood standard glaze vase with sterling silver overlay, Ohio, 1892, initialed K.C.M. for Kate C. Matchette, 6½in. high. $2,500

A Rookwood silver overlay vase, impressed artist's monogram SS, 12.5cm. high. $850

A Rookwood Pottery scenic vellum vase, Ohio, initialed by artist Harriet E. Wilcox, 1918, 8in. high. (Robt. W. Skinner Inc.) $800

ROOKWOOD

Rookwood pottery vase, Cincinnati, Ohio, 1915, with incised line and petal decoration in matte brown glaze, impressed mark 12½in. high. (Skinner Inc.) $350

Rookwood pottery scenic vellum plaque, Frederick Rothenbusch, 1915, "Late Autumn" woodland with light snowfall, 10 x 14in. (Skinner Inc.) $1,760

Rookwood pottery vase standard glaze ewer, Cincinnati, Ohio, 1896, by Matthew Daly, underglaze decoration of open petaled white roses against shaded brown green ground, 9¾in. high. (Skinner Inc.) $375

ROSEVILLE

The Roseville Pottery was established in 1892 in Roseville, Ohio, but moved in 1898 to Zanesville, where the general manager, George F Young, began making art pottery in 1900.

Their early Rozane ware was characterised by slip painting on a dark ground, finished with a high glaze, and closely resembled other art pottery being made in Zanesville at the time by the Weller and Owens pottery companies. It was renamed Rozane Royal to distinguish it from subsequent styles.

With competitors in such close proximity, however, it was necessary to develop new styles very quickly, and Roseville soon had a wide and rapidly changing range, which tended more and more towards matt glazing over relief modeling.

Roseville decorated matt umbrella stand, Ohio, circa 1910, no. 724, 20in. high. $1,500

Roseville pottery jardiniere and stand of circular bulbous form, 40in. high. $750

J. B. Owens pottery tiles, Roseville, Ohio, circa 1905, fourteen square tiles forming a continuous rectangle with Greek key pattern, 29½in. wide. (Skinner) $500

Roseville pottery jardiniere on stand, Zanesville, Ohio, early 20th century, listed as the Artcraft line, 24in. high. (Robt. W. Skinner Inc.) $400

SATURDAY EVENING GIRLS

This intriguing title (*SEG* is the usual mark) is found on the products of the Paul Revere Pottery, which was set up at the beginning of the 20th century for the purpose of training girls from poor immigrant families in Boston. The profits from the pottery were used to fund the girls' education in other subjects. The output mainly consisted of earthenware, nursery and breakfast bowls and dishes and these were decorated with birds, flowers or mottoes, often around the borders. The name Saturday Evening Girls Club is something of a misnomer, since the potters worked eight hours a day.

Saturday Evening Girls Pottery decorated motto pitcher. Boston, Massachusetts, early 20th century, 9³⁄₄ in. high. (Skinner Inc.) $2,000

Saturday Evening Girl Pottery vase, Boston, Massachusetts, 1922, with incised and painted band of tulip decoration, 6³⁄₄ in. high. (Skinner Inc.) $300

Saturday Evening Girls pottery decorated bowl, Boston, 1912, artist initialed *S.G.* for Sara Galner, 10³⁄₄ in. diam. (Robt. W. Skinner Inc.) $950

Saturday Evening Girls pottery motto plate, Mass., 1914, signed S.G. for Sara Galner, 7¹⁄₂ in. diam. (Robt. W. Skinner Inc.) $5,000

Saturday Evening Girls decorated planter, Boston, Mass., 1918, 9¹⁄₂ in. long. (Robt. W. Skinner Inc.) $650

Saturday Evening Girls pottery bowl, green glazed half-round with sgraffito interior border of yellow nasturtium blossoms, 8¹⁄₂ in. diameter. (Skinner Inc.) $935

Decorated Saturday Evening Girls pottery pitcher and bowl, Boston, 1918, both with rabbit and turtle border. (Skinner Inc.) $450

Decorated Saturday Evening Girls motto mug, Boston, 1918, with motto *In The Forest Must Always Be A Nightingale and In The Soul a Faith So Faithful That It Comes Back Even After It Has Been Slain,* 4 in. high. (Skinner Inc.) $800

A stoneware four gallon crock, by J. Norton & Co., Vermont, circa 1880, 14in. high. $1,750

A one gallon crock, by A. O. Whittemore, Havana, N.Y., strong cobalt blue design of a house or houseboat. $400

A two gallon jug, by C. E. Pharis & Co., Geddes, N.Y., cobalt blue bird holding worm in beak. $200

A five gallon churn by Woodruff, Cortland, large blue face, possibly tiger or devil head. $650

Double handled pottery floor vase, probably Zanesville Stoneware Co, Ohio, early 20th century, 18½in. high. (Skinner Inc.) $200

A stoneware storage jar, approx. 20 gallons, by West Troy Pottery, 23in. tall. $15,000

A six gallon crock, by S. Hart, Fulton, cobalt blue lineal dog carrying a basket. $1,500

Stoneware butter churn, marked 'John Burger, Rochester', circa 1860, 19in. high. $30,000

Mid 19th century three gallon stoneware jug, stamped 'S. Hart — Fulton', 13½in. high. $500

CHINA

Incised and cobalt decorated stoneware crock, impressed *W. Lundy and Co., Troy,* New York, circa 1825, 11¼ in., high. (Skinner Inc.) $5,000

Cobalt decorated stoneware jug, William H. Farrar & Company, Geddes, New York, 1841-1858 (flake at base), 11 in. high. (Skinner Inc.) $4,000

A salt-glazed stoneware incised and decorated jug, 'Corlears Hook', New York, 1800–1815, with applied line-incised handle, 17 in. high. (Christie's) $1,100

A saltglazed stoneware three-gallon jar, by Cowden & Wilcox, Penn., 1870-90, 12 in. high. (Christie's) $350

Cobalt decorated one-gallon stoneware batter jug, America, 19th century, with tin cover and spout cap, 9 in. high. (Skinner Inc.) $880

A saltglazed stoneware two-gallon batter jug, by Cowden & Wilcox, Penn., 1870-90, 11 in. high. (Christie's) $1,650

One of two 19th century salt-glazed stoneware jugs, N. Carolina, 8½ in. and 10½ in. high. (Christie's) $700

A saltglazed stoneware two-gallon jar, by G. A. Satterlee and M. Morey, 1861-85, and a two-gallon crock by P. Riedinger and A. Caire, 1857-78, 11½ in. and 9½ in. high. (Christie's) $385

Cobalt decorated stoneware jug, Boston, early 19th century, cobalt decorated at shoulder with three fish, 14½ in. high. (Skinner Inc.) $2,750

Antique three-gallon stoneware crock with cobalt decoration. (Eldred's) $176

An ash-glazed stoneware face-jug, attributed to Evan Javan Brown, Georgia, 20th century, the handle pulled from the back and ceramic chards for eyes and teeth, 6¼in. high. (Christie's) $2,420

An unmarked stoneware butter crock with cover, American, circa 1850, 8¼in. diam. (Robt. W. Skinner Inc.) $450

Cobalt decorated stoneware crock, probably Ohio or Pennsylvania, circa 1860, the four-gallon crock inscribed *Hurrah for Abe Lincoln*, 11½in. high. (Skinner Inc.) $4,400

An incised and cobalt-decorated stoneware harvest jug, New York, 1805, decorated on the obverse with incised floral vine below a fish, the reverse with a Masonic apron, inscribed and dated *J. Romer, 1805*, 7in. high. (Christie's) $6,050

Cobalt decorated six-gallon stoneware crock, impressed *Riedinger & Caire Poughkeepsie NY*, circa 1850, 13in. high. (Skinner Inc.) $1,000

A cobalt blue decorated and incised stoneware jug, New York, circa 1822, 13¾in. high. (Robt. W. Skinner Inc.) $21,000

A six-gallon salt-glazed and decorated stoneware churn, *Hubbell & Chesebro, Geddes, N.Y., 1867–1884*, cylindrical with everted neck and applied lug handles, 19½in. high. (Christie's) $800

Cobalt decorated stoneware four-gallon crock, America, 19th century, 14in. high. (Skinner Inc.) $325

TECO

The Teco pottery operated out of Terra Cotta Illinois in the early years of this century. Its output is characterised by matt green glazes which are frequently used on shapes based on natural forms.

Teco pottery vase with four handles, Terra Cotta, Illinois, circa 1910, squat, impressed twice, 6½in. high. (Skinner Inc.) $1,250

A Teco pottery four-handled vase, circa 1910, 7¼in. high. (Robt. W. Skinner Inc.) $650

Teco pottery vase, Illinois, early 20th century, flared rim, in matte buff color glaze, impressed Teco mark, 12¼in. high. (Skinner Inc.) $800

Early 20th century Teco pottery yellow bud vase, Illinois, 4½in. high. $400

A Teco pottery double-handled vase, Illinois, circa 1910, 7in. high. (Robt. W. Skinner Inc.) $350

Teco pottery brown molded vase, bullet shape on four elongated V feet, Illinois, 1909, 8½in. high. $2,000

A Teco Art pottery fluted vase, Illinois, circa 1905, 10½in. high. (Robt. W. Skinner Inc.) $1,250

A Teco pottery molded lotus flower vase, Chicago, circa 1905, designed by F. Moreau, 11½in. high. (Robt. W. Skinner Inc.) $2,500

TECO

Teco pottery handled vase, decorated by four angular quatriform handles extending to base rim, 13¹/₂in. high.
(Skinner Inc.) **$1,320**

Teco pottery wall pocket, green matt glaze on hanging vase with angular top over molded roundel, 5¹/₄in. wide.
(Skinner Inc.) **$385**

Teco Pottery vase, Terra Cotta, Illinois, circa 1909, square-shaped mouth on modeled elongated neck flaring to form bulbous base, 16¹/₂in. high.
(Skinner Inc.) **$1,100**

TIFFANY

CHARLES L TIFFANY was an American jeweler and silversmith who established the firm of Tiffany & Co in New York in 1834. Silver was produced from 1850 and won the firm an award at the Paris Universal Exposition in 1867. Tiffany produced many commemorative pieces, and is not to be confused with his son, Louis Comfort, who took over the company in 1902, when his father died.

A Tiffany pottery molded vase, New York, the mottled dark green and blue glaze on white ground, 7½in. diam., circa 1908. (Robt. W. Skinner Inc.) **$600**

Tiffany pottery vase, with mottled earth tone brown-tan-amber glaze overall, 9¹/₂in. high.
(Skinner Inc.) **$1,980**

Tiffany pottery flower bowl, heavy walled jardinière form of white clay decorated in blue, 5¹/₄in. high.
(Skinner Inc.) **$1,650**

A Tiffany Art pottery vase, New York, 1906, of cylindrical form with repeating molded lady slippers on stems, 12¼in. high. **$3,750**

Tiffany pottery bowl, raised rim bulbed pot of white clay fired with amber, blue, gray and green drip glaze overall, 6in. high.
(Skinner Inc.) **$600**

VAN BRIGGLE

Artus van Briggle was born in Felicity, Ohio in 1869. He studied painting in Cincinnati, where he also worked as a decorator of dolls' heads and vases. Around 1887 he became Director of the Rookwood Pottery, where he decorated vases with flowers in underglaze colors. It was part of Rookwood's enlightened philosophy to send talented decorators on scholarships abroad, and van Briggle benefited under this scheme with a period at the Académie Julien in Paris in 1893. On his return to Cincinnati he continued at Rookwood, while experimenting at home with the production of Chinese matt glazes.

He fell ill with tuberculosis and moved to Colorado in 1895, where he established the van Briggle Pottery Co in 1902. There he produced vases and plates decorated with stylized animal and flower forms in the Art Nouveau style. These were often relief decorated and covered in soft-colored glazes. Until his death in 1904, the pieces were entirely glazed, but later only partial glazing was introduced.

A Rookwood pottery basket, by artist Artus Van Briggle, decorated in slip underglaze with blossoms, berries and leaves, 6½in. high. (Robt. W. Skinner Inc.) $650

One of two 20th century Van Briggle pottery vases, Colorado, one 2¾in. high, the other 5½in. high. (Robt. W. Skinner Inc.) $350

Van Briggle pottery copper clad vase, Colorado, 5½in. high. $1,300

Van Briggle Pottery vase, Colorado Springs, Colorado, circa 1909, striated brown matte glaze, incised marks, 9¾in. high. (Skinner Inc.) $225

Van Briggle Pottery vase, Colorado Springs, circa 1904, decoration of narcissi, matte green glaze with yellow accents, 9⅝in. high. (Skinner Inc.) $700

Van Briggle Pottery vase, Colorado Springs, circa 1904, with molded floral design, yellow and ocher semi-matte glaze, 8½in. high. (Skinner Inc.) $700

Van Briggle pottery vase, Colorado Springs, Colorado, after 1920, relief decorated with cranes in turquoise matte glaze, 16¾in. high. (Skinner Inc.) $550

WALLEY ART

The Walley Pottery flourished around the turn of the century in the town of Sterling, Massachusetts.

Its output consisted mainly of simple forms, vases, mugs etc, designed in equally simple shapes. Decoration was often confined to the glazes, which could be mottled or streaked, and used in combinations of color such as a green drip on a brown ground. Occasionally pieces were simply molded with stylized plant and leaf forms. Grotesque mugs with molded mask faces were also produced.

Walley pottery basket-shaped vase, Massachusetts, circa 1910, 8¼in. diameter. $400

A small Walley Pottery vase, early 20th century 6½ins high. $500

An early 20th century Walley Art pottery molded vase, 6¾in. high. $650

Walley Pottery vase, Sterling, Massachusetts, early 20th century, in green drip glaze on brown ground, 9¹/₂in. high. (Skinner Inc.) $600

Late 19th century Walley pottery 'Devil' mug, impressed WJW, 5½in. high, 4in. diam. $400

WALRATH

Frederick Walrath (c1880–c1920) was an American artist potter who studied under Charles Binns. He also taught at Rochester and Columbia University, New York. His production consisted of earthenware vases and jars, decorated with linear motifs and stylized plant forms, covered in matt glazes. He exhibited in 1904 at the St Louis World Fair, and in later life worked for two years at the Newcomb College Pottery (q.v.), New Orleans. His mark consists of *Walrath Pottery*, incised, with a device of four arrows.

A Walrath pottery pitcher and five mugs, circa 1910, pitcher 6½in. high $1,500

A Walrath floral decorated vase, circa 1910, 7in. high. $1,650

WELLER

Samuel Weller (1851–1925) acquired the Lonhuda pottery at Steubenville, Ohio in the early 1890s, and moved production to his own pottery which he had established in 1882 at Zanesville. There, he continued to produce pottery in the Lonhuda style, which was now called Louwelsa. This was very like Rookwood Standard ware in appearance, and Weller continued to imitate subsequent Rookwood innovations.

A French potter, Jacques Sicard, joined the business in 1901 and produced Sicardo ware, on which a lustre decoration was applied to an iridescent ground in shades of purple, green and brown. Later, a variation, Lasa ware, was introduced with landscape decoration.

Weller worked too in imitation of French Art Nouveau styles, with relief decorations of flowers, foliage and female figures. Aurelia ware was introduced by 1904, having a brushed ground, also Jap Birdimal, with stylized natural forms as decoration.

At its height the business employed some 600 workers and by 1925 Weller owned three factories producing art pottery, garden and kitchen wares. He was succeeded by his nephew Herbert, who died in 1932, and the factory finally closed in 1949.

Marks include impressed *Weller* with the name of the style, and incised *Weller Faience*.

Weller pottery Indian portrait mug, circa 1920, 6in. high. $450

Louwelsa Weller cider pitcher with Indian portrait, Ohio, circa 1910, 12½in. high. $625

Pair of Weller 'Ivory Ware' jardinieres on stands, Zanesville, Ohio, circa 1915, 35in. high, 18in. diam. (Robt. W. Skinner Inc.) $2,500

Louwelsa Weller pottery Indian portrait vase, Ohio, circa 1915, 10¾in. high. (Robt. W. Skinner Inc.) $500

Weller pottery vase, Zanesville, Ohio, circa 1914, "Camelot" funnel shape neck on squat bulbous body, 7¾in. high. (Skinner Inc.) $275

A Weller Sicard twisted pottery vase, iridescent purples and greens with snails in the design, circa 1907, unsigned, 7½in. high. (Robt. W. Skinner Inc.) $550

BANJO CLOCKS

A Federal mahogany and giltwood presentation banjo timepiece, Mass., circa 1820, 40in. high. $2,750

An early 19th century American mahogany cased wall clock, 30in. high. $1,000

A Federal mahogany and giltwood presentation banjo timepiece, Mass., 37in. long. $2,750

Antique American banjo clock in mahogany, by A. Willard, Boston, gilt acorn finial, painted dial, reverse painted throat and tablet, 33½in. high.
(Eldred's) $2,640

Presentation banjo timepiece, Waltham Clock Co., Waltham, Massachusetts, 20th century, eagle finial, brass bezel, 43in. high.
(Skinner Inc.) $2,100

American banjo clock by J.N. Dunning (Joseph Nye Dunning), black and gilt reverse painted tablet and throat glass, painted dial, 52in. high.
(Eldred's) $3,300

A Federal mahogany giltwood and eglomise banjo clock, by Aaron Willard, 1820/25, 33¾in. high. $3,500

A Federal mahogany lyre timepiece, Henry Allen Hinckley, Massa., circa 1825, 38in. high. $3,000

Federal giltwood mahogany banjo timepiece, by Lemuel Curtis, Mass., circa 1820, 32in. high. $7,000

BANJO CLOCKS

A Federal giltwood banjo timepiece with painted dial and eight-day weight driven movement, circa 1820, 41in. high.   **$2,000**

A Federal mahogany and eglomise banjo clock, by Warren, Mass., 1815/30, 30in. high.   **$3,500**

Presentation banjo timepiece, by Waltham Clock Co., Mass., circa 1910, 37½in. high.   **$2,000**

Federal mahogany and giltwood banjo timepiece, probably Boston, circa 1820, with original painted eglomise tables, 32in. high. (Skinner Inc.)
        $2,200

Federal gilt gesso and mahogany banjo timepiece, Aaron Willard Jr., Boston, circa 1820, the circular brass molded   bezel enclosing a painted iron dial, 40in. high. (Skinner Inc.)   **$7,500**

An unusual mid 19th century American rosewood hanging wall timepiece, the 7in. circular white painted dial signed *E. Howard & Co. BOSTON*, 28½in. high.
(Christie's S. Ken)   **$522**

Classical gilt and mahogany lyre-form banjo timepiece, probably Massachusetts, circa 1820, 40in. high. (Skinner Inc.)   **$2,310**

A Federal gilt and eglomisé lyre-shaped wall clock, dial signed Aaron Willard, Boston, early 19th century, 40½in. high. (Christie's)   **$2,860**

A Federal presentation mahogany banjo timepiece, by A. Willard, circa 1820, 40½in. high.   **$2,750**

CARRIAGE CLOCKS

Silvered brass and glass carriage timepiece, probably Boston, circa 1890, 6½in. high.
$475

A porcelain mounted alarm carriage clock, the dial signed G.C. Shreve & Co., San Francisco, 6¼in. high. $1,500

Glass and brass carriage timepiece, probably Boston, circa 1890, 6¼in. high. $500

A fine and rare brass grande sonnerie and minute repeating/alarm carriage clock in oval Corinthian case, signed by the retailer *Bailey, Banks & Biddle Co., Philadelphia*, 4³/₄in. high. (Christie's S. Ken) $8,410

Late 19th century brass repeating alarm carriage clock, the dial signed E. Caldwell & Co., Philadelphia, 7½in. high. $1,300

A fine parcel gilt silver grande sonnerie carriage clock signed *Tiffany & Co., New York*, the movement probably by Drocourt, circa 1883, 8½in. high. (Christie's) $8,250

Glass and brass carriage timepiece, probably Boston, circa 1890, 7in. high. $650

Late 19th century American brass and glass carriage timepiece with eight-day movement, 9. 1/8in. high. $475

A repeating gilt brass carriage clock, circa 1890, 6½in. high. $3,000

MANTEL CLOCKS

A gilt metal timepiece, The Plato Clock, circa 1903, 6in. high. $100

Baroque Revival patinated bronze wall clock, circa 1900, the works by E. Howard & Co., Boston, the whole decorated with pierced strapwork, 37in. square. (Skinner Inc.) $3,750

Ansonia 'Triumph' oak mantel clock, New York, circa 1880, 24in. high.
                    $600

Seth Thomas brass mantel clock, 20th century, with convex front and conforming glazed sides, mercury pendulum and key, 11in. high. (Skinner Inc.) $275

Swinging doll timepiece, by Ansonia Clock Co., circa 1890, 8in. high. $800

Late 19th century pressed wood advertising timepiece, by Baird Adv. Clock Co., 31in. long. $2,000

An oak double dial calendar clock, by Waterbury Clock Co., circa 1900, 29in. long. $1,500

Black Faux marble curfew clock by W. Gilbert Clock Co., Conn., circa 1880, 17.1/8in. high. $300

A rare American globe calendar clock, signed *Patent 1860 improved by Leonard Thorn*, on molded circular base engraved with year calendar, 13½in. high. (Christie's New York) $11,000

MANTEL CLOCKS

Late 19th century ebonized wood miniature tall clock, by G. Hubbell & Son, 24in. high. **$1,500**

Handpainted opal glass hanging clock, Wavecrest-type circular frame housing, Welch Company, Forestville, Connecticut, 6in. high. (Skinner Inc.) **$275**

A cast iron blinking eye timepiece, 'Sambo', America, circa 1860, 16in. high. **$1,750**

A walnut calendar timepiece, by New Haven Clock Co., circa 1900, 32in. long. **$750**

Late 19th century nickel plated paperweight timepiece, by New Haven Clock Co., 7½in. high. **$200**

Jolly Tar wall timepiece, manufactured by Baird Clock Co., New York, 30½in. high. **$1,500**

Rare Sinclaire cut glass mantel clock, with vintage motif and stepped platform base with ribbing and diamonds, housing, 11½in. high. (Skinner Inc.) **$3,700**

Boston Beer Co. wall timepiece, manufactured by the New Haven Clock Co., circa 1900, 14in. diam. **£600**

Rosewood double dial calendar timepiece, Seth Thomas Clock Co., Thomaston, Connecticut, mid 19th century, eight-day movement, 27½in. high. (Skinner Inc.) **$700**

MANTEL CLOCKS

A grain-painted astronomical calendar clock, by Gabs Patent Welch Spring & Co., circa 1880, 30½in. long. $4,000

Early 20th century gray marble and glass Art Deco mantel clock, France, 11in. high. $500

Rosewood veneer wall regulator, by Seth Thomas, Conn., circa 1860, 31¼in. long. $750

A Gustav Stickley oak mantel clock, early 20th century, the door with faceted cut-out framing brass dial, Seth Thomas movement, 13¾in. high. (Robt. W. Skinner Inc.)$2,750

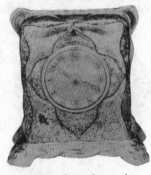

A rare mixed metal mantel clock by Tiffany & Company, New York, 1880-1885, the front with mokume panels of silver mixed with niello, brass and red metal, 9in. high. (Christie's) $18,000

L. & J. G. Stickley mantel clock, Fayetteville, New York, circa 1910, designed by Peter Heinrich Hansen, signed with Handcraft decal, 22in. high. (Skinner Inc.) $7,500

A walnut regulator wall clock, by E. Howard & Co., Boston, circa 1875, 43in. high. $4,000

A gold, rock crystal, onyx and enamel clock by Tiffany & Co. $6,000

Late 19th century 'Coca Cola' walnut regulator timepiece, by Gilbert Clock Co., 30in. long. $650

MANTEL CLOCKS

A cast iron front mantel clock, polychrome painted, America, circa 1890, 11¾in. high. **$200**

Empire mahogany ogee mantel clock by J. J. & W. Beals, Mass., circa 1840, 31in. high. **$1,000**

Ansonia porcelain mantel clock with Roman numerals. **$400**

A carved wood Art Nouveau mantel clock, by the Chelsea Clock Co., Boston, circa 1920, 18¼in. high. **$1,250**

An Arts & Crafts square oak mantel clock, by Seth Thomas Clock Co., 20th century, 12½in. high, 10½in. wide. (Robt. W. Skinner Inc.) **$1,100**

Classical Revival gilt gesso mantle timepiece, probably Atkins Clock Company, Connecticut, circa 1840, 18½in. high. (Skinner Inc.) **$1,300**

Early 20th century green onyx glass and brass mantel clock, by Ansonia Clock Co., Conn., 11in. high. **$400**

Weller Dickensware art pottery mantel clock, housed in elaborated pottery frame decorated with yellow pansies, 10in. high. (Skinner Inc.) **$440**

Art Nouveau porcelain mantel clock, elongated 'A' shape with green glaze and eight-day time and strike movement. **$350**

LONGCASE CLOCKS

Early 19th century painted and carved tallcase clock, Penn., 98in. high. (Christie's) $18,700

American mahogany long case chiming clock, 20th century, swan neck pediment above a break arch glazed door, 97in. high. (Robt. W. Skinner Inc.) $1,600

Federal mahogany and bird's-eye maple long case clock, New Hampshire, circa 1800, 86in. high. (Skinner Inc.) $1,900

A rare Federal inlaid cherrywood long case clock, dial signed *Caleb Davis,* Woodstock, Virginia, circa 1804, 97in. high. (Christie's New York) $8,250

A Federal inlaid mahogany tall case clock, dial signed by David Wood, circa 1790, 90in. high. (Christie's) $33,000

An Arts & Crafts oak tallcase clock, by the Colonial Mfg. Co., Zeeland, Michigan, circa 1914, 84in. high. (Robt. W. Skinner Inc.) $2,000

An early 19th century American cherrywood longcase clock, the 11¹/₂in. arched painted wood dial signed *L. Watson, Cincinnati,* with subsidiaries for seconds and date, 7ft. 6in. high. (Phillips) $3,700

Federal mahogany inlaid tall case clock with alarm mechanism, David Williams, Newport, Rhode Island, circa 1800, 91³/₄in. high. (Skinner Inc.) $11,000

92

LONGCASE CLOCKS

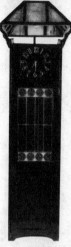

An Arts and Crafts black painted oak electric longcase clock, with a stained and leaded glass door, 76in. high.
(Christie's) $600

Federal walnut inlaid tallcase clock, Pennsylvania, circa 1770–1810, 7ft. 11in. high.
(Butterfield & Butterfield) $5,225

Arts and Crafts oak tall case clock, circa 1910, brass numerals and dial over leaded glass cabinet door, 75½in. high.
(Skinner Inc.) $935

Federal mahogany inlaid tall case clock, William Cummens, Roxbury, Massachusetts, circa 1800, 89in. high.
(Skinner Inc.) $20,900

American mahogany tall case clock with chimes, circa 1880, leaf carved swan's neck pediment over arched dial with painted moon phase, silvered chapter ring, 9ft. 5in. high.
(Skinner Inc.) $4,250

Mahogany tall case clock, William Claggett (1695–1749), Newport, Rhode Island, 1725–40), 88¼in. high.
(Skinner Inc.)
                   $25,300

Carved maple tall case clock, Stonington/Westerly, Connecticut area, circa 1800, the polychrome brass dial with niche in the arch enclosing a carved figure, 85½in. high.
(Skinner Inc.) $15,000

Tall case clock, circa 1800, in mahogany with wooden works, bonnet top, reeded quarter columns, turned feet, 93in. high.
(Eldred's) $1,320

LONGCASE CLOCKS

Mahogany carved tall case clock, Benjamin Willard, Grafton, Massachusetts, 1770, 89in. high. (Skinner Inc.) $48,400

Federal mahogany veneer tall case clock, Simon Willard, Roxbury, Massachusetts, circa 1800, 98¼in. high. (Skinner Inc.) $29,700

Grained tall case clock, Aaron Miller (d. 1777), Elizabethtown, New Jersey, 91in. high. (Skinner Inc.) $6,270

Chippendale mahogany carved tall case clock, Newport, Rhode Island, 1760–85, 86in. high. (Skinner Inc.) $73,700

Chippendale mahogany tall case clock, Pennsylvania, late 18th century, inscribed *Geo Lively, Baltimore*, 7ft. 7in. high. (Butterfield & Butterfield) $2,475

A Chippendale carved mahogany long case clock, by John Wood, Philadelphia, circa 1770, the hood with molded swan neck pediment, 96in. high, 17¼in. wide, 9½in. deep. (Christie's New York) $18,700

A Chippendale cherrywood tall-case clock, dial signed *Nathan Dean, Plainfield, Connecticut*, late 18th century, 86½in. high. (Christie's) $4,180

A Federal inlaid mahogany and flame birch tall-case clock, works by Aaron Willard, case attributed to John or Thomas Seymour, Boston, circa 1800, 103¾in. high. (Christie's) $66,000

LONGCASE CLOCKS

Queen Anne japanned tall case clock, Gawen Brown (1749–1773), Boston, circa 1760, 87in. high. (Skinner Inc.) $4,510

A Federal inlaid cherrywood tall-case clock by Christian Eby, Manheim, Pennsylvania, circa 1810, 107½in. high. (Christie's) $49,500

Federal cherry inlaid tall case clock, Concord, Massachusetts, 1800–1815, 90in. high. (Skinner Inc.) $4,400

A Federal carved mahogany tall-case clock, by Isaac Reed, Frankford, Pennsylvania, circa 1800, 91½in. high. (Christie's) $9,900

A Chippendale mahogany tall-case clock, dial and case signed *Nathaniel Mulliken, Lexington, Massachusetts,* circa 1754, 91½in. high. (Christie's) $33,000

Fine putty painted long case clock, Silas Hoadley, Plymouth, Connecticut, circa 1830, the case painted in tones of red orange and mustard on ivory, 85in. high. (Skinner Inc.) $9,000

Late Federal mahogany and mahogany veneer long case clock, William Brenneiser, Lancaster County, Pennsylvania, 1780-1830, 99½in. high. (Skinner Inc.) $2,600

A fine and important Federal inlaid mahogany long case clock, signed by Simon Willard, Roxbury, Massachusetts, circa 1805, 105¾in. high. (Christie's New York) $110,000

SHELF CLOCKS

A Federal mahogany pillar-and-scroll shelf clock, by Eli Terry & Sons, Plymouth, Connecticut, 1815–1825, on bracket feet, 31in. high.
(Christie's) $1,980

Massachusetts mahogany shelf timepiece, John Bailey, Lynn, Massachusetts, circa 1808, flaring French feet, 36in. high. (Skinner Inc.)
$4,300

Federal mahogany pillar and scroll clock, Bishop and Bradley, Waterbury, Connecticut, circa 1825.
(Skinner Inc.) $1,650

Federal mahogany pillar and scroll clock, Riley Whiting, Winchester, Connecticut, circa 1825, thirty-hour wooden movement, 30in. high.
(Skinner Inc.) $935

A Federal pillar and scroll shelf clock by Seth Thomas, Plymouth, Connecticut, circa 1805, the swan's-neck pediment centering three brass urn finials, 31in. high.
(Christie's) $3,850

Round gothic mahogany veneer shelf clock, Brewster and Ingrahams, circa 1845, with eight day brass spring movement, 19¾in. high.
(Skinner Inc.) $500

A Federal mahogany pillar-and-scroll shelf clock, by Eli Terry & Sons, Plymouth, Connecticut, 1815–1825, on bracket feet, 31in. high.
(Christie's) $1500

A Federal inlaid mahogany shelf clock by William Cummens, Roxburgh, Massachusetts, 1800–1810, with flame and urn finials above a pierced fretwork, 36¼in. high.
(Christie's) $17,600

A Federal mahogany eglomise shelf clock, by Eli Terry and Sons, Plymouth, Connecticut, circa 1820, with swan neck pediment, 30½in. high.
(Christie's New York)
$3,300

SHELF CLOCKS

Federal mahogany pillar and scroll clock, Riley Whiting, Winchester, Connecticut, circa 1820, 30in. high. (Skinner Inc.) $800

Federal mahogany inlaid shelf timepiece, probably Massachusetts, circa 1810, eight day weight driven movement, 8½in. high. (Skinner Inc.) $3,575

Federal mahogany pillar and scroll clock, Eli Terry and Sons, Plymouth, Connecticut, circa 1820, 30-hour wooden movement, 32in. high. (Skinner Inc.) $990

A Victorian carved walnut shelf-clock by Seth Thomas Company, Thomaston, Connecticut, circa 1890, of violin form carved with foliage centering a glazed cupboard door painted in gilding with musical motifs, 29in. high. (Christie's) $4,180

A late Federal mahogany pillar and scroll shelf clock, Seth Thomas, Plymouth, Connecticut, circa 1820, with a glazed cupboard door flanked by colonettes and enclosing a white dial with Arabic chapter ring, 31in. high. (Christie's) $1,540

A Federal mahogany inlaid shelf timepiece, Joseph Chadwick, Boscawen, New Hampshire, circa 1810, on ogee bracket feet, 40in. high. (Robt. W. Skinner Inc.) $5,500

A Federal walnut shelf time-piece, possibly rural Massachusetts, circa 1820, the hood with molded cornice above a glazed kidney door, 32in. high. (Robt. W. Skinner Inc.) $4,250

Rosewood shelf timepiece, probably Atkins Clock Mfg. Co., Bristol, Connecticut, circa 1855, 30-day wagon spring movement, 17½in. high. (Skinner Inc.) $1,100

Classical shelf clock, Isaac Packard, North West Bridgewater, Massachusetts, circa 1825, 30-hour wooden "Torrington-type" movement, 23¼in. high. (Skinner Inc.) $990

SHELF CLOCKS

A late 19th century oak double dial calendar shelf clock, by Waterbury Clock Co., 29in. high. $1,000

Double steeple mahogany wagon spring shelf clock, by Birge & Fuller, Conn., circa 1846, 26in. high.
    $2,250

A walnut double dial calendar shelf clock, by Seth Thomas Clock Co., 32in. high. $2,000

An Empire carved mahogany shelf clock, by M. Leavenworth & Son, Conn., 30in. high. $2,000

A Federal mahogany shelf clock, by Reuben Tower, Massa., 1836, 34½in. high. $10,000

Federal mahogany pillar and scroll clock, by Eli & Samuel Terry, Conn., circa 1825, 28½in. high. $1,250

A Federal mahogany pillar and scroll clock, by Seth Thomas, circa 1820, 30in. high. $1,500

A cast iron and mother-of-pearl shelf clock by Terry & Andrews, with painted dial, circa 1855, 15¾in..high. $350

Empire carved mahogany mirror clock by Munger & Benedict, New York, circa 1830, 39½in. high. $2,000

SHELF CLOCKS

Late 19th century oak double dial calendar shelf clock, by Waterbury Clock Co., 24in. high. **$1,000**

A rosewood shelf clock, attributed to Atkins Clock Mfg. Co., Conn., circa 1855, 18¾in. high. **$2,000**

Empire triple decker mantel clock, by Birge, Mallory & Co., circa 1840, 36in. high. **$1,000**

An Empire carved mahogany and veneer shelf clock, by Hotchkiss & Benedict, N.Y., circa 1825, 39in. high. **$1,000**

A Federal inlaid mahogany shelf clock, by David Wood, Mass., circa 1800, 33¾in. high. **$60,000**

A carved mahogany mantel clock, by Marsh, Gilbert & Co., Conn., circa 1825, 37in. high. **$1,500**

A Federal mahogany inlaid shelf timepiece, by A. Whitcombe, Massa., circa 1790, 13½in. high. **$20,000**

An Empire carved mahogany shelf clock, by Riley Whiting, Conn., circa 1825, 29½in. high. **$800**

An Empire mahogany and mahogany veneer shelf clock, by Hotchkiss & Benedict, N.Y., circa 1830, 38in. high. **$1,500**

Detective Comics No. 35,
January 1940. $10,000

Batman No. 1. $25,000

The Amazing Spiderman.
$675

Superman. $20,000

Teenage Mutant Ninja Turtles.
$300

Detective Comics No. 31,
September 1938. $10,000

Detective Comics No. 29,
June 1939. $10,000

Detective Comics No. 38.
$16,500

Iron Man and Sub Mariner.
$125

Batman No. 2, Summer Issue.
$6,750

The Incredible Hulk. $200

The Fantastic Four.
$1,100

Detective Comics No. 33,
November 1939. $13,000

Lois Lane. $750

Detective Comics No. 27, May
1939.   .$50,000

Green Lantern. $750

Action Comics No. 1, June
1938. $40,000

Giant Size X-Men, Sense
Shattering 1st Issue. $200

Justice League of America, No 8.
$80

Walt Disney No 1, 1940.
$4,000

Showcase No 4, presenting The Flash.
$5,000

Detective Comics No 35, January 1940.
$4,000

Superman, 10th Anniversary Issue, featuring the Origin of Superman.
$600

More Fun Comics No 55, May 1940.
$2,500

All Star Comics No 1, Summer Issue, 1940.
$6,000

Action Comics No 2, July 1938.
$5,500

Showcase presents Metal Men, No 40.
$55

Batman No 47, the Origin of
Batman.
$1,500

Iron Man and Sub–Mariner No 1.
$150

Daredevil No 1, The Man
Without Fear!
$600

Detective Comics No 28 June
1939.
$5,500

Batman, The Dark Knight
Returns No 1.
$100

All American Comics No 1, April
1939.
$1,500

Showcase No 6, first appearance
of Challengers of the Unknown.
$600

New Adventure Comics,
No. 27, June 1938. $300

The Flash, first appearance of
Flash in his own titled series.
$1,000

A silver-applied copper inkwell, maker's mark of Tiffany & Co., New York, 1902, the copper body applied with silver strapwork with applied flowerheads, 6³/₄in. high. (Christie's) $3,520

A Roycroft copper and brass wash handled basket, East Aurora, N.Y., circa 1920, 9in. diam. $200

A hammered copper jar with enameled cover, Boston or Worcester, Mass., circa 1915, 4½in. diam. (Robt. W. Skinner Inc.) $400

A hammered copper wall plaque, by Gustav Stickley, circa 1905, 15in. diam. $6,250

Roycroft copper American Beauty vase, East Aurora, New York, circa 1910, flared rim, original patina, signed with logo, 19¼in. high. (Skinner Inc.) $2,000

A rare copper tea kettle marked Hunneman, Boston, circa 1810, globular, with flat arched swing handle, 11in. wide. (Christie's) $2,420

Hammered copper umbrella stand, attributed to Benedict Studios, East Syracuse, New York, circa 1910, unsigned, 25in. high. (Skinner Inc.) $625

A hammered copper wall plaque, by Gustav Stickley, circa 1905, 20in. diam. $6,000

A hammered copper chamberstick, by Gustav Stickley, circa 1913, 9¼in. high. (Robt. W. Skinner Inc.) $625

A Karl Kipp copper vase, model no. 218, East Aurora, N.Y., circa 1919, 6½in. high. (Robt. W. Skinner Inc.) $300

Early 20th century Arts & Crafts hammered copper wood box with loop handles, 23½in. wide. (Robt. W. Skinner Inc.) $850

Jarvie brass candlestick, Chicago, Illinois, circa 1910, with angled handle, signed on base, 6in. high. (Skinner Inc.) $850

Metcalf Co. hammered copper vase with silver strapwork, circa 1910, silver tacked border on conical form, 12in. high. (Robt. W. Skinner Inc.) $100

Pair of relief decorated copper plaques, signed by Raymond Averill Porter, 1912 and 1913, 10½ x 9½in. (Robt. W. Skinner Inc.) $500

A hammered copper wine pitcher, no. 80, by the Stickley Bros., circa 1905, 15in. high. $350

Patinated hammered copper jardiniere, attributed to Gustav Stickley, circa 1910, 12in. diam. $800

Pair of brass candlesticks, possibly Jarvie, Chicago, circa 1910, unsigned, 6in. high, 5in. diam. (Robt. W. Skinner Inc.) $400

A triangular hammered copper umbrella stand, with single panel of stylised poppies, circa 1900, 23in. high. (Robt. W. Skinner Inc.) $375

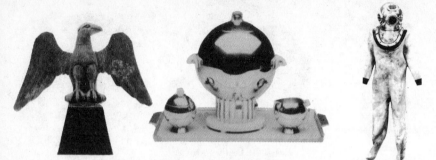

Molded copper building ornament, America, late 19th century, figure of an American eagle with outspread wings, 35 in. high with base. (Skinner Inc.) **$1,100**

Chase coffee urn, sugar, creamer and undertray, Chase Brass and Copper Co., Waterbury, Connecticut, circa 1930, 12¼ in. wide. (Skinner Inc.) **$350**

Fine early 20th century copper diving helmet, with original canvas suit, marked *San Francisco, 1915.* (Eldred's) **$2,090**

A hammered copper and repousse serving tray, attributed to Gustav Stickley, circa 1905, with simple leaf decoration, unsigned, 20 in. diam. **$800**

A fine pair of 20th century brass candlesticks, 8½ in. high. (Robt. W. Skinner Inc.) **$350**

A Gorham & Company red patinated copper and white-metal teapot, stand and burner, with ebonized turned bar handle, the body applied with white-metal flowers, blossom and butterflies, 26.7 cm. high. (Christie's) **$2,937**

Copper and enamel box, Buffalo, New York, circa 1910, red enamel floral decoration with stylized motifs in green and black enamel, 7 in. wide. (Skinner Inc.) **$400**

A bell-metal posnet by Lawrence Langworthy, Newport, Rhode Island, 1731–1739, the flaring cylindrical pot with molded lip, on three feet, 10⅞ in. high. (Christie's) **$6,600**

An Arthur Stone decorated copper bowl, Mass., circa 1910, stamped with Stone logo, 5¼ in. diam. (Robt. W. Skinner Inc.) **$5,000**

A painted cedar hen canvas-back decoy, made by L. T. Ward Bros, 1936, 15in. long. (Christie's) $3,850

A painted wooden Maine Flying Scoter decoy, by 'Gus' Aaron Wilson, circa 1880/1920, together with two black-painted wooden duck decoys. (Christie's) $4,650

A Canada Goose decoy, by George Boyd, early 20th century, 29in. long. (Christie's) $1,800

Two late 19th century painted wooden decoys, one 10in. long, the other 11½in. long. (Christie's) $330

A pair of painted wooden American Merganser decoys, a hen and drake, by L. T. Holmes, circa 1855/65. (Christie's) $93,500

Two late 19th century painted wooden decoys, 9½in. long. (Christie's) $300

A painted wooden hollow constructed Canada Goose decoy, by Chas. H. Hart, Mass., circa 1890/1915, 20½in. long. (Christie's) $4,400

A painted wooden Primitive Brant decoy, three-piece laminated construction, 18in. long. (Christie's) $300

A painted wooden oversized Golden Eye decoy, by 'Gus' Aaron Wilson, circa 1880/ 1920, 20in. long.(Christie's) $1,800

DECOYS

Carved and painted feeding rocking head black duck decoy, attributed to A.A. (Gus) Wilson, South Portland, Maine, 19¾in. long.
(Skinner Inc.) $2,090

Black-bellied plover by A. Elmer Crowell, E. Harwich, Mass., full sized, original paint. (Wm. Doyle Galleries Inc.) $12,000

Carved and painted preening black duck decoy, attributed to A.A. (Gus) Wilson, South Portland, Maine, first quarter 20th century.
(Skinner Inc.) $4,125

A life size carved and painted black duck, Birchler, circa 1925, full length 18in., 19in. high. (Robt. W. Skinner Inc.) $3,650

Eider decoy, Monhegan Island, Maine, late 19th century, hollow carved with inletted head, open braced beak with mussel, incised eye, original paint, 11in. high, 21in. long. (Skinner) $19,000

A miniature Canada goose, by A. Elmer Crowell, Mass., original paint. (Robt. W. Skinner Inc.) $1,000

Early 20th century Summer Yellow Legs carving, G. Shaw, Chatham, Mass., 5in. high, 9in. long. (Robt. W. Skinner Inc.)
                                 $1,100

Pair of Brant decoys, Southeastern Massachusetts, late 19th century, each with incised bill, metal tack eyes, 17in. long.
(Skinner Inc.) $2,700

Painted and carved swan decoy, probably coastal North Carolina or Virginia, late 19th/early 20th century, 29in. wide.
(Skinner Inc.) $375

With the opening of Disneyland Europe and the re-release of such Disney classics as Snow White and Peter Pan, there has been an upsurge in interest in the myriad objects which comprise Disneyana.

The most popular characters are without doubt Mickey Mouse, Goofy, Snow White and Donald Duck, and representations of these have been made in a wide range of materials, from games made of card to diecast and tinplate figures. There is plenty of plastic too, of course, such as large size figures of Mickey and Minnie Mouse and Donald Duck, and these are of interest to doll collectors.

In the 1950s, several British diecast toy companies made Walt Disney figures, such as a Matchbox series showing various characters riding in Matchbox cars.

With so much about, it is obviously the rarer pieces which attract a premium. One of these is a Britains lead set of Snow White and the Seven Dwarfs, first brought out in 1939, which provoked many later white metal imitations. These, however, are generally given away by the brightness of the colors. Among tinplate collectibles, Mickey Mouse mechanical figures or the clockwork Pinocchio toys brought out by Louis Marx before the Second World War are worth looking out for.

Because of the wide range of forms which they take Disneyana objects appeal to a wide range of collectors, and this of course helps increase their value.

A Wadeheath pottery Walt Disney teapot, the body molded **in relief with Grumpy and various woodland animals, 6¹/₂in. high.**
(Christie's S. Ken) $350

A Wadeheath pottery Walt Disney series jug, the body molded in relief with Dopey and various woodland animals, 8in. high.
(Christie's S. Ken) $500

Pelham Puppets, Mickey Mouse and Minnie Mouse.
$200

Fantasia, Disney, 1940, one-sheet, linen backed poster, 41 x 27in.
(Christie's East) $6,000

A set of eight Snow White and the Seven Dwarfs hand-painted porcelain toothbrush holders, 6in. and 4¹/₄in. high.
(Christie's S. Ken) $750

A large felt-covered Mickey Mouse with yellow gloves, green shoes, red shorts, a stitched smile and felt eyes, 16¹/₄in. high.
(Christie's S. Ken) $750

DISNEY

Walt Disney's Snow White and the Seven
Dwarfs. $10

Four Disney stuffed figures, comprising a velveteen Mickey Mouse and Pluto; two corduroy 'Widgets', late 1930's-40's. $750

A Mickey Mouse wicker and colored plastic cane hand bag, 25½in. high. (David Lay) $350

Child Guidance Products Inc., 126 cartridge 'Mick-A-Matic Deluxe' novelty camera in maker's original box. (Christie's) $100

American composition character doll of Pinocchio made by Ideal Novelty & Toy Co., circa 1935, 12in. high. $250

Eight polychrome molded terracotta figures of Snow White and the Seven Dwarfs: Sneezy, Sleepy, Bashful, Doc, Grumpy, Dopey and Happy, 10in. and 6in. high. (Christie's) $200

Walt Disney's 'The Jungle Book' souvenir brochure, 1967. $10

Unusual tinplate and composition Minnie Mouse and pram, probably by Wells, 7½in. long, circa 1933. $3,000

'The Three Caballeros', an original Walt Disney celluloid, signed, 18 x 16in., framed and glazed. $3,500

'Mickey Mouse Organ Grinder', tinplate toy with clockwork and musical mechanisms, by Distler, circa 1930, 6in. long. $1,250

Marx tin wind-up Merry Makers, 1930, 9in. high. $400

Marx, Walt Disney's Donald Duck Duet, boxed. $500

A set of Chad Valley Snow White and the seven dwarfs, 17in. high, the dwarfs 9½in. high. $500

Seven Walt Disney opaque glass ornaments, circa 1935, 4½in. to 7in. $1,250

Mickey Mouse, Two Gun Mickey, 1934 – Mickey With Lasso, a concept drawing, graphite pencil on paper, 9¼ x 12in.
(Christie's S. Ken) $1,000

A plush-covered Minnie Mouse with felt-covered cardboard-lined ears, holding a wire and felt flower, 16in. high, 1930's.
(Christie's S. Ken) $350

Walt Disney Studios, Snow White and the Seven Dwarfs, 1937 – 'The Seven Dwarfs', gouache on full celluloid applied to a wood veneer background, 10½ x 13¾in.
(Christie's) $2,850

Dumbo, Disney, 1941, one-sheet, linen backed poster, 41 x 27in.
(Christie's East) $4,000

A Mickey Mouse Ingersoll pocket watch, depicting Mickey Mouse on the face, the animated hour and minute-hands shaped as Mickey's arms and hands, 2½in. high.
(Christie's S. Ken) $700

Silly Symphony, Disney, 1933, one-sheet, linen backed poster, 41 x 27in.
(Christie's East) $6,000

Walt Disney Studios, Sleeping Beauty, 1959 – 'Briar Rose, woodland animals, and Prince Phillip', gouache on celluloid, a compilation of seven celluloid pieces stapled onto paper, 11½ x 13½in. (Christie's) $400

Mickey Mouse soft toy by Deans Rag Book Ltd., 1930's, 6¼in. high. $250

Walt Disney Studios, Snow White and the Seven Dwarfs, 1937 – 'Five dwarfs peering into a water trough', gouache on full celluloid applied to a wood veneer background, 9½ x 12½in. (Christie's) $3,250

Alarm clock, clockface depicting the Three Little Pigs, circa 1935, 6in. high. $500

Walt Disney, a polychrome woollen rug depicting Mickey and Minnie Mouse performing in a circus arena, 46¾ x 71in., circa 1930's. (Christie's) $650

A rubber inflatable Mickey Mouse 41cm. high. (Phillips) $50

Robin Hood, 1973, and the Rescuers 1977 — three celluloids, 'A Vulture', 'A Hen' and 'A Small Child', each gouache on celluloid, stamped 'Walt Disney Productions Certified Original Hand-Painted Movie Film Cel'. (Christie's) $400

Mickey Mouse Corporation 'Minnie Mouse' watercolor, pen and ink, initialled W.D.P. with 'Micky Mouse Corporation Produktions-Afdelingen' ink stamp 9¼ x 6¼in. (Christie's) $350

Snow White and the Seven Dwarfs, circa 1937 — eight celluloids: 'Doc', 'Sleepy', 'Sneezy', 'Snow White', 'Three Running Dwarfs', 'Happy', 'Grumpy' and 'Woodland Animals', each gouache on celluloid, one inscribed '1936 Walt Disney Productions'. (Christie's) $650

Snow White and the Seven Dwarfs, Disney, 1937, one-sheet, linen backed poster, 41 x 27in. (Christie's East) $8,000

An Art Deco style Mickey Mouse figure of cast iron finished in gilt, 5¾in. high. (Christie's) $650

Der Fuehrer's Face, Disney, 1943, one-sheet, linen backed poster, 41 x 27in. (Christie's East) $3,000

'Jiminy Cricket', original Walt Disney celluloid, framed and glazed, 16¼ x 17½in. $1,250

Back and front of tinplate Mickey Mouse mechanical bank, circa 1930, 6¾in. high. $800

Pinocchio doll, with clockwork movement within the articulated legs, circa 1942, 7½in. high. $600

Britains extremely rare set 1645, Walt Disney's Mickey Mouse, with Minnie Mouse, Goofy, Clarabelle Cow, Donald Duck and Pluto, 1939. (Phillips) $3,500

American Mickey and Minnie Mouse, plaster painted models, 9in. high, circa 1945. $325

'The Moles', a celluloid taken from 'Song of the South', framed and glazed, 12¼ x 10½in. $400

American Mickey and Minnie Mouse, two Fune-Flex painted wooden toys, circa 1931, 6¾in. high. $500

Walt Disney's 'Alice in Wonderland' Punch-Out Book, 1955. $40

Walt Disney rug in tufted cotton, showing characters from his films, 1950's, 104 x 70in. $600

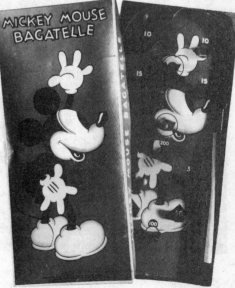

'The Three Caballeros', three plaster figures of Disney characters, circa 1950. $350

Mickey Mouse Bagatelle by Chad Valley Co. Ltd. $75

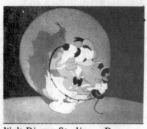

Walt Disney Studios — Peter Pan, 1953, 'Peter Pan and Wendy flying', gouache on full celluloid, framed and glazed, 12½ x 15in.(Christie's) $1,250

Walt Disney Studios — Der Fuehrer's Face, 'Donald Duck speaking into a telephone', gouache on celluloid, stamped 'Original WDP', 7½ x 9in. (Christie's) $10,000

Walt Disney Studios — Snow White and the Seven Dwarfs, 1937, gouache on celluloid, 10½ x 13¾in. (Christie's S. Ken) $2,000

A piece of Cunard White Star RMS Queen Elizabeth headed paper illustrated with a pencil drawing of Mickey Mouse, signed and inscribed *Best Wishes, Walt Disney,* 17.4 x 13.7cm. (Christie's S. Ken) $6,000

Eight hand-painted Wadeware figures of Snow White and the Seven Dwarfs, largest 7in. high. (Christie's) $750

Bambi, Disney, 1942, one-sheet, cond. A, linen backed, 41 x 27in. (Christie's East) $2,000

Walt Disney Studios — Snow White and the Seven Dwarfs, 1937, 'Dopey and Animals', gouache on celluloid with air-brush background, 5¾ x 5½in. (Christie's) $5,000

A Wadeheath pottery Walt Disney series novelty musical jug, the handle modeled as the Big Bad Wolf, printed factory mark and original paper label, 10in. high. (Christie's S. Ken) $1,000

Walt Disney Studios — Sleeping Beauty, 1959, 'Malificent with Crow', gouache on celluloid, 8 x 10in., window mounted and Walt Disney production label on reverse. (Christie's) $3,500

One of two original hand paintings on celluloid, from the Walt Disney film Snow White and the Seven Dwarfs, 6½ x 9½in. $1,500

Lead model Mickey and Minnie Mouse barrel organ group. $100

Walt Disney Studios, Snow White and the Seven Dwarfs, 1937 – 'Five Dwarfs in a heap', pencil and colored crayon animation drawing, 10 x 12in. (Christie's) $700

A felt-covered Grandmother Duck with wire glasses, wooden broomstick, and original 'Lenci' swing-tag ticket, 20in. high. (Christie's S. Ken) $2,000

A draylon plush-covered Donald Duck with yellow felt feet and a Daisey Duck with brown felt high-heeled shoes and handbag, with three smaller similarly covered Huey, Duey and Louie toys. (Christie's S. Ken) $2,500

A Japanese celluloid clockwork Popeye, with original label *Copyright King Syndicate Inc. 1929*, 8in. high. (Christie's S. Ken) $375

'Felix the Cat', large plush-covered toy with cloth bow tie, 28½in. high, circa 1930. $2,000

A painted wooden rocking Mickey Mouse swinging on a stand, made by Triang, circa 1938–9, 32¼in. long. (Christie's S. Ken) $750

'Minnie Mouse', stuffed toy by Dean's Rag Book Ltd., circa 1930, 7in. high. $400

AMERICAN CHARACTER DOLLS

The Americans were great importers of European dolls in the late 19th and early 20th century.

Of the companies who originally imported European products, many went on to manufacture their own. One such was the Amberg Co., which by 1910 had become one of the first to manufacture on a large scale dolls made entirely in the US.

Amberg employed such artists as Grace G Drayton and Jeno Juszko, who contributed the Baby Beautiful range and the New Born Babe, a two day old infant which first appeared in 1914.

Otto Ernst Denivelle worked for Amberg at the beginning of his career and designed new dolls and production methods, such as the introduction of collapsible molds for cold press composition dolls' heads. He also held some copyrights for dolls.

George Borgfeldt was one of those distributors who grew to be the largest in the country and added American manufacturers to his list of suppliers. One of the most famous Borgfeldt products was the Kewpie doll, created by Joseph Kallus from Rose O'Neill's drawings.

Another major importer turned manufacturer was Fleischaker & Baum, established in 1910 in New York. They used the trademark Effanbee and made a wide range of composition and composition and cloth dolls. These usually had sleeping eyes, either of celluloid or metal rather than glass. One of their most famous was the Baby Grumpy model, registered in 1914 and reproduced in a smaller version in 1927 as Grumpykins.

American composition character doll of Shirley Temple, circa 1935, 13in. high. $500

German all bisque character doll of Kewpie, Rose O'Neill's fantasy creature, circa 1910, 11in. high. $500

A pair of all-bisque Kewpie dolls, with jointed arms, 5½in. high, impressed O'Neill on the feet, in original boxes.
(Christie's S. Ken) $1,500

American plastic character doll, with soft head, circa 1962, 12in. high. $400

An American 'Shirley Temple' personality doll, 21in. high, circa 1935. $900

AMERICAN CHARACTER DOLLS

American composition character doll, produced by Cameo, circa 1926, 17in. high. $500

American composition character doll, 14in. high, circa 1940, in original clothes. $500

American cloth child doll, styling indicative of Art Fabric Mills, circa 1895, 13in. high. $400

American artist all bisque doll in one piece by Jeanne Orsini, New York, 1920, 7in. high. $900

American composition character baby, contained in its original cardboard trunk, 10in. high. $400

A composition doll, modeled as Shirley Temple, the straight limbed composition body dressed in outfit from the film "Miss Annie Roonie", 15in. high. (Christie's S. Ken) $225

American plastic lady doll, New York, circa 1975, 21in. high. $900

American plastic Lissy-faced character doll, circa late 1950's, 12in. high. $800

Late 19th century American cloth Folk Art doll, 23in. high in original plaid dress. $500

AMERICAN CHARACTER DOLLS

American composition character doll of Mortimer Snerd, circa 1940, 13in. high. $700

American composition personality doll by the Reliable Toy Co., circa 1935, 17in. high. $400

A painted cloth character doll with jointed velvet body, 17in. high. $500

American composition character doll of Jiminy Cricket, by the Knickerbocker Toy Co., circa 1935, 10in. high. $325

A cloth and leather figural grouping, Lucy Hiller Lambert Cleveland, Salem, Massachusetts, 1840, 15in. high. (Robt. W. Skinner Inc.) $3,500

American composition character doll 'Bobbie-Mae', circa 1940, 12in. high, in original box. $400

American composition character doll of Aunt Jemima, by Tony Sarg, circa 1925, 18in. high. $700

American artist all bisque doll 'Miss Muffet', 1981, on purple tuffet, 7in. high. $300

American plastic character doll with bendable knees, circa 1965, 7½in. high. $800

AMERICAN CHARACTER DOLLS

American artist all bisque doll 'Little Bo Peep', 1981, 10in. high. **$400**

A roly-poly Santa, Germany, probably early 20th century, 10in. high. **$250**

American cloth character doll, by Marjorie H. Buell, circa 1944, 14in. high. **$500**

American composition artist doll, designed by Dewees Cochrane in 1938, 14in. high. **$1,400**

Pair of American composition character dolls by Pat Burnell, 1976, 14in. high. **$250**

A composition shoulder headed doll, by Joel Ellis of the Cooperative Doll Co., 11in. high. **$400**

American composition child doll, with mohair wig, circa 1940, 21in. high. **$350**

American cloth character doll, made by Georgene Novelties Inc., circa 1940, 13in. high. **$500**

A bisque headed child doll with blue sleeping eyes, blonde wig and jointed body, 23in. high, probably Alt Beck & Gosschalk. (Christie's) **$1,200**

AMERICAN CHARACTER DOLLS

American cloth child doll, New York, circa 1900, 22in. high. **$900**

American plaster character Buddha-like figure, by Rose O'Neill, 5½in. high. **$75**

American plastic character doll, by Terri Lee, circa 1965, 16in. high. **$300**

American composition character doll by Effanbee, circa 1940, 17in. high, dressed in formal wear. **$700**

An autoperipatetikos cloth-headed doll, stamped Patented July 1862: also Europe 20 Dec. 1862, American, circa 1862, 9in. high. **$750**

Composition child doll by the American Doll Co., New York, circa 1940, in riding clothes, 13in. high. **$700**

American wooden character doll of Mr Peanut, 8in. high. **$150**

American cloth character doll by Charlene Kinser, 25in. high. **$150**

American papier-mache and plush character doll, circa 1909, 13in. high. **$400**

AMERICAN INDIAN DOLLS

Most primitive cultures have doll figures for various purposes, and a particularly rich tradition exists among some American Indian tribes, whose products fetch astonishing sums today.

The best known are perhaps the kachina models of the Hopi and Zuni Indians. These are made of dry cottonwood root and are painted in exact imitation of the masks worn by tribesmen who impersonate kachinas, or supernatural beings, at their annual tribal ceremonies. A huge variety of kachinas exist representing such various features as warm rain, rainbow or sun gods.

It is often difficult to tell Hopi and Zuni kachinas apart, although the Zuni versions tend to be taller and more slender than their Hopi counterparts. Their rich decoration of beads and feathers make them very popular with collectors, and many are now made especially for sale.

Originally, however, after the ceremonies it was forbidden for the kachinas to leave the village, and some were hung on the walls of houses or given to the children, who would thus gain familiarity with the rituals and traditions of the tribe.

Other types of primitive dolls commonly relate to the female life pattern, and can be carried in the hope of promoting fertility, or to ward off evil. The Ojibwa Indians, for example, had 'unlucky' figures representing a dead child. By caring for one of these, the bereaved mother could believe that she was assisting her child's passage into the next world.

Plains polychrome and fringed hide doll, Northern, 1880's, 18½in. high. $2,000

Plains beaded and fringed hide doll, Northern, 1880's, 13½in. high. $1,750

Late 19th century Hopi polychrome wood Kachina doll, possibly 'Qoia', a Navajo singer, 16½in. high. $4,500

Yuma polychromed female figure with traditional horsehair coiffure, inscribed 'Yuma, Arizona Indian 1931', 8in. high. $600

Southwestern polychrome male figure, Yuma, attached card reads 'Bought 1892 Albuquerque, New Mexico', 8¾in. high. $950

A Hopi wood Kachina doll, 'Mahuu' (locust), with black, mustard and rose decoration over a white painted body, 15¾in. high. $1,600

MADAME ALEXANDER DOLLS

Mme Alexander was a second generation US immigrant who, as a girl, helped her parents run their dolls' hospital and toyshop in the early years of this century. During the First World War she created a Red Cross figure, which was followed in the 1920s by a whole series, including some baby dolls with sleeping eyes. Most of the dolls represent characters, such as those from Dickens or Alice in Wonderland or contemporary celebrities, such as the Dionne quins. She painted the heads herself, and the hair was made of wool.

The dolls were produced in large numbers, and many went for export so they are still quite plentiful today.

American plastic character doll by Madame Alexander, circa 1958, 8in. high. $2,000

Vinyl character doll by the Alexander Doll Co., circa 1965, 13in. high. $1,000

A set of composition dolls representing the Dionne quintuplets with doctor and nurse, 7½in. high, the adults 13in. high, by Madame Alexander. $800

American plastic character doll, 'Prince Charming', by Madame Alexander, circa 1950, 18in. high. $800

American plastic character doll by Madame Alexander, 1975, 22in. high. $500

American plastic character doll by Madame Alexander, circa 1961, 14in. high. $500

American plastic character doll by by Madame Alexander, New York, circa 1966-68, 8in. high. $800

IZANNAH WALKER DOLLS

By the mid nineteenth century dolls made in the United States had come to acquire that rather distinctive homespun character which is typical of so much Americana, and styles had ceased to follow slavishly European influences.

The first notable American doll-maker was probably Izannah Walker of Central Falls, Rhode Island, who was reputedly making rag dolls as early as 1855. She did not, however, take out a patent until 1873, and under patent law it would have been illegal for her to have been producing these before her application in June of that year.

Her dolls have very characteristic hair, with the fashionable corkscrew curls of the time being painted in oil colors. Ears, fingers and other details are notable for the delicacy of their definition.

The dolls were made by stiffening several layers of stockinet which were compressed into molds. The hardened shells were then sewn together and stuffed.

American cloth character doll, produced by Izannah Walker of Rhode Island, circa 1860, 26in. high.
$4,000

American cloth character doll by Izannah Walker with corkscrew curls and painted boots, 18in. tall, circa 1875. $5,000

An Izannah Walker doll with brushed hair and painted boots, circa 1873, 17in. high. $8,000

American cloth character doll by Izannah Walker, circa 1870, 18in. high. $15,000

Izannah Walker cloth character doll with brushed hair, Central Falls, Rhode Island, 18in. tall. $5,500

Ragged cloth doll by Izannah Walker of Rhode Island, circa 1870, 18in. high. $4,000

Izannah Walker doll, Central Falls, Rhode Island, 1870-1880, molded, painted stockinette figure of a girl with corkscrew curls, 18in. high. (Skinner Inc.) $3,000

A Boston Pencil Pointer pencil sharpener. (Auction Team Koeln) $45

Painted and decorated bellows, America, 19th century, some paint loss, leather dry, 18³/₄in. high. (Skinner Inc.) $550

Prancing horse tobacco cutter, America, late 19th century, cutting blade and wooden handle mounted on a swivel, 16½in. long. (Skinner Inc.) $1,700

A Bell System hand telephone, with so-called Bell mahogany receiver for speaking and listening, circa 1880. (Auction Team Koeln) $530

A 1920s Morrisharp Art Deco style electric pencil sharpener, accompanied with letter of authenticity from Peter Noble, stating that the composer Max Steiner used the pencil sharpener when writing the score for the film Gone With The Wind. (Christie's S. Ken) $400

A carved wooden slaw cutter, Pennsylvania, Lebanon County, mid 19th century, the shaped handle pierced with six-pointed star, 58.7cm. long. (Christie's) $132

An American Candlestick desk telephone by Stromberg-Carlson, circa 1920. (Auction Team Koeln) $400

Industrial design Rocket Ship lawn sprinkler, manufactured by Allen Mfg. Co., Chicago, 9³/₄in. high. (Skinner Inc) $300

The Universal Model E 947 toaster, a rare American two sided swing toaster designed by Alonzo Warner, 1922. (Auction Team Koeln) $190

ELVIS MEMORABILIA

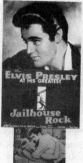

A half length publicity postcard Elvis Presley *in "Pulverdampf und heisse Lieder"* signed by subject in blue biro. (Christie's) $508

A rare set of five Elvis Presley Sun label singles comprising 'Mystery Train', 'I'm Left You're Right, She's Gone', 'Milkcow Blues Boogie', 'I Don't Care If The Sun Don't Shine' and 'That's Alright' each on the Sun label, 45 rpm. (Christie's) $3,945

Jailhouse Rock, MGM, 1957, three-sheet, linen backed, 81 x 41in. (Christie's) $1,045

Elvis Presley - An American in house platinum disc for the 1977 LP 'Moody Blue'. The award mounted above a plaque. (Phillips) $1,903

Elvis Presley's outstanding white one piece stage suit decorated with gilt studs in a 'shooting star' design all over the costume, with letter of authenticity from the suit's designer Bill Belew. (Phillips) $44,980

A large print of an oil painting by June Kelly of Elvis signed and dedicated on the front by Elvis 'Billy beautiful pal Elvis Presley', 58cm. x 48cm. (Phillips) $1,211

Elvis Presley's 'Russian Double Eagle' gold colored metal belt, intricately meshed with two eagle head fasteners. (Phillips) $4,498

Elvis Presley, a rare single-sided acetate 'Good Rockin Tonight', Memphis Recording Service label stamped W.H.B.Q. Memphis accompanied by a certificate of authenticity from The Elvis Presley Museum. (Christie's) $5,775

A single cover, 'You'll think of me/Suspicious Minds', RCA Victor, signed and inscribed 'Sincerely Elvis Presley'. (Christie's) $946

ELVIS MEMORABILIA

'Heartbreak Hotel' ten inch acetate with printed label 'Demonstration Record Not for Sale – The B.F. Wood Music Co., Mills House, London WC2'. (Phillips) $550

Elvis Presley's full length Eastern style green and gold bedrobe. (Phillips) $2,992

Elvis Presley: 'I'm left, You're right, She's Gone/Baby lets Play House', 45 rpm record on the Sun label, (Sun 217), circa May 1955. (Phillips) $411

Elvis Presley - 'That's the Way It Is' a black cotton shirt printed in shades of brown as worn in the film c.1971. (Phillips) $10,150

An Elvis Presley autograph letter, signed to a fan, *Dear Marlene,* with original envelope frankmarked Memphis, Tenn. January 24th 1961. (Christie's S. Ken) $897

A page from an autograph book signed and inscribed 'Best Wishes, Elvis Presley', 2¾ x 4½in., in common mount with a head and shoulders color machine print photograph. (Christie's) $408

A three-quarter length color machine print photograph, circa 1975, signed *Best Wishes Elvis Presley,* 9½ x 7½in. (Christie's S. Ken) $538

Elvis Presley — a casual short-sleeved shirt of white jersey decorated with black 'domino' squares and a pair of navy and white patent leather shoes by Johnston & Murphy.(Christie's) $1,208

A half-length publicity photograph circa early 1960s, signed *Best Wishes Elvis Presley* and inscribed in a different hand *To Wendy,* 9⅛ x 7⅞in. (Christie's) $581

Elvis Presley, a publicity photograph, signed. (Christie's) $567

A circular brass belt buckle, embossed with the Sun Record Company logo, inscribed *Good Rockin' Tonight (Ray Brown), Elvis Presley, Scotty and Bill,* 3in. diam. (Christie's S. Ken) $251

A black and white photograph of Elvis Presley, signed on the front, 10 x 18in. (Phillips) $374

A 10 x 8in. black and white photograph of Elvis on stage circa 1975, signed clearly on the front 'Best Wishes, Elvis Presley'. (Phillips) $481

Elvis Presley, an important autograph letter, signed, [n.d. but October 28th 1958] Hotel Grunewald, Bad Nauheim, Den Terrassenstrasse 10, to Anita Wood, telling her of his intentions to marry her. (Christie's) $7,260

A rare, early black and white promotional German postcard, signed by Elvis Presley on the front in black ink, circa 1959. (Phillips) $550

A page from an autograph book signed and inscribed *To Jerry, Best Wishes Elvis Presley,* 2¼ x 3¼in. (Christie's S. Ken) $538

Elvis Presley, a boxer's robe of cream satin, the back with appliquéd clover leaf emblem and lettering *KID GALAHAD,* with copy of Elvis Monthly Star Special number one, circa 1962 featuring Elvis wearing the robe. (Christie's) $8,712

Elvis Presley, a half-length publicity photograph circa early 1960s, signed and inscribed *To Linda Best Wishes Elvis Presley,* 6½ x 4½in. framed. (Christie's) $445

An American one sheet poster for Lolita, Metro-Goldwyn-Mayer, 1962, framed, 41¼ x 26½in.
(Christie's) $535

Marilyn Monroe — a Shannon Free Airport postcard signed *Marilyn Monroe* and *Arthur Miller*, with a previously unpublished black and white snap shot. (Christie's S. Ken) $695

Alfred Hitchcock, signed card, in old age, overmounted beneath 2.5" x 3.5" photo.
(T. Vennett-Smith) $86

A prototype robotic head of painted gold rubber for the character C-3.P.O. from the film Star Wars, 1977, incised at the base of the neck *C-3.P.O. 20TH CENTURY FOX 1977*, 12 x 9in.
(Christie's) $494

A rare school year book for the 'Class of 1949', Fairmount High School, Fairmount, Indiana, U.S.A. published by the school's Journalism Department, featuring James Dean in the graduating year.
(Christie's) $4,114

A re-issued promotional thermometer for the United Artists film Some Like It Hot of bright orange and white enamel and printed metal decorated with a caricature of Marilyn Monroe, 39 x 8in.
(Christie's) $329

A head and shoulders portrait photograph, signed and inscribed on margin *To S.M. Swamy with my best wishes Charlie Chaplin 1.9.42*, 12¼ x 8¾in.
(Christie's) $370

A bowler hat lined in silk with manufacturer's details *G.A. Dunn & Co. Ltd*, additionally signed *Malcolm McDowell* and inscribed in a separate hand, worn by McDowell in the leading role of the 1971 Warner film A Clockwork Orange.
(Christie's) $3,703

A Souvenir of New York calendar for 1953 featuring a color reproduction of the famous nude portrait of Marilyn Monroe by Tom Kelly, titled *Golden Dreams*, 15½ x 9½in.
(Christie's) $329

Michael J. Fox/Back to the Future Part II, a Mattel Hoverboard of fluorescent pink plywood covered in pink three-dimensional effect vinyl decorated with various Mattel stickers, 19¹/₂in. long.
(Christie's) $4,937

A stetson of fawn colored hatter's plush, accompanied by a letter of authenticity from Gerald A. Fernback stating that 'John Wayne presented . . . his personal stetson when visiting London in February 1951'. (Christie's)
                               $4,000

Aliens, a grotesque Alien creature head of polyurethane foam with isocylate coating finished in acrylic airbrush, 36¹/₂in. long, used in the 1986 Twentieth Century Fox film Aliens.
(Christie's) $1,646

Noel Coward, a full-length dressing gown of black and gold silk, accompanied by a letter of authenticity stating that the robe was given to fellow actor Ronnie Ward at Drury Lane when Ward shared a dressing room with his friend Noel Coward.
(Christie's) $2,468

A novelty souvenir clock for the film Indiana Jones & The Last Crusade, made out of a film box, signed by *Steven Spielberg, George Lucas, Alison Doody, Denholm Elliott, Tom Stoppard, Harrison Ford* and eleven other members of the cast and crew, 11³/₄ x 11³/₄in.
(Christie's) $987

A red and white striped cotton jacket fastening with three white buttons, stamped *M.G.M. WARDROBE* and inscribed *Gene Kelly* inside collar, possibly worn by Kelly in the 1952 M.G.M. film Singing In The Rain.
(Christie's) $370

A late Regency stained satin birch spoonback chair, marked with Paramount Studios invoice number *A 5158* and stenciled with artist's name *Marlene Dietrich*.
(Christie's) $5,760

The Last Sitting, a set of ten limited edition Bert Stern color portrait photographs taken in 1962, six weeks before Marilyn Monroe's death, printed in 1978.
(Christie's) $4,114

A single-breasted tailcoat of charcoal gray wool, with *Metro-Goldwyn-Mayer* woven label inscribed with production number and artist's name *Groucho Marx*.
(Christie's) $3,497

An Art Deco style Mickey Mouse figure of cast iron finished in gilt, 5¾in. high. (Christie's) $651

George Bernard Shaw/Danny Kaye — a rare 16mm. black and white film, 10 minutes long, sold with copyright. (Christie's) $35,321

Walt Disney Studios — Sleeping Beauty, 1959, 'Malificent with Crow', gouache on celluloid, 8 x 10in., window mounted and Walt Disney production label on reverse. (Christie's) $2,974

A half-length still of Mae West signed and inscribed in white ink 'Miss Seena Owen Come up and see me sometime, Mae West', 10 x 8in. (Christie's) $297

Eight hand-painted Wadeware figures of Snow White and the Seven Dwarfs, largest 7in. high. (Christie's) $650

Emile T. Mazy, 'Portrait of Charlie Chaplin', signed, dated 1917, oil on canvas, framed, 27¼ x 21¼in. (Christie's) $1,022

One of a complete set of eight 1970 reproduction front of house stills for 'Giant', with four original 1956 front-of-house stills, for the same film. (Christie's)Twelve $167

James Dean — one of a complete set of eight front-of-house stills for 'Rebel Without A Cause', 1955. (Christie's)
          Eight $260

Ronald Reagan — a poly-chrome film poster, for 'Hell's Kitchen', printed in America by Continental Litho Corp., Cleveland, 41 x 27in.(Christie's) $483

FILM MEMORABILIA

Walt Disney Studios — Peter Pan, 1953, two similar multi-cel set ups, both gouache on full celluloid, one framed and glazed, 12½ x 15¾in. (Christie's) $836

A stetson of fawn-colored hatter's plush with indistinct signature 'Tom Mix' on brim, the inside leather band stamped 'Made by John B. Stetson Company especially for Tom Mix'. (Christie's) $1,022

Walt Disney Studios — Peter Pan, 1953, 'Wendy', a half-length close-up, gouache on celluloid, 12½ x 16in., framed and glazed; with three other celluloids of Wendy.(Christie's) $520

A piece of paper signed 'Marilyn Monroe Miller' attached to the reverse of a previously unpublished photograph of Marilyn Monroe with her husband Arthur Miller arriving at London airport 1956. (Christie's) $1,394

An autograph letter signed from Eli Wallach to a fan, dated Oct. 3rd, 1960, telling him 'I'm currently filming "The Misfits" with Clark Gable, Marilyn Monroe, and Montgomery Clift — since you're collecting autographs, I took the liberty of asking them to sign as well — Sincerely, Eli Wallach'. (Christie's) $8,923

A half-length publicity photograph, signed and inscribed 'To Honey Frances thanks for the pointers Antony Curtis', 10 x 8in. (Christie's) $74

Walt Disney Studios — Snow White and the Seven Dwarfs, 1937, 'Dopey and Animals', gouache on celluloid with airbrush background, 5¾ x 5½in. (Christie's) $4,089

James Dean — one of a complete set of eight front-of-house stills for 'East of Eden', 1955. (Christie's) Eight $260

A good head and shoulders portrait photograph with manuscript inscription 'Montgomery Clift', 10x8in. (Christie's) $223

133

Metro-Goldwyn-Mayer Studios — Tom and Jerry, 'Robin Hoodwinked', gouache on full celluloid applied to a water-color background, 7¼ x 10in. (Christie's) $1,115

A bowler hat, the inside leather band with manuscript inscription in black ink 'Thanks Harry! Stan Laurel', allegedly worn by Stan Laurel during his 1947 stage tour of Britain. (Christie's) $15,801

Metro-Goldwyn-Mayer Studios — Tom and Jerry, 'Muscle Beach Tom', gouache on full celluloid applied to a water-color background, 8½ x 11½in. (Christie's) $1,208

A 'Marilyn Monroe Drawing Aid', the perspex draftsman's 'aid' shaped as the seated figure of Marilyn Monroe with instructions in red lettering, 8½ x 4¼in. (Christie's) $1,022

A decollete full-length evening dress of gold lame in 'Grecian style', owned by Marilyn Monroe and worn by her on the occasion of the Royal Film Premier for 'The Battle of the River Plate', October 29th, 1956, when she was presented to H.M. Queen Elizabeth II. (Christie's) $5,205

A model of the head of the fantasy half man, half fish, from the 1954 film 'The Creature from the Black Lagoon', of molded rubber, 11 x 9½in., possibly a prototype for the head of 'The Creature'. (Christie's) $1,487

A good half-length portrait photograph by Coburn with manuscript inscription 'To Pat Dixon Sincerely Gary Cooper', 13½ x 10½in. (Christie's) $520

Laurel and Hardy — a head and shoulders publicity photograph signed and inscribed on the margin *Hello Gerald! Stan Laurel* and *Oliver Hardy*, 8 x 10in. (Christie's S. Ken) $834

Montgomery Clift, good signed 8" x 10", head and shoulders, apparently obtained in person at the Connaught Hotel, London. (T. Vennett-Smith) $477

Walt Disney Studios — Der Fuehrer's Face, 'Donald Duck speaking into a telephone', gouache on celluloid, stamped 'Original WDP', 7½ x 9in. (Christie's) $9,024

A bowler hat allegedly owned by Oliver Hardy and given by him to Max Miller. (Christie's) $2,230

Walt Disney Studios — Peter Pan, 1953, 'Peter Pan and Wendy flying', gouache on full celluloid, framed and glazed, 12½ x 15in.(Christie's) $1,115

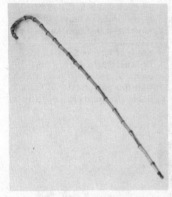

A bamboo cane with metal tip, allegedly given by Charlie Chaplin to a relative of the vendor, 33¾in. long. (Christie's) $1,078

A promotional thermometer for the United Artists film 'Some Like It Hot', decorated with a picture of Marilyn Monroe, her white dress blowing in the breeze, circa 1959, 39 x 8in. (Christie's) $6,507

Ken Konno, two portrait studies of Lauren Bacall and Humphrey Bogart, signed by artist, airbrush, pen and acrylic, both 29½ x 22in. (Christie's) $297

A head and shoulders portrait photograph with manuscript inscription 'Marilyn Monroe', 5 x 4in. (Christie's) $1,115

A theatre programme for 'The Teahouse Of The August Moon' at the Martin Beck Theatre, signed on the cover by Marilyn Monroe and Joe Di Maggio. (Christie's) $1,115

Marilyn Monroe — a poly-chrome film poster for 'Bus Stop', 20th Century Fox, printed in England by Stafford & Co., Nottingham and London, 30 x 20in. (Christie's) $1,208

Sergio Gargiulo, 'Clark Gable and Vivien Leigh in 'Gone with the Wind', original poster artwork, signed and dated '44, pastel, 16¼ x 12in. (Christie's) $700

A U.S.A. Air Corps officer's peak cap with manufacturers details 'Fighter by Bancroft' stamped inside, the cap worn by Clark Gable in the 1949 Metro-Goldwyn-Mayer film 'Command Decision' and a typescript letter from the editor of Picture Show to Mr Browne, congratulating him on his '. . . postcard entry which wins this unique prize of Clark Gable's uniform cap'. (Christie's) $970

A 'translucent' evening dress of 'gold' and 'silver' sequins, the bodice with shoe-string straps, the skirt slit to the thigh, worn by Joan Collins as Alexis Colby, 1981. (Christie's) $1,220

Edith Head 'Ginger Rogers in Tender Comrade', signed, charcoal, pencil and colored crayon costume design, titled by artist and inscribed 'Embroidered organdie', 11¼ x 8¾in. (Christie's) $530

A pair of elaborate costumes of various materials, worn by dancers in the 1978 Universal Studios film 'The Wiz', accompanied by a still showing similar costumes. (Christie's) $325

A rare album containing ninety-four snap-shots of film stars and film studios in Los Angeles, California, 1917-1918, subjects include Charlie Chaplin, Mary Pickford, and various camera-men and directors. (Christie's) $1,300

A one piece running suit of yellow, gray and scarlet 'lycra', and a color still of Arnold Schwarzenegger wearing the suit in the 1987 Tri Star film 'The Running Man'. (Christie's) $650

Ronald Reagan, 'Law and Order' and 'Tropic Zone', two polychrome film posters, Universal productions and Paramount Pictures, both 30 x 40in. (Christie's) $1,425

A two piece 'pant suit' of gold lurex reputedly worn by Marilyn Monroe, and given to Jean O'Doul, the wife of Joe Di Maggio's personal manager; accompanied by a copy of a letter from James Gold O'Doul. (Christie's) $2,850

R. R. Bombe, 'Portrait of Marlene Dietrich', signed, ink inscription dated 15.11.59, watercolor and pencil, 18 x 14in. (Christie's) $185

Two luggage labels each stamped 'S.S. President Roosevelt, Hong Kong to Yokohama, 12 Jun 1964', one inscribed with passenger's details 'Judy Garland', both signed by Judy Garland, signed by Alfred Hitchcock on reverse and annotated with a self-portrait caricature. (Christie's) $325

A 1920's style sleeveless evening dress of black silk chiffon, worn by Betty Grable for publicising the 1940 Twentieth Century Fox film 'Tin Pan Alley'. (Christie's) $120

A photographer's contract comprising a typescript receipt form acknowledging payment and authorising 'Earl S. Moran, . . . to use my photograph for advertising purposes . . . ' inscribed in blue ink with payment details, '$15.00', date 'Los Angeles 26 April '49', and model's name and address, 'Marilyn Monroe, 1301 Nr Harper'. (Christie's) $4,885

A velvet and felt Dean's Mickey Mouse with yellow felt hands, yellow cardboard-lined feet, red shorts, felt ears and printed smile, 11½in. high, early 1930s.
(Christie's)   **$194**

A set of sixteen Mazda Mickey Mouse Lights, each colored plastic Christmas tree light transfer-printed with Disney characters, made in England by The British Thomson-Housten Co. Ltd. in original box, 9½ x 16½in.
(Christie's)   **$133**

An illustrated premiere program for Walt Disney's Snow White and the Seven Dwarfs, Cathay Circle Theatre, Los Angeles, California, December 21st, 1937.
(Christie's)   **$288**

Jean Simmons, a close-fitting, trained evening dress of ruby red crêpe-de-Chine, designed by R. St. John Roper and worn by Jean Simmons in Steven Sondheim's production A Little Night Music, 1975.
(Christie's)   **$350**

A printed souvenir menu for the Grand Order of Water Rats House Dinner, Savoy Hotel, London, September 21st 1947, with illustrated cover featuring cartoon portraits of guests of honor Laurel and Hardy, autographed by subjects in blue ink, 6¾ x 14¾in.
(Christie's)   **$1,954**

Wizard of Oz, a guardsman's bearskin cap with metal plume-ring on left side, 15in. high, thought to have been worn by one of the Wicked Witch's Winkie guards, in the 1939 M.G.M. film The Wizard of Oz, 8¼ x 10¼in.
(Christie's)   **$3,703**

A pair of painted rubber pointed ear tops, 2¼in. high, worn by Leonard Nimoy to create the appearance of Mr Spock's Vulcan ears in the T.V. series, 5¼ x 9¼in. framed.
(Christie's)   **$1,646**

A Wadeheath nursery bowl, featuring Mickey Mouse and Pluto, 6½in. diameter.
(Christie's)   **$103**

Bruce Davidson, "The new face of Marilyn Monroe", circa 1960, gelatin silver print, 6¾ x 9⅞in.
(Butterfield & Butterfield)   **$880**

Liberty, MGM, 1929, one-sheet, linen backed, 41 x 27in.
(Christie's) $6,600

A painted plaster portrait model of Christopher Reeve as Superman in a flying pose, 26in. long.
(Christie's) $494

A plush and velvet Dean's Donald Duck with white hands, yellow cardboard-lined feet, blue velvet hat and jacket trimmed with ribbon and glass eyes, 8in. high.
(Christie's) $288

A cloth Mickey Mouse dressed as a cowboy with sheepskin and leather chaps, original swing-tag ticket and *Knickerbocker Toy Co.* printed label glued to Mickey's right foot, 11in. high, circa 1935.
(Christie's) $453

Jessica Tandy, a pair of gilt frame spectacles, signed *Imperial G.F.*, worn by Jessica Tandy in the 1989 Warner Brothers film, Driving Miss Daisy.
(Christie's) $720

An American one sheet poster for The Empire Strikes Back, Twentieth Century Fox, 1981, signed by *Harrison Ford, Dave Prowse, Billy Dee Williams, Carrie Fisher, Mark Hamill, Peter Mayhew, Anthony Daniels, Kenny Baker* and *George Lucas*, framed, 40¹/₂ x 26³/₄in.
(Christie's) $1,748

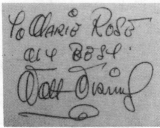

Mickey Mouse, a rare early 1930s German lithographic tinplate mechanical bank with lever action eyes and extending tongue operated by pressing Mickey's right ear, probably made by Saalheimer & Strauss, 7in. high.
(Christie's) $15,427

Walt Disney, a piece of card signed and inscribed, *To Marie Rose, Our Best Walt Disney*, 3¹/₂ x 4³/₄in.
(Christie's) $391

A velvet and felt Dean's Mickey Mouse with white felt hands and yellow leather-soled feet, white shorts, felt ears, printed smile and comic eyes, 8¹/₂in. high, early 1930s.
(Christie's) $247

An illustrated handbill advertising the Maid of the Mist Steamboat ..., signed *Marilyn Monroe* in blue ink, 1952, 4 x 6in.
(Christie's S. Ken) **$2,528**

Marilyn Monroe — a polychrome film poster Gentlemen Prefer Blondes, printed by The Haycock Press, London, 30 x 40in. (Christie's S. Ken) **$278**

A Ketubbah/Jewish marriage contract, inscribed with the bride and groom's names Arthur Miller and Marilyn Monroe, the secular date July 1, 1956.
(Christie's S. Ken) **$13,692**

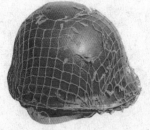

A shirt of cream silk woven with purple stripes worn by Rudolph Valentino as Ahmed – The Sheik in the early scenes of his last film, The Son of the Sheik, United Artists, 1926.
(Christie's S. Ken) **$8,426**

A worn black leather wallet, stamped inside with gilt lettering *James Dean*, made by Rolfs, 7 x 4in., accompanied by an affidavit confirming the provenance.
(Christie's S. Ken) **$10,533**

A 1950s bathing outfit comprising a one-piece bathing suit in black cotton decorated with P.V.C. polka dots, with handwritten labels stitched inside, inscribed *M. Monroe*, designed for the film There's No Business Like Show Business, Twentieth Century Fox, 1954.
(Christie's) **$22,110**

A black chiffon cocktail dress, made by Chanel accompanied by a still of Delphine Seyrig wearing the dress in the 1961 film Last Year in Marienbad.
(Christie's S. Ken) **$674**

An American G.I.'s World War II combat helmet initialled inside R.G.; a unit list from the film Yanks, and a still of Richard Gere wearing a similar helmet.
(Christie's S. Ken) **$674**

A hand-made sixteen-plait bull-whip of kangaroo hide with 106in. long lash – used by Harrison Ford as Indiana Jones in all three Stephen Spielberg/George Lucas adventure films.
(Christie's S. Ken) **$23,172**

A page from an autograph book signed and inscribed 'Rudolph Valentino, London Aug 2 1923', additionally signed by Valentino's wife 'Natacha Valentino'. (Christie's) $400

Ronald Reagan, a single breasted tweed jacket, fully lined, with 'Warner Bros.' woven label, accompanied by a still of Reagan wearing the jacket in the 1947 Warner Brothers film 'Stallion Road'. (Christie's) $1,730

A complete set of eight 'Gone with the Wind' front of house stills; with two promotional programs and two poly-chrome film posters. (Christie's) $265

A painted sign applied with cardboard cut-out letters 'W. C. Fields . . . Poppy', and photomontage portrait of W. C. Fields, advertising the 1936 Paramount Pictures film 'Poppy', 29¾ x 39½in. (Christie's) $160

Metro-Goldwyn-Mayer Studios Tom and Jerry — 'Barbecue Brawl', gouache on full celluloid applied to a water-color background, 8½ x 11¼in. (Christie's) $1,320

Marilyn Monroe 'Let's Make Love', a polychrome film poster, 20th Century Fox, printed in England, 30 x 40in. (Christie's) $610

An ornate headdress of gilt metal, paper, and fiber and an autographed photograph of autographed photograph of Ava Gardner wearing the headdress in the 1976 Twentieth Century Fox film 'The Blue Bird'. (Christie's) $305

A tailored blouse of pink rose silk, with '20th Century Fox' woven label inside; the blouse reputedly worn by Marilyn Monroe in the 1960 Twentieth Century Fox film 'Let's Make Love'. (Christie's) $4,884

A tiara of simulated diamonds and pearls set in white metal; with a quantity of ornate hair pins, all used to decorate Ava Gardner's hair in her role as the Empress Elizabeth of Austria-Hungary in the 1968 Corona film 'Mayerling'. (Christie's) $610

Laurel and Hardy — a half length publicity photograph signed and inscribed *Hello Clive! Stan Laurel* and *Oliver Hardy*, 5 x 7in. (Christie's S. Ken) $452

Marilyn Monroe — a re-issue promotional thermometer of bright orange and yellow enamel, for the United Artists film Some Like It Hot, made in the USA, 13 x 7¼in. (Christie's S. Ken) $79

Spencer Tracy, signed album page, with three attached photos, annotated in another hand 'Died Hollywood'. (T. Vennett-Smith) $76

A collection of autographs from four of the leading characters in the 1939 MGM film The Wizard of Oz, in common mount with a reproduction still from the four characters standing, 23¼ x 15¼in. (Christie's S. Ken) $782

Stan Laurel and Oliver Hardy — a pair of bowler hats, both with *Hal Roach Studios Wardrobe Department,* accompanied by a typescript letter, signed, dated *February 2nd 1938.* (Christie's S. Ken) $17,380

Laurel and Hardy — a three-quarter length photograph of Stan Laurel playing the banjo whilst he unwittingly hits Oliver Hardy in the eye, signed and inscribed, 10 x 8in. (Christie's S. Ken) $869

Marilyn Monroe — a typescript letter, signed, dated *April 17, 1958,* to Charles Henry Crowther, on Marilyn Monroe headed paper, thanking Crowther for sending a copy of the Golden Treasury. (Christie's S. Ken) $1,130

Bert Stern, 'The Last Sitting', a portfolio of 10 Ektacolor prints, 1962, printed 1978, each measuring 19 x 18½in., each signed and numbered. (Butterfield & Butterfield) $3,300

Dorothy Wilding, Tallulah Bankhead, autographed portrait, 1930, gelatin silver print, 8 x 6in., signed and inscribed in ink *For my darling Helen Love and Blessings Tallulah* on recto. (Christie's) $449

Joan Crawford, signed color postcard, three quarter length. (T. Vennett-Smith) **$42**

Audrey Hepburn, signed 8" x 10", head and shoulders from 'My Fair Lady'. (T. Vennett-Smith) **$86**

Harold Lloyd, signed and inscribed sepia 3" x 2", head and shoulders. (T. Vennett-Smith) **$69**

Rudolph Valentino, signed and inscribed sepia 8" x 10", half length, as Vladimir Dubrovsky from 'The Eagle'. (T. Vennett-Smith) **$859**

A half length portrait photograph of Marilyn Monroe by Cecil Beaton, 9¼ x 9¼in., mounted on card, signed and inscribed, with original envelope frankmarked *Beverly Hills Calif. March 9th 1960.* (Christie's S. Ken) **$3,824**

Cary Grant, signed 7.5" x 10" synopsis sheet for 'Indiscreet', to front cover, featuring caricature of Grant and Bergman. (T. Vennett-Smith) **$86**

Edward G. Robinson, good signed and inscribed sepia 8" x 10", head and shoulders smoking pipe, photo by Elmer Fryer of Hollywood. (T. Vennett-Smith) **$118**

A brass key ring, one side inscribed with the MGM lion trade mark, the other inscribed *Dressing Room 24 Clark Gable,* 2¼in. diam. (Christie's S. Ken) **$417**

Humphrey Bogart — a half length film still signed on the margin *Humphrey Bogart,* 10¼ x 8in. (Christie's S. Ken) **$869**

A good head and shoulders portrait photograph signed and inscribed 'Sincerely Gary Cooper', 9 x 7in. (Christie's) $225

A half-length portrait photograph signed and inscribed 'To Phyllis from Clark Gable', 9½ x 7¾in. (Christie's) $305

A good half-length publicity photograph, signed and inscribed 'To Betty from Ronald Reagan', 7 x 5in. (Christie's) $445

Rita Hayworth and Maureen O'Hara, two good portrait photographs, each signed and inscribed by subject 'To Teresa', both 14 x 11in. (Christie's) $240

A head and shoulders portrait photograph signed 'Sincerely Boris Karloff', 7 x 5in; with a rare half-length publicity photograph of Lon Chaney in the role of 'The Wolf Man' 1940. (Christie's) $400

A good head and shoulders portrait photograph, with manuscript inscription 'To Hazel Betts Cordially Carole Lombard', 14 x 11in. (Christie's) $284

A good head and shoulders portrait photograph with manuscript inscription 'To Rose Marie Betts with kindest regards Gary Cooper 1938', 14 x 11in. (Christie's) $142

A collection of ten publicity photographs, each signed and inscribed 'To Phyllis . . . ' subjects include Grace Kelly, Ingrid Bergman, Mel Ferrer, Ava Gardner, Gene Kelly, Robert Taylor, Lana Turner, Stewart Granger, largest 10 x 8in. (Christie's) $485

A good head and shoulders portrait photograph by Laszlo Willinger, with photographer's ink credit on reverse, and manuscript inscription 'Best wishes always to Hazel Betts, Clark Gable', 13 x 11in. (Christie's) $200

A head and shoulders publicity photograph, signed and inscribed on margin *Best Always! Stan Laurel and Oliver Hardy,* 8 x 10in. (Christie's S. Ken) **$1,011**

A head and shoulders publicity photograph, circa 1956, signed and inscribed by subject *To Charles, Marilyn Monroe,* 10 x 8in. (Christie's S. Ken) **$5,898**

A publicity photograph of Vivien Leigh as Scarlett O'Hara, signed by subject, and an illustrated Atlanta, première program for Gone With The Wind, 1939. (Christie's S. Ken) **$843**

Cher, signed 8" x 10", three quarter length standing, as Rusty Dennis from 'Mask', apparently obtained in person at a London Hotel. (T. Vennett-Smith) **$57**

A rare full-length photograph on board R.M.S. 'Queen Elizabeth', signed on margin *Stan Laurel and Oliver Hardy,* 4³/₄ x 3³/₄ in. (Christie's S. Ken) **$295**

A three-quarter length portrait still of subject in the 1941 film Manpower, signed *Marlene Dietrich* in blue ink, 9¹/₂ x 7¹/₂ in. (Christie's S. Ken) **$463**

A head and shoulders publicity photograph signed and inscribed *To Marjorie From Ronald Reagan "Good Luck" Always,* 10 x 8in. (Christie's S. Ken) **$165**

A film still from Star Trek III, The Search For Spock, signed and inscribed by four members of the production including *Gene Roddenberry, Harve Bennett* and *Leonard Nimoy,* 9 x 12in. (Christie's) **$332**

A head and shoulders publicity photograph, circa 1956, signed and inscribed by subject in white ink, *To Briget Warmest Regards, Marilyn Monroe,* 10 x 8in. (Christie's S. Ken) **$4,634**

Douglas Fairbanks Snr — a piece of paper signed and inscribed *Don Q. To Louella Parsons with great admiration and regard from Douglas Fairbanks 1925.* (Christie's S. Ken) **$348**

The Three Stooges, signed and inscribed 8" x 10" by Moe, Larry and Shemp, each individually, with first names only, slight corner creasing. (T. Vennett-Smith) **$621**

Mae West, signed postcard, head and shoulders, Picturegoer No. 781, corner crease. (T. Vennett-Smith) **$76**

Betty Grable, signed and inscribed, slight smudging. (T. Vennett-Smith) **$82**

Douglas Fairbanks Snr., signed 6.5" x 8.5", three quarter length standing. (T. Vennett-Smith) **$115**

Gary Cooper, signed 6.5" x 8.5", head and shoulders. (T. Vennett-Smith) **$191**

A three-quarter length photograph of Katharine Hepburn by Bob Willoughby on the set of the film The Lion In Winter, 1967, signed and inscribed, 12½ x 9¼in. (Christie's S. Ken) **$348**

Shirley Temple, signed 8" x 10", three quarter length with, but not signed by, Victor McLaglen from 'Wee Willie Winkie'. (T. Vennett-Smith) **$124**

William Holden, signed 8" x 10", head and shoulders, four pinholes to white border and corner creasing. (T. Vennett-Smith) **$92**

Fred Astaire, signed sepia postcard, head and shoulders in bow tie.
(T. Vennett-Smith) $95

Laural and Hardy, signed and inscribed sepia 7" x 5", half length, very slight surface crease.
(T. Vennett-Smith) $592

Tyrone Power, signed color postcard.
(T. Vennett-Smith) $67

Clark Gable, signed and inscribed postcard, head and shoulders.
(T. Vennett-Smith) $344

Boris Karloff, signed 8" x 10", head and shoulders, slight creasing.
(T. Vennett-Smith) $191

Ben Turpin, signed 4.5" x 7.75", head and shoulders in characteristic pose wearing bowler hat.
(T. Vennett-Smith) $936

Gary Cooper — a half length portrait photographer signed and inscribed *Sincerely Gary Cooper*, 9 x 7in., circa 1937.
(Christie's S. Ken) $261

Mae West, signed 8" x 10", head and shoulders, modern reproduction signed in later years.
(T. Vennett-Smith) $76

A half length portrait photograph of Bela Lugosi, signed and inscribed *To My Friend Ginger in Rememberance, Bela Lugosi*, 10 x 8in. (Christie's S. Ken) $322

One of a pair of American 19th century fire pumper water buckets, 12in. high. $1,000

A pair of painted leather fire buckets, Newport, Rhode Island, 1843, 12¼in. high. $1,500

A leather fire bucket, America, circa 1806, 13¼in. high. $2,750

Painted and decorated leather fire bucket, New England, 1806, decorated with oval reserve, having draped figure of Mercury blowing a trumpet against a smoke filled sky, inscribed J. Peirce Active 1806, 12¾in. high. (Skinner) $27,000

Leather fire bucket, New England, early 19th century, painted dark green and decorated in polychrome with full-length figure of George Washington holding a globe, dated 1800, 12½in. high. (Skinner) $10,000

A fine painted leather ceremonial parade fire bucket, branded by John Fenno, Boston, circa 1790, with enclosed leather swing handle, 13½in. high. (Christie's) $1,980

A painted leather fire bucket, America, 1822, 12½in. high. (Robt. W. Skinner Inc.) $8,500

Pair of 19th century painted leather fire buckets, New England, 13½in. high. $1,250

Painted and decorated leather fire bucket, Waltham, Massachusetts, early 19th century, ground painted green and decorated with scrolling devices, 12½in. high. (Skinner Inc.) $400

A painted and decorated leather fire bucket, Ipswich, Massachusetts, dated 1803, inscribed S. Newman, Ipswich Fire Society, 30.8cm. high. (Robt. W. Skinner Inc.) $1,300

A 19th century pair of painted and decorated leather fire buckets, New England, 12.3/8in. high. (Robt. W. Skinner Inc.) $1,600

American, 19th century fire bucket, painted green with *City of Boston, Ward No. 11 – Fireman No. 3, 1826* in yellow lettering, 13in. high. (Eldred's) £477

Painted and decorated leather fire bucket, Nantucket Island, Massachusetts, dated 1847, the green ground decorated with black and yellow banding, 12in. high. (Skinner Inc.) $1,200

Pair of painted leather fire buckets, Waltham, Massachusetts, 19th century, green painted ground inscribed *Waltham Fire Club H. Hammond 1842*. (Skinner Inc.) $650

A painted and decorated leather fire bucket, branded I. Fenno, Boston, Massachusetts, dated 1826, the painted ocher ground decorated with a shield-shaped reserve with standing figure of a Massasoit Indian, 13in. high. (Robt. W. Skinner Inc.) $5,500

A leather fire bucket, red painted rim, body painted black, legend reads 'No. 11 Daniel Waldo, 1756', Mass., 11in. high. (Robt. W. Skinner Inc.) $650

Pair of painted and decorated fire buckets, branded *C. Lincoln*, probably Waltham, Massachusetts, 13in. high. (Skinner Inc.) $1,000

A painted leather fire bucket, America, 11¾in. high. (Robt. W. Skinner Inc.) $850

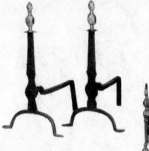

A pair of Federal late 18th/early 19th century bell metal andirons, 24in. high. $1,600

A pair of brass and iron knife-blade andirons, American, circa 1800, 22¼in. high. $950

A pair of brass andirons, probably by R. Wittingham, N.Y., circa 1810, 25in. high. $1,650

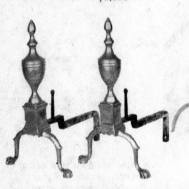

A pair of brass andirons with a shovel and poker, New York, 1800-15, 22in. high. $1,000

Pair of 19th century American iron andirons with arched supports, 19in. high. $350

Pair of Federal brass andirons and matching tools, 1800-20, 17in. high. $1,200

American pair of Federal brass andirons, circa 1810, 17in. high. $500

A pair of Federal brass andirons, 1800-10, 27in. high. $1,750

Pair of Federal brass andirons, Phila., 1800-10, 29in. high. $3,250

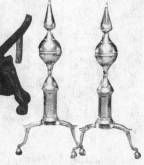

A pair of engraved brass andirons by Richard Whittingham, New York, 1800–1820, on spurred arched legs, 20in. high.
(Christie's) $3,850

A pair of Federal steeple top faceted plinth brass andirons with matching shovel and tongs, New York, 1790-1810.
(Christie's New York) $9,680

A pair of Chippendale brass and iron firetools attributed to Daniel King, Philadelphia, circa 1760, the tongs with penny grips, 28in. high.
(Christie's) $2,860

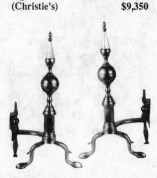

A pair of Chippendale brass andirons, American, late 18th century, each with a ball-and-flame finial over a baluster and ring-turned support, 21¹/₂in. high.
(Christie's) $9,350

Pair of large patinated bronze figural andirons of American Indians by Louis Potter, first quarter 20th century, Roman Bronze Works, New York, 22in. high.
(Butterfield & Butterfield) $4,950

A pair of Federal brass andirons, mid-Atlantic States, 1790–1810, each with a faceted steeple finial over a molded sphere, 24in. high.
(Christie's) $1,320

Pair of signed brass andirons, America, early 19th century, 22in. high.
(Skinner Inc.) $2,000

A pair of brass andirons, probably New York, 1790–1810, each with steeple-top above a ball with mid-band over a faceted hexagonal plinth, 22in. high.
(Christie's) $1,320

Pair of knife blade andirons, America, circa 1780, 25½in. high. (Robt. W. Skinner Inc.) $800

BEDS

"Tady" headboard, designed by Ferruccio Tritta, produced by Studio Nove, New York, offset geometric design marquetry of walnut and ebony, 63¹/₂in. wide. (Skinner Inc.) $1,200

Lifetime Furniture day bed, Hastings, Michigan, circa 1910, shaped crest rail over nine vertical slats at each end joined by seat and lower rail forming three arches, 77¾in. long. (Skinner Inc.) $1,650

Gustav Stickley day bed, circa 1902–03, no. 216, wide crest rail over five vertical slats, with cushion, signed with large red decal, 31in. wide. (Skinner Inc.) $2,400

Late 18th/early 19th century pine deception bedstead, Penn., in the form of a slant-front desk with four sham graduated long drawers, the back enclosing a hinged bedstead, 48in. high, 93in. long. (Christie's) $880

Antique American Sheraton field bed in maple with pine headboard, turned posts, with canopy, 50in. wide. (Eldred's) $1,320

A late Federal carved mahogany high post bedstead, Massachusetts, 1810-1820, the footposts spiral turned with acanthus and waterleaf carved inverted balusters, 58in. wide. (Christie's New York) $2,860

Gustav Stickley double bed, circa 1907, no.. 923, tapering vertical posts centering five wide slats, signed, 57¹/₂in. wide. (Skinner Inc.) $3,300

A late Federal figured maple bedstead, 62in. wide, overall. $3,000

An Arts & Crafts inlaid bed, attributed to Herter Bros., oak burl and other veneers, 26½in. wide. $2,000

BEDS

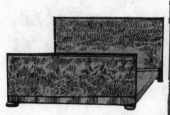

An Art Deco burl and ash bed, American, circa 1930, 4ft. 6in. wide. **$750**

A Federal figured maple and ebonized high-post bedstead, Mass., 1810-20, 59in. wide. (Christie's) **$1,430**

A classical mahogany sleigh bed, New York, 1820–1840, on rectangular molded feet and casters, 60¾in. wide. (Christie's) **$1,870**

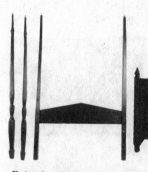

Federal mahogany tall post bed, New England, circa 1800, square tapering headposts flank head board, reeded footposts, 55in. wide. (Skinner Inc.) **$2,310**

Fine Aesthetic inlaid, gilt-incised and carved walnut and burled walnut three-piece bedroom suite by Herter Brothers, New York, circa 1880. (Butterfield & Butterfield) **$22,000**

A Chippendale mahogany tall post bed, Goddard-Townsend School, Rhode Island, circa 1770, 54in. wide, 86in. high. (Robt. W. Skinner Inc.) **$7,000**

Fine American Renaissance figured maple and rosewood three-piece bedroom suite comprising a bedstead, nightstand, and dresser, by Herter Brothers, New York, circa 1872. (Butterfield & Butterfield) **$12,100**

American maple faux bamboo bed, circa 1880, headboard, footboard, side rails, turned finials, incised details, 72½in. long. (Skinner Inc.) **$900**

George III style mahogany tester bed, raised on Marlborough legs, approximate height 94½in. (Skinner Inc.) **$2,000**

153

BLANKET CHESTS

Dower chest, Pennsylvania, early 19th century, the rectangular molded top over a dovetailed case with painted decorations, on molded base, 51in. wide. (Robt. W. Skinner Inc.) $1,500

A red painted blanket chest, possibly Pennsylvania, 19th century, the rectangular top with batten edges, 43in. wide. (Christie's) $1,980

Painted and decorated six-board chest, New England, 19th century, all-over green paint with colored panels decorated with Rufus Porter-type trees, 43in. wide. (Skinner Inc.) $1,900

Painted pine, oak and maple paneled joined chest, probably Hampshire County, Massachusetts, circa 1720, 30in. wide. (Skinner Inc.) $6,600

A Queen Anne painted pine two-drawer blanket box, the lift-lid above three false drawers and two working drawers, probably Mass., circa 1750, 38¾in. wide. (Robt. W. Skinner Inc.) $2,400

Oak and pine carved and paneled chest over drawers, Hadley area, Massachusetts, 1690–1710, 49½in. wide. (Skinner Inc.) $10,450

Grain painted and decorated six-board chest, New England, early 19th century, grained ocher and umber original decoration, 40in. wide. (Skinner Inc.) $2,475

Child's painted and decorated blanket box, Pennsylvania, first quarter 19th century, decorated with red, yellow, black and green, 15in. wide. (Skinner Inc.) $11,000

Paint decorated dower chest, Pennsylvania, late 18th century, the overhanging top with molded edge (feet added; repainted), 54in. wide overall. (Skinner Inc.) $800

BLANKET CHESTS

Painted pine blanket box, possibly New York, early 19th century, the lift top opens to a well with open till, 47in. wide. (Skinner Inc.) $3,100

Grain painted six-board chest, New England or New York State, early 19th century, red and yellow graining to simulate mahogany, 36in. wide. (Skinner Inc.) $375

Painted six-board chest, New England, early 19th century, lidded till, red paint, shaped bootjack ends, 47½in. wide. (Skinner Inc.) $425

Painted blanket chest, New England, circa 1830, the top opens to paper lined interior, with lidded molded till above two drawers, 39in. wide. (Skinner Inc.) $3,575

Grain painted blanket chest, New England, second quarter 19th century, all-over ocher and burnt umber simulated mahogany graining, 38in. wide. (Skinner Inc.) $1,400

Grain painted pine blanket chest, New England, 18th century, the molded top overhangs a dovetailed case with a well, 43¼in. wide. (Skinner Inc.) $27,000

Painted pine blanket box, probably Connecticut River Valley, circa 1840, the rectangular hinged top opens to an interior with lidded till, 25¾in. high. (Robt. W. Skinner Inc.) $1,400

Painted and decorated poplar six board chest, Soap Hollow, Somerset County, Pennsylvania, 1875, probably by John Sala, Sr., (1810-1882) 46in. wide. (Skinner Inc.) $3,200

Painted pine blanket box, probably New Hampshire, first half 19th century, original blue paint, one original pull, 45¾in. wide. (Skinner Inc.) $1,430

BLANKET CHESTS

A paint-decorated poplar and maple blanket-chest, Pennsylvania, 19th century, the hinged and molded rectangular top opening to a compartment fitted with a till, 38⅝in. long. (Christie's) $15,000

Painted dower chest, Pennsylvania, late 18th century, all-over blue-green paint, some original brasses, 50½in. wide. (Skinner Inc.) $1,200

A painted and grained pine blanket box, New England, circa 1810. (Robt. W. Skinner. Inc.) $1,300

Grain painted pine blanket chest, probably New England, 18th century, the over-hanging top with thumb molded edge, 42in. wide. (Skinner Inc.) $2,500

A red pine painted joined blanket chest, America, circa 1820, 37½in. wide. $800

Late 18th/early 19th century Chippendale tiger maple two drawer blanket chest, New England, 38¾in. wide. (Christie's) $2,640

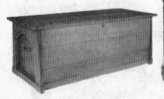

Oak chest, designed by George Washington Maher, circa 1912, green colored oak, cedar lined, brass handles, ends with fielded panels incorporating the motif of *Rockledge*, 60in. wide. (Skinner Inc.) $2,000

Painted dower chest, probably Pennsylvania, early 19th century, original worn green paint, old replaced brasses and hinges, 45¼in. wide. (Skinner Inc.) $1,400

Late 18th/early 19th century painted pine blanket chest, Penn., 50in. wide. (Christie's) $3,300

BLANKET CHESTS

Early 19th century grain painted blanket box, New England, 38¼in. wide. (Robt. W. Skinner Inc.) $750

Grain painted and decorated six-board chest, Albany County, New York, 1810–35, the sides and front grained to simulate mahogany, 42in. wide. (Skinner Inc.) $1,900

Early 19th century grain painted pine six board chest with hinged lid, probably New England, 47¾in. wide. (Robt. W. Skinner Inc.) $1,800

An oak and poplar chest with drawer, probably Conn., 1690-1710, 48½in. wide. (Christie's) $20,900

A painted blanket chest, Pennsylvania, dated 1760, 21in. high, 51½in. wide, 24½in. deep. (Christie's) $385

A grain painted blanket box, the molded lift-top on dovetailed base and cut-out bracket feet, Conn., circa 1850, 40½in. wide. (Robt. W. Skinner Inc.) $650

Grain painted and stencil decorated six-board chest, probably Schoharie County, New York, circa 1830, red and black graining in simulation of rosewood, 40in. wide. (Skinner Inc.) $440

A Chippendale blue painted and decorated blanket chest, signed Johannes Rank, Dauphin County, 1794, the blue painted rectangular top with two orange bordered square reserves, 51½in. wide. (Christie's) $4,620

Grain painted six-board chest, New England, early 19th century, the yellow ocher and burnt umber fanciful graining in imitation of mahogany, 38½in. wide. (Skinner Inc.) $850

BOOKCASES

Renaissance Revival walnut bureau bookcase, circa 1870, drop-front desk enclosing a fitted interior, 51in. wide. (Robt. W. Skinner Inc.) $1,500

Arts and Crafts bookcase, Jamestown, Ohio, circa 1912, cut out gallery flanked by two cabinet doors, 51½in. wide. (Skinner Inc.) $1,600

Shop of the Crafters inlaid bookcase, Cincinnati, Ohio, 1906, with pierced detail over two glass doors, 28¼in. wide. (Robt. W. Skinner Inc.) $2,000

A classical mahogany desk-and-bookcase, probably New York, circa 1820–1840, the upper section with cove-molded pediment above a crossbanded frieze over a pair of Gothic-glazed cupboard doors, on acanthus-carved paw feet, 45½in. wide. (Christie's) $4,180

A Federal mahogany bookcase, Philadelphia, 1790–1810, the two bookcase sections each with double cupboard doors glazed in a Gothic-arch pattern enclosing adjustable shelves, on a molded base, 119in. wide. (Christie's) $24,200

A small Federal carved cherry glazed bookcase on chest, probably Connecticut, circa 1800, the upper case with moulded and dentiled broken pediment, 32½in. wide. (Robt. W. Skinner Inc.) $45,000

Oak bookcase, 20th century, gallery top, shelf with double keyed tenon over median shelf with single keyed tenons, 28⅛in. wide. (Skinner Inc.) $250

A classical mahogany library-case, New York, 1810–1830, on foliate-carved and gadrooned bun feet, 47½in. wide. (Christie's) $3,850

An Aesthetic ebonized and inlaid cherrywood book-case by Herter Bros., N. Y., circa 1880-85, 63½in. wide. $15,000

A mahogany dental cabinet by the American Cabinet Co Two Rivers Wisconsin, the upper part with three glazed-door compartments, 40¼ in. wide. (Christie's S. Ken) $1,351

American Aesthetic movement rosewood, marquetry and parcel gilt side cabinet, circa 1875–85, Herter Brothers, New York, 66¾ in. wide. (Skinner Inc.) $19,800

Renaissance Revival walnut cabinet, third-quarter 19th century, carved broken pediment crest with bust of Shakespeare, 54½ in. wide. (Skinner Inc.) $4,500

Walnut inlaid wall cabinet, Chester County area, Pennsylvania, 1720–60, tulip and berry line inlay on drawer front, 24¾ in. high. (Skinner Inc.) $6,000

A Federal walnut cabinet on chest, Pennsylvania, 1800-1820, in two sections, the upper cabinet with molded cornice above two recessed panel covered doors, on French feet, 41¼ in. wide. (Christie's New York) $9,900

American Dutch-style bombe-fronted walnut and oak glazed display cabinet, 6ft. wide, 7ft. 6in. high. (Giles Haywood) $1,640

An Arts & Crafts oak cabinet with repousse hammered copper panels, circa 1900, 31¾ in. wide. (Robt. W. Skinner Inc.) $1,000

Renaissance style walnut corner cabinet, late 19th century, carved throughout with scrolling acanthus leaves and masks, 59½ in. wide. (Robt. W. Skinner Inc.) $1,100

Rare classical mahogany veneer artifact cabinet, Boston, circa 1820, upper case with ratchets to receive shelves, lower case has ten graduated pull-out drawers, 44in. wide. (Skinner Inc.) $3,400

CANDLESTANDS

Federal tiger maple candlestand, New England, early 19th century, refinished, 27½ in. high. (Skinner Inc.) $1,500

Mahogany veneered octagonal tilt top candlestand, Rhode Island, early 19th century, cross banded veneer and cockbeading in outline, 28¾ in. high. (Skinner Inc.) $1,900

Grain painted candlestand, New England, early 19th century, faux rosewood, 25¼ in. high. (Skinner Inc.) $2,100

A late Federal carved mahogany tilt-top candlestand, New York, 1815-1835, on sabre legs, 30½ in. high. (Christie's) $1,210

A Country Chippendale cherry carved candlestand, Connecticut, circa 1780, the square tray top with applied molded edge, 26 in. high. (Robt. W. Skinner Inc.) $3,100

A Federal mahogany tilt-top candlestand, Western New Hampshire, circa 1810, oval top on an incised vase and ring turned stem, 22 in. wide. (Robt. W. Skinner Inc.) $4,000

A Country Federal birch candlestand, possibly New Hampshire, circa 1810, 27¼ in. high. (Robt. W. Skinner Inc.) $325

Paint decorated Federal candlestand, New Hampshire attributed to the Dunlap family of cabinetmakers, 1780-1810, 26½ in. high. (Skinner Inc.) $8,000

A Country Federal mahogany and cherry inlaid candlestand, Upper Connecticut River Valley, 1800, 28½ in. high. (Robt. W. Skinner Inc.) $1,300

CANDLESTANDS

Chippendale mahogany dish top inlaid candlestand, Connecticut River Valley, late 18th century, 26in. high.
(Skinner Inc.) $5,225

Painted maple, cherry and ash candlestand, New Hampshire, 18th century, original red wash on base, 27in. high.
(Skinner Inc.) $4,400

Painted birch candlestand, possibly Shaker, New England, 1830–1845, all over original red paint, 26½in. high.
(Skinner Inc.) $3,025

A Country Federal tiger maple inlaid tilt top candlestand, New England, circa 1810, the rectangular top with ovolo corners, 28¼in.high. (Robt. W. Skinner Inc.) $1,100

A Federal tiger maple candlestand, New England, circa 1810, top 17 x 17½in. (Robt. W. Skinner Inc.) $1,300

A Chippendale cherrywood candle-stand, New England, 1760–1780, the circular top above a column and urn-turned pedestal and tripartite base with cabriole legs, 28in. high. (Christie's) $3,080

A Chippendale walnut dish-top stand, Phila., 1770-90, 20¾in. diam. (Christie's) $8,250

Federal painted and decorated candlestand, probably New England, on a tripod base with an arris leg, mid 19th century, 28in. high. (Skinner Inc.) $850

Federal cherry candlestand, New England, early 19th century, refinished, 16½in. diameter (Skinner Inc.) $1,000

DINING CHAIRS

Grained Windsor chair for stand-up desk, New England, early 19th century, original red and black graining, 46in. high. (Skinner Inc.) **$522**

A rare Queen Anne stained maple side chair, Connecticut, 1740-1760, on cabriole legs with squared knees and pad feet, 43in. high. (Christie's New York) **$44,000**

One of a set of six painted and decorated Windsor chairs, Pennsylvania, circa 1835, original light green paint, 33⅝in. high. (Skinner Inc.)

(Six) **$1,900**

A Queen Anne maple side chair, Massachusetts, 1730-1750, with carved yoke crest above a solid vase shaped splat, 42in. high. (Christie's New York) **$3,520**

Very important inlaid walnut and ebony chair, designed by Greene & Greene, executed in the workshop of Peter Hall for the living room of the Robert R. Blacker house, Pasadena, California, circa 1907. (Skinner Inc.) **$34,000**

Joseph P. McHugh and Co. oak side chair, New York, early 20th century, shaped lower leg, 36in. high. (Skinner Inc.) **$375**

A painted Windsor fan-back side-chair, New England, 1780–1800, the serpentine bowed crestrail with shaped ears above seven spindles flanked by baluster-turned stiles, 37¼in. high. (Christie's) **$990**

A William and Mary maple side chair, Boston, Massachusetts, circa 1710, the carved, molded crest rail over molded square stiles, 45½in. high. (Robt. W. Skinner Inc.) **$11,000**

A Chippendale carved walnut slipper chair, Philadelphia 1740-1760, on short cabriole legs with trifid feet, 37¾in. high. (Christie's New York) **$4,400**

162

DINING CHAIRS

A Chippendale cherrywood side chair with a square slip seat, Mass,, 1780-1800, 38in. high. (Christie's).$715

Painted fan-back Windsor side chair, New England, 1780–1800, black paint, 35³/₄in. high. (Skinner Inc.) $330

One of a set of six stenciled green-painted side chairs, probably New York, circa 1820, 33¼in. high. (Christie's) $2,860

Chippendale carved mahogany side chair, Philadelphia, 1750–90, old refinish, 39¹/₂in. high. (Skinner Inc.) $130,000

A Queen Anne carved mahogany side chair, Newport, Rhode Island, 1740-1770, the shaped crest with central shell carving, 38½in. high. (Robt. W. Skinner Inc.) $57,000

A Chippendale walnut side chair, America, probably Southern 1760-1790, the serpentine crest rail with molded raked terminals. (Robt. W. Skinner Inc.) $900

One of two black-painted Queen Anne side-chairs, New York, late 18th century, each with yoked crestrail over a vase-shaped splat, 41¹/₂in. high. (Christie's) (Two) $1,760

A cherry, Country Chippendale, upholstered side chair, Upper Connecticut River Valley, circa 1790, 38in. high. (Robt. W. Skinner Inc.) $475

An 18th century mid American red walnut dining chair, the balloon shaped back with solid vase splat. (Phillips) $2,700

163

FURNITURE

A rush-seated oak sidechair, by Joseph P. McHugh & Co., N.Y., circa 1900, 36in. high. (Robt. W. Skinner Inc.) $400

William and Mary banister back side chair, New England, 18th century, dark varnish, replaced splint seat. (Skinner Inc.) $950

One of a set of twelve Federal maple side-chairs, New York, 1790–1810, each with a scrolling concave crestrail over a conforming slat and caned trapezoidal seat, 33¹/₂in. high. (Christie's) (Twelve) $5,500

Queen Anne walnut carved side chair, Newport, Rhode Island, circa 1760, refinished, 38in. high. (Skinner Inc.) $7,150

Chippendale mahogany carved side chair, probably Delaware, late 18th century, refinished. (Skinner Inc.) $2,600

Queen Anne carved walnut upholstered side chair, Rhode Island, circa 1750, refinished, worn old leather upholstery. (Skinner Inc.) $8,500

One of a fine set of six antique American Federal mahogany scrollback dining chairs in the manner of Duncan Phyfe, on reeded splayed legs, probably New York, circa 1810. (Selkirk's) (Six) $5,100

Chippendale mahogany carved side chair, Massachusetts, 1775–85, needlepoint slip seat, 38in. high. (Skinner Inc.) $2,420

Painted decorated child's bowback Windsor side chair, New England, 1790–1810, gold striping on light blue ground, 24³/₄in. high. (Skinner Inc.) $1,800

DINING CHAIRS

Queen Anne walnut side chair, Massachusetts, circa 1780, the serpentine crest rail with scrolled ears, 37¾in. high. (Skinner Inc.) $2,200

A Federal mahogany side-chair, New York, 1790–1810, the molded serpentine crestrail above a shield-shaped back, 37¾in. high. (Christie's) $2,640

Chippendale mahogany carved side chair, Pennsylvania or Delaware River Valley, 1745–60, 38¾in. high. (Skinner Inc.) $1,870

Antique American Queen Anne side chair in maple, vase shaped back splat, rush seat, turned legs ending in Spanish feet, 42½in. high. (Eldred's) $275

A Chippendale mahogany side-chair, Newport, 1760–1780, the serpentine crestrail centered by diapering flanked by molded scrolling ears over a scrolling, pierced vase-shaped splat, 37¼in. high. (Christie's) $4,400

One of a pair of Chippendale carved mahogany side chairs, Massachusetts, circa 1790, refinished. (Skinner Inc.) $500

Queen Anne side chair, New Hampshire, circa 1800, original stained surface with later varnish, replaced splint seat, 43½in. high. (Skinner Inc.) $2,700

A Chippendale mahogany side chair, probably Massachusetts, circa 1770-1800, the serpentine crest with raked molded terminals. (Robt. W. Skinner Inc.) $375

A fine Chippendale carved walnut side chair, Philadelphia, circa 1760, with a serpentine crest-rail centered by a shell flanked by foliate boughs and shell-carved ears over fluted stiles, 41¾in. high. (Christie's) $110,000

EASY CHAIRS

Chippendale mahogany and walnut easy chair, Southern New England, 1760–90, 45in. high.
(Skinner Inc.) **$12,100**

American iron campaign folding arm chair, 19th century, with pale gray buttoned leather upholstery.
(Butterfield & Butterfield) **$550**

An adjustable back armchair, attributed to J. Young & Co., circa 1910, 31½in. wide.
(Robt. W. Skinner Inc.) **$900**

An upholstered oak armchair with cut out sides, circa 1905, 28¾in. wide. (Robt. W. Skinner Inc.) **$1,400**

Stainless steel and leather lounge chair, with head roll, supported by leather buckled straps on X-shape stainless steel frame, 29½in. high.
(Skinner Inc. **$550**

A Federal inlaid mahogany lolling-chair, Massachusetts, 1790–1810, with downswept line-inlaid supports above a padded trapezoidal seat, 46in. high.
(Christie's) **$10,450**

One of a fine and large pair of American modern gothic walnut and oak parlor chairs, attributed to Daniel Pabst, the design attributed to Frank Furness, circa 1877.
(Butterfield & Butterfield) **$1,870**

A Plail Bros. barrel-back armchair, Wayland, N.Y., circa 1910, 33in. high. (Robt. W. Skinner Inc.) **$1,100**

Antique American Chippendale wing chair in mahogany, square legs.
(Eldred's) **$660**

EASY CHAIRS

Queen Anne walnut carved easy chair, Pennsylvania, circa 1740–60, shell-carved knees and pad feet with carving, 20th century upholstery, 41in. high. (Skinner Inc.) $53,900

An American Arts & Crafts oak reclining chair with reclining mechanism, in the manner of A. H. Davenport of Boston. (Phillips) $300

Federal mahogany lolling chair, New England, circa 1800, with molded arms and legs, old surface, 42in. high. (Skinner Inc.) $5,100

A Queen Anne walnut easy chair on cabriole legs with pointed slipper feet, N.Y., 1735-55. (Christie's) $22,000

One of a matched pair of American horn open armchairs, on quadripartite supports and sharply pointed feet, late 19th century. (Christie's)

(Two) $3,360

American 19th century style spoon back armchair, on squat cabriole legs and scrolled feet, upholstered in red and ivory fabric. (County Group) $575

One of a pair of Chippendale mahogany upholstered armchairs, Charlestown, New Hampshire, circa 1795, attributed to Bliss and Horswill. (Robt. W. Skinner Inc.)
Two $28,000

Rococo Revival rosewood laminated side chair, attributed to J. H. Belter, circa 1860, on carved seat rail and cabriole legs, 33¾in. high. (Skinner Inc.) $425

A Country Federal child's mahogany wing chair, New England, circa 1770, 30¼in. high. (Robt. W. Skinner Inc.) $5,500

EASY CHAIRS

Federal mahogany easy chair, New England, circa 1790, the tapering molded legs with stretchers, 47in. high. (Skinner Inc.) **$4,510**

A Federal mahogany lolling chair, Mass., circa 1815, 44in. high. (Robt. W. Skinner Inc.) **$5,500**

A Chippendale mahogany easy chair, Penn., 1780-1800, 47¾in. high. (Christie's) **$8,800**

A Chippendale mahogany easy chair, Salem, Massachusetts, 1770-1790, on square corner molded legs joined by a molded H-stretcher, 33in. wide. (Christie's New York) **$8,250**

Fancy wicker armchair, by Heywood Bros. & Co., Mass., 39in. high. (Robt. W. Skinner Inc.) **$1,600**

A Federal mahogany barrel back easy chair, Philadelphia, 1800-1815, with curving wings above scrolled arms, 47½in. high. (Christie's New York) **$5,500**

A Federal mahogany easy chair, American, 1790-1810, with arched crest flanked by shaped wings, 45¾in. high. (Christie's New York) **$1,650**

Fine antique American Chippendale wing chair with mahogany frame, chamfered straight legs with stretchers, red brocade damask upholstery, 44in. high. (Eldred's) **$3,410**

A Chippendale upholstered wing chair, New England, circa 1810, 45¾in. high. (Robt. W. Skinner Inc.) **$1,800**

ELBOW CHAIRS

A laminated mahogany arm-
chair, circa 1900, 45in. high.
(Robt. W. Skinner Inc.)
$700

Turned great chair, New
England, all-over dark red stain,
worn leather upholstered seat,
44$\frac{1}{2}$in. high.
(Skinner Inc.) $3,250

Painted turned slat back armchair, New England, last
quarter 17th century, rush
seat, 42in. high overall.
(Skinner Inc.) $12,000

A William and Mary painted
banister back armchair, probably Massachusetts, circa 1750,
the cut out splat above five split
banister spindles, 46in. high.
(Robt. W. Skinner Inc.) $1,500

Queen Anne walnut armchair,
Rhode Island, mid 18th century, the yoked crest above a
vasiform splat, 39$\frac{1}{2}$in. high.
(Skinner Inc.) $46,000

Painted writing arm Windsor
chair, Connecticut, 1780-
1800, with baluster and ring
turned splayed legs. (Skinner
Inc.) $7,000

A comb back Windsor arm-
chair, Pennsylvania, late 18th
century, on flaring baluster
turned and cylindrical legs
with ball feet, 42in. high.
(Christie's New York) $4,400

Painted ash and maple child's
ladderback highchair, New
England, 18th century,
original black paint (missing
foot rest), 38$\frac{1}{2}$in. high.
(Skinner Inc.) $3,250

A blue-painted Windsor sack-
back armchair, New England,
late 18th century, the arching
crestrail above seven spindles
and shaped arms over baluster-
turned supports and a shaped
plank seat, retains 19th century
paint, 43$\frac{1}{2}$in. high.
(Christie's) $10,450

ELBOW CHAIRS

Handcraft Furniture slant back Morris chair, circa 1910, No. 497, stationary back with wide arms over five vertical slats, 41in. high.
(Skinner Inc.) $2,310

A Chippendale carved walnut roundabout chair, Rhode Island, 1760–1780, with a serpentine slip-seat and cabriole front leg carved with a scallop shell and pendant bellflower, 31¾in. high.
(Christie's) $49,500

A Queen Anne mahogany armchair, Mass., circa 1750, 42in. high. (Robt. W. Skinner Inc.) $60,000

A fine and rare black painted high chair, Delaware River Valley, 1730-1760, with four graduated and arched slats, on turned front feet, 38in. high.
(Christie's) $6,050

Two of a set of ten Federal carved mahogany chairs, Philadelphia or Baltimore, circa 1800–1810, on square tapering legs joined by H-stretchers.
(Butterfield & Butterfield)
                    $8,800

A Chippendale walnut armchair, Pennsylvania, 1750–1780, the serpentine crestrail with scrolling ears centering a shell above a spurred vase-shaped splat and serpentine, scrolling arms, 41½in. high.
(Christie's) $27,500

A Federal mahogany arm chair, Salem, Massachusetts, 1790-1810, the rectangular back with reeded crest, stiles and three vertical bars, 32¼in. high.
(Christie's New York) $2,200

Child's painted sack-back Windsor chair, New England, late 18th century, painted black, 25in. high.
(Skinner Inc.) $400

A Federal carved mahogany armchair, with scrolling molded tablet crestrail flanked by reeded stiles over X-shaped molded ribs, 35in. high.
(Christie's) $2,420

ELBOW CHAIRS

Painted low back Windsor armchair, Philadelphia area, 1765–80, dark green later paint, 28in. high. (Skinner Inc.) $750

Painted ladderback armchair, England or America, 18th century, (significant paint loss and restoration), 48½in. high. (Skinner Inc.) $175

Antique American sack-back Windsor armchair, Rhode Island, 18th century, in pine, maple and other woods. (Eldred's) $468

Slat back maple child's high chair, Philadelphia or the Delaware River Valley, 1720-1760, old color, old twisted hemp seat, 39in. high. (Skinner Inc.) $6,000

Two late Federal carved mahogany chairs, New York, 1810-1815, each with tablet crest rail above a carved lyre, 32½in. high. (Christie's New York) $24,200

A Country Queen Anne transitional tiger maple armchair, New England, mid 18th century, the yoked crest above vasiform splat, 41¼in. high. (Robt. W. Skinner Inc.) $4,500

Plail Co. barrel back armchair, Wayland, New York, circa 1910, spring cushion seat over wide front seat rail, 40in. high. (Skinner Inc.) $1,100

Chippendale birch high chair, probably Massachusetts, circa 1780, the shaped crest rail above vase splat, 36½in. high. (Robt. W. Skinner Inc.) $2,900

Painted maple slat back armchair, New Jersey or Hudson River Valley, 1725-1775, 40in. high. (Skinner Inc.) $1,300

171

ELBOW CHAIRS

Antique American corner commode chair in maple, square legs, slip seat, 32in. high. (Eldred's) $248

Queen Anne maple carved arm chair, Connecticut River Valley, 18th century, 36in. high. (Skinner Inc.) $4,950

Roundabout maple chair, New England, 18th century, old refinish, 30in. high. (Skinner Inc.) $3,750

A Federal white-painted and parcel-gilt armchair, Philadelphia, circa 1790, the arching molded crestrail decorated with acorns amid oak leaves over a padded tapering back flanked by reeded baluster-turned stiles, 36in. high.(Christie's) $52,800

Child's painted and decorated settee, America, circa 1840, light green ground with green and yellow pinstriping and pink roses, 24³/₄in. wide. (Skinner Inc.) $1,300

A rare Queen Anne maple armchair, probably Rhode Island, 1740-1760, on lambrequin scrolled cabriole legs with pad feet, 39½in. high. (Christie's New York) $12,100

Antique American plank seat Windsor armchair with bamboo turnings. (Eldred's) $100

A Queen Anne walnut armchair, Pennsylvania, 1740–1760, the scrolling arms with incurved supports above a trapezoidal slip seat concealing the support for a chamber pot, 42½in. high. (Christie's) $3,080

Painted turned child's high chair, Bergen County, New Jersey, late 18th century, worn old green paint, replaced rush seat. (Skinner Inc.) $700

ROCKING CHAIRS

An American Arts & Crafts stained oak rocking chair, in the manner of David Kendal for Phoenix Furniture. (Phillips) $175

A child's spindle back arm rocker, unsigned, circa 1915, 24¼in. high. (Robt. W. Skinner Inc.) $400

Shaker maple armed rocker, New Lebanon, New York, circa 1850, old splint seat over-upholstered, 44¾in. high. (Skinner Inc.) $10,450

A painted bow back Windsor rocking chair, probably New England, circa 1830, the bowed crest rail above seven tapering incised spindles. (Robt. W. Skinner Inc.) $700

Early 20th century wicker arm rocker, 31in. wide. (Robt. W. Skinner Inc.) $225

Shaker child's maple rocking chair, Mt. Lebanon, New York, circa 1870, the horizontal shawl bar over three arched slats, 27½in. high. (Skinner Inc.) $1,800

Hand forged steel rocker, 20th century, bent steel, with tufted upholstered suede back and seat, 45in. high. (Skinner Inc.) $250

Plail Bros. barrel-back rocker, with spring cushion seat, N.Y., circa 1910, 31½in. high. (Robt. W. Skinner Inc.) $700

Painted and decorated Salem rocking chair, by J. D. Pratt, Lunenburg, Massachusetts (minor paint loss), 43½in. high. (Skinner Inc.) $1,400

173

CHESTS OF DRAWERS

A fine Chippendale cherrywood reverse serpentine chest of drawers, Connecticut, 1760-1780, the rectangular top with serpentine molded edge, 38¾in. wide. (Christie's New York) $71,500

A Chippendale carved mahogany reverse-serpentine chest of drawers, Massachusetts, 1775–1790, with molded edge reverse-serpentine front above a conforming case, 41in. wide. (Christie's) $8,250

A Federal carved mahogany chest of drawers, Salem, Massachusetts, 1810-1820, with four cockbead molded long drawers flanked by spiral turned columns, 44in. wide. (Christie's New York) $3,520

A fine Chippendale carved mahogany block front chest of drawers, Massachusetts, 1760–1780, with four graduated long drawers over conforming base molding above a shell-carved pendant, on ogee bracket feet, 37⅜in. wide. (Christie's) $22,000

A late Federal mahogany veneer chest-of-drawers, New York, 1810–1820, the rectangular top above a conforming case fitted with a crossbanded long drawer veneered in imitation of three short drawers, 46½in. wide. (Christie's) $2,200

A Chippendale maple chest-of-drawers, New England, 1760–1780, the molded rectangular top above a conforming case fitted with four thumbmolded graduated long drawers, 38½in. wide. (Christie's) $1,320

A Federal inlaid cherrywood bow front chest of drawers, New England, 1790-1810, the bowed top with inlaid cross-banding, on French feet, 40¾in. wide. (Christie's New York) $3,520

A Chippendale cherrywood reverse serpentine chest of drawers, signed by George Belden, Hartford, Connecticut, circa 1790, the molded rect-angular top with an oxbow front edge, 34¾in. wide. (Christie's New York) $20,900

A Federal mahogany and figured maple veneered chest-of-drawers, Boston, Massachusetts, 1790–1810, on bracketed turned tapering feet, 42in. wide. (Christie's) $5,500

174

CHESTS OF DRAWERS

Federal mahogany veneer and cherry inlaid bowfront bureau, Connecticut River Valley, circa 1800, 41in. wide. (Skinner Inc.) $3,500

Federal grain painted chest of drawers, New England, circa 1820s, the scrolled back board above the two tiered bureau, 39in. wide. (Skinner Inc.) $3,500

Chippendale mahogany veneer serpentine chest of drawers, Philadelphia, circa 1789, probably the work of Jonathan Gostelowe (1744–1795), 48in. wide. (Skinner Inc.) $23,100

Chippendale wavy birch bowfront chest of drawers, Massachusetts, circa 1780, the rectangular top with bow front and beaded edge, 35in. high. (Robt. W. Skinner Inc.) $11,000

Eastlake lockend walnut chest of drawers, late 19th century, superstructure of mirrored cabinet and raised galleried shelves, 35¼in. wide. (Skinner Inc.) $1,200

A mahogany chest of American Queen Anne Boston style with molded waved rectangular top, the block front with four graduated long drawers, on cabriole legs and claw-and-ball feet, 32½in. wide. (Christie's) $5,363

Federal mahogany veneered inlaid bureau, New England, circa 1810, drawer front crossbanded in curly maple, 39½in. wide. (Skinner Inc.) $1,300

Federal mahogany inlaid bureau, Middle Atlantic States, 1795–1810, old surface, replaced brasses, 44½in. wide. (Skinner Inc.) $4,250

Grain painted chest, New England, early 19th century, faux mahogany with simulated indistinct stringing, 41¾in. wide. (Skinner Inc.) $1,000

Antique American lift-top blanket chest in pine, painted black, two drawers, bracket feet, 37in. wide.
(Eldred's) $550

Chippendale cherry oxbow chest of drawers, Connecticut, circa 1780, with three reverse serpentine graduated drawers, 44in. wide. (Skinner Inc.) $1,500

Chippendale mahogany block-front bureau, Boston, Massachusetts, 1760–90, refinished, brasses appear original, 34¾in. wide.
(Skinner Inc.) $36,300

Chippendale tiger maple chest of drawers, Rhode Island, late 18th century, the rectangular molded edge top above four thumb-molded edge-graduated long drawers, 38in. wide.
(Butterfield & Butterfield)
                            $7,150

A Federal mahogany bow-front chest-of-drawers, Eastern Connecticut, 1790–1810, the rectangular top with bowed front over a conforming case, on French feet, 43½in. wide.
(Christie's) $2,640

Federal cherry inlaid chest of drawers, possibly Pennsylvania, circa 1800, the projecting molded top above row of inlaid diamonds, 43¾in. high.
(Skinner Inc.) $1,100

Federal mahogany veneer and cherry chest of drawers, Connecticut River Valley, circa 1800, brasses replaced, 41in. wide.
(Skinner Inc.) $2,310

A Federal inlaid mahogany chest-of-drawers, New York, 1790–1810, on flaring bracket feet, appears to retain original brasses, 45¼in. wide.
(Christie's) $2,200

Chippendale mahogany oxbow bureau, Connecticut, circa 1790, cockbeaded drawers, replaced brasses, 35in. wide.
(Skinner Inc.) $6,600

CHESTS OF DRAWERS

Chippendale mahogany chest of drawers, on molded bracket base, brasses are old replacements, old refinish, 38½in. wide. (Skinner Inc.) **$17,000**

A Chippendale mahogany serpentine chest-of-drawers, Massachusetts, 1760–1780, on short bracketed cabriole legs with ball-and-claw feet, appears to retain original brasses, 38in. wide. (Christie's) **$30,800**

Antique American Hepplewhite bowfront chest in cherry, cock beaded drawer fronts, French feet, brass knobs, 41in. wide. (Eldred's) **$1,540**

Queen Anne painted pine blanket chest, New England, circa 1750, the molded lift lid above case of two false and two working thumb molded drawers, 40in. wide. (Skinner Inc.) **$6,000**

Painted birch chest of drawers, Northern New England, circa 1800, drawers beaded, all over original red paint, 43¾in. wide. (Skinner Inc.) **$3,850**

Antique American Sheraton four-drawer bureau, circa 1800, in mahogany and maple, back splash, cock beaded drawers, shaped apron, peg feet, 39½in. wide. (Eldred's) **$605**

Painted Chippendale chest of drawers, New England, mid 18th century, document drawer, old red paint, 37¾in. wide. (Skinner Inc.) **$2,200**

A Chippendale curly maple five-drawer chest, New England, circa 1780, 37¼in. wide. (Robt. W. Skinner Inc.) **$1,000**

Chippendale mahogany reverse serpentine chest of drawers, Massachusetts, 1760–80, drawers with cockbeaded surrounds, 39¼in. wide. (Skinner Inc.) **$13,200**

CHESTS OF DRAWERS

Federal bird's-eye maple and mahogany veneered bow-front bureau, New England, early 19th century, 41¼in. wide. (Skinner Inc.) **$1,045**

A Chippendale fruitwood reverse serpentine chest of drawers, Mass., circa 1780, 38in. wide. **$20,000**

Federal mahogany inlaid bowfront bureau, probably New York, circa 1800, the rectangular inlaid top with bowed front, 41¾in. wide. (Skinner Inc.) **$1,600**

A Chippendale carved cherrywood serpentine chest-of-drawers, probably Lyme, Connecticut, 1780–1800, with serpentine front and molded edges, on ogee bracket feet with elaborately double-scrolled brackets, 39¼in. wide. (Christie's) **$28,600**

Federal inlaid mahogany bow-front chest of drawers, Massachusetts, circa 1790–1810, on flaring French feet, 39in. wide. (Butterfield & Butterfield) **$2,750**

A Country Chippendale tiger maple blanket chest, New England, circa 1760, 37¾in. wide. (Robt. W. Skinner Inc.) **$9,500**

A Federal mahogany and mahogany veneer bowfront bureau, circa 1800, 35½in. wide. **$1,200**

Painted pine blanket chest, New England, circa 1750, old red paint, replaced brasses, 38¾in. wide. (Skinner Inc.) **$1,500**

A Queen Anne tiger maple chest of drawers, New England, circa 1750, 36in. wide. **$4,500**

CHESTS OF DRAWERS

Federal mahogany inlaid butler's desk, probably Middle Atlantic States, circa 1800, refinished, brasses replaced, 42in. wide. (Skinner Inc.) $1,700

A Federal inlaid mahogany bowfront dressing bureau, the top drawer fitted with a mirror, 38in. wide. $5,000

A Federal mahogany inlaid butler's desk on French feet, with replaced oval brass pulls, 44in. wide. $2,500

A Chippendale poplar blanket chest, New England, circa 1780, 37¾in. wide. (Robt. W. Skinner Inc.) $950

Painted pine wall cabinet, America, early 18th century, the rectangular case with applied double arched molding, 18in. wide. (Skinner Inc.) $3,700

A Chippendale cherrywood block-front chest-of-drawers, Connecticut, circa 1775, with blocked front edge above a conforming case fitted with four graduated long drawers above a molded base, on ogee bracket feet, 37½in. wide. (Christie's) $9,900

An American Federal mahogany and maple dressing bureau in the manner of John and Thomas Seymour of Boston, on turned tapering reeded legs, 38½in. wide. (Christie's) $5,759

A Federal mahogany and mahogany veneer bureau, possibly carved by Samuel F. McIntire, circa 1810, 42½in. wide. $3,500

Child's whalebone and exotic woods inlaid mahogany chest of drawers, America, 19th century, 27½in. wide. (Skinner Inc.) $4,950

179

CHESTS OF DRAWERS

A fine Federal inlaid mahogany bowfront chest of drawers, Massachusetts, 1790-1810, the bowfront top edged with lozenge pattern inlay, 41¾in. wide. (Christie's New York) $7,700

A Chippendale cherry and pine four-drawer bureau on ogee bracket feet, Conn., circa 1780, 39½in. wide. (Robt. W. Skinner Inc.) $4,250

A Chippendale mahogany chest-of-drawers, Penn., circa 1780, 38in. wide. (Robt. W. Skinner Inc.) $3,500

A Federal inlaid and flame birch veneered mahogany chest of drawers, Portsmouth, New Hampshire, 1790–1810, the rectangular top with bowed front edged with crossbanding and stringing, on French feet, 40in. wide. (Christie's) $27,500

A grain painted pine five-drawer chest, New England, circa 1780, 37¾in. wide. (Robt. W. Skinner Inc.) $6,000

A fine Chippendale mahogany reverse serpentine chest of drawers, Massachusetts, 1760–1780, with four graduated long drawers with cockbead surrounds over a conforming base molding, on ogee bracket feet, 37in. wide. (Christie's) $10,700

A Federal inlaid mahogany bow front chest of drawers, New England, 1790-1810, on flared French feet, 42in. wide. (Christie's) $2,640

Fine American Renaissance inlaid maple and rosewood tall chest of drawers by Herter Brothers, New York, circa 1872, 37in. wide. (Butterfield & Butterfield) $20,900

A Chippendale curly maple chest-of-drawers, probably New Hampshire, 1775-1810, 39in. wide. (Christie's) $6,600

CHESTS OF DRAWERS

Federal maple with bird's-eye maple and mahogany veneer chest of drawers, New Hampshire, circa 1800, brasses probably original, 42¼in. wide. (Skinner Inc.) $1,000

Birch chest of drawers, New England, circa 1800, refinished, original brass pulls, 36in. wide. (Skinner Inc.) $2,000

Federal mahogany veneered bowfront bureau, Pennsylvania, early 19th century, replaced brasses, signed on back *W.H. Spangler, Ephrata. Pa.*, 42in. wide. (Skinner Inc.) $1,600

A Chippendale mahogany veneer chest-of-drawers, Salem, Massachusetts, 1760–1780, the moulded serpentine top over a conforming case fitted with four cockbeaded graduated long drawers, on ogee bracket feet, 42in. wide. (Christie's) $11,000

Fine pine grained and bird's-eye maple painted apothecary chest, New England, 19th century, with rectangular gallery above thirty-two small graduated drawers, 6ft. ½in. high. (Butterfield & Butterfield) $27,500

A Chippendale mahogany block-front chest-of-drawers, Boston, Massachusetts, 1760–1780, the molded rectangular top with blocked and shaped front above a conforming case, on bracket feet, appears to retain original brasses, 36in. wide. (Christie's) $55,000

A Federal mahogany and bird's eye maple chest of drawers, Salem, Massachusetts, 1800-1815, the rectangular top with reeded edge and outset rounded corners, 42in. wide. (Christie's New York) $3,520

Small Chippendale mahogany chest of drawers, Massachusetts, late 18th century, the four graduated drawers with cock-beaded surrounds, 36in. wide overall. (Skinner Inc.) $18,000

A Chippendale birch reverse serpentine chest of drawers, Massachusetts, circa 1780, on claw and ball feet, 41in. wide. (Robt. W. Skinner Inc.) $9,500

Chippendale style cherry chest on chest, America, circa 1900, 88¹/₂in. high. (Skinner Inc.)   **$5,000**

Chippendale maple carved chest on chest, New England, circa 1780, old refinish, some original brass, 38³/₄in. wide. (Skinner Inc.)   **$13,200**

Chippendale mahogany carved chest on chest, New London County, Connecticut, 1760–80, on a serpentine lower case, 44¹/₄in. wide. (Skinner Inc.)   **$30,800**

A Queen Anne maple chest-on-chest, in two sections, New Hampshire, 1740-70, 41in. wide. (Christie's)   **$14,300**

The John Mills family Chippendale cherrywood chest-on-chest, by Major Dunlap, New Hampshire, circa 1780, 41½in. wide. (Christie's)
$66,000   £39,903

A Chippendale maple chest-on-chest, Mass., circa 1780, 38in. wide. (Robt. W. Skinner Inc.)   **$8,750**

Chippendale birch chest on chest, New Hampshire, circa 1780, old refinish, brasses and escutcheons replacements, 38in. wide. (Skinner Inc.)   **$8,000**

Chippendale carved cherrywood and birch bonnet-top chest on chest, New England, late 18th century, on ball-and-claw feet centring a foliate-carved pendant, 38in. wide. (Butterfield & Butterfield)
$4,125

A Chippendale figured maple chest-on-chest, New Hampshire, 1760–1790, carved with a fan centered by a pair of short drawers over four long drawers, the lower section with four long drawers, 34¹/₄in. wide. (Christie's)   **$17,600**

A Queen Anne tiger maple
high chest of drawers, Salem,
Massachusetts, 1730-1760,
the center fan carved above a
scalloped skirt, 38¼in. wide.
(Christie's) $27,500

**Queen Anne cherry high chest
of drawers, Rhode Island or
Connecticut, 1750–70, brasses
appear original, 46in. wide.
(Skinner Inc.) $8,800**

A Queen Anne cherry high-
boy on four cabriole legs,
Conn., circa 1770, 37¼in.
wide. (Robt. W. Skinner Inc.)
$11,500   £6,845

A Queen Anne maple high
chest of drawers, New England,
1740-1760, the upper case
with molded swan neck pediment centering three ball and
spire finials, 38¾in. wide.
(Christie's New York) $26,400

**The important Gilbert family
matching Queen Anne walnut
high chest of drawers and
dressing table, Salem,
Massachusetts, 1750–1770, on
cabriole legs with pad feet, 38in.
wide. (Christie's) $165,000**

A Queen Anne curly maple
bonnet top highboy, New
England, circa 1770, 36¾in.
wide. (Robt. W. Skinner
Inc.) $3,500

Queen Anne maple high chest
of drawers, Salem, Massa-
chusetts, 1740-1760, on cut
out skirt joining four cabriole
legs, 37¾in. wide. (Skinner
Inc.) $16,000

A Queen Anne walnut high chest
of drawers, Pennsylvania,
1740–1760, the upper section
with coved cornice above three
short and three long thumb-
molded drawers, 41½in. wide.
(Christie's) $16,500

Maple high chest on frame,
Goffstown, Bedford or
Henniker, New Hampshire,
probably by Major John or
Lieutenant Samuel Dunlap, late
18th century, 77½in. high.
(Skinner Inc.) $18,000

CORNER CUPBOARDS

Classical carved walnut
veneered glazed corner cabinet,
Ohio, 1830–40, refinished, brass
replaced, 55in. wide.
(Skinner Inc.)   **$4,125**

A painted pine Federal
corner cupboard, America
or England, circa 1800,
49in. wide. (Robt. W.
Skinner Inc.)   **$3,000**

Federal cherry glazed corner
cupboard, probably Fairfield
County, Ohio, circa 1820–35, the
lower case with a single shelf,
replaced brasses, 41½in. wide.
(Skinner Inc.)   **$4,400**

A fine Chippendale carved
walnut corner cupboard,
probably Lancaster County,
Pennsylvania, 1760-1780,
the upper part with molded
swan neck pediment, 91½in.
high. (Christie's New York)
          $8,800

A Federal carved mahogany
corner cupboard, mid-Atlantic
States, 1800-1810, with overhanging broken molded
cornice above two paneled
cupboard doors, 80½in. high.
(Christie's New York) **$3,300**

A Chippendale mahogany
corner-cupboard, Philadelphia,
1760–1780, the upper section
with broken pitched pediment
with molded dentiled cornice
filled with lattice-work, on ogee
bracket feet, 54½in. wide.
(Christie's)   **$33,000**

A Federal pine corner cupboard, New England, mid-19th
century, with molded cornice,
90in. high. (Christie's) **$3,520**

A Federal red-painted corner-
cupboard, Northern New
England, early 19th century, the
upper section bowed with
molded cornice hung with
spherules over a frieze , 56½in.
(Christie's)   **$11,000**

Federal cherry glazed inlaid
corner cupboard, probably
Pennsylvania, early 19th
century, refinished, 47in. wide.
(Skinner Inc.)   **$3,250**

Federal carved pine corner
cupboard, mid-Atlantic States,
early 19th century, the lower
molded panel doors opening to
one shelf over a molded base,
46¹/₂in. wide.
(Butterfield & Butterfield)
$2,475

Cherry corner cupboard, Ohio,
circa 1840, glazed doors open to
a two-shelved interior above a
single drawer, 56in. wide.
(Skinner Inc.) $1,650

Federal cherrywood corner
cupboard, mid-Atlantic States,
early 19th century, the two
hinged glazed doors opening to
three shelves above a molded
waist, 4ft. 3in. wide.
(Butterfield & Butterfield)
$2,750

A grain painted corner cupboard, mid-Atlantic States,
mid-19th century, with
coved cornice above an egg-
and-dart molding, 87in.
high. (Christie's) $2,860

A Chippendale painted poplar
corner cupboard, mid-Atlantic
States, 1760–1780, the upper
part with a molded cornice
with canted corners above a pair
of arched glazed cupboard
doors, 82in. high.
(Christie's) $2,640

Country Federal poplar corner
cupboard, possibly Pennsylvania, circa 1825, in two
sections, the projecting molded cornice above cockbeaded
glazed door, 45in. wide. (Robt.
W. Skinner Inc.) $2,300

A Federal grain-painted corner
cupboard, Pennsylvania, early
19th century, with scalloped
cornice above a glazed cupboard door, 84in. high.
(Christie's) $6,600

Late Federal carved birch
corner cupboard, early 19th
century, with swan's neck
cresting centering three urn-
shaped finials, 45in. wide.
(Butterfield & Butterfield)
$3,300

Federal pine corner cupboard,
New England, early 19th
century, the hinged paneled
doors opening to shelves, on
bracket feet, 47in. wide.
(Butterfield & Butterfield)
$2,090

CUPBOARDS

A Country Federal pine step-back cupboard, circa 1800, 50in. wide. (Robt. W. Skinner Inc.) $800

Pine paneled cupboard, North America, first half 19th century, the two doors on rat-tail hinges, 46in. wide. (Skinner Inc.) $3,080

Grain painted and bird's-eye maple decorated pine apothecary cupboard, New Ipswich, New Hampshire, early 19th century, 51in. wide. (Skinner Inc.) $13,500

Fine American Renaissance parcel-gilt, stained and burled maple armoire by Herter Brothers, New York, circa 1872, the mirrored door above a single drawer, 46¹/₂in. wide. (Butterfield & Butterfield) $5,500

Walnut glazed cupboard, Pennsylvania, circa 1810, the flaring cornice molding above two glazed cupboard doors, 85in. high. (Skinner Inc.) $3,250

A fine Shaker maple cupboard with chest of drawers, Mount Lebanon, New York, mid-19th century, the molded top above a paneled cupboard door opening to a single shelf, 94in. high. (Christie's) $22,000

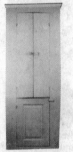

Country Federal glazed tiger maple cupboard, Western Pennsylvania or Ohio, 19th century, 45¹/₄in. wide. (Skinner Inc.) $3,500

Painted slant back cupboard, New England, early 19th century, later glass pulls, green paint, 81¹/₂in. high. (Skinner Inc.) $2,900

Painted cupboard, probably Georgia, mid 19th century, opens to a two-shelved interior, all over original red paint and pulls, 59¹/₂in. wide. (Skinner Inc.) $4,950

Pine glazed stepback cupboard, Pennsylvania, circa 1840, refinished, replaced pulls, 51in. wide.
(Skinner Inc.) $2,475

Classical Revival mahogany veneer commode, Eastern America, mid 19th century, brasses replaced, 25¹/₂in. wide.
(Skinner Inc.) $900

Painted glazed cupboard, New England, first quarter 19th century, black paint, cream interior, brasses replaced, 56¹/₄in. wide.
(Skinner Inc.) $1,900

Country Federal cherry two-part cupboard, possibly Pennsylvania, circa 1820, on shaped bracket feet (refinished, replaced pulls, restoration), 46in. wide. (Skinner Inc.)
$1,500

Chippendale walnut step back cupboard, possibly Pennsylvania, late 18th/early 19th century, in two parts, the upper section with molded cornice above two glazed doors, 6ft. 8in. wide.
(Butterfield & Butterfield)
$4,675

Pine slant back cupboard, New England, 18th century, four thumb molded shelves, old stain and varnish, 75in. high. (Skinner Inc.) $5,500

Antique American two-part step-back cupboard in pine, upper section with two glazed doors, lower section with two paneled doors, 76in. high.
(Eldred's) $1,100

Painted pine stepback cupboard, New England, early 19th century, old wooden pulls and catches, old red paint with later varnish, 7 3¼in. high. (Skinner Inc.) $3,750

Joined, paneled and painted oak court cupboard, probably Massachusetts, 17th century, refinished, 50in. wide.
(Skinner Inc.) $12,100

CUPBOARDS

A rare Federal grain painted step-back cupboard, Vermont, early 19th century, the entire surface painted olive with brown sponge painted grain decoration, 63½ in. wide. (Christie's New York) $44,000

Pine stepback cupboard, Canadian Provinces, 18th century, the molded cornice above two raised panel cupboard doors, 58 in. wide. (Skinner Inc.) $3,250

American Rococo Revival walnut and burl walnut credenza and overmantel mirror, third-quarter 19th century, raised on a plinth base, 59½ in. wide. (Skinner Inc.) $2,300

Carved pine buffet, Canadian Provinces, 18th century, the rectangular top above two molded single drawers and two carved diamond point cupboard doors, 58¾ in. wide. (Skinner Inc.) $3,900

Mahogany cupboard with cockle shell doors, 20th century, cut out crest on arched gallery top, 34½ in. wide. (Robt. W. Skinner Inc.) $325

An 18th century carved pine buffet, Canada, 58 in. wide. (Robt. W. Skinner Inc.) $1,000

A Federal blue-painted cupboard with two glazed doors, possibly N. Jersey, 1775-1810, 50 in. wide. (Christie's) $7,150

An 18th century Chippendale pine step-back cupboard in two sections, Penn., 73½ in. wide. (Christie's) $13,200

George III oak corner cupboard, second half 18th century, with a reeded frieze above two sets of paneled doors flanked by reeded angles, 4ft. 3in. wide. (Butterfield & Butterfield) $2,750

Shop-O'-The-Crafters slant front desk, Ohio, circa 1906, style no. 279, signed with paper label, 42in. wide. (Robt. W. Skinner Inc.) **$600**

Grain painted standing desk, probably Pennsylvania, circa 1825–40, original yellow ocher and burnt umber feather graining, 32in. wide. (Skinner Inc.) **$1,210**

Heywood Wakefield painted wicker desk, late 19th century, shelved superstructure above a rectangular writing surface, 37in. wide. (Skinner Inc.) **$800**

Federal mahogany veneer lady's desk, New England, circa 1810, old refinish, pulls replaced, 38¼in. wide. (Skinner Inc.) **$850**

A rare Queen Anne japanned kneehole bureau, probably Boston area, 1730-1750, with a central recessed bank of five graduated drawers, 34¼in. wide. (Christie's) **$264,000**

A Chippendale carved mahogany block-front and shell-carved bureau-table, Goddard or Townsend Workshops, Newport, Rhode Island, 1750–1760, with a coved frieze and long blocked drawer carved with three shells above a recessed kneehole, 36¾in. wide. (Christie's) **$115,500**

An Arts and Crafts oak writing cabinet, the shaped rectangular top with curved three-quarter gallery above open recess, fall flap and short drawers, 94cm. wide. (Christie's) **$750**

A Chippendale walnut desk, the hinged lid with molded bookrest opening to a fitted interior, probably Virginia, 1760-80, 36in. wide. (Christie's) **$6,050**

A lady's oak desk with fall-front, circa 1890, 28½in. wide. (Robt. W. Skinner Inc.) **$650**

DESKS

Chippendale cherry slant top desk, Norwich-Colchester, Connecticut area, 1760–1800, replaced brasses, 41¼ in. wide. (Skinner Inc.) $2,800

A Chippendale walnut slant-front desk with fitted interior, Penn., 1760-80, 41 in. wide. (Christie's) $3,300

Chippendale maple desk, New England, late 18th century, replaced hardware, 35¼ in. wide. (Skinner Inc.) $3,520

Federal cherry inlaid slant lid desk, New England, circa 1800, the interior of small drawers and valanced compartments, 40in. wide. (Skinner Inc.) $2,200

A   Chippendale figured maple slant-front desk, Pennsylvania, 1770–1780, the rectangular top above a molded slant-lid enclosing an elaborately fitted interior, on ogee bracket feet, 41in. wide. (Christie's) $18,700

Maple grained desk, Southern New England, circa 1800, the interior with valanced compartments and recessed panel prospect door, old refinish, 38½ in. wide. (Skinner Inc.) $5,000

Chippendale mahogany veneered slant lid desk, probably Massachusetts, circa 1800, on molded bracket base, replaced pulls, 39¾ in. high. (Skinner Inc.) $3,500

Chippendale tiger maple slant front desk, New England, late 18th century, the lid with thumb-molded-edge, opening to a compartmentalised interior with six valenced pigeonholes, 37in. wide. (Butterfield & Butterfield) $4,400

Chippendale mahogany carved slant lid desk, Massachusetts, 18th century, refinished, old brasses, 41¾ in. wide. (Skinner Inc.) $4,750

DESKS

Chippendale tiger maple slant lid desk, New England, circa 1800, the interior has small drawers and open valanced compartments, 40½in. wide. (Skinner Inc.) $5,500

A Chippendale mahogany block-front slant top desk with fitted interior, Salem, Mass., 1760-90, 43½in. wide. (Christie's) $22,000

Chippendale sycamore slant lid desk, New England, late 18th century, a stepped interior of small drawers, 36in. wide. (Skinner Inc.) $3,080

Chippendale maple and cherrywood slant front desk, New England, late 18th century, the thumb-molded edge slant lid enclosing a compartment interior with six valenced pigeonholes centering two document drawers, 40¼in. wide. (Butterfield & Butterfield) $3,025

A Queen Anne cherrywood desk-on-frame, probably New Hampshire, 1760–1780, the upper section with thumbmolded slant-lid opening to a fitted interior with five valanced pigeonholes, on short cabriole legs, 41in. wide. (Christie's) $8,250

Antique American Chippendale slant lid desk in mahogany, seashell, herringbone and line inlay, four graduated drawers, fitted interior with an inlaid prospect door and four small drawers, 37in. wide. (Eldred's) $1,210

A fine Queen Anne tiger maple slant lid desk, Massachusetts, circa 1750, on scrolled cabriole legs ending in pad feet, 37½in. wide. (Robt. W. Skinner Inc.) $53,000

A Chippendale carved mahogany slant front desk, signed *Joseph Davis*, Newburyport, Massachusetts, circa 1775, on ball and claw feet, 40in. wide. (Christie's New York) $7,700

Chippendale mahogany carved block front desk, North Shore, Massachusetts, 1770–90, old refinish, replaced brasses, 40¾in. wide. (Skinner Inc.) $14,000

A Chippendale mahogany reverse serpentine slant-front desk, Massachusetts, 1760–1780, on short cabriole legs with ball-and-claw feet, 43¾in. wide. (Christie's) $4,950

Chippendale carved maple desk, New Hampshire, attributed to the Dunlaps, 1780-1800, on an ogee bracket molded base, 35in. wide. (Skinner Inc.) $51,000

A Chippendale cherrywood slant-front desk, Eastern Connecticut, 1760–1780, the slant lid enclosing an interior fitted with a shell-carved small drawer over two shaped small drawers flanked by fluted pilasters, 40¾in. wide. (Christie's) $14,300

A Country Chippendale cherry slant front desk, probably Charlestown, New Hampshire, 1760-1780, 36in. wide. (Robt. W. Skinner Inc.) $22,000

A diminutive Chippendale carved cherrywood slant-front desk, Woodbury, Connecticut, 1760–1780, the rectangular top above a thumb-moulded slant lid opening to a fitted interior with fan-curved and fluted prospect door flanked by document drawers, 39in. wide. (Christie's) $77,000

A Federal inlaid mahogany lady's writing-desk, Boston, 1790–1810, the lower section with applied mid-molding over a hinged felt-lined writing surface above four crossbanded graduated long drawers, on bracket feet, 20in. wide. (Christie's) $8,800

A Chippendale carved cherry-wood reverse serpentine desk, Massachusetts, 1780-1800, with thumb molded slant lid enclosing a compartmented interior, 44¼in. wide. (Christie's New York) $10,450

Charles Rohlfs dropfront oak desk, Buffalo, New York, circa 1907, shaped gallery top above slant front, 25½in. wide. (Robt. W. Skinner Inc.) $3,000

A Chippendale mahogany slant front desk, Massachusetts, circa 1780, with shaped bracket feet and remnants of central drop, 40in. wide. (Robt. W. Skinner Inc.) $12,000

A mid 19th century American Wooton Desk Co. burr-walnut paneled office desk. (Locke & England) $8,476

A Chippendale tiger maple slant lid desk, the fall-front reveals a stepped interior, New England, circa 1780, 36in. wide. (Robt. W. Skinner Inc.) $4,500

Chippendale carved serpentine mahogany slant lid desk, North Shore Massachusetts, 1785–1800, the prospect door with mirror and fan carving, 42in. wide. (Skinner Inc.) $13,000

A Chippendale tiger maple slant lid desk, Rhode Island, circa 1780, the slant lid opens to reveal an interior of valanced compartments and small end-blocked drawers, 38in. wide. (Robt. W. Skinner Inc.) $17,000

Rare Charles Rohlfs carved drop front desk with swivel base, Buffalo, New York, 1900, Gothic style, signed with logo, 25½in. wide. (Skinner Inc.) $12,000

A Federal inlaid cherrywood slant-front desk, Maryland or Pennsylvania, circa 1790, the rectangular top above a slant lid with line inlay centering an inlaid patera opening to a fitted interior with a corner fan-inlaid prospect door, 38in. wide. (Christie's) $11,000

Federal style cherrywood slant-front desk, Pennsylvania, 19th century, the thumb-molded edge slant-lid opening to a compartmentalised interior with eight small drawers, 39¾in. wide. (Butterfield & Butterfield) $1,870

A painted Country birch slant top desk, probably Western Massachusetts, circa 1780, the fall front reveals a stepped interior of valanced compartments, 38in. wide. (Robt. W. Skinner Inc.) $14,000

Fine Queen Anne tiger maple slant lid desk, New Hampshire, circa 1750, the slant lid opens to a double tier stepped interior, old finish, 37½in. wide. (Skinner Inc.) $55,000

DESKS

A Chippendale mahogany slant-front desk with fitted interior, N.Y., 1760-90, 44¼ in. wide. (Christie's) $4,400

Chippendale birch slant lid desk, New England, circa 1800, the interior of small drawers and valanced compartments, 41½ in. wide. (Skinner Inc.) $1,600

Federal mahogany inlaid slant lid desk, New England, circa 1810, on shaped inlaid base with French feet, 38in. wide. (Skinner Inc.) $1,800

A Chippendale mahogany slant top desk, the fall-front reveals a fitted interior, Mass., circa 1780, 40in. wide. (Robt. W. Skinner Inc.) $5,500

Antique American Chippendale slant lid desk in tiger maple, fitted interior with six drawers and seven pigeon holes, four drawers with molded fronts, 40in. wide. (Eldred's) $5,940

A Chippendale birch reverse-serpentine front desk, Mass., 1765-85, 42½ in. wide. (Christie's) $10,450

A Chippendale maple slant top desk, the fall-front opening to reveal a fitted interior, circa 1790, 36in. wide. (Robt. W. Skinner Inc.) $1,600

An antique Federal period mahogany slantfront desk of desirable small size, decorated with line inlay, the flap enclosing a fitted interior, 34in. wide. (Selkirk's) $3,000

A Chippendale carved figured maple slant front desk, Rhode Island, 1760-80, 38in. wide. (Christie's) $12,650

DESKS

An American walnut roll-top desk, with a D-shaped tambour top enclosing a fitted interior with three frieze drawers below. (Christie's S. Ken)
$2,310

A fine Chippendale carved mahogany block-front desk, Boston, 1760-1780, the case with four graduated and blocked long drawers, 43in. wide. (Christie's) $71,500   £42,235

Chippendale mahogany block front desk, late 18th century, base restoration including four repaired feet, 36½in. wide. (Skinner Inc.) $2,800

Chippendale walnut slant-front desk, Pennsylvania, circa 1770-1790, the thumb-molded edge slant lid opening to a compartmentalised interior, 41in. wide. (Butterfield & Butterfield) $3,850

A Chippendale figured maple slant front desk, New England, 1760-1780, with thumb molded slant lid opening to a fitted interior with six valanced pigeonholes, 93.7cm. (Christie's New York) $12,100

Federal walnut inlaid slant-front desk, Pennsylvania, early 19th century, the thumb-molded edge top with string quarter fan-inlay opening to a compartmentalised interior, 42in. wide. (Butterfield & Butterfield) $2,200

Country Queen Anne maple desk on frame, New England, circa 1740, the slant lid opens to reveal interior with compartments and drawers, 34in. wide. (Skinner Inc.) $4,250

A Queen Anne maple inlaid slant top desk, New England, 18th and 19th century, the slant lid with burl panels centering a sun motif, 34¾in. wide. (Robt. W. Skinner Inc.) $17,000

Chippendale carved tiger maple slant lid desk, New Hampshire, late 18th century, stepped interior of small drawers and valanced compartments, 37½in. wide. (Skinner Inc.) $9,900

DESKS & BOOKCASES

A small Chippendale mahogany desk bookcase, Mass., circa 1780, 34in. wide. (Robt. W. Skinner Inc.) $14,000

A Chippendale mahogany blockfront secretary desk, circa 1780, 42in. wide. (Robt. W. Skinner Inc.) $50,000

Federal cherry desk and bookcase, Southern New England, early 19th century, two-shelved divided upper interior, 41¹/₂in. wide. (Skinner Inc.) $3,300

A Chippendale mahogany desk and bookcase, possibly Charleston, S. Carolina, 1760-90, 53in. wide, 109in. high. (Christie's) $242,000

Federal cherry and flame birch veneer desk and bookcase, New England, circa 1815, refinished, replaced brasses, 40in. wide. (Skinner Inc.) $3,750

A Classical rosewood desk and bookcase, probably Boston 1825-1835, on flaring hexagonally faceted legs above a shaped medial shelf, 50½in wide. (Christie's New York) $14,300

Chippendale cherry desk and bookcase, Connecticut, late 18th century, refinished, replaced brasses, 36¹/₄in. wide. (Skinner Inc.) $2,500

Federal mahogany glazed desk and bookcase, New England, circa 1810, refinished, brasses old replacements, 40¹/₂in. wide. (Skinner Inc.) $2,200

An antique American Renaissance Revival figured walnut cylinder desk and bookcase, the top member with architectural pediment, circa 1880, 8ft. 1in. high. (Selkirk's) $1,900

196

HANGING CUPBOARDS

A poplar hanging cupboard, Ephrata, Penn., 1743-60, 18½in. wide, 24½in. high. (Christie's) $990

Country Chippendale walnut corner cabinet, Pennsylvania, circa 1780, the shaped backboard joining three-quarter round shelves, 24in. wide. (Skinner Inc.) $7,000

Mid/late 18th century Chippendale poplar hanging cupboard, Penn., 36½in. high, 27in. wide. (Christie's) $1,045

KAS

A William and Mary gumwood kas, New York, 1725–1755, the upper part with an elaborately molded bold cornice above two fielded panel double cupboard doors enclosing two shelves, 65¹/₂in. wide. (Christie's) $4,950

A maple and walnut kas, in two sections, N.Y., or N. Jersey, 1750-1800, 72in. wide. (Christie's) $4,400

Pine wardrobe or Kas, Hudson River Valley or Delaware, circa 1750, on large turnip feet painted black, 59½in. wide. (Skinner Inc.) $6,500

LINEN PRESSES

A Chippendale red gum linen press, New York State, 1750-1800, on a molded base with bracket feet, 51½in. wide. (Christie's) $4,180

A Chippendale figured maple linen-press, Pennsylvania, 1760–1780, the upper section with elaborately molded cornice about two arched paneled cupboard doors fitted with three shelves, on bracket feet, 48in. wide. (Christie's) $14,300

Chippendale cherry linen press, Eastern America, circa 1780, the molded cornice above two paneled doors, 42in. wide. (Skinner Inc.) $3,700

Painted pine fireboard, possibly Central Massachusetts, circa 1815, depicting fruit and flowering boughs in a vase, 37½in. wide. (Skinner Inc.) **$26,000**

A Victorian wooden fencing, Maine, circa 1850, 39½in. high, total length 172in. **$600**

Painted three panel floor screen, depicting an elephant family moving through the jungle, signed *Ernest Brierly*, 8ft. wide. (Skinner Inc.) **$2,500**

A wood and copper phone screen, circa 1910, 12in. high, 13in. wide. (Robt. W. Skinner Inc.) **$150**

Paint decorated three-paneled folding screen, America, 19th century, each section decorated with rocaille and a laden compote within scrolled border, 5ft. high. (Skinner Inc.) **$330**

Arts and Crafts fireplace screen, circa 1910, triptych design comprised of three repousse copper panels decorated with stylized fish and naturalistic motifs, in hammered copper and riveted frame, 38in. wide. (Skinner Inc.) **$500**

A late Federal rosewood firescreen, probably Boston, mid-19th century, with three hinged rectangular panels over trestle supports with hipped downswept legs, 40½in. high. (Christie's) **$1,320**

A wrought-iron and pierced copper fire-screen, circa 1900, 34½in. wide. (Robt. W. Skinner Inc.) **$325**

An inlaid oak three-paneled screen, designed by Harvey Ellis for Gustav Stickley, circa 1903-04, 66¾in. high, each panel 20in. wide. (Robt. W. Skinner Inc.) **$20,000**

A Federal ladies' secretaire, Salem, Massachusetts, 1790-1810, with tambour doors enclosing a compartmented interior, 30½in. wide. (Christie's New York) $2,640

A Federal mahogany veneered inlaid secretary/desk, Mass., circa 1800, 38in. wide. (Robt. W. Skinner Inc.) $2,750

A fine and rare Classical mahogany and bird's eye maple secretaire a abattant, Philadelphia, 1820-1830, on acanthus carved lion's paw feet, 36½in. wide. (Christie's New York) $46,200

A Federal inlaid mahogany secretary-bookcase, North Shore, Massachusetts, 1790–1810, the shaped cornice flanked by reeded plinths surmounted by two brass urn finials above two glazed cupboard doors with geometric line-inlaid mullions, on French feet, 43in. wide. (Christie's) $12,100

A fine and rare Classical secretaire bookcase, New York, 1822-1838, the double glazed cupboard doors with gothic pattern mahogany and giltwood muntins, 58in. wide. (Christie's New York) $41,800

An American maple Federal secretaire bookcase, the raised cornice with three urn finials above a pair of arched glazed doors, with hinged baize-lined writing slope below, 19th century, 31in. wide. (Christie's) $3,455

Country Federal grain painted secretary desk, second-quarter 19th century, with faux mahogany grained interior, 39½in. wide. (Skinner Inc.) $6,750

A Federal mahogany butler's-desk, New York, early 19th century, fitted with a pair of cockbeaded short drawers above a crossbanded secretary drawer, on turned tapering reeded legs and brass ball feet, 51½in. wide. (Christie's) $3,850

Federal mahogany veneered glazed secretary, New England, 1830's, interior with four open compartments above small drawers, 37½in. wide. (Skinner Inc.) $2,200

SETTEES & SOFAS

Federal mahogany sofa, New England, early
19th century, old refinish, 74¼in. long.
(Skinner Inc.) $950

Federal mahogany sofa, probably New
England, circa 1810, refinished, 80in. long.
(Skinner Inc.) $700

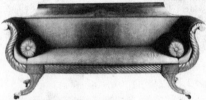

Classical mahogany and maple veneer sofa,
probably Boston, circa 1815, refinished, 80in.
wide.
(Skinner Inc.) $1,800

Painted and carved country sofa, probably
Pennsylvania, 19th century, original olive
green paint, 73½in. wide.
(Skinner Inc.) $1,700

Painted and stencil decorated Windsor day
bed, New England, circa 1820's, fold-out
hinged sleeping area supported by four
wooden pinned legs, allover original yellow
paint with gold and black fruit and leaf
decoration, fold-out, 49½ x 80⅝in.,
(Skinner Inc.) $1,600

A Federal inlaid mahogany sofa-frame,
Baltimore, 1790–1810, the serpentine crestrail
curving to molded downswept arms above a
serpentine seatrail flanked by oval reserves
inlaid with shaded foliage over square tapering
legs, 78½in. wide.
(Christie's) $22,000

Federal mahogany inlaid sofa, New Hampshire, circa 1815, attributed to John
Gould, Jr., the swelled reeded legs on casters,
79in. wide. (Skinner Inc.) $2,750

A Classical carved mahogany sofa, Boston,
1820-1830, on carved saber legs with leafy
feet, 35in. high, 85in. wide (Christie's New
York) $7,700

SETTEES & SOFAS

Federal carved mahogany sofa, possibly New England, circa 1800, refinished, 76in. long. (Skinner Inc.) $1,200

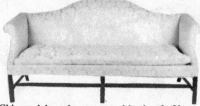

Chippendale mahogany camel-back sofa, New York, 18th century, refinished, 76in. wide. (Skinner Inc.) $8,250

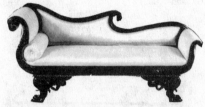

A Classical carved mahogany small recamier, attributed to Quervelle, Philadelphia, circa 1820, on anthemion carved paw feet, 72in. long. (Christie's New York) $8,800

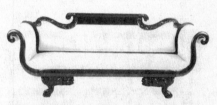

Classical Revival carved mahogany veneered upholstered sofa, light green silk watered moreen upholstery, 86½in. long. (Skinner Inc.) $800

Federal carved mahogany triple chairback settee, early 19th century, the triple shield back with carved and pierced urn-shaped splats with outstretched shaped arms, 4ft. 6in. wide. (Butterfield & Butterfield) $3,025

An antique baroque revival walnut chairback settee with three oval padded backrests within carved motifs of scrolls, grapevines, birds and cartouche crestings, 19th century, 68in. wide. (Selkirk's) $1,000

Painted and decorated settee, Pennsylvania, early 19th century, all-over light green paint with stencil decoration, 72in. wide. (Skinner Inc.) $750

Late classical mahogany carved sofa, probably New York, mid 19th century, green and gold silk upholstery, 84in. wide. (Skinner Inc.) $1,045

SETTEES & SOFAS

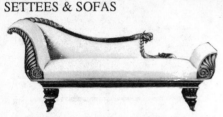

A Classical carved and giltwood meridienne, New York, 1825-1835, the scrolling half back carved with a lion's head terminal, 85in. wide. (Christie s New York) $5,500

Federal mahogany carved sofa, Salem, Massachusetts, circa 1810, refinished, 75¾in. wide. (Skinner Inc.) $1,320

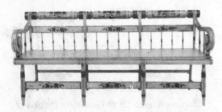

A painted and decorated settee, the rolled crest rail above three slats and twelve spindles, Penn., circa 1825, 76in. long. (Robt. W. Skinner Inc.) $2,750

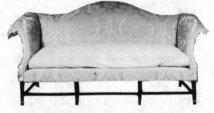

A Federal mahogany sofa, New York or Philadelphia, 1785-1810, on square, tapering legs with spade feet, 91in. long. (Christie's New York) $17,600

Fine small classical carved and parcel gilt mahogany and marble sofa, Philadelphia, circa 1820–1830, on Ionic marble columns with gilt capitals and bases on turned feet, 4ft. 7in. long. (Butterfield & Butterfield) $3,850

Rococo Revival walnut upholstered settee, third-quarter 19th century, grape vine and floral carved serpentine molded crest rail, raised on cabriole legs, 66in. wide. (Skinner Inc.) $1,100

An antique American Classical Revival carved mahogany upholstered settee carved with cornucopia and foliate motifs with molded seat rail on paw feet, 7ft. 5in. wide. (Selkirk's) $1,650

Classical carved mahogany veneer sofa, New York, circa 1820–30, molded veneer crest rail with scrolled arms above leaf carved arm supports, 71½in. wide. (Skinner Inc.) $1,540

SETTEES & SOFAS

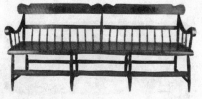

Painted and decorated settee, Pennsylvania, 1830–50, all over old light green paint with stencil decoration and striping, 75¼in. wide. (Skinner Inc.) **$1,760**

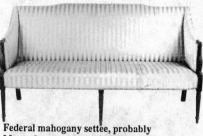

Classical mahogany veneered and carved sofa, Boston, circa 1830, embossed green velvet upholstery, old refinish, 72in. wide. (Skinner Inc.) **$2,860**

American Empire mahogany settee, second quarter 19th century, with carved griffin heads, acanthus carved scrolled arms, 60½in. long. (Skinner Inc.) **$1,300**

Federal mahogany settee, probably Massachusetts, circa 1810, (blue silk upholstery with water stain) 66½in. wide. (Skinner Inc.) **$5,750**

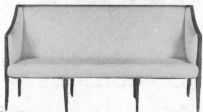

Fine Federal carved mahogany sofa, possibly by Slover and Taylor, New York, circa 1800–1815, on square tapering reeded legs ending in brass and wood wheel casters, 6ft. 6in. long. (Butterfield & Butterfield) **$14,300**

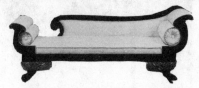

Classical carved mahogany sofa, Boston, circa 1820–1825, the molded and concave shaped crest terminating in rosette and punchwork scrolls, 6ft. 10in. long. (Butterfield & Butterfield) **$990**

A late Federal carved mahogany sofa, New York, circa 1825, the upswept crestrail carved with a basket of fruit flanked by griffins and tasseled swags over a padded back, on cornucopia-bracketed paw feet with casters, 86in. wide. (Christie's) **$11,000**

A classical mahogany and parcel-gilt recamier, New York, 1810–1820, with serpentine-molded crestrail terminating in a rosette over a padded back and flaring molded arms carved with rosettes, on gilt foliate bracketed hairy paw legs and casters, 83½in. wide. (Christie's) **$3,300**

SIDEBOARDS

A Federal inlaid mahogany sideboard with serpentine front, Baltimore, 1790-1810, 72in. wide. (Christie's) **$41,800**

A Federal inlaid mahogany sideboard, Pennsylvania, 1790-1810, on square tapering legs, 72in. wide. (Christie's) **$16,500**

A Federal mahogany sideboard, New England, 1790–1810, the serpentine top above a conforming case fitted with a serving slide lined with stenciled leather, on Marlborough legs with pendant husk and cuff inlay, 61in. wide. (Christie's) **$60,500**

Unusual Limbert sideboard, Grand Rapids, Michigan, circa 1903, gallery top, three short drawers over three cabinet doors, single long drawer below, round copper and brass pulls, 59¼in. wide. (Skinner Inc.) **$1,600**

A Federal inlaid mahogany sideboard, Mid-Atlantic States, 1790–1810, the rectangular top with serpentine front edge, on square tapering legs with pendant husks and cuff-inlay, 65½in. wide. (Christie's) **$8,800**

George III style mahogany pedestal sideboard, mid-19th century, the serpentine-edged top above three frieze drawers, one pedestal with a cupboard door enclosing slides, the other with a shelf and a drawer, 6ft. 1in. wide. (Butterfield & Butterfield) **$2,750**

A Federal inlaid mahogany sideboard, the serpentine top edged with line inlay, 72¾in. wide. Mass., 1790-1815. (Christie's)
$16,500

A Federal inlaid mahogany sideboard with bowed serpentine top, Mass., 1790-1810, 72¾in. wide. (Christie's) $6,600

L. & J.G. Stickley sideboard, circa 1910, no. 738, rectangular plate rack on corresponding top, two long drawers flanked by cabinet doors, 60in. wide.
(Skinner Inc.) $4,100

Federal carved mahogany sideboard, New York, circa 1815–1820, the rectangular top with Palladian arched splashboard flanked by reeded columns with acorn finials, 6ft. ½in. wide. (Butterfield & Butterfield) $1,650

A classical parcel gilt mahogany sideboard, New York, 1820–1830, the rectangular top backed by a splashboard with broken pediment centering a pinecone finial over a pair of crossbanded short drawers, on paw feet, 61¾in. wide.
(Christie's) $3,080

Gustav Stickley sideboard, circa 1902, No. 967, gallery top over two short drawers and single long drawer, two cabinet doors below, iron hardware, 60in. long.
(Skinner Inc.) $6,050

SIDEBOARDS

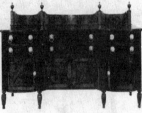

Federal mahogany veneer sideboard, New York, circa 1800, three inlaid drawers above a central cupboard flanked by bottle drawers and end cupboards, 67½in. wide. (Skinner Inc.) $8,000

A late Federal mahogany sideboard on tapering leaf carved feet, Mass., 1800-10, 78in. wide. $750

Federal mahogany veneered inlaid sideboard, Massachusetts, circa 1790, right cupboard door simulated, right end with hinged cupboard door, 67in. wide. (Skinner Inc.) $7,500

A classical mahogany and parcel-gilt sideboard, New York State, first quarter 19th century, the rectangular molded top with upswept scrolling three-quarter splashboard over a conforming case fitted with a pair of bolection-molded short drawers, 49½in. wide. (Christie's) $2,860

A Louis XVI style ebonized sideboard with bronze and ormolu mountings, America, 1865-70, approx. 69in. wide. $3,000

Renaissance Revival walnut sideboard, circa 1870, upper case with carved crest above a pair of glazed doors, 46½in. wide. (Skinner Inc.) $500

Renaissance style oak sideboard, circa 1860, with three frieze drawers and three cabinet doors carved throughout, 84½in. wide. (Robt. W. Skinner Inc.) $700

Small Federal cherry inlaid sideboard, New England, circa 1815, 44in. wide. $2,500

Walnut sideboard, circa 1870, backsplash with carved crest above shelves and mirror on a molded white marble top, 82in. high. (Skinner Inc.) $1,700

STANDS

Federal bird's-eye maple veneered sewing table, Massachusetts, 1790-1810, with two maple veneered cockbeaded drawers, 27½in. high. (Skinner Inc.) $1,400

Chrome and bakelite smoking stand, Brooklyn, New York, circa 1930, with chrome topped ashtray and supports, 20¾in. high. (Skinner) $200

Maple light stand, New England, circa 1800, refinished, replaced pull, 28in. high. (Skinner Inc.) $650

Arts & Crafts umbrella stand, probably Europe, early 20th century, shaped flat sides with spade trailing to circle cut-out, 22in. wide. (Skinner Inc.) $300

Painted cherry stand, Connecticut River Valley, early 19th century, the scrolled two board top above a base with single beaded drawer, 26in. high. (Skinner Inc.) $3,750

Painted and mahogany veneer stand, Massachusetts or New Hampshire, 1800-15, top and base painted with original red stain, 18in. wide. (Skinner Inc.) $4,840

A late Federal figured maple two drawer stand, Pennsylvania, 1810-1820, on tapering baluster and ring turned legs, 17½in. wide. (Christie's) $2,640

A grain painted pine and poplar etagere, New England, circa 1820, 35½in. wide. (Robt. W. Skinner Inc.) $450

A Country Federal grain painted maple tray table, possibly New Hampshire, circa 1820, top 17 x 16½in. (Robt. W. Skinner Inc.) $3,250

STANDS

A Federal mahogany etagère, Boston, 1790–1810, on turned tapering feet with brass cup feet and casters, 53in. high, 17½in. wide.
(Christie's) **$3,300**

Bent plywood tea cart, mid 20th century, top fitted with beverage holder, centering tray, bent wood legs joined by lower median shelf, 20in. wide.
(Skinner Inc.) **$250**

A three-tiered muffin stand, by Charles Rohlfs, Buffalo, N.Y., 1907, 34in. high.
(Robt. W. Skinner Inc.)
$1,400

A Federal inlaid mahogany two-drawer stand, Portsmouth, New Hampshire, 1790–1810, the rectangular top with outset rounded corners over a conforming case fitted with two crossbanded drawers, 18¾in. wide.
(Christie's) **$26,400**

A fine and rare figured mahogany veneer cellarette, attributed to Duncan Phyfe, New York, 1815-1825, of sarcophagus form, with gilt leaf carved lion's paw feet, 25¼in. high.
(Christie's New York) **$13,200**

American Renaissance inlaid maple and rosewood nightstand by Herter Brothers, New York, circa 1872, the later faux marble top within a molded walnut border, 17in. wide.
(Butterfield & Butterfield)
$990

A County Federal tiger maple light stand, New England, circa 1810, the square overhanging top above four square tapering legs, 27¾in. high. (Robt. W. Skinner Inc.) **$850**

Federal mahogany canterbury, probably New York, 1820's, pulls appear original, 19in. high.
(Skinner Inc.) **$1,650**

A Federal mahogany stand, Salem, Massachusetts, 1790–1810, on square tapering molded legs joined by X-stretchers, 14¼in. wide.
(Christie's) **$2,090**

208

STOOLS

One of a pair of early 19th
century late Federal mahogany
footstools, 12¾in. long.
(Christie's) $7,700

A Federal carved mahogany
window seat, attributed to the
shop of Duncan Phyfe, N.Y.,
1810-20, 40in. wide.
(Christie's) $26,400

Classical Revival maho-
gany stool, possibly New
York, circa 1825, 21in.
wide. $500

A Classical mahogany piano
stool, New York, 1800 1815,
the upholstered circular seat
turning above a threaded support, 14in. diam. (Christie's
New York) $700

A pair of late Federal mahogany
foot-stools, New England, 1800–
1820, each with padded
rectangular top above a reeded
apron with baluster and ring-
turned legs, 12in. wide.
(Christie's) $660

A classical carved and gilt
mahogany piano stool,
Baltimore, 1820–1830, on three
acanthus-carved and gilt paw
feet, 32⅞in. high.
(Christie's) $2,420

A Classical mahogany stool,
Boston, 1820-1830, on a
scrolled curule base joined
by a turned stretcher, 20in.
wide. (Christie's New York)
          $1,870

One of a pair of Windsor stools,
New England, 1800-1820, the
oval tops on bamboo turned
splayed tapering legs, 13in.
high. (Skinner Inc.)
          $13,000

A black-painted Windsor footstool stamped *J. Stanyan*,
Pennsylvania, 1790–1820, on
bamboo-turned splayed legs
joined by stretchers, 12¾in.
wide.
(Christie's) $550

Four piece suite of Heywood-Wakefield wicker seat furniture, a settee, armchair and two side chairs, raised on circular legs. (Skinner Inc.) $1,000

Three-piece Art Deco living room suite, by Collins and Alkman Corporation, circa 1929, wood mohair upholstery with wood veneer accents and feet, couch upholstery in shades of burgundy with gold piping. $2,000

Harden three-piece suite, circa 1910, including settee, armchair and rocker, concave crest rail over five vertical slats, bent arm over four vertical slats, spring cushion seat. (Skinner Inc.) $1,000

Part of a four-piece Harden & Co. livingroom set, comprising: settee, rocker and two armchairs, settee 54in. wide, circa 1910. (Robt. W. Skinner Inc.) $2,250

A Limbert oak dining room set comprising a pedestal table with four boxed leaves, diameter 54in., and a set of four dining chairs, circa 1910. (Skinner's) $3,500

Early 20th century Plail & Co., barrel-back settee and matching armchairs, 46¼in. long. (Robt. W. Skinner Inc.) $5,500

CARD TABLES

A Federal inlaid mahogany card table, North Shore, Massachusetts, 1800–1810, the serpentine top with outset rounded corners and inlaid edge folding above a conforming apron, 35½in. wide. (Christie's) **$1,980**

Classical carved veneered brass inlaid table, probably New York, circa 1820s, the green marble top with triple banded edge, 33in. wide. (Skinner Inc.) **$6,500**

Federal mahogany veneer carved card table, Salem, Massachusetts, circa 1820, leaf carving on a star punched background, 38¾in. wide. (Skinner Inc.) **$1,045**

Classical mahogany carved card table, New England, early 19th century, 35in. wide. (Skinner Inc.) **$425**

A Federal inlaid mahogany card table, Mass., 1800-15, 34in. wide. (Christie's) **$1,320**

A Federal mahogany inlaid card table, probably Mass., circa 1790, 35in. wide. (Robt. W. Skinner Inc.) **$2,750**

Federal mahogany inlaid demilune card table, probably Rhode Island, circa 1800, refinished, 33¾in. wide. (Skinner Inc.) **$1,000**

Federal carved mahogany card table, New York, circa 1810–1815, on an acanthus carved pedestal above a quadripartite base, 36½in. wide. (Butterfield & Butterfield) **$3,850**

A Federal inlaid mahogany card table on four tapering legs, Baltimore, 1790-1810, 36¼in. diam. (Christie's) **$3,850**

CARD TABLES

Classical carved mahogany
veneer card table, Middle
Atlantic States, circa 1830, some
refinish, 36in. wide.
(Skinner Inc.) $1,000

Federal mahogany inlaid card
table, Rhode Island, circa 1800,
old refinish, 35³/₄in. wide.
(Skinner Inc.) $4,200

Classical mahogany and
rosewood veneer card table,
probably Boston, circa 1815,
refinished, 36in. wide.
(Skinner Inc.) $850

Federal inlaid birch and
mahogany card table, New
England, circa 1800–1810, on
square tapering line inlaid legs,
36in. wide.
(Butterfield & Butterfield)
$1,320

Rare small mahogany serpentine
Chippendale card table,
probably Rhode Island, circa
1760 (minor imperfections),
24in. wide. (Skinner Inc.)
$7,500

A Federal inlaid mahogany
card table with D-shaped
top, Mass., 1790-1810, 34in.
wide. (Christie's) $4,400

Federal mahogany and maple
veneer card table, New England,
circa 1800, old refinish, 35³/₄in.
wide.
(Skinner Inc.) $2,600

Classical mahogany carved
veneered card table, New
England, circa 1830, with
curving legs ending in brass paw
feet, 35¼in. wide.
(Skinner Inc.) $715

Federal cherry veneered card
table, Southern Massachusetts,
circa 1810, on four ring turned
reeded tapering legs ending in
turned feet, 35¼in. wide.
(Skinner Inc.) $2,600

CARD TABLES

Federal mahogany card table with mahogany and birch veneers, Portsmouth, New Hampshire, circa 1800, 36in. wide.
(Skinner Inc.) $9,500

Federal mahogany inlaid card table, Massachusetts, circa 1810, refinished, 35½in. wide.
(Skinner Inc.) $2,640

Federal mahogany veneered card table, New England, early 19th century, refinished, 36½in. wide.
(Skinner Inc.) $750

Late Classical carved mahogany card table, probably New York State, circa 1830, old surface, 36¾in. wide.
(Skinner Inc.) $1,100

A classical mahogany veneer card-table, attributed to Duncan Phyfe, New York, 1820–1830, the crossbanded D-shaped hinged top swiveling above a conforming apron, 35½in. wide.
(Christie's) $3,300

A Chippendale carved mahogany card table, Rhode Island or Massachusetts, 1770-1790, with hinged serpentine top, 32in. wide. (Christie's New York) $2,750

A fine Federal inlaid mahogany card table, Massachusetts, 1790-1810, on square tapering line-inlaid legs with inlaid cuffs, 91cm. wide. (Christie's New York) $2,420

A Federal carved mahogany card table, attributed to Henry Connelly, circa 1810, 36in. wide. (Christie's) $2,640

Classical Revival carved mahogany card table, Salem, Massachusetts, circa 1820, the rectangular top with reeded edge, 35½in. wide.
(Skinner Inc.) $2,500

CARD TABLES

Federal mahogany veneered card table, probably Connecticut, circa 1820, the serpentine top with ovolo corners, 36in. wide. (Skinner Inc.) $1,300

Classical mahogany card table, New York or New Jersey, circa 1830, refinished, 36in. wide. (Skinner Inc.) $1,900

Federal mahogany and mahogany veneer inlaid card table, New York, circa 1800, refinished, 35¾in. wide. (Skinner Inc.) $2,600

Federal mahogany inlaid card table, Newport, Rhode Island, circa 1800, on four square tapering front legs; two back legs swing to support the top. (Skinner Inc.) $20,000

Federal mahogany and bird's-eye maple card table, probably Massachusetts, circa 1810–1815, on a lyre-form support on down-curving legs, ending in square brass casters, 33½in. wide. (Butterfield & Butterfield) $3,300

A Federal inlaid mahogany card-table, Rhode Island, 1790–1810, the hinged D-shaped top with lightwood banding over a conforming frieze centered by a fluted vase issuing bellflowers and rosettes, 36¼in. wide. (Christie's) $13,200

Federal mahogany and birch veneer card table, Massachusetts or New Hampshire, circa 1800, 35¾in. wide. (Skinner Inc.) $7,000

A Classical gilt stenciled mahogany card table, New York, 1825-1835, on four acanthus carved legs with lion's paw feet, 36in. wide. (Christie's New York) $2,090

Federal mahogany inlaid card table, Newport or Providence, Rhode Island, circa 1790, 36in. wide. (Skinner Inc.) $2,750

"Bonnie" dining table, designed by Ferruccio Tritta, produced by Studio Nove, New York, on three columnar supports, 56in. diameter.
(Skinner Inc.) $2,600

Renaissance Revival walnut center table, third quarter 19th century, stamped *W. Gertz*, with carved laurel leaf frieze, 28¾in. long. (Skinner Inc.)
$3,250

Renaissance Revival rosewood and marble center table, third quarter 19th century, 42in. wide.
(Skinner Inc.) $2,090

A painted 'Windsor' tavern table, possibly Rhode Island, circa 1780, 28in. wide.
(Robt. W. Skinner Inc.)
$6,000

Classical mahogany veneer center table, New York, 1810–30, marble top on a conforming skirt with canted corners over a four-column pedestal, 33½in. wide.
(Skinner Inc.) $1,100

A classical mahogany veneer center-table, New York, early 19th century, with a molded circular fossiled black marble top above a crossbanded conforming frieze, with scrolling feet, 29½in. high.
(Christie's) $3,080

Queen Anne figured maple tavern table, New England, 18th century, the oval top above a rectangular case on circular tapering legs, 36½in. wide.
(Butterfield & Butterfield)
$1,650

Renaissance Revival walnut center table, third quarter 19th century, the inset marble top above a carved pedestal with four fluted supports, 30½in. high.
(Skinner Inc.) $1,000

Marquetry and laminated wood center table, 20th century, inlaid with various woods, raised on cabriole legs, 29¾in. diameter.
(Skinner Inc.) $750

CENTER TABLES

A William and Mary maple tavern table, New England, circa 1730, 34in. diam. $6,000

Late 19th century Renaissance Revival inlaid mahogany center table, America, 45½in. wide. $1,500

An 18th century maple tavern table with breadboard ends, New England, the top 40 x 24½in. (Robt. W. Skinner Inc.) $2,700

Rosewood center table, late 19th century, raised on single baluster form pedestal supported by three griffon headed C-scroll legs, 26in. high. (Robt. W. Skinner Inc.) $450

A tiger maple hutch table, North America, 18th century, on molded stepped, shoe feet, 45½in. wide. (Robt. W. Skinner Inc.) $5,100

One of a pair of cast iron tables, circa 1900, circular mahogany top raised on three legs, headed by caryatids, 29in. high. (Skinner Inc.) Two $600

Carved Lotus center table, executed by John Bradstreet, Minneapolis, circa 1905, original black finish, unsigned, 30in. diam. (Skinner Inc.) £15,432

A rococo Revival laminated rosewood lamp table, by J. B. Belter, New York, circa 1855, 26in. diam. $25,000

A Renaissance Revival marble top parlor table, by T. Brooks Cabinet & Upholstery Warehouse, circa 1865, the white oval top 37in. long. $1,750

DRESSING TABLES

Queen Anne cherry dressing table, Connecticut, 1750–80, brass replaced, 33in. wide. (Skinner Inc.) $17,600

A yellow painted pine dressing table with stencil and foliate designs, New England, circa 1825, 34in. wide. (Robt. W. Skinner Inc.) $800

A rare Queen Anne figured maple dressing table, Delaware River Valley, 1750-1770, on square tapering cabriole legs with Spanish feet, 39in. wide. (Christie's New York) $41,800

A fine Queen Anne carved mahogany dressing table, Salem, Massachusetts, 1740-1760, on cabriole legs with pad feet, 34in. wide. (Christie's New York) $66,000

A Chippendale carved walnut dressing-table, Philadephia area, 1760–1780, on cabriole legs with carved knees and ball-and-claw feet, 33¹/₂in. wide. (Christie's) $46,200

Rare William and Mary japanned maple and pine dressing table, Boston area, 1710-1715 (one leg and foot, an old replacement), 34in. wide. (Skinner Inc.) $45,000

A Chippendale carved walnut dressing table, Phila., 1765-85, 36in. wide. (Christie's) $253,000

A Federal carved mahogany dressing table, New York, 1800–1815, the stepped rectangular top with four short drawers surmounted by a rectangular frame containing a conforming plate on serpentine dolphin supports, 63¹/₄in. high. (Christie's) $2,200

A Queen Anne cherrywood dressing table, New England, 1740–1760, with a molded rectangular top above a long drawer and three short drawers over an arched apron, 32¹/₂in. wide. (Christie's) $8,800

DRESSING TABLES

Chippendale carved walnut highboy base, Pennsylvania, 18th century, 20th century top, refinished, replaced brasses, 38½in. wide. (Skinner Inc.) **$800**

A Chippendale tiger maple dressing table on cabriole legs, probably Penn., circa 1780, 33¾in. wide. (Robt. W. Skinner Inc.) **$20,000**

Queen Anne dressing table, New England, 18th century, refinished, replaced brasses, 33in. wide. (Skinner Inc.) **$12,000**

A Queen Anne cherry dressing table, Upper Connecticut River Valley, circa 1785, 34½in. wide. (Robt. W. Skinner Inc.) **$11,000**

Federal mahogany carved and inlaid dressing bureau, Boston or North Shore, Massachusetts, circa 1810, supported by fluted posts and scrolled side arms, 38½in. wide. (Skinner Inc.) **$15,400**

A Queen Anne inlaid walnut dressing table, New England, 1730-1750, the rectangular top with molded edge above one long drawer over three short drawers, 32½in. wide. (Christie's) **$3,080**

Queen Anne mahogany and mahogany veneered dressing table, probably Rhode Island, circa 1770, the molded over-hanging top above cockbeaded case, 30½in. wide. (Skinner Inc.) **$10,000**

Chippendale carved walnut dressing table, Pennsylvania, circa 1770, with shaped skirt and shell carved legs ending in trifid feet, 35in. wide. (Skinner Inc.) **$4,125**

Queen Anne cherry dressing table, probably Connecticut, circa 1770, the rectangular overhanging top with shaped corners and molded edge, 35¾in. wide. (Robt. W. Skinner Inc.) **$15,000**

DROP LEAF TABLES

Queen Anne tiger maple drop leaf table, New England, on cabriole legs ending in pad feet, 48in. wide. (Skinner Inc.) $6,600

Federal cherry inlaid breakfast table, New England, circa 1810, refinished, 18¼in. wide. (Skinner Inc.) $500

A Queen Anne maple dining table with oval drop-leaf top, Rhode Island, circa 1760, 50in. wide open. (Robt. W. Skinner Inc.) $7,500

Federal mahogany carved and veneered drop leaf table, Rhode Island, circa 1815, one working and one simulated drawer, 45¼in. wide. (Skinner Inc.) $1,320

Country Queen Anne maple dining table, New England, mid 18th century, the rectangular drop leaf top above a shaped skirt, 26¾in. high. (Skinner Inc.) $3,000

Classical mahogany veneer breakfast table, probably Boston, circa 1815, the drop leaves over four curving beaded legs, 42in. wide. (Skinner Inc.) $750

Queen Anne mahogany drop leaf table, Massachusetts, 1750-1780, with hinged square leaves over a shaped skirt, 27in. high. (Skinner Inc.) $5,500

Fine American custom-made butterfly table in the 17th century style, one drawer, 28in. high. (Eldred's) $523

Chippendale cherry drop leaf table, New England, circa 1780, with beaded edges and replaced brass, refinished, 36in. wide. (Skinner Inc.) $550

DROP LEAF TABLES

A Queen Anne cherrywood drop leaf table, probably Connecticut, 1740-1760, on cabriole legs with pad feet, 28in. high. (Christie's New York) **$1,870**

Queen Anne maple drop leaf table, Rhode Island, circa 1760, the rectangular top with rounded leaves, 26in. high. (Skinner Inc.) **$1,700**

Queen Anne painted maple drop leaf dining table, New England, 1760–80, extended 42¼in. (Skinner Inc.) **$3,575**

Diminutive Queen Anne maple drop leaf table, New England, circa 1750, on four cabriole legs terminating in pad feet, 25¼in. high. (Skinner Inc.) **$3,500**

A Federal figured maple drop-leaf table, New England, 1800–1820, the rectangular top with two drop leaves above a plain apron, on square tapering legs, 55½in. wide. (Christie's) **$4,400**

A Classical carved mahogany breakfast table, New York, 1815-1825, the clover shaped top with two drop leaves, 29½in. high. (Christie's New York) **$5,500**

A Chippendale mahogany drop-leaf table, Salem, Massachusetts, 1760–1780, the molded oval twin-flap top above an arching, shaped skirt on cabriole legs and ball-and-claw feet, 53in. wide. (Christie's) **$8,800**

A Chippendale cherrywood drop-leaf table, with wavy stretchers, Conn., 1760-80 (Christie's) **$1,980**

A Queen Anne mahogany drop-leaf table, New England, circa 1750, the hinged oval top with twin drop-leaves over a flat-arched apron and cabriole legs, 46½in. wide. (Christie's) **$2,420**

DROP LEAF TABLES

A Chippendale mahogany dining table with two drop-leaves, Phila., 1765-85, 55in. long. (Christie's) **$1,320**

Late Federal rosewood veneer, gilt and brass inlaid breakfast table, attributed to Charles-Honore Lannuier, N.Y., circa 1815, 46in. long, extended. (Christie's) **$71,500**

A Chippendale mahogany card table with scalloped front skirt, Mass., circa 1770, 31½in. wide, open. (Robt. W. Skinner Inc.) **$6,100**

A Federal painted maple dining table with rounded drop leaves, New England, circa 1800, 42in. wide. (Robt. W. Skinner Inc.) **$4,000**

A Queen Anne maple drop leaf table, Massachusetts, 1730-1750, with shaped skirts and cabriole legs, 42½in. wide, extended. (Robt. W. Skinner Inc.) **$61,000**

A Queen Anne mahogany drop-leaf table, Newport, 1740-60, 47.7/8in. wide. (Christie's) **$4,950**

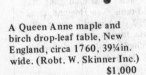

A Queen Anne maple and birch drop-leaf table, New England, circa 1760, 39¼in. wide. (Robt. W. Skinner Inc.) **$1,000**

A Queen Anne cherrywood drop leaf table, Massachusetts, 1740-1760, on cabriole legs with pad feet, 26½in. high. (Christie s New York) **$5,500**

Queen Anne maple and birch dining table, Rhode Island, circa 1760, tapering legs ending in high pad feet, 59in. wide. (Robt. W. Skinner Inc.) **$4,900**

222

GATELEG TABLES

Maple gateleg table, Massachusetts, circa 1740, old scrubbed top on early base, 42½in. wide. (Skinner Inc.) $3,250

A William and Mary walnut gateleg table, probably New England, circa 1740, 56in. wide. (Robt. W. Skinner Inc.) $3,700

A rare pine gateleg table, probably Southern, 18th century, the rectangular top with two drop leaves, on turned feet, 29^{1}/$_{3}$in. high. (Christie's New York) $2,200

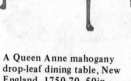

A Queen Anne mahogany drop-leaf dining table, New England, 1750-70, 50in. deep with leaves open. (Christie's) $8,800

A William and Mary maple gateleg table with oval drop-leaf top, New England, circa 1740, 41in. long, 51in. wide. (Robt. W. Skinner Inc.) $2,500

Painted maple gateleg table, New England, 18th century, dark red stain, beaded skirt, 29^{3}/$_{4}$in. wide. (Skinner Inc.) $3,850

Antique American William & Mary gate-leg table in maple and curly maple, drawer of pine and poplar secondary woods, top open 49in. x 61in. (Eldred's) $2,860

A Queen Anne maple drop leaf dining table, New England, 1740-1760, on cabriole legs with pad feet. 44in. wide. (Christie's) $2,420

William and Mary walnut gate-leg table, Massachusetts, 1715-1740, the rectangular top with half round hinged leaves, 28½in. high. (Skinner Inc.) $20,000

LARGE TABLES

Federal mahogany veneer two-part dining table, circa 1815, refinished, 93in. long.
(Skinner Inc.) $2,090

Large six drawer library table, circa 1915, rectangular top over six drawers, large post legs with side stretchers, 86in. long.
(Skinner Inc.) $1,000

A mahogany dining-table in three sections, the end-sections with rectangular single drop-leaf, the central section with two drop-leaves, on square tapering reeded legs, 160in. long.
(Christie's) $2,657

A Federal mahogany accordion-action dining table, New York, 1790–1810, the rounded rectangular top extending to include five extra leaves over a straight apron and baluster and ring-turned supports, on downswept molded saber legs, 147in. wide, extended.
(Christie's) $22,000

A Federal inlaid mahogany two-part dining table, probably Baltimore, 1800–1810, in two parts, each with D-shaped ends and rectangular drop leaves, on five square tapering legs edged with stringing, 48in. wide.
(Christie's) $14,300

Drop-leaf table, George Nakishima for Widdicomb Furniture, Grand Rapids, Michigan, circa 1955, 73³/₄in. wide.
(Skinner Inc.) $1,500

Walnut and cherry tavern table, probably New York State, 18th century, old surface, 53¹/₂in. wide.
(Skinner Inc.) $2,300

Queen Anne maple dining table, probably Rhode Island, circa 1760, old refinish, 47¹/₄in. wide.
(Skinner Inc.) $3,000

FURNITURE

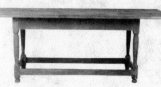

Painted pine and maple tavern table, probably New England, 18th century, base with red stain, top scrubbed, 72in. long. (Skinner Inc.)   **$2,500**

Federal cherry and mahogany veneer two-part dining table, New England, early 19th century, refinished, 88⅝in. wide. (Skinner Inc.)   **$1,430**

Federal carved mahogany two-part dining table, New England, circa 1815–1825, the D-shaped top with one drop leaf, on ring-turned and foliate carved legs, length extended 7ft. 9in. (Butterfield & Butterfield)   **$1,540**

A Country maple and pine painted harvest table, New England, circa 1800, 72in. long. (Robt. W. Skinner Inc.)   **$2,800**

A fine Classical mahogany two part dining table, Boston, 1820-1830, on molded saber legs with cylindrical feet, 29¼in. high. (Christie's New York)   **$28,600**

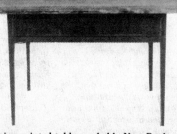

A pine painted table, probably New England, early 19th century, the overhanging scrubbed two board top with breadboard ends, 50in. wide. (Robt. W. Skinner Inc.)   **$1,900**

Country Federal mahogany two part dining table, New England, circa 1820, the D-end tops with molded edge and hinged drop leaves, extended 91in. (Skinner Inc.)   **$4,250**

Shaker cherry ministry dining table, probably Enfield, New Hampshire or Harvard, Massachusetts, first half 19th century, the cherry two-board scrubbed top above an arched maple base, 84in. long. (Skinner Inc.)   **$82,500**

OCCASIONAL TABLES

A Queen Anne cherrywood tea-table, probably Northampton or Hatfield, Massachusetts, 1740–1760, the deeply scalloped molded top above a rectangular frame, 35in. wide. (Christie's) $38,500

Chippendale mahogany carved tilt top tea table, probably Connecticut, circa 1780, 34½in. wide. (Skinner Inc.) $2,500

Chippendale mahogany carved tea table, Newport, Rhode Island, 1760–80, old surface, 33in. diameter. (Skinner Inc.) $11,000

A fine Chippendale carved mahogany tea table, Philadelphia, 1760–1780, with circular dished and molded rim top revolving and tilting above a tapering columnar and compressed ball-turned pedestal, 27½in. high. (Christie's) $27,500

Federal carved mahogany server, New England, circa 1815–1820, on ring-turned, reeded and rope twist legs joined by a serpentine shaped shelf ending in brass casters, 36in. wide. (Butterfield & Butterfield) $1,210

A classical green-painted and gilt-stenciled side-table, attributed to John Needles, Baltimore, early 19th century, on a quadripartite base with foliate bracketed X-shaped supports, on turned tapering feet, 37in. wide. (Christie's) $6,600

A Queen Anne figured maple octagonal tilt-top tea table, Conn., 1730-40, 33in. wide, 26in. high. (Christie's) $19,800

A late Federal carved mahogany serving table, New York, 1815-1825, the reeded rectangular top with outset rounded corners, 36in. wide. (Christie's New York) $3,300

Chippendale mahogany carved tilt-top tea table, Boston, 1760–80, old surface, 35in. diameter. (Skinner Inc.) $4,100

OCCASIONAL TABLES

Maple tea table, Rhode Island, 1740–90, refinished, 36⅞ in. wide.
(Skinner Inc.) $3,000

A Country Chippendale maple tea table, New England, circa 1780, 33½ in. wide. (Robt. W. Skinner Inc.) $850

Chippendale walnut tilt top table, Middle Atlantic States, circa 1800, refinished, 28½ in. diameter.
(Skinner Inc.) $600

A mahogany veneered side table, designed by Frank L. Wright, circa 1955, 21½ in. wide, red decal on back. (Robt. W. Skinner Inc.)
                    $850

A Queen Anne cherry and walnut tea table, probably Rhode Island, circa 1760, the rectangular breadboard overhanging top with exposed tenons, 30 in. wide. (Robt. W. Skinner Inc.) $30,000

Painted pine hutch table, Massachusetts, 18th century, the round two board top above a two board seat, 49 in. diam. (Skinner Inc.) $4,750

Country maple and pine tea table, New England, 18th century, on tapering turned legs, 25½ in. high. (Skinner Inc.) $1,200

A Classical carved mahogany and mahogany veneer sofa table, probably New York, circa 1820, 35½ in. wide. (Robt. W. Skinner Inc.) $7,500

American Renaissance figured maple and rosewood sewing table by Herter Brothers, New York, circa 1872, on stylized feet, 34½ in. wide.
(Butterfield & Butterfield)
                    $1,045

OCCASIONAL TABLES

Chippendale walnut tilt-top tea table, Pennsylvania, late 18th century, old surface, 27½in. diameter. (Skinner Inc.) $880

Painted and decorated Windsor table, New England, early 19th century, later orange paint with buff color accent, 29¼in. wide. (Skinner Inc.) $715

Chippendale tiger maple bird cage tilt top tea table, on tripod cabriole leg base, 19½in. diam. (Skinner Inc.) $3,200

A Federal mahogany tilt top stand, Salem, Massachusetts, 1790-1810, on tripod cabriole legs with pad feet, 69cm. high. (Christie's New York) $1,210

William and Mary cherry and pine hutch table, Hudson River Valley, circa 1750, 44in. diam. (Robt. W. Skinner Inc.) $6,400

A Chippendale carved mahogany scallop top tea table, Pennsylvania, 1765-1785, on tripod cabriole legs with ball and claw feet, 28in. high. (Christie's New York) $13,200

Chippendale carved walnut tilt top tea table, Connecticut, 1760-1780, on a cabriole leg tripod base, 34in. diam. (Skinner Inc.) $3,250

A Federal mahogany serving-table, New York, circa 1810, the rectangular top with outset rounded front corners and reeded edge, on turned tapering legs and brass feet, 35¾in. wide. (Christie's) $3,300

Chippendale mahogany tilt top tea table, New England, circa 1780, the circular top above a birdcage support, 34in. diam. (Skinner Inc.) $2,000

OCCASIONAL TABLES

Pine and maple hutch table, New England, 18th century, the circular top tips above block and bulbous turned arms, 27½in. high. (Skinner Inc.) $1,700

A late Federal mahogany serving-table, Boston, circa 1815, on spirally-turned legs with turned feet and casters, 39½in. wide. (Christie's) $4,400

Painted Queen Anne tavern table, Rhode Island, 18th century, scrubbed top on original red washed base, 38in. wide. (Skinner Inc.) $12,000

Fine painted country maple tea table, New England, circa 1800, rectangular top with shaped corner overhangs, 27in. high. (Skinner Inc.) $10,000

Antique American tavern table in pine and other woods, oval top, cut-out apron, molded square tapered legs, 25in. high. (Eldred's) $193

A rare Chippendale mahogany tilt top tea table, attributed to John Goddard, Newport, Rhode Island, 1760-1790, on three arched legs, 69.5cm. high. (Christie's New York) $28,600

Chippendale mahogany carved tilt top table, Philadelphia, circa 1765, old refinish, bird cage fixed in place, 32in. diameter. (Skinner Inc.) $11,000

Chippendale cherry tilt top tea table, Norwich, Connecticut, 1760-1790, on cabriole leg tripod base, 26½in. high. (Skinner Inc.) $1,300

Pine tavern table, New England, 18th century, old refinish, oval top, 34in. long. (Skinner Inc.) $1,600

Tiger maple and cherry breakfast table, New England, circa 1800, refinished, brass replaced, 28¼in. high. (Skinner Inc.) $1,700

Federal cherry inlaid Pembroke table, New England, circa 1810, with stringing on the skirts and legs, 34½in. wide. (Skinner Inc.) $1,320

A Federal cherrywood Pembroke table, New England, 1800–1810, the rectangular top with two D-shaped drop-leaves above a long drawer, on square tapering legs, 35½in. long. (Christie's) $1,100

A Federal inlaid mahogany Pembroke-table, Mid-Atlantic States, 1790–1810, the hinged oval top with twin drop-leaves over a conforming cockbeaded frieze drawer flanked by tablet inlay on square-tapering legs, 38¼in. wide. (Christie's) $3,080

A Federal mahogany Pembroke-table, New York, 1790–1810, the rectangular top with clover-leaf shaped drop leaves over a frieze drawer, on square tapering legs, 31in. wide. (Christie's) $2,640

A Federal mahogany Pembroke-table, New York, 1790–1810, on square tapering legs joined by serpentine X-stretchers, 31in. wide. (Christie's) $5,500

Chippendale walnut Pembroke or breakfast table, probably Philadelphia, circa 1800, pierced fret cross stretchers, 28¾in. high. (Skinner Inc.) $6,000

Federal cherry breakfast table, New England, early 19th century, single drawer with beading and replaced brass, 36in. wide. (Skinner Inc.) $660

A Chippendale mahogany Pembroke table, possibly Penn., circa 1780, the shaped top with serpentine leaves, 31in. wide. (Robt. W. Skinner Inc.) $1,300

Federal cherry breakfast table, New England, circa 1810, refinished, replaced brass pull, 32½in. wide. (Skinner Inc.)   **$800**

A Federal inlaid mahogany Pembroke table, Rhode Island, 1790–1810, the hinged oval top with molded edge decorated with stringing over a bowed frieze drawer with lightwood banding, 31in. wide. (Christie's)   **$15,400**

A Federal inlaid mahogany Pembroke table, New York, 1790-1810, the rectangular top with bowed ends and line inlaid edge, 41in. wide (leaves open). (Christie's)   **$5,500**

Federal mahogany inlaid Pembroke table, Rhode Island, circa 1790-1810, on four square tapering inlaid legs terminating in spade feet, measures 32 x 40½in. (Skinner Inc.)   **$4,250**

A Federal figured maple Pembroke table, eastern Connecticut or Rhode Island, 1795–1825, on square tapering legs joined by an X-shaped stretcher, 29³/₈in. high. (Christie's)   **$6,050**

A Federal mahogany Pembroke-table, New York, 1790–1810, the oval hinged top with molded edge and D-shaped drop leaves over a cockbeaded bowed frieze drawer, on square tapering legs, 31³/₄in. wide. (Christie's)   **$1,760**

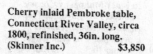

A late Federal figured maple and cherrywood Pembroke table, signed by A. J. Baycock, Brookfield, Madison County, New York, 1810-1830, on spirally reeded tapering cylindrical legs, 28¼in. high. (Christie's New York)   **$3,850**

Cherry inlaid Pembroke table, Connecticut River Valley, circa 1800, refinished, 36in. long. (Skinner Inc.)   **$3,850**

A Federal figured maple Pembroke table, New York or Bermuda, 1800-1820, the rounded rectangular top with two drop leaves, 28in. high. (Christie's New York)   **$3,080**

231

PIER TABLES

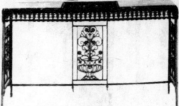

A Classical carved and gilt stenciled mahogany marble top pier table, Philadelphia, 1825-1835, on scroll supports with acanthus knees, 42in. wide. (Christie's New York) $4,620

Early 20th century Art Deco cast and wrought iron parcel gilt pier table, France, 53in. wide. (Robt. W. Skinner Inc.) $1,300

Classical pier table, New York, circa 1820, with mirror above carved gilded leafage and paw feet, 36in. wide. (Skinner Inc.) $3,250

A classical mahogany pier-table, probably New York, circa 1825, the rectangular crossbanded top above a frieze with brass string inlay and a mirrored back-plate, 42³/₄in. wide. (Christie's) $2,640

American Renaissance carved walnut pier mirror and console, executed for the south wall of the main floor hall, Thurlow Lodge, Menlo Park, California by Herter Brothers, New York, circa 1872, 15ft. 6in. high. (Butterfield & Butterfield) $22,000

A classical gilt-stenciled mahogany pier-table, New York, 1815–1830, the rectangular white and gray marble top with canted corners over a conforming bolection-molded frieze centred by a rosette, 45in. wide. (Christie's) $6,600

A Classical rosewood marble top pier table, Philadelphia, 1820-1830, with ormolu medallion and leafage above gilt scrolled supports, 42in. wide. (Christie's New York) $7,700

Regency Mahogany Console Table, c. 1810, D-shaped top raised on circular carved tapering legs, 31¹/₄in. long. (Skinner Inc) $2900

One of a pair of Empire mahogany marble-top pier tables, probably Boston, circa 1830, 49in. wide. (Christie's) $4,400

WORK TABLES

Painted and grained work table, possibly Pennsylvania, second quarter 19th century, with smoke grained top, 25½ in. wide. (Skinner Inc.) **$2,200**

Classical carved mahogany veneered work table, probably New York, 1820s, two working and two simulated drawers, 15½ in. wide. (Skinner Inc.) **$425**

Classical mahogany and mahogany veneer work table, Rhode Island, circa 1830, on a veneered swiveling pedestal, 20¾ in. wide. (Skinner Inc.) **$450**

A Federal figured maple work table, on ball and ring turned reeded tapering legs with ball turned feet, 27½ in. high. (Christie's New York) **$2,420**

A Classical stenciled rose-wood work table, New York, 1815-1825, on four gilt acanthus leaf carved lion's paw feet, the top and corners with gilt stenciling, 29¼ in. high. (Christie's New York) **$6,600**

A late Federal mahogany drop leaf work table, New England, 1810-1830, on spirally reeded and ring turned legs, 44½ in. wide, leaves open. (Christie's) **$1,210**

A classical mahogany work-table, New York, circa 1830, the square top with outset polygonal hinged ends opening to deep compartments over two cockbeaded small drawers, 30½ in. high. (Christie's) **$935**

Classical carved mahogany veneered work table, Boston, 1820-30, the central fitted veneered drawer above similar frame drawer for the wooden work bag, 30½ in. high. (Skinner Inc.) **$1,800**

A classical carved mahogany work table, Philadelphia, 1815-1825, on four saber legs with carved scrolled knees and cast foliate brass casters, 20 in. wide. (Christie's) **$3,850**

WORK TABLES

A late Federal mahogany work-stand, Philadelphia, 1800-1820, on baluster turned and reeded legs on peg feet, 16¾in. wide. (Christie's) $2,090

A Federal mahogany work-table, New York, 1800–1815, on a turned pedestal and quadripartite base on downswept molded legs, on paw feet with casters, 25¼in. wide. (Christie's) $3,300

Classical carved mahogany veneer work table, Salem, Massachusetts, circa 1820, the top drawer fitted with writing surface, 18¾in. wide. (Skinner Inc.) $770

Federal mahogany and maho-gany veneer work table, Massa-chusetts, circa 1800, the rectan-gular top with ovolo corners, 21½in. wide. (Robt. W. Skin-ner Inc.) $2,900

A Classical gilt stenciled mahogany work table, New York, 1820-1830, on acanthus carved lion's paw feet with casters, 23in. wide. (Christie's New York) $3,520

A Federal mahogany sewing-table, Salem, Massachusetts, 1790–1810, the serpentine top above a conforming case with a cockbeaded drawer fitted with a velvet-lined writing surface over an additional drawer and sliding work-bag, 19½in. wide. (Christie's) $8,250

A late Federal carved mahogany work-table, Salem, Massachusetts, 1800–1820, the rectangular top with outset rounded corners, on spirally-turned tapering legs and ball feet, 21¾in. wide. (Christie's) $1,320

A classical carved mahogany work-table, attributed to A. Querville, Philadelphia, 1815–1825, the hinged rectangular top with molded edge above a fitted interior, on four carved paw feet with waterleaf-carved knees and casters, 23in. wide. (Christie's) $3,850

A Country Federal inlaid cherry work table, New England, circa 1800, top 20 x 19¼in. (Robt. W. Skinner Inc.) $3,500

WORK TABLES

Federal mahogany veneer work stand, New England, circa 1810, old refinish, 16½in. wide. (Skinner Inc.) **$3,300**

Federal mahogany veneered work table, New York, 1810–30, top drawer fitted, replaced brasses, 22½in. wide. (Skinner Inc.) **$4,000**

A Federal mahogany work table, Boston, Massachusetts, 1810-1820, on molded saber legs with castors, 51.1cm. wide, closed. (Christie's) **$3,300**

Federal mahogany veneered work table, Boston or North Shore, circa 1800, the mahogany veneered top with four carved ovolo corners, 18½in. wide. (Skinner Inc.) **$3,000**

An Academy painted tiger maple work table, New England circa 1815, the rectangular over hanging top edged in tiny flowers, 43,5cm. wide. (Robt. W. Skinner Inc.) **$7,250**

Classical cherry and rosewood veneer gilt-stenciled worktable, Middle Atlantic States, circa 1815, 20¾in. wide. (Skinner Inc.) **$1,500**

A rare Federal mahogany veneered inlaid work table, probably Seymour workshop, Boston, Massachusetts, 1795-1810, 18in. wide. (Robt. W. Skinner Inc.) **$44,000**

Classical Revival mahogany veneered carved work table, probably New York or New Jersey, circa 1830m, with brass inlay, 24in. wide. (Skinner Inc.) **$700**

A Classical grain painted and stenciled work table, New York, 1825-1835, the rectangular top with drop leaves, 28¾in. high. (Christie's New York) **$2,640**

Chippendale painted tall blanket chest, New England, circa 1800, the top opens to a well with three drawers below, old dark red paint, 37½in. wide. (Skinner Inc.) $3,025

Queen Anne maple chest on frame, New Hampshire, circa 1760, old refinish, brasses probably original, 38in. wide. (Skinner Inc.) $7,700

Maple tall chest, probably New York state, circa 1800, refinished, replaced brasses, 41¼in. wide. (Skinner Inc.) $1,900

A Federal inlaid figured maple tall chest of drawers, New England, 1790-1810 with cove molded cornice, on French feet, 44½in. wide. (Christie's New York) $8,800

A Queen Anne painted maple tall chest on a tall bracket base, New England, circa 1750, 36in. wide. (Robt. W. Skinner Inc.) $6,500

A Chippendale tiger maple tall chest on bracket feet, replaced brasses, New England, circa 1790, 38½in. wide. (Robt. W. Skinner Inc.) $5,500

Queen Anne maple tall chest, Salisbury, New Hampshire area, School of Bartlett Cabinetmaking, circa 1800, refinished, 36in. wide. (Skinner Inc.) $4,000

A Federal inlaid walnut tall chest of drawers, Pennsylvania, 1790-1810, on flared French feet, 43¾in. wide. (Christie's) $5,280

Maple tall chest on frame, New Hampshire, circa 1780, on cabriole legs ending in pad feet, brasses replaced, 36in. wide. (Skinner Inc.) $9,000

TALL CHESTS

Antique American Chippendale six-drawer tall chest in maple, graduated drawers, molded cornice, bracket base, 38in. wide.
(Eldred's) $1,870

Cherry and maple tall chest, Thetford, Vermont, circa 1800, refinished, replaced brasses, 38¹/₄in. wide.
(Skinner Inc.) $4,000

Maple and pine tall chest, New England, circa 1800, refinished, replaced brasses, 36in. wide.
(Skinner Inc.) $3,300

Pine blanket chest, probably New England, early 19th century, refinished, replaced brass, 38¹/₂in. wide.
(Skinner Inc.) $700

A Chippendale maple tall chest-of-drawers with original pulls, circa 1780, 36in. wide.
(Robt. W. Skinner Inc.)
                             $6,500

A Country Chippendale pine blanket chest, New England, circa 1780, the molded lift top above a case of two false thumb-molded drawers and three working drawers, 36¾in. wide. (Robt. W. Skinner Inc.)
                             $1,500

Painted chest on frame, New Hampshire, circa 1830, with six graduated thumb molded drawers, on cabriole legs with arris pad feet, 36in. wide.
(Skinner Inc.) $151,000

A Federal tiger maple tall chest, Pennsylvania, circa 1810, the rectangular top with flaring cornice, 40in. wide. (Robt. W. Skinner Inc.) $3,750

Chippendale maple tall chest of drawers, Rhode Island, late 18th century, the molded cornice above the thumb-molded edge, on bracket feet, 39¹/₄in. wide.
(Butterfield & Butterfield)
                             $3,575

WASHSTANDS

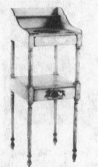

A painted and decorated washstand, New England, circa 1830, 15¼in. wide.   **$500**

Country Federal tiger maple corner washstand, New England, circa 1810, the shaped backboards above cut out shelf, 40½in. high. (Skinner Inc.)   **$2,500**

A Federal mahogany carved washstand, probably Mass., circa 1815, 20in. wide.   **$3,000**

A late Federal mahogany washstand, New York, 1815-1825, the shaped splashboard above a medial shelf over a pierced and fitted D-shaped top.   **$1,750**

Shaker painted pine washstand, Harvard, Massachusetts, 19th century, the hinged lid opens to a storage compartment above a cupboard, 36in. wide. (Skinner Inc.)   **$11,000**

A Federal mahogany washstand, circa 1795, 39in. high, 23in. wide.   **$850**

Antique American Sheraton washstand in mahogany, shaped backsplash, drawer in base, turned legs, 18½in. wide. (Eldred's)   **$220**

Federal mahogany and bird's-eye maple veneer corner chamber stand, Massachusetts, early 19th century, 21in. wide. (Skinner Inc.)   **$2,090**

Federal mahogany veneered Beau Brummel, probably Eastern United States, circa 1820, on turned tapering legs, 40in. high. (Skinner Inc.)   **$6,000**

WASHSTANDS

Classical Revival mahogany washstand, probably Boston, circa 1815, 18¼in. diam. (Robt. W. Skinner Inc.)
$3,600

Shaker pine, tiger maple and butternut washstand, 20¼in. wide. (Robt. W. Skinner Inc.)
$10,000

Federal mahogany corner washstand on splay feet, 21½in. wide, circa 1800.
$1,250

A Federal carved mahogany wash basin stand, Boston, 1800–1810, with reeded and shaped splash board above a rectangular top with reeded edge fitted for three wash bowls, 30½in. wide. (Christie's)
$1,430

Antique American kitchen cupboard in pine, backsplash top, two small drawers over two paneled cupboard doors, bracket feet, 48in. high. (Eldred's)
$660

A Federal inlaid mahogany and birch-veneered wash-stand, Portsmouth, New Hampshire, 1790–1810, the rectangular top pierced with three circular openings and edged with a three-quarter gallery, 35½in. high. (Christie's)
$22,000

A Federal inlaid mahogany corner stand, the top with a pierced brass gallery, probably New York, 1800-15, 34½in. high.
$3,000

A 19th century painted pine washstand, painted old pink over other colors, America, 15½in. wide. (Robt. W. Skinner Inc.)
$800

A Classical Revival mahogany washstand, probably Boston, circa 1815, 17½in. diam. (Robt. W. Skinner Inc.)
$16,500

LIMBERT

Charles Limbert was a furniture designer and maker, working in Grand Rapids, Michigan, around 1900–10,. He must have been well acquainted with the two Stickley brothers, George and Albert, who were also active in the town at that period, and Limbert's output owes much to the inspiration of Gustav Stickley.

Limbert worked mainly in the Mission style, named from the furniture supposedly found in the Franciscan missions in California. His work is characterised by its simple, sturdy design, with exposed pegs and tenon ends often as the only decoration.

Limbert oak day bed, Michigan, circa 1910, shaped headrest and wide skirt accommodating spring cushions, square raised feet, 79in. long.
(Robt. W. Skinner Inc.) $650

A magazine stand with cutouts, Michigan, 1910, 20in. wide. (Robt. W. Skinner Inc.)
$800

**Limbert dining table, circa 1910, circular top over arched skirt connecting to four square legs, 51in. diameter.
(Skinner Inc.)** $1,100

Round table with caned pedestal base, probably Michigan, circa 1915, unsigned, (refinished), 36½in. diam. (Robt. W. Skinner Inc.)
$450

Limbert double oval table with cut out base, Grand Rapids, Michigan, circa 1907 (bangs and stains on surface). (Robt. W. Skinner Inc.)
$5,000

Limbert octagonal plant stand with cut-outs, Michigan, circa 1910, on box base with double trapezoidal cut-outs, 28½in. high. (Skinner Inc.)
$2,000

**Lifetime Furniture sideboard, Grand Rapids, Michigan, circa 1910, mirrored backboard, three central drawers flanked by cabinet doors over long lower drawer, 60½in. wide.
(Skinner Inc.)** $600

A cane-sided plant stand, probably Limbert, circa 1910, 23in. high, the top 16in. sq. (Robt. W. Skinner Inc.)
$600

LIMBERT

A Limbert mirrored oak sideboard, Michigan, circa 1910, 54in. wide. (Robt. W. Skinner Inc.) $1,250

Limbert open-arm adjustable back rocker, circa 1910, no. 518, flat-arm over elongated corbels, original upholstered spring cushion seat, branded mark, 36¾in. high. (Skinner) $1,250

Limbert oak window bench, Grand Rapids, Michigan, 1907, with original leather cushion, branded mark (minor nicks), 24in. wide. (Skinner Inc.) $12,500

Three pieces of Limbert furniture, Grand Rapids, Michigan, circa 1910, open arm rocker, and matching armchair, both with straight crest rail, open-arm settle, with straight crest rail. (Skinner Inc.) (Three) $1,250

Limbert open book rack, Michigan, circa 1910, flat sides centering three open shelves, 28in. high. (Robt. W. Skinner Inc.) $800

Limbert round tall pedestal, circa 1906, no. 267, 32½in. high, 14in. diam. (Robt. W. Skinner Inc.) $1,250

A Limbert oval table with cut-out sides, Grand Rapids, Michigan, circa 1907, no. 146, 45in. long. (Robt. W. Skinner Inc.) $1,250

LIMBERT

A Limbert single door china cabinet, no. 1347, Grand Rapids, Michigan, circa 1907, 34¼in. wide. (Robt. W. Skinner Inc.) **$2,000**

A Limbert sideboard with arched mirrored backboard with corbel detail, Michigan, circa 1910, 47¾in. wide. **$1,400**

Limbert cellarette, circa 1908, no. 751, rectangular top projecting over single drawer with square copper pulls, 24³⁄₄in. wide. (Skinner Inc.) **$1,100**

Oak liquor cabinet with copper slide, probably Michigan, circa 1910, with fitted compartments, unsigned, 40¾in. high. (Skinner Inc.) **$700**

Unusual Limbert sideboard, Grand Rapids, Michigan, circa 1903, gallery top, three short drawers over three cabinet doors, single long drawer below, round copper and brass pulls, 59¼in. wide. (Skinner) **$1,750**

Limbert miniature bookcase with heart cut-out gallery, circa 1910, 24in. wide. **$1,500**

Octagonal plant stand with cutouts, Michigan, circa 1910, probably Limbert, with double trapezoidal cut-outs, 28in. high. (Skinner Inc.) **$725**

A Limbert mirrored sideboard, no. 1453 3/4, circa 1910, 48in. wide. **$900**

Limbert octagonal plant stand, style no. 251, circa 1910, 24¼in. high. (Robt. W. Skinner Inc.) **$1,400**

MISSION FURNITURE

The Mission Style of furniture which was immensely popular around the beginning of the 20th century was essentially the major American expression of the Arts & Crafts style which had recently evolved in England.

Its name derives from the fact that it was supposed to reflect the style of furniture found in the old Franciscan missions of California, and it was seen as a revival of medieval and functional designs.

Most pieces were made in oak, and the forms were rectilinear and as simple and functional as possible. Obvious signs of handiwork, such as exposed mortice and tenon joints were characteristic of the style. Mission furniture was often used in furniture schemes alongside Tiffany glass, Navajo rugs and Morris chairs.

The style flourished until around 1920, and mass-produced pieces are often found.

Mission oak double bed with exposed tenons, circa 1907, 58½in. wide. (Robt. W. Skinner Inc.) $2,500

A Mission oak magazine/wood carrier, circa 1910, 18in. high, 15¼in. wide. (Robt. W. Skinner Inc.) $500

Mission rectangular oak sideboard, circa 1910, 72in. wide. $1,500

Early 20th century Mission oak magazine stand with cut out arched sides, 49in. high. (Robt. W. Skinner Inc.) $600

Mission oak two-door china closet, no. 2017, circa 1910, 46½in. wide. (Robt. W. Skinner Inc.) $500

One of a pair of mahogany Mission oak beds, possibly Roycroft, circa 1912, 42in. wide. (Robt. W. Skinner Inc.) $800

Mission oak 'knock-down' table, unsigned, circa 1910, 30in. diam. (Robt. W. Skinner Inc.) $275

ROYCROFT

Elbert Hubbard (1856–1915) was an American soap manufacturer who became fired with enthusiasm for the Arts & Crafts movement after a visit to Britain in 1894. In 1895 he established the Roycroft shops, a craft community based in East Aurora, NY, to produce pieces in the Arts & Crafts style.

Thus they were one of the major manufacturers of Mission style furniture, mainly in oak and mahogany, often with leather seats and copper studs on armchairs. They also produced, between 1905–12, a kind of deck chair, with three slats in the back, which was known as the Morris chair. Their pieces were known as Aurora colonial furniture from 1905. In 1908 a copper workshop was set up, making bookends, trays, inkwells etc. Following his visit to England, Hubbard also bought a printing press, on which he printed some fine books, such as The Song of Songs, on handmade paper.

A Roycroft oak piano bench, N.Y., circa 1910, signed with logo, 36in. long. (Robt. W. Skinner Inc.) $2,750

Roycroft magazine pedestal, circa 1906, no. 080, overhanging square top, canted sides with keyed tenons, five shelves, carved oak leaf design, 64in. high.
(Skinner) $4,000

Roycroft pedestal base lamp table, East Aurora, New York, circa 1910, with four curving legs joining in the middle, 29½in. high. (Skinner Inc.) $2,000

A Roycroft oak library table, East Aurora, New York, circa 1910, having two drawers and square tapered legs with shaped feet, 48in. wide. $2,000

NATVRE
B   Y
RALPH
WALDO
EMERSON

Nature by Ralph Waldo Emerson, published by the Roycrofters, East Aurora, New York, 1905, good condition. (Robt. W. Skinner Inc.) $250

Roycroft oak magazine pedestal, East Aurora, N.Y., circa 1910, 48in high. $2,000

Roycroft oak umbrella stand, East Aurora, New York, circa 1910, signed with logo, (finish partially removed) 29¾in. high. (Robt. W. Skinner Inc.) $600

FURNITURE

Roycroft oak upholstered footstool, New York, circa 1910, no. 048, needlepoint cover, 10in. high. (Skinner Inc.) $450

A Roycroft oak bridal chest, East Aurora, New York, circa 1912, with extended serpentine sides, 36½in. wide. (Robt. W. Skinner Inc.) $7,500

Roycroft pedestal base dining table, East Aurora, New York, circa 1910, signed with logo, no leaves, 48in. diam. (Robt. W. Skinner Inc.) $2,500

Roycroft Little Journeys book stand, circa 1910, rectangular overhanging top over two lower shelves, keyed tenons, 26¼in. wide. (Skinner) $750

Roycroft "Ali Baba" bench, circa 1910, oak slab seat with some exposed bark underneath, plank ends joined by long center stretcher, 42in. long. (Skinner) $1,650

Roycroft mirrored dressing table, East Aurora, New York, circa 1910, with swing handles, tapering MacMurdo feet, signed with orb, 39in. wide. (Skinner Inc.) $1,100

Roycroft oak chiffonier, East Aurora, New York, circa 1907, signed with *Roycroft* across front, 42in. wide. (Skinner Inc.) $7,500

Unusual Roycroft sewing table, East Aurora, New York, circa 1910, incised with logo, (some stains, one knob broken) 30in. wide. (Robt. W. Skinner Inc.) $2,000

Roycroft 'Little Journeys' bookrack, circa 1910, rectangular overhanging top, two lower shelves with keyed tenons through vertical side plats, 26¼in. wide. (Skinner) $465

GEORGE & ALBERT STICKLEY

Two of the famous Stickley family, George and Albert, set up their furniture workshop in Grand Rapids, Michigan in 1901. There, they produced furniture which owed much to the Craftsman style. (The Craftsman was a magazine published by their brother Gustav, which advocated the principles of the Arts & Crafts movement).

It was marketed as Quaint Furniture, and is generally inferior in terms of material, workmanship and design, to that turned out by their elder brother.

The Quaint, or Fanciful style was the name also given to the British trade version of the Art Nouveau style which flourished between c. 1895–1905. It combined elements of Anglo-Japanese, Arts & Crafts, Glasgow School and continental Art Nouveau furniture and was characterized by painted and inlaid floral motifs, heart-shaped apertures and ornate hinges.

With regard to decoration, 18th century forms were often used as the basic inspiration. Cabinets and armchairs had thin legs, and often six or eight of them, with low stretchers. Especially popular were versions of the Windsor chair and asymmetrical sofas. The woods used were mainly polished rosewood, fumed oak and cheap woods stained green or purple.

At its best Quaint furniture was restrained in form and decoration, whereas cheaper imitations tended to be over elaborate. Names of designers and manufacturers associated with the style include William Birch, George Ellwood, J S Henry and E G Punnett.

A Stickley Bros. sideboard, Grand Rapids, Michigan, 1912, 60in. wide. (Robt. W. Skinner Inc.) $600

Stickley Brothers inlaid settle, Grand Rapids, Michigan, circa 1901, inlaid with flowers, leaves, grasses and other naturalistic motifs, unmarked, 51¾in. high. This settle, advertised in 1901, was influenced by the English Arts and Crafts movement.
(Skinner) $3,250

A Stickley Bros. slat-back settle, signed with paper label, Quaint, circa 1910, 72in. wide. (Robt. W. Skinner Inc.) $5,000

GEORGE & ALBERT STICKLEY

Stickley Bros. set of drawers with swinging mirror, circa 1910, 38in. wide. $800

Hinged oak box with glass lining, attributed to Stickley Bros., Michigan, circa 1910, 15½in. wide. $800

Stickley Brothers chest of drawers, circa 1912, rectangular swivel mirror, two short drawers over three long drawers, 44in. wide. (Skinner Inc.) $400

Stickley Bros. inlaid mahogany two-seater settee, Michigan, circa 1920.
$2,000

Stickley Brothers costumer, Grand Rapids, Michigan, circa 1914, no. 187, four iron hooks on post with corbeled cross-stretcher base, 68in. high. (Skinner Inc.) $225

A Stickley Bros. spindle sided footstool, circa 1907, with stretchers centering seven spindles each side, unsigned, 20½in. wide. (Robt. W. Skinner Inc.)
$3,000

'Quaint Furniture' cafe table with copper top, Grand Rapids, Michigan, circa 1915, no. 2615, signed with metal tag, 18¼in. diameter. (Skinner Inc.) $700

A marquetry paneled oak smoking rack, possibly Stickley Bros., Michigan, circa 1910, style no. 264-100, 22in. high, 24in. wide. (Robt. W. Skinner Inc.)
$200

Stickley Brothers flip-sided sewing table, Grand Rapids, Michigan, circa 1912, rectangular box with applied handle, 18in. wide. (Skinner Inc.) $425

GUSTAV STICKLEY

The Arts & Crafts Movement found one of its greatest exponents in the USA in Gustav Stickley (1857–1942). He was the eldest of six brothers who all went into furniture making, though he at first trained as a mason.

In his youth he designed mainly chairs in the American Colonial style, but in 1898 he founded the firm of Gustav Stickley of Syracuse, New York, which specialised in the Arts & Crafts or Mission style of furniture (from the furniture supposedly found in the old Franciscan missions in California). He also published a magazine 'The Craftsman' which popularised this new style.

Like Art Nouveau, of which this was the American version, the style was seen as being a return to the simple functional style of the medieval period. Oak was the most popular wood, and construction was simple, often with obvious signs of handiwork, such as exposed mortice and tenon joints. Chairbacks were usually constructed as a series of flat vertical or horizontal boards.

Interestingly five of the brothers went into the same line of business, and the relationship between them seems to have been a highly political one. George and Albert worked in Grand Rapids, Michigan from 1891, and formed the firm of Stickley Bros. Co. around 1901. Their furniture is similar to the Craftsman style, often characterized by through tenons, but it was generally inferior in quality in terms of wood, design and finish. It was marketed as Quaint Furniture. They also produced independent designs similar to English cottage furniture.

A Gustav Stickley oak bed, designed by Harvey Ellis, 59½in. wide. (Robt. W. Skinner Inc.) $30,000

Gustav Stickley oak and wrought iron secretary, designed by Harvey Ellis, circa 1904, 56in. wide. (Robt. W. Skinner Inc.) $17,500

A three-sectioned oak screen, by Gustav Stickley, circa 1913, each panel 21½in. wide, 66in. high. (Robt. W. Skinner Inc.) $10,000

An oak wastebasket, by Gustav Stickley, 1907, 14in. high, 12in. diam. (Robt. W. Skinner Inc.) $2,000

Gustav Stickley two-door wardrobe, circa 1907, two paneled doors with copper pulls opening to reveal two compartments, 34¹/₈ in. wide. (Skinner Inc.) $5,000

Open-sided music stand, circa 1907, similar to Gustav Stickley no. 670, four tapering posts, centering four shelves with gallery, unsigned, 39in. high. (Skinner Inc.) $1,000

GUSTAV STICKLEY

The other two brothers, Leopold and J. George, were at first employed by Gustav but left his employment to found L. & J.G. Stickley at Fayetteville, in 1900. They too based their designs on Craftsman furniture, sometimes using veneers and laminated members, and their pieces are identifiable by the name L. & J.G Stickley in red. They were open to other influences, however, which may help to account for their survival, and made furniture designed by Frank Lloyd Wright, the Morris chair, and by 1914 were turning out reproduction furniture as well.

When one refers to 'Stickley' it is undoubtedly Gustav who springs most readily to mind. Certainly he was the most original designer of the family, he was also the purist, and his pieces are often austere in their unadorned simplicity. His brothers were perhaps more realistic in seeing that their products also had to find a market, and they were readier to compromise in terms of putting some embellishments on the basic style. It may have been Gustav's unwillingness to compromise his ideals that led to the break with Leopold and J. George, and it may also be why, by 1915, he was bankrupt. He attempted to soldier on, selling new lines based loosely on 18th century styles, or in bright colors, but to no avail. It was left to L. & J.G. to buy him out in 1916, when the business became the Stickley Manufacturing Co. Under this name it is still active, chiefly producing American Colonial reproduction furniture in cherrywood.

A Gustav Stickley spindle-sided baby's crib, no. 919, circa 1907, 56½in. long. (Robt. W. Skinner Inc.) $1,650

A Gustav Stickley plate rack, circa 1904, 48in. wide. $3,000

Pair of Gustav Stickley oak twin beds, 40in. wide. (Robt. W. Skinner Inc.) $5,000

A Gustav Stickley oak music cabinet, the ten pane single door with amber glass, circa 1912, 47¼in. high. (Robt. W. Skinner Inc.) $3,000

Gustav Stickley one door china closet, circa 1907, no. 820, 36in. wide. (Robt. W. Skinner Inc.) $2,000

An inlaid oak secretary, designed by Harvey Ellis for Gustav Stickley, circa 1903-04, 42in. wide. (Robt. W. Skinner Inc.) $100,000

GUSTAV STICKLEY BOOKCASES

A two-door oak bookcase, twelve panels to each door, by Gustav Stickley, circa 1904, 48in. wide. (Robt. W. Skinner Inc.) $7,500

A Gustav Stickley oak bookcase, the door with wrought iron lock plate and drop loop handle, 98cm. wide. (Christie's) $2,500

A Gustav Stickley double-door bookcase, no. 719, circa 1912, 60in. wide. (Robt. W. Skinner Inc.) $4,500

Gustav Stickley leaded two-door bookcase, designed by Harvey Ellis, circa 1904, no. 716, 42¾in. wide. (Robt. W. Skinner Inc.) $3,000

A rare and important Gustav Stickley inlaid two door bookcase, designed by Harvey Ellis, circa 1903-1904, signed with red decal in a box, 55¾in. wide. (Robt. W. Skinner Inc.) $50,000

Gustav Stickley two-door bookcase, circa 1910, no. 716, gallery above eight-pane doors, 42in. wide. (Robt. W. Skinner Inc.) $2,500

A Gustav Stickley two-door bookcase, no. 718, signed with large red decal, circa 1904-05, 54in. wide. (Robt. W. Skinner Inc.) $5,000

Gustav Stickley leaded single door bookcase, designed by Harvey Ellis, circa 1904, no. 700, 36in. wide. (Robt. W. Skinner Inc.) $10,000

Gustav Stickley double door bookcase, Eastwood, New York, circa 1907, gallery top over two doors each with eight panes, 48in. wide. (Skinner Inc.) $2,500

GUSTAV STICKLEY CHAIRS

Rare Gustav Stickley oak Eastwood chair, circa 1902-1904, signed with a red decal in a box, 36in. wide. (Skinner Inc.) $20,000

A Gustav Stickley child's arm rocker, no. 345, signed with small red decal and paper label, circa 1904-06. (Robt. W. Skinner Inc.) $600

A Gustav Stickley willow armchair, circa 1907, 39in. high, 31in. wide. (Robt. W. Skinner Inc.) $600

Gustav Stickley mahogany bow armchair, circa 1907, no. 336, 36in. high. (Robt. W. Skinner Inc.) $2,250

A tall spindle-back armchair, no. 386, by Gustav Stickley, 49½in. high. (Robt. W. Skinner Inc.) $12,500

A Gustav Stickley bird's-eye maple wide slat cube chair, circa 1903-04, no. 328. (Robt. W. Skinner Inc.) $3,000

Gustav Stickley fixed back armchair, circa 1907, no. 324, flat arm over six vertical slats, 39in. high. (Robt. W. Skinner Inc.) $1,000

A Gustav Stickley slat-sided cube chair, no. 331, circa 1910, 25¼in. wide. (Robt. W. Skinner Inc.) $6,000

A Gustav Stickley bow armchair, no. 335, circa 1905, signed with small red decal, 37½in. high. (Robt. W. Skinner Inc.) $7,000

GUSTAV STICKLEY CHAIRS

A tall back, slat sided rocker with leather spring cushion by Gustav Stickley, 41½in. high. **$900**

Rare leather sling seat arm chair, Toby Furniture Co., Chicago, circa 1900, design attributed to Gustav Stickley, unsigned, 33in. wide. (Skinner Inc.) **$3,500**

A Gustav Stickley spindle-sided cube chair, no. 391, circa 1907, 26in. wide. (Robt. W. Skinner Inc.) **$18,000**

Gustav Stickley revolving office chair, no. 361, circa 1904, signed with decal in a box, 28in. wide. (Robt. W. Skinner Inc.) **$1,750**

Two of a set of five Gustav Stickley dining chairs with rush seats, circa 1907, 37in. high. (Robt. W. Skinner Inc.) **$2,000**

A Gustav Stickley willow armchair, circa 1910, the tall back with square cut-outs centered by flat arms, unsigned, 42¾in. high. (Robt. W. Skinner Inc.) **$4,000**

A bent arm spindle Morris chair, no. 369, by Gustav Stickley, with adjustable back, 24in. high. (Robt. W. Skinner Inc.) **$15,000**

A Gustav Stickley oak 'Eastwood' chair with original rope support for seat, circa 1902. (Robt. W. Skinner Inc.) **$28,000**

One of a set of six Gustav Stickley dining chairs, including one armchair, circa 1907, 18in. wide. (Robt. W. Skinner Inc.) **$4,500**

GUSTAV STICKLEY CHAIRS

A Gustav Stickley adjustable back drop armchair, no. 369, circa 1907, signed with red decal, 38in. high. (Robt. W. Skinner Inc.) $5,000

Gustav Stickley inlaid oak side chair. $2,000

Gustav Stickley Morris chair, circa 1910, no. 332, adjustable back, five vertical slats, straight seat rail, unsigned, 40in. high. (Skinner Inc.) $4,000

A leather upholstered dining chair, no. 355, by Gustav Stickley, circa 1910, 33¼in. high. (Robt. W. Skinner Inc.) $1,000

Two of six V-back dining chairs, complete with dining table, by Gustav Stickley, circa 1907. (Robt. W. Skinner Inc.) $4,500

A leather upholstered dining armchair, by Gustav Stickley, circa 1910, no. 355A, 36¼in. high. (Robt. W. Skinner Inc.) $2,000

Gustav Stickley 'rabbit ear' armchair, 1901-02, signed, 41½in. high. (Robt. W. Skinner Inc.) $800

A Gustav Stickley bent arm spindle Morris chair, circa 1907, with spring cushion seat. (Robt. W. Skinner Inc.) $15,000

One of six Gustav Stickley dining chairs, circa 1907, three horizontal slats, new seats in cream colored leather, 37½in. high. (Skinner Inc.) (Six) $3,000

GUSTAV STICKLEY CHESTS

A nine-drawer tall chest with cast bronze faceted pulls, by Gustav Stickley, circa 1904-06, 36in. wide. (Robt. W. Skinner Inc.) $7,500

An experimental Gustav Stickley cedar-lined chest, circa 1901-02, 27¾in. wide. $10,000

Gustav Stickley six-drawer chest, circa 1907, no. 902, reverse V splashboard, two half-drawers over four graduated drawers, signed with red decal, 52½in. high.(Skinner Inc.)$4,500

Gustav Stickley chest of drawers, circa 1907, two half drawers over three long drawers, 37in. wide. (Robt. W. Skinner Inc.) $2,250

Early Gustav Stickley six-drawer chest, circa 1902-04, no. 902, reverse V splashboard, two half-drawers over four graduated drawers with square wooden pulls, 40in. wide. (Skinner) $4,500

A Gustav Stickley work cabi-net, circa 1905-7, with two cabinet doors over two drawers with square wooden pulls, 36in. high. (Robt. W. Skinner Inc.) $15,000

Gustav Stickley smoker's cabinet, circa 1907, over-hanging top above single drawer and cabinet door, 20in. wide. (Robt. W. Skinner Inc.) $2,000

A Gustav Stickley nine-drawer tall chest, no. 913, circa 1907, 36in. wide, 50in. high. (Robt. W. Skinner Inc.) $5,000

A Gustav Stickley chest-of-drawers, no. 901, with wooden pulls, circa 1907, 37in. wide. (Robt. W. Skinner Inc.) $1,500

GUSTAV STICKLEY DESKS

A Gustav Stickley drop-front desk, the doors opening to reveal a fitted interior, circa 1906, 38in. wide. (Robt. W. Skinner Inc.)
$3,000

Early Gustav Stickley drop front desk, 1902-04, step-down gallery, chamfered drop front with copper strap hinges over two open shelves, 52in. high. (Skinner)
$6,500

Gustav Stickley drop-front desk with cabinet doors, circa 1902-04, 32¾in. wide. (Robt. W. Skinner Inc.)
$5,000

An early Gustav Stickley chalet desk, circa 1901-2, the arched gallery top with pierced corner cut-outs and keyed tenon sides, 45¾in. high. (Robt. W. Skinner Inc.)
$2,000

Gustav Stickley slant lid desk, Eastwood, New York, circa 1907, gallery top, slant lid front over single drawer with brass v-pulls, 30in. wide. (Skinner Inc.)
$1,000

An inlaid oak drop-front desk, designed by Harvey Ellis for Gustav Stickley, 1903-04, style no. 706, 30in. wide. (Robt. W. Skinner Inc.)
$20,000

An oak drop-front desk, by Gustav Stickley, circa 1912, 32in. wide. (Robt. W. Skinner Inc.)
$1,500

Gustav Stickley desk, circa 1912, letter file with two small drawers on rectangular top over two half drawers, 22¾in. wide. (Skinner Inc.)
$750

A Gustav Stickley desk, no. 721, circa 1912, 29in. high. (Robt. W. Skinner Inc.)
$500

GUSTAV STICKLEY
SETTEES & COUCHES

Gustav Stickley even arm settle, circa 1907, no. 208, straight rail over eight vertical slats on back, three on each end, with Southwestern designs, 76in. long. (Skinner Inc.) $9,000

A Gustav Stickley paneled settle, no. 189, signed with large red decal with signature in a box, 1901-03, 84in. long. (Robt. W. Skinner Inc.) $7,500

A Gustav Stickley tall spindleback settee, no. 286, signed with decal, circa 1906, 48in. wide. (Robt. W. Skinner Inc.) $40,000

A Gustav Stickley bird's-eye maple wide slat settee, no. 214, circa 1903-04, 50¼in. wide. (Robt. W. Skinner Inc.) $4,500

Gustav Stickley knock-down settee, New York, circa 1907, 12in. wide horizontal back slat, 84in. long. (Skinner Inc.) $9,000

An oak hall settle with leather covered spring cushion seat, by Gustav Stickley, 56in. wide. (Robt. W. Skinner Inc.) $3,500

A Gustav Stickley slat-back settle, no. 206, circa 1904-06, 60in. wide. (Robt. W. Skinner Inc.) $17,500

An early Gustav Stickley settle with arched slats, 1901-03, 60in. wide. (Robt. W. Skinner Inc.) $27,500

GUSTAV STICKLEY
SIDEBOARDS

Rare Gustav Stickley sideboard, circa 1902, the top shelf galleried on three sides, unsigned, 48in. wide. (Skinner Inc.) $3,750

Gustav Stickley desk, circa 1902-03, rectangular top over two banks of four short drawers, 54in. wide. (Skinner Inc.) $2,250

An oak chest with plate rack by Gustav Stickley, circa 1904, 69½in. wide. $5,500

Gustav Stickley oak sideboard, circa 1907, 56in. wide. $2,000

An oak sideboard, by Gustav Stickley, 1907, 66in. wide. (Robt. W. Skinner Inc.) $1,500

Gustav Stickley sideboard, circa 1907-12, no. 816, plate rack on rectangular top, long drawer over two central drawers, 48in. wide. (Skinner Inc.) $2,000

Gustav Stickley eight-legged sideboard, circa 1904, no. 817, with plate rack, 70in. wide. (Robt. W. Skinner Inc.) $10,000

Early Gustav Stickley sideboard, no. 967, with long copper strap hardware and square copper pulls, 60in. wide. (Robt. W. Skinner Inc.) $12,000

GUSTAV STICKLEY STANDS

A Gustav Stickley V-top bookrack, signed with red decal in a box, 1902-04, 31in. wide, 31in. high. (Robt. W. Skinner Inc.) $1,750

Gustav Stickley oak plant stand, circa 1903, 28in. high. $2,000

Gustav Stickley open slat-sided bookshelf, circa 1909, 27in. wide. (Robt. W. Skinner Inc.) $1,100

Gustav Stickley Toby magazine stand, circa 1904, square top with corbel supports, unsigned (top reglued), 43in. high. (Skinner Inc.) $800

Gustav Stickley inlaid tiger maple open music stand, circa 1904, no. 670, signed with Eastwood label, 39in. high. (Robt. W. Skinner Inc.) $10,000

Gustav Stickley hall tree, circa 1902–03, with four wrought iron hooks, 74in. high. (Skinner Inc.) $2,250

A Gustav Stickley three-drawer bedside stand, style no. 842, copper hardware with loop handles, circa 1907, 29½in. high. (Robt. W. Skinner Inc.) $1,500

An early Gustav Stickley leather fire-screen, 1902, 35in. high, 31in. wide. (Robt. W. Skinner Inc.) $2,500

A Gustav Stickley slat-sided folio stand, no. 551, 1902-03, 40½in. high, 29½in. wide. (Robt. W. Skinner Inc.) $3,500

GUSTAV STICKLEY STOOLS

A Gustav Stickley mahogany footstool, no. 302, signed with red decal, 1905-05, 4½in. high. (Robt. W. Skinner Inc.) **$1,100**

Gustav Stickley footstool with cross stretcher base, circa 1902, no. 725, arched sides with leather upholstery and tacks, 16½in. wide. (Skinners) **$1,350**

A Gustav Stickley footstool with notched feet, style no. 726, circa 1902-04, 12¼in. wide. (Robt. W. Skinner Inc.) **$800**

A Gustav Stickley upholstered footstool with tacked leather surface, no. 300, circa 1905, 20½in. wide. (Robt. W. Skinner Inc.) **$2,000**

A Gustav Stickley mahogany footstool, circa 1904-1906, with upholstered seat, arched seat rail and exposed tenons, 20¼in. wide. (Robt. W. Skinner Inc.) **$600**

A leather upholstered footstool, no. 300, by Gustav Stickley, 20in. wide, circa 1905. (Robt. W. Skinner Inc.) **$1,000**

Gustav Stickley spindle-sided footstool, circa 1907, no. 395, 15in. high. (Robt. W. Skinner Inc.) **$300**

An oak piano bench with cut-out handles, by Gustav Stickley, circa 1907, 36in. wide. (Robt. W. Skinner Inc.) **$2,000**

A leather topped footstool, by Gustav Stickley, 20¼in. wide. (Robt. W. Skinner Inc.) **$1,350**

GUSTAV STICKLEY TABLES

A Gustav Stickley hexagonal leather-top table, no. 624, circa 1910-12, 48in. diam. (Robt. W. Skinner Inc.)
$8,000

Gustav Stickley table, circa 1912–16, no. 626, round top on four legs, joined by arched cross stretchers with finial, 40in. diameter. (Skinner Inc.) $1,250

A Gustav Stickley round library table, no. 633, circa 1904, 48in. diam. (Robt. W. Skinner Inc.)
$2,500

A Gustav Stickley square table with cut corners, no. 612, circa 1905-06, signed with small red decal, 29¾in. sq. (Robt. W. Skinner Inc.)
$1,250

An occasional table with cut corners, possibly early Gustav Stickley, circa 1902-04, 29in. high. (Robt. W. Skinner Inc.)
$1,250

An occasional table, no. 609, by Gustav Stickley, circa 1904-05, unsigned, 36in. diam. (Robt. W. Skinner Inc.)
$1,000

Gustav Stickley tabouret, no. 603, circa 1907, round top on four square legs, cross stretcher base, 18in. diameter. (Skinner Inc.)   **$800**

A leather top library table with three drawers, by Gustav Stickley, 66½in. wide.   **$3,000**

Gustav Stickley round oak table, circa 1904, 24in. diam.
$2,000

GUSTAV STICKLEY
TABLES

Gustav Stickley hexagonal top library table, circa 1904, no. 625, 48in. diam. (Robt. W. Skinner Inc.) **$7,500**

A mirrored dressing table with circle pulls, by Gustav Stickley. **$2,500**

A spindle-sided table with lower shelf, by Gustav Stickley, circa 1905, 36in. wide. **$6,000**

A Gustav Stickley round leather-top table, no. 645, circa 1907, 36in. diam. (Robt. W. Skinner Inc.) **$2,500**

Gustav Stickley table with twelve Grueby tiles, 1902-1904, four flat rails framing 4in. green tiles, 24in. wide. (Skinner Inc.) **$20,000**

Early Gustav Stickley table, circa 1902–03, no. 439, round top with four cut-in leg posts, 30in. diameter. (Skinner Inc.) **$1,250**

Gustav Stickley round library table, circa 1907, no. 636, with diagonal chamfered legs and arched cross stretcher with keyed tenons, unsigned, 48in. diameter. (Skinner Inc.) **$1,500**

An oak director's table with trestle base, by Gustav Stickley 96½in. long. **$18,000**

A drop-leaf table, by Gustav Stickley, no. 638, circa 1912, 42in. long, 40in. wide, open. (Robt. W. Skinner Inc.) **$3,000**

261

L & J G STICKLEY

Leopold and J George Stickley were younger brothers of the famous Gustav, with whom they obviously enjoyed a somewhat complicated relationship. They were at first employed by him in his firm at Syracuse, New York, but in 1900 left to found their own establishment, L & J G Stickley at Fayetteville. Like Gustav, they based their designs on Craftsman furniture, sometimes using veneers and laminated members, and their pieces are identifiable by the name L & J G Stickley in red.

Unlike Gustav, however, they were also open to other influences, and were perhaps more realistic in seeing that their products also had to find a market. They were certainly readier to compromise in terms of putting some embellishments on the basic style. They later made furniture designed by Frank Lloyd Wright and by 1914 were turning out reproduction pieces as well.

They bought out their elder brother in 1916, when the firm, still in existence today, became the Stickley Manufacturing Co.

L. & J.G. Stickley davenport bed, circa 1912, no. 285, seat rail slides out opening to a bed, 77in. long.
(Skinner Inc.) $1,750

L. & J. G. Stickley oak double bed, Fayetteville, New York, circa 1910, signed, 50in. high, 58in. wide.
(Skinner Inc.) $6,000

L. & J. G. Stickley china closet, circa 1912, no. 746, overhanging top above two doors with six smaller panes above single glass panel, 62in. high.
(Skinner) $5,000

An L. & J. G. Stickley slatted double-bed, signed with red (Handcraft) decal, 58in. wide.
(Robt. W. Skinner Inc.)
$12,000

L. & J. G. Stickley square drink stand, Fayetteville, New York, circa 1910, signed with Handcraft decal, 27in. high. (Skinner Inc.) $750

L. & J.G. Stickley settle, circa 1912, no. 216, straight crest rail, seven vertical slats across back, 72in. wide.
(Skinner Inc.) $2,500

L. & J.G. Stickley footstool, Syracuse and Fayetteville, New York, circa 1918, no. 397, signed with decal, 20in. wide.
(Skinner Inc.) $500

L & J.G. STICKLEY
BOOKCASES

A double door bookcase, by L. & J. G. Stickley, circa 1912, 48¾in. wide. $3,000

L. & J. G. Stickley single door bookcase, circa 1907, no. 643, gallery top with exposed key tenons over single door, 36in. wide. (Robt. W. Skinner Inc.) $2,500

L. & J. G. Stickley three door bookcase, circa 1906, no. 647, gallery top and exposed key tenons over three doors, unsigned, 70in. wide. (Robt. W. Skinner Inc.) $5,000

An L. & J. G. Stickley two-door bookcase, no. 654, circa 1910, 50in. wide. (Robt. W. Skinner Inc.) $3,500

L. & J. G. Stickley narrow bookcase with adjustable shelves, circa 1912, no. 652, 22in. wide. (Robt. W. Skinner Inc.) $2.500

Onondaga double door bookcase, by L. & J. G. Stickley, circa 1902-04, 56½in. high. (Robt. W. Skinner Inc.) $2,750

L. & J. G. Stickley two door bookcase, Fayetteville, New York, circa 1907, unsigned, (escutcheons replaced) 42in. wide. (Skinner Inc.) $4,000

L. & J. G. Stickley two-door bookcase, style no. 645, circa 1912, 49in. wide. (Robt. W. Skinner Inc.) $3,500

L. & J. G. Stickley single door bookcase with keyed tenons, no. 641, circa 1906, 36in. wide. (Robt. W. Skinner Inc.) $3,000

L & J.G. STICKLEY CHAIRS

An L. & J. G. Stickley adjustable back flat armchair, no. 412, circa 1909, 35in. wide. (Robt. W. Skinner Inc.) $3,000

L. & J.G. Stickley rocker, circa 1910, no. 837, concave crest rail over four vertical slats, spring cushion seat, 39in. high. (Skinner Inc.) $500

L. & J.G. Stickley adjustable back armchair, Fayetteville, New York, c. 1909, no. 470, flat arm with arched support, 27½in. wide. (Skinner Inc) $1,000

L. & J. G. Stickley tall back armchair, with spring cushion seat, no. 837, circa 1907, 44in. high. (Robt. W. Skinner Inc.) $750

Two of a set of six Stickley Bros. dining chairs, including one armchair, circa 1908. (Robt. W. Skinner Inc.) $1,250

A slat sided armchair with cushion seat, by L. & J. G. Stickley, circa 1912. $1,750

L. & J. G. Stickley fixed back armchair, circa 1912, with upholstered spring cushion seat with back cushion, unsigned, 32in. high. (Robt. W. Skinner Inc.) $5,250

L. & J. G. Stickley slat-sided armchair, circa 1912, style no. 408, 26½in. diam. (Robt. W. Skinner Inc.) $1,750

L. & J.G. Stickley fixed back armchair, Fayetteville, New York, circa 1910, no. 438, four horizontal back slats, 24½in. high. (Skinner Inc.) $750

L & J.G. STICKLEY DESKS

Gateleg dropfront desk, circa 1912, arched gallery top and flat sides, branded *The Work of L. & J. G. Stickley,* 31½in. wide. (Robt. W. Skinner Inc.) $1,000

An L. & J. G. Stickley flat top writing desk, circa 1905, 40in. wide. (Robt. W. Skinner Inc.) $700

An L. & J. G. Stickley drop-front writing desk, no. 613, writing surface with fitted interior, circa 1910, 32in. wide. (Robt. W. Skinner Inc.) $800

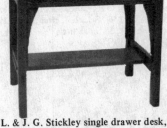

L. & J. G. Stickley writing desk and chair, circa 1912, desk no. 610, chair no. 913, letter rail on rectangular top over single drawer, lower shelf with kneehole; chair with curved crest rail, both branded "The Work of L. & J. G. Stickley". $650

L. & J. G. Stickley single drawer desk, Fayetteville, New York, circa 1910, no. 520, rectangular top, single drawer with copper pulls, with short corbel supports, lower median shelf through-tenon, 36in. wide. (Skinner Inc.) $900

MAGAZINE RACKS

An L. & J. Stickley magazine rack, no. 45, circa 1912, 44½in. high. (Robt. W. Skinner Inc.) $1,600

L. & J. G. Stickley magazine and bookcase, circa 1910, 48in. wide. $2,000

An L. & J. G. Stickley slat-sided magazine rack, no. 46, circa 1910, signed with decal, 42in. high. (Robt. W. Skinner Inc.) $2,500

L & J.G. STICKLEY
SETTEES & COUCHES

Rare L. & J. G. Stickley spindle 'Prairie' settle, circa 1912, no. 234 the broad even sided flat crest rail over spindles, two section seat, unsigned, 86in. wide. (Robt. W. Skinner Inc.) $90,000

An L. & J. G. Stickley slat-back settle, style no. 281, with spring cushion seat, circa 1912, 76in. wide. (Robt. W. Skinner Inc.) $2,500

A panelled prairie settle with spring cushion seat, by L. & J. G. Stickley, circa 1912, 29in. deep. (Robt. W. Skinner Inc.) $1,500

L. & J.G. Stickley prairie settle, Fayetteville, New York, circa 1912, no. 220, wide flat arms and crest rail supported by corbels over inset panels, 84½in. wide.
(Skinner Inc.) $20,000

SIDEBOARDS

L. & J. G. Stickley sideboard, circa 1912, paneled plate rail with corbels, (refinished, some stains and scratches) 54in. wide. (Skinner Inc.) $1,800

An oak sideboard with plate rack and slightly arched apron, by L. & J. G. Stickley, 54in. wide. (Skinner Inc.) $800

L. & J. G. Stickley sideboard, circa 1910, no. 738, rectangular plate rack on corresponding top, two long drawers flanked by cabinet doors, 60in. wide. (Skinner Inc.) $4,500

L. & J. G. Stickley sideboard, circa 1912, no. 734, plate rack with corresponding rectangular top over three drawers flanked by cabinet doors over single long drawer, 48in. wide. (Skinner Inc.) $2,000

L & J.G. STICKLEY
STANDS

An open-sided music stand, possibly by Stickley, circa 1907, 39in. high. (Robt. W. Skinner Inc.) $500

L. & J. G. Stickley dinner gong, Fayetteville, New York, 1912, arched frame supporting circular bronze gong. (Robt. W. Skinner Inc.) $8,500

A drink stand, by L. & J. G. Stickley, no. 587, circa 1912, 16in. sq. (Robt. W. Skinner Inc.) $700

TABLES

An L. & J. G. Stickley occasional table, no. 543, circa 1912, 29¼in. diam. (Robt. W. Skinner Inc.) $400

A tabouret with cut corners, by L. & J. G. Stickley, no. 560, circa 1912, 16in. wide. (Robt. W. Skinner Inc.) $800

L. & J. G. Stickley oak server with open plate rack, circa 1912, no. 750, 48in. wide. (Robt. W. Skinner Inc.) $700

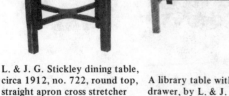

L. & J. G. Stickley dining table, circa 1912, no. 722, round top, straight apron cross stretcher base tenoned through square legs, with three leaves, 48in. diameter. (Skinner) $1,500

A library table with one drawer, by L. & J. G. Stickley, signed with Handcraft label, 42in. wide. (Robt. W. Skinner Inc.) $1,000

L. & J.G. Stickley dining table, circa 1912, no. 720, circular top, straight apron, supported on five tapering legs, with four extension leaves, 48in. diameter. (Skinner Inc.) $1,800

BASKETS

Steuben art glass basket, flared rim on reticulated glass woven basket of pomona green crystal, 8in. diam. (Robt. W. Skinner Inc.) $175

Mount Washington cameo glass bride's basket, shaped rim on flared half-round bowl of opal glass layered in pink, 9½in. high. (Robt. W. Skinner Inc.) $175

Steven & Williams Victorian glass basket, applied crimped amber glass rim and handles on transparent blue folded pedestaled bowl, 6in. high. (Skinner Inc.) $225

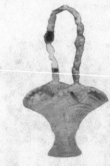

Mount Washington Crown Milano bride's basket, tricorn crimped rim on round opal body, silver plated pedestal base dated 'Feb. 6, 1896', 12½in. high. (Robt. W. Skinner Inc.) $2,100

An amberina bride's basket and holder, set into a silver plated basket with applied leaves and cherries, 9in. high. (Robt. W. Skinner Inc.) $650

Tiffany silver and cut glass basket, flared horizontal stepped and cane cut flower basket mounted with floral handle, 13in. high. (Skinner Inc.) $1,980

BONBONS

Steuben blue Aurene bonbon, crimped extended rim on round bowl of cobalt blue, signed 'Aurene', 6¼in. diam. $1,300

Webb Alexandrite berry bowl and underplate, circa 1910, both pieces with crimped rim on shallow form, 6in. diam. $1,000

Tiffany glass Floriform dish, gold iridescent bowl form with scalloped and crimped irregular rim, marked 'L.C.T' diam. 4½in. $225

BOTTLES

Cathedral type pickle bottle, minor stain along 1in. of bottom, 33cm., America, 1870-1875. $150

'J. Lake/Schenectady N.Y.' ten pin soda bottle, cobalt blue, heavy collared mouth, iron pontil mark, 8in. high, America, 1845-1860. $350

Rare 'Fortune Sequattir' sealed spirits bottle, deep olive green, sheared mouth with applied string rim, pontil scar, 9in. high, Europe, 1760-1780. $250

'National Bitters' ear of corn figural bitters bottle, medium amber, 12½in. high, America, 1860–80.
(Skinner Inc.) $225

Very rare Stiegel-type bottle, the flattened globular chunky body, with 12 diamond ogival pattern, 12oz., made at the Henry William Stiegel's American Flint Glass Manufactory, Manheim, Pennsylvania, 1770-1774. (Skinner Inc.) $3,900

'AM Bininger & Co.' labeled cannon shaped whiskey bottle, label *Great Gun Gin* with woman holding flag and man with goblet and rifle, 12½in. high, America, 1861–1864.
(Skinner Inc.) $950

Huckleberry bottle, tall cylinder with upper body, neck ribbed, deep golden amber, 11in. high, New England, 1850-1870. $400

Rare 'Bennett & Carroll/ No. 120 Wood St./Pitts Pa' flattened whiskey bottle, golden amber, 8¼in. high, America, 1845-1860. $250

'Browns Celebrated Indian Herb Bitters' bottle, Indian figural, honey amber, smooth base, 12¼in., America, 1865-1880. $225

BOTTLES

Greeley's Bourbon Bitters bottle, barrel, puce amber, smooth base, 9¼in. high, America, 1860-1880. (Robt. W. Skinner Inc.) **$125**

Fire grenade rack with four grenades, with brass label 'Pyro-Ball/International/Staten Island/ New York City'. (Skinner Inc.) **$125**

Pillar molded bar bottle, conical with eight heavy pillars, gray, pontil scar, 12in., Pittsburgh area, 1850-1870. (Robt. W. Skinner Inc.) **$1,900**

Ribbed pinch bottle, deep sapphire blue, tooled lip pontil scar, 8½in., Germany/ Austria, mid 18th century. (Robt. W. Skinner Inc.) **$500**

Warners 'Log Cabin-Extract-Rochester NY' labeled medicine bottle, with box in mint condition, 8⅛in. high. (Skinner Inc.) **$130**

'Browns/Celebrated/Indian Herb Bitters' figural Indian bitters bottle, patented February 11,1868, amber, 12⅜in. high, America, 1870–80. (Skinner Inc.) **$200**

Morse's Celebrated Syrup, Providence, R.I., medicine bottle, whittled, flattened sides, 9½in., America, 1855-1865. (Robt. W. Skinner Inc.) **$500**

Fire grenade, patented Aug. 8, 1871, square with round panels, original contents, cobalt blue, 5⅞in. high. (Skinner Inc.) **$175**

J & A Dearborn, N. Y., Albany Glassworks, New York, soda bottle, extremely rare, cobalt blue, 7¼in., 1848-1856. (Robt. W. Skinner Inc.) **$450**

BOTTLES

Rare "Dr. Kilmer's Swamp Root Kidney Liver and Bladder Remedy", Binghamton, NY, light olive yellow, flat collar with smooth base, 8in. high, America, 1870–90.
(Skinner Inc.) $99

Pottery book figural bottle, Bennington type, white body with brown mottling, 5½in., America, 1850-1875. (Robt. W. Skinner Inc.) $225

Martha Washington Hair Restorer bottle with full label and contents, colorless, 7in., America, 1870-1880. (Robt. W. Skinner Inc.) $160

'Dr. Caldwells/Herb Bitters' bottle, triangular, amber, sloping collar with ring-smooth base, 12½in. high, America, 1870–80.
(Skinner Inc.) $125

'E.G. Booz's', figural Whiskey bottle, cabin shape, beveled roof edge variety, Whitney Glassworks, Glassboro, New Jersey, 1870–80, 7¾in. high.
(Skinner Inc.) $950

'Reeds/Bitters' bottle, lady's leg, bubbly glass, amber, sloping collar with bevel-smooth base, 12½in. high, America, 1820–80.
(Skinner Inc.) $175

The Fish Bitters bottle, amber, applied lip, smooth base, 11½in. high, America, 1870-1880.
(Robt. W. Skinner Inc.) $125

'Barnums/Hard Fire/Ext-Diamond' fire grenade, patented June 25, 1869, square with indented round panels, aqua, 6in. high.
(Skinner Inc.) $275

Skull figural poison bottle, crossed bones on base, cobalt blue, tooled lip-smooth base, 4⅛in. high.
(Skinner Inc.) $1,300

271

BOTTLES

'Warners/Safe/Remedies Co.'
labeled medicine bottle, full
label with contents and neck
label, 6 fl. oz., golden amber,
7³/₈ in. high.
(Skinner Inc.) $80

Anna-type pottery railroad
guide pig, large railroad map
around body, mint condition,
4in. high, probably Anna
Pottery, Anna, Illinois, 1890.
(Skinner Inc.) $3,700

'Greeley's Bourbon/Bitters'
labeled bitters bottle, barrel
shape, 95% label, light smokey
olive green, 9¹/₈ in. high,
America, 1860–80.
(Skinner Inc.) $550

Cathedral pickle bottle, square,
fancy panels, rolled lip-smooth
base, 12in. high, America, 1860–
70.
(Skinner Inc.) $55

Skull figural poison bottle, deep
cobalt, 4¹/₄ in. high, America,
1880–90.
(Skinner Inc.) $950

Labeled blacking bottle,
*Leonard and King's Sponge
Blacking, Methuen, Mass*, deep
olive amber, sheared lip-pontil
scar, 5in. high.
(Skinner Inc.) $253

'Hathaways/Celebrated/
Stomach/Bitters' labeled bitters
bottle, square, amber, 80%
black and white label, 10in. high,
America, 1870–80.
(Skinner Inc.) $150

"Browns/Celebrated/Indian
Herb Bitters" bottle, Indian
queen figural, one of three
known, aqua, 12¹/₈ in. high,
America, 1860–80.
(Skinner Inc.) $6,875

Bininger barrel whiskey bottle,
dark amber, double collared lip-
pontil scar, 8in. high, America
1861–64.
(Skinner Inc.) $155

BOTTLES

Paneled cologne bottle, 12-sided, rare rolled over lip, deep emerald green, smooth base, 4³/₄ in. high, New England, 1860–80.
(Skinner Inc.) $400

'Suffolk Bitters' – 'Philbrook and Tucker' figural pig bitters bottles, medium golden amber, flattened collared lip, 10 in. high, America, 1870–80.
(Skinner Inc.) $450

'Rohrers-Expectoral/Wild/ Cherry/Tonic' medicine bottle, amber, sloping collar with bevel-iron pontil, 10³/₄ in. high, America, 1860–70.
(Skinner Inc.) $100

Early snuff bottle, rectangular with beveled edges, oliver green, applied lip-smooth base, 6³/₄ in. high, New England, early 19th century.
(Skinner Inc.) $175

Midwestern globular bottle, 24-ribs swirled to the left, deep golden amber, rolled lip-pontil scar, 7³/₄ in. high, 1820–50.
(Skinner Inc.) $325

Early utilitarian bottle, cylinder with slightly wider base, applied string ring below lip, olive green, pontil scar, 5⁷/₈ in. high, 1780–1830.
(Skinner Inc.) $550

"McKeevers Army Bitters" bottle, drum figural, amber, sloping collar-smooth base, 10¹/₂ in. high, America, 1860–80.
(Skinner Inc.) $1,980

'EG Booz's/Old Cabin/Whiskey' bottle, cabin shaped, deep golden amber, quart, Whitney Glassworks, Glassboro, New Jersey, 1860's.
(Skinner Inc.) $1,100

Moses figural Poland Springs mineral water bottle, unusual flared lip, green, 10⁷/₈ in. high.
(Skinner Inc.) $175

BOTTLES

E. G. Booz's Old Cabin Whiskey bottle, honey amber, 7¾in., Whitney Glassworks Glasshouse, New Jersey, 1860-1870. (Robt. W. Skinner Inc.) $900

David Andrews vegetable/jaundice/bitters bottle, with sloping shoulders, 8¼in., America, 1850-1865. (Robt. W. Skinner Inc.) $460

Lancaster Glass Works NY soda bottle, very rare, medium sapphire blue, 1855-1865. (Robt. W. Skinner Inc.) $150

Pineapple Bitters bottle, W & Co., NY, amber, double collared lip, 8½in., probably New Jersey Glasshouse, 1850-1860. (Robt. W. Skinner Inc.) $200

Rare 'W. Ludlow' seal spirits bottle, dark olive green, sheared mouth with wide string rim, pontil scar, 12½in. high, possibly America, circa 1760. (Robt. W. Skinner Inc.) $450

T.C. Pearsall on seal spirits bottle, some of the original wax on lip, olive green, 10½in. high, perhaps America, 1780-1795. (Robt. W. Skinner Inc.) $425

Fancy peppersauce bottle, square with five stars vertically placed in three panels, 21.92cm. high, probably Midwest America, 1845-1860. (Robt. W. Skinner Inc.) $150

'Turner Brothers, New York' whiskey bottle, barrel shaped, brownish amber, flattened collared lip, smooth base, 10in. high, America, 1860-1880. (Robt. W. Skinner Inc.) $100

Pressed bar bottle, amethyst, oversized doughnut lip, polished pontil, 11in., probably Bakewell Pears and Co., Pittsburgh, 1860-1880. (Robt. W. Skinner Inc.) $650

274

BOTTLES

"Bakers Orange Grove-Bitters" labeled bitters bottle, full front and back labels, olive amber, 9¹/₂in. high, America, 1870's. (Skinner Inc.) $374

Beiser and Fisher pig figural whiskey bottle, amber, double collared lip smooth base, 9½in. America, 1865-1875. (Robt. W. Skinner Inc.) $200

Bininger's Regulator whiskey bottle, clock shape, honey amber, 6in., America, 1861-1864. (Robt. W. Skinner Inc.) $200

Pineapple Bitters bottle, citron, double collared lip, pontil scar, 8½in., probably New Jersey, 1850-1865. (Robt. W. Skinner Inc.) $2,700

Harrisons Columbian Ink master ink bottle, 11¼in. high, probably Whitney Bros. or Isabella Glassworks, New Jersey, 1855-1865. (Robt. W. Skinner Inc.) $24,000

Large chestnut bottle, olive amber, sloping collar, pontil scar, 10¼in. high, New England, 1790-1830. (Robt. W. Skinner Inc.) $150

Large barrel bottle, wide opening, emerald green, tooled lip, smooth base, 9¾in., America, 1870-1885. (Robt. W. Skinner Inc.) $75

Rohrer's Expectoral Wild Cherry Tonic bottle with label, pyramid shape, 10½in. high, America, 1860-1865. (Robt. W. Skinner Inc.) $375

'Dr H. B. Skinner/Boston' medicine bottle, rectangular with beveled corners, olive amber, flared mouth, 6in. high, New England, 1840-1860. (Robt. W. Skinner Inc.) $100

BOTTLES

Santa Claus figural bottle, Husted on lower side, colorless round flat collar-smooth base, 12¹/₂in. high, 1880–1900. (Skinner Inc.) **$30**

"Suffolk Bitters" figural pig bitters bottle, yellow amber, double collar, 10in. long, America, 1860–80. (Skinner Inc.) **$385**

'Mohawk Whiskey Pure Rye' Indian figural whiskey bottle, original red sealing wax around half of lip, 12⁵/₈in. high, America, 1870–80. (Skinner Inc.) **$650**

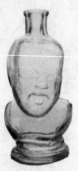

Crying baby figural bottle, colorless, (one small chip on underside of base), 6in. high, 1875–90. (Skinner Inc.) **$100**

Early geometric smelling bottle, daisy pattern, corrugated edges, medium amethyst, 2in. high, possibly Keene Marlboro Street Glassworks, Keene, New Hampshire, 1815–30. (Skinner Inc.) **$308**

'S.O. Dunbar/Taunton/Mass' medicine bottle, with frayed and stained label reading *Fluid Magnesia, prepared by S.O. Dunbar, Taunton, Mass*, 5⁵/₈in. high, America, 1840–60. (Skinner Inc.) **$230**

W. & Co./NY pineapple shaped bitters-type bottle, olive yellow, double collared lip, iron pontil, 8¹/₂in. high, America, 1855–65. (Skinner Inc.) **$990**

Fancy cologne bottle, square with upward diamond-like points on edge, excellent deep amethyst color, 6³/₈in. high New England, 1860–80. (Skinner Inc.) **$550**

Pineapple figural bitters bottle, bright medium green, double collared lip-iron pontil, 8¹/₂in. high, America, 1855–65. (Skinner Inc.) **$1,100**

BOTTLES

Fancy barber's bottle, nine panels on bulbous body with diamond design, cranberry, with colorless petaled applied lip, 6¹/₂ in. high.
(Skinner Inc.) $70

Tea kettle ink bottle, barrel shaped, medium sapphire blue, no closure, 2¹/₄ in. high.
(Skinner Inc.) $550

Melon sided barber bottle, opalized yellow green, rolled lip-smooth base, 7¹/₄ in. high.
(Skinner Inc.) $70

"H.P. Herb Wild Cherry Bitters" bottle, with original foil around lip and neck, medium amber, 10¹/₄ in. high, America, 1870's.
(Skinner Inc.) $231

Pineapple figural bitters-type bottle, bright yellow amber, double collared lip-pontil scar, 8¹/₂ in. high, probably Whitney Glassworks, Glassboro, New Jersey, 1850–60.
(Skinner Inc.) $275

Blown ink bottle, deep emerald green with a tint of olive, whittled, sloping collar with flaring base-pontil scar, 5¹/₄ in. high, America, 1820–50.
(Skinner Inc.) $83

Corset waisted cologne bottle, unusual shape, ten panels, medium amethyst, tooled lip-smooth base, 6¹/₂ in. high, New England, 1850–70.
(Skinner Inc.) $286

Early snuff bottle, rectangular with chamfered corners, mouth slightly offset, deep green, very bubbly glass, 4⁵/₈ in. high, probably New England, 1800–40.
(Skinner Inc.) $250

'Log Cabin/Sarsaparilla/ Rochester NY' sarsaparilla bottle, golden amber, round blob lip-smooth base, 9 in. high, America, 1885–1895.
(Skinner Inc.) $50

BOTTLES

Mount Washington peachblow bottle, flared and raised rim on vertically ribbed body of rose pink to blue, total height 5 in. $650

'Old Sachem/Bitters/Wigwam Tonic' bottle, barrel shaped, light golden yellow, 9½ in. high. America, 1860-1880. $550

Mount Washington amberina bottle, flared flat rim, dark fuchsia to amber color, faceted amber stopper, total height 5½ in. $200

'A.B.L. Myers AM/Rock Rose/ New Haven' medicine bottle, emerald green, crude blob lip, iron pontil, 9½ in. high, America, 1860 1870. $500

An amethyst glass pattern-molded Stiegel-type perfume bottle, probably Pennsylvania, third quarter 18th century, the body with enlarged diamond-daisy motif, 5 in. high. (Christie's) $4,400

'Tr. Cannab. I' label under glass apothecary bottle, cylindrical, base embossed 'W. N. Walton Patd Sep 23 1862', cobalt blue, 8½ in. high, America, 1860-1890. $350

'Red Star/Stomach Bitters' bottle, fluted shoulder and base, amber, sloping collar, smooth base, 11½ in. high, America, circa 1900. $250

Rare 'Bennington/Battle' figural book bottle, brown, cream and green flint enamel, 11 in. high, 1840-1880. $650

Rare 'E. Smith/Elmira/N.Y.' soda bottle, cylindrical, cobalt blue, heavy collared mouth, iron pontil mark, half pint, America, 1845-1860. $325

BOWLS

Pairpoint cobalt blue center bowl, with raised pedestal foot, brilliant crystal clarity, 14¼in. diam. $300

Tiffany gold Favrile center bowl, crimped and scalloped ten rib molded bowl with overall iridescence, 10¹/₂in. diam. (Skinner Inc.) $950

Early 20th century American two-part cut glass punch bowl, 14¼in. diam. $900

Tiffany favrile pastel blue centerbowl, rare ten-lobed transparent blue vessel striped with opaque opal-blue, 8¹/₂in. diameter. (Skinner Inc.) $2,750

Free blown milk pan, with pouring spout, aqua, folded lip-pontil scar, 18in. wide, America, mid 19th century. (Skinner Inc.) $275

South Jersey type footed bowl, freeblown thickly made, 15.5cm. wide, probably South Jersey, or Pittsburgh area glasshouse, 1820-1850. (Robt. W. Skinner Inc.) $300

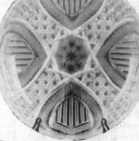

Rare American brilliant cut glass shield bowl, possibly commemorating President McKinley, 10in. diam. (Skinner Inc.) $650

Freeblown swagged cuspidor, wide flaring lip, bowl with swag decoration, possibly Ellenville Glassworks, New York. (Robt. W. Skinner Inc.) $1,800

Steuben amethyst silverina center bowl, elliptical form with mica-flecked diamond decoration, 12¹/₂in. wide. (Skinner Inc.) $770

An American cut glass caviar bowl with outer ice bowl and white metal mounts, early 20th century, 13in. diam. (Tennants) $2,652

Freeblown bowl, with witch ball cover, widely flaring lip, applied solid foot, greenish aqua, 8in. high. (Skinner Inc.) $300

Pattern molded bowl, broken swirl, 16-ribs swirling to the right, lead glass, sapphire blue, pontil scar, 4⁷/₈in. wide, possibly early Pittsburg piece. (Skinner Inc.) $300

GLASS

CANDLESTICKS

Pair of early candlesticks, columnar with petal socket, colorless, 9¼ in., probably Boston & Sandwich Glassworks, Sandwich, Massachusetts, 1850-1865. $125

Tiffany gold iridescent candlelamp, twisted stem ten-rib candlestick with opal glass oil font, 12½ in. high. (Skinner Inc.) $1,320

Pair of dolphin candlesticks, single step base, 10¼ in., Boston & Sandwich Glass Co., Sandwich, Massachusetts, 1845-1870. (Robt. W. Skinner Inc.) $3,800

Pair of pressed glass candlesticks, Sandwich Glass Company, Massachusetts, 1850–65, 9 in. high. (Skinner Inc.) $950

Pair of early 20th century Dominick & Haff sterling silver and cut glass candlesticks, threaded into Classical Revival bases, 13½ in. high. $1,500

Pair of cranberry to clear candlesticks, classic baluster form with faceted paneling, 9½ in. high. (Skinner Inc.) $100

Early candlestick, rare color translucent purple-blue, probably Boston & Sandwich Glassworks, Sandwich, Massachusetts, 1850-1865. $300

A pair of Steuben threaded candlesticks, squat holders of bright Bristol yellow accented with dramatic black threading, 4½ in. high. $250

Tiffany gilt bronze blown out candelabrum, three-branch candle holders with green favrile glass liners, 12½ in. high. (Skinner Inc.) $1,760

Tiffany bronze and blown-out glass chamberstick, circa 1915, 6in. high.
$1,500

A Tiffany 'Favrile' glass candlestick in iridescent gold, 4½in. high.
$300

Tiffany bronze and favrile candlestick, elaborate four branch candelabrum with green glass blown into slit candlecups, 11½in. high.
(Skinner Inc.)
$3,025

Carder Steuben twisted candlestick, solid twist colorless shaft with dished pedestal foot and vasiform candlecup, 15in. high.
(Skinner Inc.)
$550

Four pressed glass Clambroth candlesticks, Sandwich Glass Company, Massachusetts, 1840–60, all with petal bobeches, 7in. high.
(Skinner Inc.)
$350

A Sandwich Clambroth and blue glass dolphin candlestick, circa 1820, 10in. high.
$350

A pair of Steuben candlesticks, swirled sticks of clear green with hollow teardrop shaft, 10in. high. $300

A pair of Tiffany Favrile pastel candle holders, lavender opalescent optic pattern with squared bobeche rim, 3½in. high.
$500

Pair of gold Aurene candlesticks, baluster and ring-turned shaft on cupped pedestal foot, 8¼in. high.
$700

CANDY CONTAINERS

Rabbit family candy container, with all original gold paint, no closure.
(Skinner Inc.) $400

Piano candy container, with tin closure, mint condition.
(Skinner Inc.) $150

Rocking horse with clown candy container, bluish tinted glass, no closure, few base chips.
(Skinner Inc.) $90

Kewpie candy container, standing by barrel with 100% paint, perfect closure with coin slot.
(Skinner Inc.) $145

Village log cabin candy container, complete with glass liner.
(Skinner Inc.) $500

Rabbit pushing chick in shell cart candy container, excellent example, all original complete paint.
(Skinner Inc.) $425

Telephone candy container, with cork top and cardboard shield *when empty have me refilled at H B Waters & Co., Boston, Mass,* 5¹/8 in. high.
(Skinner Inc.) $350

Liberty Motors airplane candy container, excellent condition with 100% paint, complete.
(Skinner Inc.) $3,500

Crowing chicken candy containers, with all original paint, colorful contents and closure.
(Skinner Inc.) $220

Duck with large bill candy container, with most of its original paint.
(Skinner Inc.) $125

Opera glass candy container, opaque white glass, tin screw on closures, perfect condition.
(Skinner Inc.) $150

Uncle Sam's hat candy containers, with original paint, one small base chip.
(Skinner Inc.) $30

Pairpoint mounted compote of white and clear glass hand-painted within with floral designs and ladybugs, 9in. high. **$300**

Hairpin pressed compote, with loop pattern base, wafer attachment, colorless, 5³/₄in. high, England, 1840–60. (Skinner Inc.) **$138**

Unusual Mt. Washington Amberina compote, with tooled scalloped rim, applied pedestal and foot, extremely deep fuchsia and dark amber color , 5in. high. (Skinner Inc.) **£366**

Mt. Washington Napoli Compote, colorless glass bowl, handpainted on exterior with pink water lilies against green background, 11in. high. (Skinner) **$468**

Early 20th century cut glass compote on round foot with starburst bottom, America, 7in. diam. **$300**

Cranberry Art Glass Compote, simulated overshot tree-of-life surface with gilt decorated cut-out shaped rim and hollow-stem foot, 10¼in. high. (Skinner) **$600**

One of a pair of Portland clear overshot glass compotes, late 19th century, 8¾in. high. **$700**

Carder Steuben Compote with fruit finial, verre de soie covered compote 3343 with frosted Celeste blue twisted stem, 6in. high. (Skinner) **$2,500**

Early 20th century cut glass compote with flaring bowl, America, 10½in. diam. **$450**

DECANTERS

Opaque blue glass cruet, by Northwood Glass Co., Indianan, circa 1900, 7in. high. $750

An Art Deco electroplated and cut-glass two-division tantalus with central locking carrying handle, 11½ in. high. $1,200

Broken chain decorated decanter, colorless lead glass, 8in., probably Thomas Cains Phoenix Glassworks, Boston, 1820-1830. (Robt. W. Skinner Inc.) $125

Blown three mold decanter, colorless, pontil scar, quart, probably New England, 1825-1840. (Robt. W. Skinner Inc.) $100

Blown three-mold decanter, olive amber, sheared lip-pontil scar, pint, 1815–30. (Skinner Inc.) $385

Early engraved decanter, thinly blown, well engraved with florals, pontil scar, 8¾in. high, possibly Pittsburgh district, 1820–40. (Skinner Inc.) $176

Blown three mold decanter, type two stopper, colorless, pontil, quart, New England, 1825-1835. (Robt. W. Skinner Inc.) $100

Gold decorated glass decanter and eight wine goblets having round reserves with courting scenes. (Du Mouchelles) $350

Blown three-mold decanter, with unusual ribbed Tam o'Shanter stopper, deep sapphire blue, flaring lip-pontil scar, 1825–40. (Skinner Inc.) $660

DECANTERS

Blown three-mold decanter, stopper, colorless, pontil scar, quart, New England, 1825–40. (Skinner Inc.) $154

Early 20th century kew blas decanter, Union Glass Co., Mass, 13½in. high.
$350

Blown three-mold decanter, pint, stopper, three pairs of quilled neck bands, colorless, pontil scar, New England, 1825–40. (Skinner Inc.) $143

Blown three mold decanter, with original stopper, type 2, colorless, flaring lip, pontil scar, quart, New England, 1830-1845. $200

An Art Deco glass decanter set, comprising: a decanter of tapering, faceted form with six cylindrical, faceted glasses en suite. $500

A cut glass and silver-gilt claret jug by William B. Durgin Company, Concord, New Hampshire, circa 1900, 12½in. high. $7,150

Blown three-mold decanter, mint, stopper, colorless, pontil scar, New England, 1825–40. (Skinner Inc.) $440

Gorham Sterling and ruby-colored cut glass decanter, repoussé melon-form cover on an ovoid body cut with fruiting vine, 9in. high.
(Skinner Inc.) $2,970

A large glass decanter and stopper, American, early 19th century, with a lobed stopper moulded with diapering, 14¾in. high.
(Christie's) $1,210

GLASS

DISPENSERS

'Orange-Julep' syrup dispenser, circa 1920, 14¼in. high. $750

'Hires' syrup dispenser, Phila., patented 1920, 14¼in. high. $500

'Cherry Chic' syrup dispenser, manufactured by J. Hungerford Smith, New York, circa 1925, 11½in. high. $1,750

FLASKS

A double eagle historical pint flask, GII-40, bright green, sheared mouth-pontil scar, Kensington Glass Works, 1830-38. $325

Double Eagle historical flask, vertically ribbed body, emerald green, double collared lip, pontil scar, Louisville Glass works, Kentucky, 1855-1865. $1,600

A Masonic eagle historical pint flask, golden amber, White Glass Works, 1820-40. $300

A scroll pint flask, GIX-11, golden amber, sheared mouth-pontil scar, 1845-60. $250

A vertically ribbed chestnut flask, golden amber, sheared mouth-pontil scar, 4½in. high, 1820-40. $200

One of two half pint Adams-Jefferson portrait flasks, GI-114, olive amber, sheared mouth-pontil scars, 1830-50. $275

286

Washington Taylor portrait flask, smoky mauve sheared lip pontil scar, quart, Dyottville Glassworks, Pennsylvania, 1840-1860. (Robt. W. Skinner Inc.) $1,200

Scroll flask, bright tobacco amber, sheared lip-pontil scar, quart, America, 1840–60. (Skinner Inc.) $150

Sunburst flask, olive amber, pint, Keene Marlboro St. Glassworks, Keene, New Hampshire, 1822-1830. (Robt. W. Skinner Inc.) $300

Concentric ring eagle historical flask, light green, sheared lip-pontil scar, approximate pint, probably New England Glassworks, Cambridge, Massachusetts, 1820s–30's. (Skinner Inc.) $4,000

Franklin-Dyott portrait flask, deep amber, sheared lip-pontil scar, pint, Kensington Glassworks, Philadelphia, 1826–30. (Skinner Inc.) $1,900

Stiegel type flask, 16oz., deep amethyst, sheared lip, pontil scar, 5½ in., possibly Stiegel's American Flint Glass Manufactory, Manheim, Pennsylvania, 1770-1774. (Robt. W. Skinner Inc.) $3,700

Whimsey flask, chestnut-form with X-pinched rigaree pattern on each side, olive green, sheared lip-pontil scar, 7¼ in. high, New England, early 19th century. (Skinner Inc.) $1,500

Flora Temple pictorial flask, crudely applied lip, smooth base, pint, Whitney Glassworks, Glassboro New Jersey, 1859-1865. (Robt. W. Skinner Inc.) $200

Pitkin-type flask, 36 ribs swirled to the left, olive amber, sheared lip-pontil scar, 5in. high, New England, 1790–1830. (Skinner Inc.) $190

FLASKS

Eagle-tree historical flask, deep golden amber, sheared lip-pontil scar, half-pint, America, 1820's. (Skinner Inc.) $1,210

Sunburst flask, light olive amber, sheared lip-pontil scar, pint, Coventry Glassworks, Coventry, Connecticut, 1820's. (Skinner Inc.) $275

Hunterman-fisherman pictorial flask, aqua, round collar with ring-pontil scar, calabash, American 1850–60. (Skinner Inc.) $70

'Success to the Railroad' historical flask, bubbly glass, good color, deep forest green, possibly Mt. Vernon Glassworks, New York, late 1820's. (Skinner Inc.) $150

Sunburst flask, mint condition, no wear, medium apricot puce, sheared lip-pontil scar, half-pint, America, 1830–50. (Skinner Inc.) $5,225

'Biningers/Travelers Guide' pocket flask, teardrop shape, medium golden amber, double collared lip-smooth base, 6³⁄₄in. high. (Skinner Inc.) $180

Baltimore/Glassworks sheaf of grain pictorial flask, calabash, medium sapphire blue, double collared lip-pontil scar, Baltimore Glassworks, circa 1850. (Skinner Inc.) $3,960

Free blown decorated flask, with four applied bands of quilled rigaree, deep olive amber, sheared lip-pontil scar, 5in. high, possibly South Jersey glasshouse, early 19th century. (Skinner Inc.) $55

'Travelers/Companion' historical flask, medium golden amber, dark striations throughout, possibly Westford Glassworks, Westford, Connecticut, 1857–73. (Skinner Inc.) $125

Kossuth-tree portrait flask, olive yellow, sloping collar with bevel-pontil scar, calabash, America, 1850–60.
(Skinner Inc.) $330

Nailsea-type flask, opaque white with large cranberry loopings, folded over lip-pontil scar, 7³/₄in. high, 1870–80.
(Skinner Inc.) $176

Waisted scroll flask, thinly blown, nice sharp impression, aqua, pint, probably Pittsburg district, 1830's.
(Skinner Inc.) $325

Washington-Taylor portrait flask, deep emerald green, sheared lip-pontil scar, quart, Dyottville Glassworks, Philadelphia, 1840's.
(Skinner Inc.) $880

Jenny Lind bust lyre flask, aqua, sheared lip-pontil scar, pint, McCarty & Torreyson, Wellsburg, West Virginia, 1840–60.
(Skinner Inc.) $825

'Lafayette' liberty cap portrait flask, medium olive green, sheared lip-pontil scar, pint, Covenry Glassworks, Coventry, Connecticut, 1820's.
(Skinner Inc.) $250

"Success to the Railroad" historical flask, deep green, sheared lip-pontil scar, pint, Keene Marlboro Street Glassworks, Keene, New Hampshire, circa 1830.
(Skinner Inc.) $209

Emil Larson type flask, inverted swirled diamond, amethyst, sheared lip-pontil scar, 5⁵/₈in. high, 1930's.
(Skinner Inc.) $110

Washington-Taylor portrait flask, medium sapphire blue, sheared lip-pontil scar, quart, Dyottville Glassworks, Philadelphia, Pennsylvania, 1847–55.
(Skinner Inc.) $1,700

JARS

Potter and Bodine's Air Tight
Fruit Jar, barrel shaped, wax
seal groove, pint, Bridgeton
Glassworks, Bridgeton, New
Jersey, 1858-1863. (Robt. W.
Skinner Inc.) $700

A Mount Washington/Pairpoint
cracker jar, decorated in the
Crown Milano manner with
blossoms and leaves, 6½in. high.
                $500

A Pairpoint art glass pickle
jar and holder, cranberry colored jar decorated with enamel-
led aster blossoms, 13in. high.
                $250

Potter & Bodine's Air Tight
Fruit Jar, barrel shape, wax
seal groove, 1½ quart size,
Bridgeton Glassworks, New
Jersey, 1858-1863. (Robt. W.
Skinner Inc.) $325

Bear figural pomade jar,
removable head, deep amethyst,
3¾in. high, New England,
1870–90.
(Skinner Inc.) $130

Mason's Patent, Nov. 30th,
1858, fruit jar, honey amber,
ground lip, smooth base, half
gallon, America, 1870-1880.
(Robt. W. Skinner Inc.) $130

Early rum jar, tall square
container with tapering sides,
deep olive green, 11in. high,
probably America, late 18th
century. (Robt. W. Skinner Inc.)
                $850

Mt. Washington jeweled crown
Milano biscuit jar, square form
with applied glass beads in fan
and circle designs, 8in. high.
(Skinner Inc.) $950

Sand jar, America, late 19th
century, colorful sand
arranged in geometric patterns
centering an eagle with American
flag, 9in. high. (Skinner Inc.)
                $2,100

Smith Bros. enamel decorated creamer, Mass., circa 1890, 3.3/8in. high. **$225**

Lemonade set of jug and six glasses with blue glass decoration, 1930s. (Muir Hewitt) **$275**

Freeblown creamer, high arched lip, ear handle with crimping, 3¾in., possibly South Jersey/Pittsburgh area, 1830-1850. (Robt. W. Skinner Inc.) **$500**

A cut glass and silver-gilt claret jug, marked by Theodore B. Starr, New York, circa 1900, the glass ovoid with melon-reeding, 11⅝in. high. (Christie's) **$1,760**

A Tiffany iridescent gold Favrile glass jug and four glasses, circa 1910, jug 21.5cm. high, glasses 10.5cm. high. **$1,000**

New England Amberina Pitcher and two tumblers, with strongest 'chocolate blue' color at rim and spout, 7in. high. (Skinner Inc.) **$600**

Gorham Sterling and two-color cut glass claret jug, ovoid body with green and ruby cutting, 10½in. high. (Skinner Inc.) **$2,640**

Art Nouveau lemonade set, green art glass tankard pitcher and six matching tumblers with raised gold enamel stylized blossoms, 12½in. high. (Skinner Inc.) **$413**

Crimped foot handled jug, globular body, with thick crude handle, 6½in., probably South Jersey glasshouse, 1820-1840. (Robt. W. Skinner Inc.) **$550**

MILK BOTTLES

Square tin-top milk bottle, with embossed line and liquid measurement on side, 'Climax patd 1898', pint. (Skinner Inc.) $80

Thatcher's milk bottle, 'Absolutely Pure Milk' with man milking cow and 'The Milk Protector Thatcher Mfg. Co.' (Skinner Inc.) $275

'Pure Milk' milk jar, very rare tin screw top with handle, Adlam patent on base, colorless. (Skinner Inc.) $850

A.G. Smalley handled milk bottle, no side embossing, colorless , quart size. (Skinner Inc) $124

Tin-type dairy bottle, with embossed Indian's head, no cap seat, 'Indian Head Farm/ Framingham, Massachusetts' (Skinner Inc.) $100

Rare cream separator milk bottle, colorless with red pyroglazed 'Deluxe Cream Separator'. (Skinner Inc.) $350

Square tin-top milk bottle, 'NL Martin, Boston' 'Climax 107' on base, (light haze, some acid lettering on side), quart. (Skinner Inc.) $375

'Langs Creamery', Buffalo, New York, milk bottle, UD51-12, green, quart. (Skinner Inc.) $300

'Alta Crest Farms' milk bottle, green, (light wear), quart. (Skinner Inc.) $700

GLASS

MILK BOTTLES

A.G. Smalley handled milk bottle, rare half-pint size, side embossing reads 'this bottle to be washed and returned', colorless . (Skinner Inc.)　　　　**$400**

'Big Elm/Dairy/Company' milk bottle, green, quart. (Skinner Inc.)　　　**$250**

A.G. Smalley handled milk bottle, with embossing on side, colorless , quart size. (Skinner Inc.)　　　**$140**

Alta Crest milk bottle, crown top with blue pyroglazed, 'Patent 1929' on base, colorless, quart. (Skinner Inc.)　　**$70**

'Alta Crest Farms' milk bottle, UD51-1, green, with paper seat cap, and Alta Crest top cover. (Skinner Inc.)　　**$700**

'Brighton/Place Dairy' milk bottle, UD51-3, green, quart. (Skinner Inc.)　　**$325**

'Weckerle' milk bottle, green, quart. (Skinner Inc.)　　**$150**

Rare milk pail, 'pat. glass pail, Boston, Massachusetts, June 24, 84' on base, tin band around lip with handle. (Skinner Inc.)　　**$275**

Rare cream separator, square pyroglaze deluxe, colorless, quart. (Skinner Inc.)　　**$400**

MISCELLANEOUS

Rare spill holder, Sandwich star pattern, 13.02cm.,. probably Boston & Sandwich Glassworks, Massachusetts, 1840-1860. (Robt. W. Skinner Inc.) $900

Tiffany Studios double inkwell, designed as a treasure chest in Venetian pattern with two ink bottle receptacles, 5in. x 3in. (Skinner Inc.) $425

Rare Steuben gazelle luminaire, molded Art Deco pressed glass figure mounted on conforming black plinth housing electrical fittings, 13in. high. (Skinner Inc.) $495

One of a pair of early witch ball stands, hollow feet, with witch balls, golden amber, tooled lips-pontil scars, 12¼in. high, possibly Whitney Glassworks, Glassboro, New Jersey, mid 19th century. (Skinner Inc.)   (Two) $495

Early blown and decorated tankard, aqua with white loopings, applied solid handle, pontil scar, 7in. high, possibly a South Jersey glasshouse, mid 19th century. (Skinner Inc.) $413

Nailsea-type vase and witch ball, colorless with white loopings, pontil scar, 16in. high, possibly Pittsburgh or New Jersey glasshouse, 1840–60. (Skinner Inc.) $1,210

Swirling cut glass cheese dish, brilliant swirling pattern serving plate and matching high dome cover with faceted knob top, 8in. high. (Skinner Inc.) $550

Early pressed spillholder, inverted diamond with oval, amethyst, polished pontil, 4½in., New England, 1840–60. (Skinner Inc.) $468

Large hat whimsey, blown three mold, rare, made by Clevenger Brothers, circa 1930, aqua, 8in. wide, New Jersey. (Skinner Inc.) $50

MISCELLANEOUS

Handel ware humidor, flat sided opal glass jar with knobbed cover attached with hinged rim, 7½in. high. (Robt. W. Skinner Inc.) $500

Sinclaire cut glass scenic platter, "silver thread' cutting centers moose medallion, rim features four game birds, 14½in. wide. (Skinner Inc.) $3,100

Tiffany blue goblet, of dark cobalt blue glass with overall iridescence and mirror finish below, 7in. high. (Robt. W. Skinner Inc.) $425

Tiffany decorative rondel, the round flat disk of dark cobalt blue favrile glass with strong blue iridescence,16¼in. diam. (Robt. W. Skinner Inc.) $1,900

George Washington commemorative glass pane, America, last quarter 19th century, acid etched cobalt blue to frost, 20in. wide. (Skinner Inc.) $468

American cut glass charger with sawtoothed scalloped rim, 14in. diam. $1,500

A Tiffany 'Favrile' iridescent glass Seal molded with the bodies of three scarab beetles, 4.5cm. high. (Phillips) $750

Pair of Tiffany Company Commemorative goblets, designed as thistles, impressed 'Engineers Club December 9th 1907', 7½in. high. (Skinner Inc.) $550

Phrenology head inkwell, milk glass head and font, cast iron frame, America, 1855–75. (Skinner Inc.) $2,750

PITCHERS

Early freeblown pitcher, thinly blown, applied handle with multiple crimping at bottom, Pittsburgh area glasshouse, 1820–50.
(Skinner Inc.) $60

Lily pad decorated pitcher, solid, uncrimped foot, aqua, 6½in. high. (Robt. W. Skinner Inc.) $375

Very rare lily pad decorated pitcher, a beautiful early piece, 7in. high, probably South Jersey glasshouse, early 19th century. (Robt. W. Skinner Inc.)
                    $2,400

Rare pillar molded pitcher, cranberry body with clear cased cranberry blown handle, 9½in., possibly Pittsburgh area, 1850-1870. (Robt. W. Skinner Inc.) $8,800

Overshot champagne pitcher, gooseneck form, 10½in., probably Boston & Sandwich Glass, Sandwich, Massachusetts, 1870-1887. $100

Early pattern molded pitcher, with eight large panels around the lower portion, deep sapphire blue, pontil scar, 6in. high, possibly New England, 1840–50. (Skinner Inc.) $495

Carder Steuben gold Aurene pitcher, broad bulbous vessel with applied conforming handle, 9¾in. high. $950

Mount Washington Royal Flemish pitcher, with extensive marine decoration including realistic fish, seashells and oceanic plant-life, 8½in. high. $2,000

Crown Milano enamel decorated cream pitcher, Mt. Washington Glass Co., circa 1893, 4¼in. high. $550

An amberina syrup pitcher with silverplated undertray, New England Glass Company, 5½in. high.   **$500**

Exceptional freeblown pitcher, round handle, applied crimped foot, deep blue, 6½in. high, probably South Jersey, possibly Whitney Glassworks, 1835-1850. (Robt. W. Skinner Inc.)   **$1,100**

Wheeling peach blow drape pattern pitcher, Hobbs, Brockunier & Co., circa 1886, 4½in. high.   **$400**

Early blown pitcher, eleven bands of threading around lip, applied handle, aqua, pontil scar, 6¼in. high, possibly a New York State glasshouse, 1830–50. (Skinner Inc.)   **$231**

Extremely rare Hawkes presentation pitcher, carved with the likeness of 'Thomas G. Hawkes', signed by the artist 'W.H. Morse', 15in. high. (Skinner Inc.)   **$4,000**

Early blown pitcher, double incised rim, applied foot and handle, deep sapphire blue, 6¾in. high, possibly South Jersey glasshouse, 1840–50. (Skinner Inc.)   **$413**

Liberty Bell centennial pitcher, applied ribbed handle, three piece mold, colorless, 9in. high. (Skinner Inc.)   **$500**

Threaded art glass pitcher, tinted in cranberry and amber, circa 1890, 8½in. high.   **$275**

An amberina miniature cream pitcher, New England Glass Co., Mass., circa 1880, 2½in. high.   **$275**

Blown vase, deep cobalt blue, rolled over lip, pontil scar, 8in., probably New England, probably mid 19th century. (Robt. W. Skinner Inc.) $550

Steuben green jade vase, flared rim on oval spirally ribbed body of pastel green jade, 6¾in. high. (Robt. W. Skinner Inc.) $200

An aurene vase by Steuben Glass Works, New York, circa 1920, 8in. high. $2,250

A Steuben green jade vase, Corning, New York, circa 1920, 10½in. high. $650

Blue aurene vase by Steuben Glass Works, N.Y., circa 1910, signed, 10½in. high. $1,000

Tiffany favrile cameo carved vase, rare double carved and applied baluster form vessel of frosted crystal, 10¹/₂in. high. (Skinner Inc.) $7,150

Rare paneled vase, so-called Stiegel type, twelve panels, 8½in., probably New England, 1840-1860. (Robt. W. Skinner Inc.) $1,700

A Mount Washington lustreless vase, opal glass handpainted with clusters of pink and white forget-me-nots, 11in. High. (Robt. W. Skinner Inc.) $150

Early 20th century red Tiffany glass vase with pulled blue iridescent design, 3¼in. high. $3,000

Early 20th century Tiffany
Art glass vase, New York,
4¼in. high. $1,000

Royal Flemish enamel decorated glass vase, Mt. Washington
Glass Co., circa 1885, 6.7/8in.
high. $1,250

Rare swagged vase with ball
cover, aqua, 7in., pontil scar.
(Robt. W. Skinner Inc.) $700

Tiffany red miniature vase,
classic oval of brilliant red
favrile, decorated with three
gold and blue triple-pulled and
hooked feather designs, 3¹/₂in.
high.
(Skinner Inc.) $4,500

A Tiffany Favrile glass Jack-in-
the-Pulpit vase, covered in a
greenish-golden iridescence with
pink tinged rim, (tiny rim chip),
with engraved signature L. C.
Tiffany-Favrile, 51.6cm. high.
(Christie's) $8,415

Satin glass portrait vase,
attributed to American
Decorator Company, probably
Gillinder, marked in white on
base 'Cameo', 8in. high.
(Skinner Inc.)
                      $550

A free-hand ware vase by
the Imperial Glass Co.,
Ohio, 1920's, 5.7/8in. high.
                      $450

Tiffany blue iridescent Art
glass vase, New York, circa
1900, 3¾in. high. $2,000

Early 20th century Quezal
Art Glass vase, New York,
signed, 8¼in. high. $800

VASES

Tiffany Cypriote vase, basic green body overlaid with blue-black metallic iridised glass and three lustrous gold leaf-form decorations, 6¹/₂in. high. (Skinner Inc.) $10,000

Steuben dark jade blue grotesque vase, quatriform ribbed bowl, 11¹/₂in. wide. (Skinner Inc.) $3,850

Pressed vase, three printie block pattern, gaffered rim, no wafer, canary, 9in. high, New England Glass Co., Cambridge, Massachusetts, 1840–60. (Skinner Inc.) $165

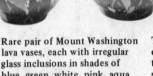

Roycroft silver washed vase with Steuben glass insert, East Aurora, New York, no. 248 in the 1926 catalog, 6in. high. (Skinner Inc.) $250

Rare pair of Mount Washington lava vases, each with irregular glass inclusions in shades of blue, green, white, pink, aqua and some red, 8in. high. (Robt. W. Skinner Inc.) $3,500

Tiffany Tel El Amarna vase, classic baluster footed form of transparent aquamarine-green, subtly ribbed, with applied flared gold iridescent raised cuff, 9¹/₂in. high. (Skinner Inc.) $3,300

An important Tiffany 'Favrile' iridescent glass vase, decorated below the shoulders with a band of café-au-lait/lemon swirls against pale peacock blue with shades of green and violet, 29.5cm. high. (Phillips) $12,250

Pair of Bohemian type engraved vases, engraved with grapes, florals and leaves, 10½in. high, possibly Boston & Sandwich Glassworks, Massachusetts, 1880s. (Robt. W. Skinner Inc.) $200

Rare Mount Washington jeweled Royal Flemish vase, decorated with enameled and gilt bordered blossoms, buds, autumn leaves and thorny stems, 9in. high. (Robt. W. Skinner Inc.) $1,400

The one-sheet from 'The Devil is a Woman' offered here has an unusual history to it. One of the employees at Morgan Litho, where the poster was printed, was Hoy G. Fisher, who did the color separations. He was so taken with its beauty that he took a copy of it straight off the press before it was folded and preserved it unfolded through the years. One-sheet posters from major studios are almost never found unfolded.

'The Devil is a Woman', Paramount, 1935, one-sheet, unfolded, 41 x 27in. (Christie's East)

$46,200

Angel, Paramount, 1937, one-sheet, linen backed, 41 x 27in. (Christie's East) $2,860

The New Frontier, Republic, 1935, one-sheet, linen backed, 41 x 27in. (Christie's East) $5,720

Dimples, 20th Fox, 1936, one-sheet, linen backed, 41 x 27in. (Christie's East) $2,640

Her Wedding Night, Paramount, 1930, one-sheet, linen backed, 41 x 27in. (Christie's East) $3,300

Flying Pat, Paramount, 1920, one-sheet, linen backed, 41 x 27in. (Christie's East) $1,870

The Mysterious Dr. Fu Manchu, Paramount, 1929, one-sheet, linen backed, 41 x 27in. (Christie's East) $2,530

Red Headed Woman, MGM, 1932, one-sheet, linen backed, 41 x 27in. (Christie's East) $10,780

Shall We Dance, RKO, 1937, one-sheet, linen backed, 41 x 27in. (Christie's East) $6,050

The Young Rajah, Paramount, 1922, one-sheet, linen backed, 41 x 27in. (Christie's East) $3,410

The Unknown, MGM, 1927, one-sheet, linen backed, 41 x 27in.
(Christie's East) $12,100

The Grim Game, Paramount-Artcraft, 1919, one-sheet, linen backed, 41 x 27in.
(Christie's East) $12,650

Go Into Your Dance, First National, 1935, one-sheet, linen backed, 41 x 27in.
(Christie's East) $3,520

Doubling for Romeo, Goldwyn, 1922, one-sheet, linen backed, 41 x 27in.
(Christie's East) $1,870

The Round Up, Paramount, 1920, one-sheet, linen backed, 41 x 27in.
(Christie's East) $4,400

Tarzan and his Mate, MGM, 1934, one-sheet, linen backed, 41 x 27in.
(Christie's East) $5,720

Son of the Golden West, FBO, 1928, one-sheet, linen backed, 41 x 27in.
(Christie's East) $1,870

The Suitor, Vitagraph, 1920, one-sheet, linen backed, 41 x 27in.
(Christie's East) $1,045

Prodigal Daughters, Paramount, one-sheet, linen backed, 41 x 27in.
(Christie's East) $1,430

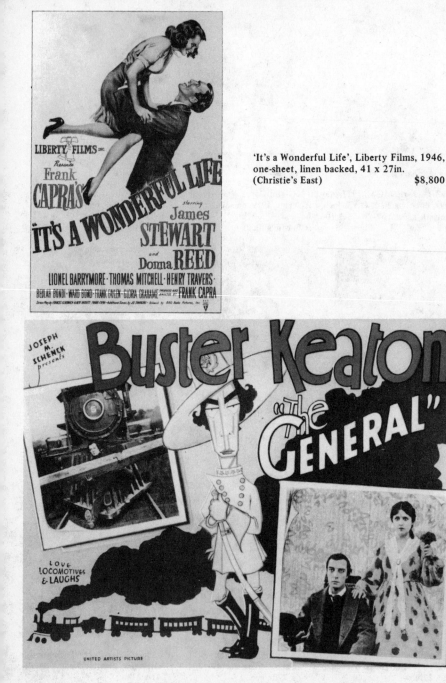

'It's a Wonderful Life', Liberty Films, 1946, one-sheet, linen backed, 41 x 27in. (Christie's East) $8,800

'The General', United Artists, 1926, half-sheet, unfolded, 22 x 28in. (Christie's East) $13,200

'King Kong', RKO, 1933, original French poster, linen backed, 63 x 47in. (Christie's East) $14,300

'The Walking Dead', Warner Brothers, 1936, six-sheet, linen backed, 81 x 81in. (Christie's East) $28,600

What Do Men Want?, Lois Weber Productions, 1921, one-sheet, linen backed, 41 x 27in.
(Christie's East) $5,700

The Toll Gate, Paramount-Artcraft, 1920, one-sheet, linen backed, 41 x 27in.
(Christie's East) $2,600

The Siren Call, Paramount, 1921, one-sheet, linen backed, 41 x 27in.
(Christie's) $1,000

The Gilded Lily, Paramount, 1921, one-sheet, linen backed, 41 x 27in.
(Christie's East) $1,750

Forbidden, Columbia, 1932, one-sheet, linen backed, 41 x 27in.
(Christie's East) $1,850

Victory, Paramount-Artcraft, 1919, one-sheet, linen backed, 41 x 27in.
(Christie's East) $875

Know Your Men, Fox, 1921, one-sheet, linen backed, 41 x 27in.
(Christie's East) $1,650

A Dog's Life, First National, 1918, one-sheet, linen backed, 41 x 27in.
(Christie's East) $17,600

Minnie, First National, 1922, one-sheet, linen backed, 41 x 27in.
(Christie's East) $550

The Big Parade, MGM, 1927, one-sheet, linen backed, 41 x 27in.
(Christie's East) $2,750

Don't Shove, Pathe, 1919, one-sheet, linen backed, 41 x 27in.
(Christie's East) $1,200

The Woman Alone, Gaumont British, 1936, one-sheet, linen backed, 41 x 27in.
(Christie's East) $2,200

The Bait, Paramount, 1921, one-sheet, linen backed, 41 x 27in.
(Christie's East) $1,000

The Wild Party, Paramount, 1929, one-sheet, linen backed, 41 x 27in.
(Christie's East) $3,000

Charlie Chan's Chance, Fox, 1931, one-sheet, linen backed, 41 x 27in.
(Christie's East) $2,200

An Amateur Devil, Paramount, 1921, one-sheet, linen backed, 41 x 27in.
(Christie's East) $820

The Rough Diamond, Fox, 1921, one-sheet, linen backed, 41 x 27in.
(Christie's East) $1,200

East is West, First National, 1922, one-sheet, linen backed, 41 x 27in.
(Christie's East) $3,750

'The Old Dark House', Universal, 1932, set of eight lobby cards, each 11 x 14in.
(Christie's East) $12,100

'Things to Come', United Artists, 1936, six-sheet, linen backed, 81 x 81in. (Christie's East)
$22,000

'The Sin of Nora Moran', Majestic
Pictures, 1933, one-sheet, linen
backed, 41 x 27in.
(Christie's East) $19,800

'The Circus', United Artists,
1928, one-sheet, linen backed,
41 x 27in.
(Christie's East) $18,700

The Son of the Sheik, United Artists, 1926, half-sheet, unfolded, 22 x 28in.
(Christie's East) $2,750

Citizen Kane, RKO, 1941, half-sheet, unfolded, 22 x 28in.
(Christie's East) $3,850

The Jazz Singer, Warner Brothers, 1927, 24-sheet, linen backed, 9 x 20 feet.
(Christie's East) $18,700

Platinum Blonde, Columbia, 1930, three-sheet, linen backed, 81 x 41in.
(Christie's East) $4,620

Manhattan Melodrama, MGM, 1934, half-sheet, unfolded, 22 x 28in.
(Christie's East) $3,190

The American Venus, Paramount, 1926, six-sheet, linen backed, 81 x 81in.
(Christie's East) $3,740

The Pilgrim, First National, 1923, six-sheet, linen backed, 81 x 81in. (Christie's East) $12,650

Way Out West, MGM, 1937, half-sheet, unfolded, 22 x 28in. (Christie's East) $3,190

The Cabinet of Dr. Caligari, Goldwyn, 1921, one-sheet, linen backed, 41 x 27in. (Christie's East) $37,400

American Entertainment Co., ca. 1900, one-sheet, linen backed, 28 x 41in. (Christie's East) $3,740

The Wizard of Oz, MGM, 1939, half-sheet, unfolded, 22 x 28in. (Christie's East) $11,000

She Done Him Wrong, Paramount, 1933, six-sheet, linen backed, 81 x 81in. (Christie's East) $5,720

'The Perils of Pauline', Eclectic Film, 1914, one-sheet, linen backed, 41 x 27in.
(Christie's East) $6,600

'Frankenstein', Universal, 1931, original Spanish poster, unfolded, 41 x 27in.
(Christie's East) $11,000

'The Walking Dead', Warner Brothers, 1936, half-sheet, unfolded, 22 x 28in. (Christie's East)
$3,520

Alice the Peacemaker, Winkler, 1924, one-sheet, paper backed, 41 x 27in.
(Christie's) $22,000

Turning the Tables, Paramount-Artcraft, 1919, one-sheet, linen backed, 41 x 27in.
(Christie's) $1,650

Devil's Harvest, unknown, ca. 1940's, one-sheet, linen backed, 41 x 27in.
(Christie's) $990

The Cat's Meow, Pathe, 1924, one-sheet, linen backed, 41 x 27in.
(Christie's) $770

Devil Dogs of the Air, Warner Brothers, 1935, three-sheet, linen backed, 81 x 41in.
(Christie's) $5,720

The Fleet's In, Paramount, 1928, one-sheet, linen backed, 41 x 27in.
(Christie's) $2,200

The Phantom of the Opera, Universal, 1925, one-sheet, paper backed, 41 x 27in.
(Christie's) $38,500

The Pilgrim, First National, 1923, one-sheet, linen backed, 41 x 27in.
(Christie's) $6,600

20th Century, Columbia, 1934, one-sheet, linen backed, 41 x 27in.
(Christie's) $23,100

Dr. Jekyll and Mr. Hyde,
Paramount, 1932, window card,
22 x 14in.
(Christie's) $7,700

City Lights, United Artists,
1931, three-sheet, linen backed,
81 x 41in.
(Christie's) $23,100

The Maltese Falcon, Warner
Brothers, 1941, one-sheet, linen
backed, 41 x 27in.
(Christie's) $5,500

The Oregon Trail, Republic,
1936, one-sheet, linen backed, 41
x 27in.
(Christie's) $10,450

Creature from the Black
Lagoon, Universal, 1954, one-
sheet, linen backed, 41 x 27in.
(Christie's) $4,620

The Unholy Three, MGM, 1925,
one-sheet, linen backed, 41 x
27in.
(Christie's) $4,400

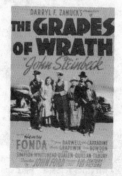

Casablanca, Warner Brothers,
1943, one-sheet, linen backed,
41 x 27in.
(Christie's) $5,720

The Grapes of Wrath, 20th
Century Fox, 1940, one-sheet,
linen backed, 41 x 27in.
(Christie's) $5,280

Star of Midnight, RKO, 1935,
one-sheet, linen backed, 41 x
27in.
(Christie's) $7,700

'Babe Comes Home', First National,
1927, lobby card, 11 x 14in.
(Christie's East) $3,740

'Citizen Kane' is widely considered by film critics to be the greatest film ever made. (It has won every poll). Yet it was a failure on its original release. Perhaps it was too innovative and different for audiences of the day. The six-sheet poster attempted to show the main theme of the film, the enigma of Charles Foster Kane. The six-sheet offered here is widely believed to be one of two currently known to exist.

'Citizen Kane', RKO, 1941, six-sheet, linen backed, 81 x 81in. (Christie's East) $22,000

In 1924, Douglas Fairbanks starred in 'The Thief of Bagdad', one of the greatest fantasy films ever made. United Artists recognized this and commissioned its finest poster artist at the time to create a one-sheet showing the film's most magnificent scene, depicting Fairbanks flying over the city of Bagdad on a flying horse.
'The Thief of Bagdad', United Artists, 1924, one-sheet, paper backed, 41 x 27in.
(Christie's East) $30,800

'The Canary Murder Case', Paramount, 1929, one-sheet, paper backed, 41 x 27in.
(Christie's East) $28,600

Society Dog Show, Disney, 1939, one-sheet, linen backed, 41 x 27in.
(Christie's) $10,450

40,000 Miles with Lindbergh, MGM, 1928, one-sheet, linen backed, 41 x 27in.
(Christie's) $5,500

The Devil is a Woman, Paramount, 1935, one-sheet, linen backed, 41 x 27in.
(Christie's) $16,500

The Birth of a Nation, Epoch Producing Corp., 1915, one-sheet, linen backed, 41 x 27in.
(Christie's) $28,600

The War of the Worlds, Paramount, 1953, six-sheet, linen backed, 81 x 81in.
(Christie's) $5,280

The Westerner, United Artists, 1940, three-sheet, linen backed, 81 x 41in.
(Christie's) $5,500

East is West, First National, 1922, one-sheet, linen backed, 41 x 27in.
(Christie's) $880

The Red Shoes, J. Arthur Rank, 1948, original English poster, linen backed, 41 x 27in.
(Christie's) $1,760

Bluebeard's 8th Wife, Paramount, 1923, one-sheet, linen backed, 41 x 27in.
(Christie's) $14,300

The Master Mystery, Octagon Films, 1919, one-sheet, linen backed, 41 x 27in.
(Christie's) $16,500

Out West, Paramount-Arbuckle, 1918, one-sheet, linen backed, 41 x 27in.
(Christie's) $5,280

Sawing a Lady in Half, Clarion Photoplays, 1922, one-sheet, linen backed, 41 x 27in.
(Christie's) $2,420

Werewolf of London, Universal, 1935, insert, paper backed, 36 x 14in.
(Christie's) $4,620

Rebel without a Cause, Warner Brothers, 1955, six-sheet, linen backed, 81 x 81in.
(Christie's) $4,400

Moon Over Miami, 20th Century Fox, 1941, three-sheet, linen backed, 81 x 41in.
(Christie's) $13,200

Steamboat round the Bend, Fox, 1935, one-sheet, linen backed, 41 x 27in.
(Christie's) $1,100

Blonde Venus, Paramount, 1933, original Belgian poster, linen backed, 30 x 24in.
(Christie's) $10,450

Horse Feathers, Paramount, 1932, one-sheet, linen backed, 41 x 27in.
(Christie's) $5,280

'The 39 Steps', Gaumont British, 1935, one-sheet, paper backed, 41 x 27in. (Christie's East) $14,300

'Tarzan of the Apes', First National, 1918, one-sheet, linen backed, 41 x 27in. (Christie's East) $30,800

'Queen Christina', MGM, 1934, one-sheet,
linen backed, 41 x 27in.
(Christie's East) $5,280

'The Wizard of Oz', MGM, 1939, half-sheet, unfolded, paper backed, 22 x 28in.
(Christie's East) $19,800

Tanned Legs, RKO, 1929, one-sheet, linen backed, 41 x 27in.
(Christie's) $2,200

The Mummy, Universal, 1932, Title lobby card, 11 x 14in.
(Christie's) $10,450

Under the Yoke, Fox, 1918, one-sheet, linen backed, 41 x 27in.
(Christie's) $825

Queen Christina, MGM, 1933, three-sheet, linen backed, 81 x 41in.
(Christie's) $17,600

Atom Man vs. Superman, Columbia, 1950, six-sheet, linen backed, 81 x 81in.
(Christie's) $8,250

The Wizard of Oz, MGM, 1939, three-sheet, linen backed, 81 x 41in.
(Christie's) $25,300

Captain January, 20th Century Fox, 1936, one-sheet, linen backed, 41 x 27in.
(Christie's) $2,200

Son of Frankenstein, Universal, 1939, one-sheet, linen backed, 41 x 27in.
(Christie's) $14,300

Behind the Mask, Columbia, 1932, one-sheet, linen backed, 41 x 27in.
(Christie's) $770

The Old Dark House, Universal, 1932, one-sheet, 41 x 27in. (Christie's) $48,400

King Kong, RKO, 1933, three-sheet, linen backed, 81 x 41in. (Christie's) $57,200

The Wolf Man, Universal, 1941, one-sheet, 41 x 27in. (Christie's) $17,600

An American in Paris, MGM, 1951, three-sheet, linen backed, 81 x 41in. (Christie's) $1,980

A Dog's Life, First National, 1918, six-sheet, linen backed, 81 x 81in. (Christie's) $35,200

Dracula, Universal, 1931, insert, 36 x 14in. (Christie's) $33,000

The Bellhop, Vitagraph, 1921, one-sheet, linen backed, 41 x 27in. (Christie's) $715

Citizen Kane, RKO, 1941, one-sheet, linen backed, 41 x 27in. (Christie's) $22,000

Disraeli, Warner Brothers, 1929, one-sheet, paper backed, 41 x 27in. (Christie's) $770

William Powell and Ginger Rogers were the male and female epitome of grace and wit. Both had long and illustrious careers, yet their professional paths crossed only once, when they co-starred in 'Star of Midnight' in 1935.

'Star of Midnight', RKO, 1935, three-sheet, linen backed, 81 x 41in. (Christie's East) $13,200

324

Surveyor's cased brass compass, New York, circa 1840, 15in. long. $750

Orrery 'Trippensee Planetarium, Detroit, Michigan', early 20th century, painted wood, various metals and printed paper, 25½in. wide. (Skinner Inc.) $750

A very rare J. N. Williams US check writer for Automatic Bank Punch Co., New York City, 1885. (Auction Team Koeln) $289

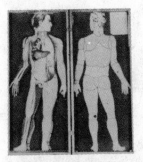

Anatomical teaching device, 'Smiths's New Outline Map of the Human System, Anatomical Regions, No. 2', manufactured by American Manikan Co., Peoria, Illinois, 1888, 44in. high. (Robt. W. Skinner Inc.) $900

A terrestrial globe, by Gilman Joslin, Boston, Massachusetts, early 19th century, the stand on ring and baluster turned legs joined by an X-stretcher, 14in. high. (Christie's New York) $1,650

A brass compound microscope for the American market, signed I. P. Cutts, Sheffield, retailed by McAllister & Bro., Philadelphia, circa 1825, on folding tripod base, 31cm. length of box. (Christie's) $2,090

The Portable Astronomical Pantoscope, original US patent 1865. Shows 'position of the heavenly bodies in relation to the horizon, the equator and the ecliptic!' (Auction Team Köln) $4,332

Rare American Momsen lung, the first well-known submarine escape device. (Eldred's) $88

Ship's wheel type kaleidoscope stamped, *C.D. Bush, Claremont, NH*, brass and leather wrapped barrel, 13½in. high. (Eldred's) $770

American celestial globe, J. Wilson & Sons, 1826, Albany St. New York, on a mahogany tripod base, 36½in. high. (Skinner Inc.) $1,200

A brass surveyor's vernier compass, signed Benj'n Pike Jr., 294 Broadway, N.Y. N.Y., mid-19th century, the shaped strap with two detachable slit sights, 14¾in. (Christie's) $880

Stereo daguerreotype, America, circa 1854, ¼ plate thermoplastic case with Mascher's Patent lens board. $500

A brass Martin type orrery with tellurium of American interest, signed T. Blunt, London, 22cm. diam. (Christie's) $15,400

An American Stereoscopic Co. Brewster pattern hand held stereoscope with gilt tooled leather covered body. (Christie's S. Ken) $305

A rare American kaleidoscope by G.C. Bush, Providence, Rhode Island, "Patent reissued Nov 11 1873", with textured pasteboard tube and brass collar incorporating object case filled with colored glass, last quarter 19th century, 10¼in. long. (Christie's) $1,980

An American lacquered brass monocular microscope, signed E. H. & F. H. Tighe, Detroit, circa 1885, length of tube 5in. $800

Rosewood stereo viewer, table top, manufactured by Alex. Becker, N.Y., circa 1859. $800

Surveyor's brass transit with wooden case, silvered dial marked 'Blunt & Co., N.Y.', circa 1845, 12in. high. $800

One of a pair of cast iron hall trees, America, circa 1875, 75in. high. $1,000

A wrought iron foot scraper, probably Pennsylvania, mid-19th century, modeled in the form of a ram, 34.6cm. long. (Christie's) $4,620

A cast fountain, J. W. Fiske, Ironworks, New York, late 19th century, young boy and girl beneath an open umbrella, 27in. high. (Skinner Inc.) $3,250

An American 19th century painted iron trade sign, 40in. high, 15in. wide. $3,000

A pair of cast iron figural andirons, America, late 19th/early 20th century, caricature figures of a black man and woman, 16½in. high. (Robt. W. Skinner Inc.) $1,200

A wrought iron Conestoga wagon box hasp, Pennsylvania, early/mid-19th century, the triangular crest above a double row of two pierced circles, 14½in. long. (Christie's) $462

Late 19th century cast iron fountain, stamped 'Robert Wood & Co. Makers Phila.', 40in. high. $4,000

Late 18th century cast iron bake kettle, original fitted cover with deep flange, 13¼in. deep. $600

Mid 19th century cast iron interior plant stand, America, 43in. high. $2,000

'Sailor', a painted iron figure of a Newfoundland, cast by Bartlett and Hayward, American, 19th century, 36³/₈ x 65¹/₂in.
(Christie's) $19,800

Oriental cast iron gate, Baltimore area, 19th century, 20in. high, 28in. long.
(Skinner Inc.) $700

A painted cast iron trade sign, American, 19th century, modeled in the form of a top hat, 7in. high. (Christie's New York) $2,200

A pair of painted cast iron hitching post finials, American, second half 19th century, each modeled as a horse head, 12³/₄in. high.
(Christie's) $1430

Cast iron architectural ornament, America, late 19th/early 20th century, in the form of an eagle with outstretched wings, 21in. high.
(Skinner Inc.) $700

Pair of painted cast iron garden figures, Whitman Foundry, Whitman, Massachusetts, late 19th/early 20th century, 64in. high.
(Skinner Inc.) $8,500

A rare Mickey Mouse cast white metal money box, indistinct registration number 50611?, 5¹/₄in. high.
(David Lay) $1,080

A cast iron stove plate, probably by Mary Ann Furnace, York County, Pennsylvania, circa 1761, depicting two tulip and heart decorations, 24½in. high.
(Christie's) $990

Four piece wrought iron fireplace set, attributed to Gustav Stickley, circa 1905, with strapwork log holder, unsigned, 33½in. high.
(Skinner Inc.) $6,000

Antique American wood and iron candle mold, designed for twenty-four candles, 22in. wide. (Eldred's) **$633**

Cast iron Old South Church still bank, America, late 19th/early 20th century, with original paint and paper label, 13in. high. (Skinner Inc.) **$4,675**

Cast iron garden ornament in the form of a Newfoundland dog, America, mid 19th century, 55in. long. (Skinner Inc.) **$23,100**

Cast-iron painted blackamoor tether, American, 19th century, the standing figure dressed in a white shirt and black pants, 44in. high. (Butterfield & Butterfield) **$1,650**

A pair of painted figures of hounds, cast by J.W. Fiske, American, 19th century, 48 x 46¹⁄₂in. (Christie's) **$38,500**

Cast iron painted urn, circa 1900, bears makers mark *Kramer Brothers Foundry, Dayton, Ohio,* on a square pedestal, 42in. high. (Skinner Inc.) **$700**

Cast iron stove plate, Pennsylvania, c. 1750, 'Dance of Death', pattern, the inscription translated 'Here fights with me the bitter death/And brings me in death's stress' 22in. x 24in. (Skinner Inc.) **$500**

Cast iron State Seal of New York, America, late 19th century, the figure of an eagle with outstretched wings perched upon a scrolled cartouche, 34in. wide. (Robt. W. Skinner Inc.) **$2,200**

Elihu Vedder wrought iron fireback, New York, 1882, The Sun God, cast with the face of a man surrounded by flowing hair, 27¾in. wide. (Skinner Inc.) **$3,100**

A late 19th century cast
iron Newfoundland figure
dog, 65in. long. $15,000

Late 18th century
wrought iron broiler,
probably Pennsylvania,
20in. long. $600

Late 19th century American
cast iron elk figure, 49in.
wide. $4,000

A molded polychrome
tobacconist figure, Wm.
Demuth, N.Y., circa 1890,
67½in. high without base.
(Robt. W. Skinner Inc.)
            $11,000

A pair of mid 19th century
American painted cast iron
dressing glasses, 21in. high.
            $1,000

Fine cast iron doorstop of a
trained bear climbing a tree,
marked *Warwick* on lower front,
13½in. high.
(Eldred's) $231

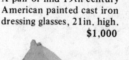

A cast iron funeral gate by
James Monahan, Savannah,
Georgia, late 19th century,
centering a reticulated weeping
willow tree, 33 x 27¾in.
(Christie's) $1,210

A cast iron painted mill weight,
American, late 19th/early 20th
century, modeled as a bob-
tailed standing horse, 16½in.
high. (Christie's) $440

A cast iron architectural ornament, American, early 20th century, modeled in the form of
a Classical head, 22in. high.
(Christie's) $770

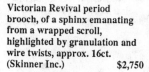

Victorian Revival period brooch, of a sphinx emanating from a wrapped scroll, highlighted by granulation and wire twists, approx. 16ct. (Skinner Inc.) $2,750

Red, white and blue rhinestone brooch in the form of the American flag centrally set with a mini glass Coca-Cola bottle, dated 1976. (Robt. W. Skinner Inc.) $360

Diamond turtle brooch, set throughout with round diamonds, est. total weight 11.50ct., with emerald set eyes. (Skinner Inc.) $9,075

Carved shell cameo brooch, depicting the profile of a woman, mounted in a 14ct. gold frame with raised floral design. (Skinner Inc.) $1,980

Victorian ear pendants, composed of hinged plaques, highlighted by wire twist and granulated gold completed by ball fringe, 14ct. gold. (Skinner Inc.) $1,430

Enamel and diamond tiger head pendant, Alling & Co., highlighted by round diamonds, suspended from a 14ct. gold link chain. (Skinner Inc.) $1,430

'Euphoria', a Memphis enameled chromed metal necklace on rubber cord, designed by Ettore Sottsass Jnr. for Acme. (Christie's) $292

18ct. gold, ruby and diamond pin, Tiffany & Co., in the shape of a feather, highlighted by rubies and a diamond. (Skinner Inc.) $440

Pair of gold coin earrings, five dollar U.S. gold coins, one dated 1898, the other 1900, in gold bezels. $490

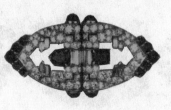

Art Nouveau pin, 14ct. gold, depicting the face of a woman with flowing hair. (Skinner Inc.) $450

Art Deco sapphire and diamond double clip brooch, triangular-shaped clips set throughout with round and fancy-cut diamonds. (Skinner Inc.) $10,175

Art Nouveau pin of a peacock against a sunset background, 14ct. gold. (Skinner Inc.) $450

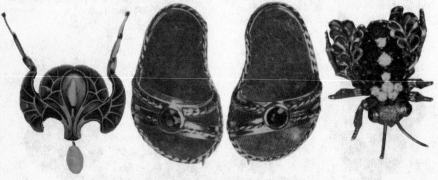

Ruby and diamond fly brooch, set with carved rubies, round diamonds and cabochon-cut green onyx, 18ct. gold. (Skinner Inc.) $1,540

A plique-a-jour pendant with pearl drop and sterling silver chain, circa 1910, 15in. long. (Robt. W. Skinner Inc.) $400

14ct. gold Madonna sandal clips, attributed to Paul Flato, each set with a garnet, originally advertised in the October 15 1940 issue of Vogue magazine. (Skinner Inc.) $1,980

Victorian hardstone cameo brooch, depicting the profile of a woman, mounted in a gold frame, 18ct. gold. (Skinner Inc.) $880

18ct. yellow gold knot brooch, Tiffany & Co., Italy, 31 dwt. (Skinner Inc.) $2,090

Art Nouveau locket, centered by a cabochon-cut sapphire with a raised floral design, 14ct. gold. (Skinner Inc.) $770

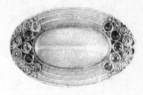

Frank Gardner Hale gold and silver brooch with opals, Boston, circa 1917, a gold scroll filigree setting, 1½in. long. (Skinner Inc.) $2,300

Art Deco diamond bow pin, pave-set with 105 diamonds weighing approx. 3.00kt. and highlighted by caliber cut onyx. (Robt. W. Skinner Inc.) $4,500

A Tiffany & Co. two-color gold, sapphire and moonstone oval brooch, 3.3cm. across. (Phillips) $1,250

An emerald clover brooch, Tiffany & Co., set with twenty-five square-cut emeralds, weight approx. 8.50 carats. $10,000

An enameled gold diamond-set lapel watch and a butterfly brooch signed *M. Scooler, New Orleans*, with nickel keyless lever movement jeweled through the center 18ct gold cuvette, blue enameled dial with white enamel Arabic chapters, circa 1890, 23.5mm. diameter. (Christie's) $3,520

Pink tourmaline and gold pendant, attributed to Margaret Vant, Boston, circa 1925, shield shaped open gold filigree form, 2in. wide. (Skinner Inc.) $850

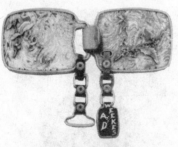

Enamel locket, 1860s, depicting a dragon, highlighted by cabochon rubies and rose-cut diamonds, 18ct. gold. (Skinner Inc.) $6,600

A rare early Mokume cloak clasp by Tiffany & Co., New York, 1876, in the Japanese taste, 6½in. wide, extended, 3 oz. 10 dwt. (Christie's) $3,000

14ct. yellow gold and ruby pin, circa 1940's, Cartier, New York, fluted leaf highlighted by five round rubies. (Skinner Inc.) $1,100

Cut overlay glass lamp with pressed glass base, New England, circa 1870, white glass heightened with gilt, 40in. high. (Skinner Inc.) $425

Art Deco lamp, circa 1925, fan-shape mica covered metal shade with patinated metal standard and base, 13³/₈in. high. (Skinner Inc.) $600

A slag glass and gilt metal table lamp, America, circa 1910, 23½in. high, shade 17¾in. diam. $800

Leaded glass table lamp, umbrella-form shade of segmented white glass panels with swag and blossom elements, 18in. diameter. (Skinner Inc.) $400

A leaded slag glass and oak table lamp, early 20th century, the square hipped shade with colored glass panels, 22in. high. (Robt. W. Skinner Inc.) $1,500

Copper and mica table lamp, Upstate New York, circa 1910, mushroom topped flaring shade with four mica panels, 29in. high. (Skinner Inc.) $3,750

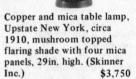

Hammered copper and mica table lamp, early 20th century, with three mica panels on urn shape standard. (Skinner Inc.) $400

Copper oil lamp, executed by Mary Steere Batchelder, 39 Hancock St., Boston, circa 1907, 13in. high. (Skinner Inc.) $1,750

A 1930's Modernist chromium plated table lamp, the domed metal stepped shade with white painted reflector, 42cm. high. (Christie's) $2,000

Glass and brass table lamp, with reverse painted border design in yellow with stylized green and red floral motif, 16in. diameter. (Skinner Inc.) **$700**

Rare Limbert copper and mica Prairie School table lamp, Michigan, circa 1913, branded on foot, 19in. high, 24in. wide. (Skinner Inc.) **$50,000**

An Art Nouveau bronze and leaded glass shade on bronze base, 22½in. high. (Christie's) **$1,500**

A Moe Bridges parrot lamp, with reverse handpainted scene of two exotic birds centered in a summer landscape, 23in. high. (Robt. W. Skinner Inc.) **$5,000**

A Fulper pottery 'Vase-Kraft' table lamp, circa 1915, 18in. high, 16½in. diam. (Robt. W. Skinner Inc.) **$7,500**

Copper and mica table lamp, circa 1910, flaring shade with four mica panels divided by copper straps, 26in. high. (Skinner Inc.) **$2,000**

Wilkerson table lamp, leaded conical shade with red, yellow, orange and pink blossoms, 29in. high. (Skinner Inc.) **$5,775**

Hammered copper and mica table lamp, probably Upstate New York, with strapwork dividing four panels, 20in. high. (Skinner Inc.) **$2,000**

An Art Deco frosted glass lamp painted in colors with banding and linear decoration, 31cm. high. (Phillips) **$650**

A hammered copper table lamp with mica shade, Old Mission Kopperkraft, San Francisco, circa 1910, 13¾in. high, 15in. diam. (Robt. W. Skinner Inc.) $3,250

Hampshire pottery lamp, Keene, New Hampshire, circa 1910, with incised key device in matt green glaze, 10in. high. (Skinner Inc.) $413

Gone-with-the-Wind glass lamp shade, with etched and gilt enameled alternating dragon and wreath with quiver decoration, 9½in. high. (Skinner Inc.) $450

Millefiore Art Glass miniature lamp, mushroom cap shade and matching glass lamp shaft, mounted with gilt metal and "Bryant" electrical fittings, 11in. high. (Skinner Inc.) $1,200

Pair of fire engine side lamps, De Voursney Bros. 9 Broome Street, New York, late 19th century, each with two blue, one red and clear etched glass panels, 19½in. high. (Skinner Inc.) $2,100

Free blown petticoat oil lamp, wide flaring folded foot, large crimped handle, with thumb rest, pontil scar, 9½in. high, possibly New England, early 19th century. (Skinner Inc.) $770

Mount Washington cameo glass lamp base, pink to white, mounted in brass and gilt metal lamp fittings, 8in. diameter. (Skinner Inc.) $375

A copper and leaded glass piano lamp, cone-shaped slag glass shade, incised mark 'KK', 13¾in. high. (Robt. W. Skinner Inc.) $450

Arts & Crafts oak and slag glass table lamp, circa 1910, pyramidal shade lined with green slag glass, 26in. high. (Skinner Inc.) $800

One of a pair of oak and leaded glass wall lanterns, circa 1910, 23in. long. (Robt. W. Skinner Inc.) **$1,250**

A hammered copper and mica table lamp, circa 1910, 14¾in. high. (Robt. W. Skinner Inc.) **$1,600**

Copper and mica table lamp, early 20th century, mica paneled shades, petal form sockets, 18½in. high. (Skinner Inc.) **$1,210**

An art glass table lamp, open Tam o' Shanter shade of green iridescent pulled and swirled damascene design cased to opal-white glass, 19½in. high. (Robt. W. Skinner Inc.) **$2,000**

Leaded glass table lamp, Wilkerson-type amber-centred white clematis blossom leaded shade on two-socket black and gilt metal base, 20in. high. (Skinner Inc.) **$325**

Bradley-Hubbard paneled table lamp, of eight curved ribbed glass panels reverse painted with a border of tulip blossoms and stylized leaf designs, 24in. high. (Robt. W. Skinner Inc.) **$900**

Late 19th century peach-blow fairy lamp on three-legged brass stand, possibly Mt. Washington, 8½in. high. **$800**

R. Guy Cowan Pottery table lamp, Cleveland, Ohio, circa 1925, metal shade of square flaring form, simulating mica, 19½in. high. (Skinner Inc.) **$1,000**

Early 20th century leaded cased glass lantern in vintage pattern, 13¼in. high, 9in. wide. (Robt. W. Skinner Inc.) **$625**

BENEDICT STUDIOS

The Benedict Studios flourished in East Syracuse, New York State in the early years of the 20th century.

Their lamps are often unsigned, but are characterized by the frequent use of copper and mica, a mineral often used as a substitute for glass.

A mica and hammered copper table lamp, possibly Benedict Studios, New York, early 20th century, 19in. diam. (Robt. W. Skinner Inc.) $3,000

Copper and mica piano lamp, attributed to Benedict Studios, East Syracuse, New York, circa 1910, unsigned, 21½in. high. (Skinner Inc.) $2,250

BRADLEY & HUBBARD

The American glass makers Bradley & Hubbard worked out of Meriden, Connecticut, in the early 20th century. Their table lamps often feature metal pedestal bases with domed shades of iridescent or painted glass.

Their mark is usually Bradley & Hubbard Mfg Co within a triangle, set round an oil lamp.

A Bradley & Hubbard table lamp with gold iridescent shade, Mass., circa 1910, 15in. high. (Robt. W. Skinner Inc.) $900

Reverse painted and gilt metal table lamp, by Bradley & Hubbard, circa 1910, 23¼in. high. $1,200

GRUEBY

Lamps did not feature largely in the short lived pottery venture launched by William Grueby in Boston Mass. in 1897, tiles and vases forming his principal lines. Some were produced in the early years of this century, and these feature the typical Grueby glazes, matt, opaque and mainly in shades of yellow brown, and of course dark green. Shades, and sometimes also parts of the base, were produced by other manufacturers.

A Grueby pottery lamp with Bigelow & Kennard leaded shade, circa 1905, 17¾in. diam. $4,000

Grueby pottery two-color lamp base, Boston, circa 1905, bronze foot signed Gorham Co., 18in. high. (Robt. W. Skinner Inc.) $15,000

GUSTAV STICKLEY

Gustav Stickley, the noted Arts & Crafts furniture designer, also ventured into lamp production. His offerings are very much what one would expect – frequent use of hammered copper, with clear signs of hand craftsmanship, simple lines, with little in the way of embellishment.

In his youth he designed mainly chairs in the American Colonial style, but in 1898 he founded the firm of Gustav Stickley of Syracuse, New York, which specialised in the Arts & Crafts or Mission style of furniture (from the furniture supposedly found in the old Franciscan missions in California). He also published a magazine 'The Craftsman' which popularised this new style.

Like Art Nouveau, of which this was the American version, the style was seen as being a return to the simple functional style of the medieval period.

HAMPSHIRE

The Hampshire Pottery was founded in 1871 at Keene, New Hampshire, by J S Taft, and produced earthenware for domestic use and souvenirs for tourists. There was also some majolica production. Decoration often consisted of transfer printing in black. Lamp bases figured among their output and these can often be found teamed up with glass shades from other stables.

A patinated wrought-iron and textured amber glass chandelier, attributed to Gustav Stickley, 28in. diam. $7,000

One of a pair of Gustav Stickley wall lanterns, circa 1910, no. 225, wrought iron lanterns with heart cut-out design, suspended from wrought iron hooks with spade shape mounts, 10in. high. (Skinner Inc.) $2,000

A copper and amber glass lantern, style no. 324, by Gustav Stickley, circa 1906, 15in. high, globe 5¼in. diam. (Robt. W. Skinner Inc.) $8,000

A Gustav Stickley hammered copper lamp with willow shade, circa 1905, signed, 22in. high, 20in. diam. (Robt. W. Skinner Inc.) $2,000

Hampshire pottery lamp with leaded shade, circa 1910, 19½in. high, 16in. diam. (Robt. W. Skinner Inc.) $1,000

Early 20th century Hampshire pottery lamp with leaded Handel shade, 21in. high, 16in. diam. (Robt. W. Skinner Inc.) $1,000

HANDEL

The Handel Company was established by Philip Handel at Meriden, Connecticut around 1885, and from 1900–1930 a branch also operated in New York City. The company produced Art Nouveau and other styles of art glass vessels, but came to be known principally for their leaded glass shades for gas and electric lighting. Many styles closely followed the designs of Tiffany, but were very much less expensive.

Handel moonlight desk lamp, with reverse painted pine forest landscape scene centering a full moon, shade 8¼in. long. (Robt. W. Skinner Inc.) $2,000

A Handel brass table lamp, with silvered reflective interior on brass finished three socket standard, 26in. high. (Robt. W. Skinner Inc.) $750

Leaded glass table lamp, attributed to Handel, of mottled green brickwork banded with border of bright pink apple blossoms, 23in. high. (Robt. W. Skinner Inc.) $1,250

Handel parrot lamp, domical Teroma glass shade signed *Handel 7128,* and by artist *Bedigie,* handpainted interior with three colorful parrots, 18in. diam. (Robt. W. Skinner Inc.) $27,500

Handel leaded glass table lamp, Meriden, Connecticut, late 19th century (some leading damage, base polished to high copper gloss), 24in. high. (Skinner Inc.) $1,500

An early 20th century Handel lamp on Hampshire pottery base, with Mosserine shade, 20in. high. (Robt. W. Skinner Inc.) $1,250

Handel type pond lily desk lamp, early 20th century, green slag and white leaded glass full blossom shade, 13¾in. high. (Skinner Inc.) $600

A Handel leaded glass lamp shade with Hampshire Pottery base, early 20th century, signed, 1851, 21in. high. (Robt. W. Skinner Inc.) $4,250

HANDEL

Handel leaded glass table lamp with cone shade. 23½in. high. $3,250

Handel moonlight boudoir lamp, with reverse painted landscape scene with mountains and rolling meadows, 14in. high. (Robt. W. Skinner Inc.) $2,250

Handel type table lamp, painted and decorated, with rust floral design, shade 16in. diameter.
     $1,500

Handel reverse painted lamp, hand painted on the interior with wide multicolored border band of predominantly lavender and fuchsia red scrolls, shade diam. 18in. (Robt. W. Skinner Inc.) $5,000

A Handel adjustable desk lamp, with green glass shade, circa 1920, 12¾in. high. (Robt. W. Skinner Inc.) $900

Handel reverse painted scenic table lamp, Meriden, Connecticut, early 20th century, with brilliant sunset colored tropical island scene, 21in. high. (Skinner Inc.) $3,000

Handel banded poppy table lamp, reverse painted with wide border band of orange poppy blossoms, buds, pods and leaves, shade diam. 18in. (Robt. W. Skinner Inc.)
     $6,000

A Handel leaded glass table lamp, the domed circular shade having rows of honey colored marbled glass segments on the upper section, 59cm. high. (Phillips London) $6,500

A Handel scenic table lamp, handpainted on the interior with a scenic landscape of summer birches and poplar trees, 23in. high. (Robt. W. Skinner Inc.) $3,000

HANDEL

Handel scenic boudoir lamp, hexagonal ribbed textured glass, mounted on bronzed metal *Handel* signed base, 14in. high. (Skinner Inc.) $2,310

One of a pair of leaded glass and patinated metal wall lanterns, possibly Handel, circa 1910, hexagonal verdigris framework, 18in. high. (Skinner Inc.) $2,600

Handel treasure island lamp, textured glass dome shade reverse painted with tropical moonlit coastline scene, 27in. high. (Skinner Inc.) $10,175

Handel-type floral table lamp, dome shade of green and amber leaded slag glass arranged with a wide band of violet blossoms, 23in. high. (Skinner Inc.) $650

Handel-type piano-desk lamp, adjustable roll cylinder shade of leaded green slag glass segments, 14in. high. (Skinner Inc.) $605

One of a pair of Handel wall sconces, early 20th century, oval hammered back plate, suspending cylindrical frosted glass buckle shade, 8^{1}/4in. high. (Skinner Inc.) $850

Leaded glass table lamp, with four repeating clusters of lavender iris blossoms and green spiked leaves, shade diam. 18in. (Robt. W. Skinner Inc.) $550

Handel daffodil table lamp, conical glass shade of sand-textured surface exterior painted with realistic daffodil, 27in. high. (Skinner Inc.) $4,250

Handel scenic table lamp, textured glass shade reverse painted with riverside clusters of tall trees before a mountainous horizon, 24in. high. (Skinner Inc.) $7,150

PAIRPOINT

The Pairpoint Manufacturing Co. started out as electroplaters in New Bedford Mass. in 1880. In 1900, they merged with the mount Washington Glass Co. to become the Pairpoint Corp., making glass only.

Their products were not much influenced by the innovations of Tiffany and Frederick Carder of the Steuben Glassworks, and they continued producing Victorian inspired floral designs.

Late 19th century Pairpoint reverse painted table lamp, Mass., base and shade signed, 21in. high. $1,200

Early 20th century pairpoint puffy boudoir lamp, Mass., 8in. high. $2,000

Early 20th century Pairpoint reverse painted table lamp, New Bedford, base signed and numbered 3011, 22¾in. high. (Robt. W. Skinner Inc.) $2,000

Rare Pairpoint blown-out puffy apple tree lamp, with extraordinary large blown glass shade handpainted on the interior, 15½in. diameter. (Skinner Inc.) $25,000

An early 20th century Pairpoint table lamp with blown-out shade, New Bedford, 14in. diam. (Robt. W. Skinner Inc.) $2,000

A Pairpoint scenic table lamp, handpainted with four nautical scenes of tall ships separated by seashell panels, 23in. high. (Robt. W. Skinner Inc.) $3,000

Pairpoint puffy boudoir lamp, reverse painted blown-out glass shade with colorful pink and lavender pansies, roses and asters, 14½in. high. (Skinner Inc.) $2,000

Pairpoint seascape table lamp, colorfully reverse painted Directoire shade with expansive full round ocean scene, 16in. diam. (Robt. W. Skinner Inc.) $4,500

PAIRPOINT

Pairpoint puffy rose table lamp with tree trunk base, shade 8in. diameter. $2,750

Pairpoint floral and butterfly puffy table lamp, signed, 18in. high. $6,000

Pairpoint reverse painted open top table lamp, signed, 16in. diameter. $4,000

Pairpoint blown-out puffy lilac and trellis lamp, reverse painted with four panels of pink and lavender blossoms against latticework background, 18in. diam. (Robt. W. Skinner Inc.) $7,000

Pairpoint butterflies and roses puffy lamp, quatriform blown-out glass dome, drilled and mounted to gilt metal petal-moulded base, 20½in. high. (Skinner Inc.) $5,200

Pairpoint floral table lamp, large flared "Exeter" glass shade with broad apron of stylized blossoms of pink, beige and amber, 22in. high.
(Skinner) $1,600

A Pairpoint boudoir lamp, with panels of floral sprays mounted on silvered metal standard, 15in. high. (Robt. W. Skinner Inc.) $550

Pairpoint bird-in-tree lamp, handpainted in a highly stylized frieze centering a bird with colorful plumage, 18in. high. (Skinner Inc.) $1,500

Pairpoint seascape boudoir lamp, reverse painted dome shade with whimsical Viking ships, 14½in. high. (Robt. W. Skinner Inc.) $2,000

344

PAIRPOINT

Pairpoint seascape table lamp, reverse painted flared *Exeter* shade with tropical island scene, 26in. high.
(Skinner Inc.) $2,090

Pairpoint seascape table lamp, "Exeter", four ocean scenes enhanced by scallop shell and dolphin panels, 20in. high.
(Skinner Inc.) $1,400

Pairpoint Puffy Poppy Bonnet lamp, deeply blown-out glass shade reverse painted with a profusion of multicolored blossoms and buds, 22in. high.
(Skinner) $10,000

Pairpoint puffy papillon lamp, quatriform blown out shade with four clusters of colorful rose blossoms centering multicolored butterflies painted within, 18in. high.
(Skinner Inc.) $4,840

Pairpoint Scenic Planter lamp, squat mushroom cap Vienna shade reverse painted with two landscape reserves of New England village and sailboat scene, 14in. high.
(Skinner) $2,500

Pairpoint blown-out puffy lamp, squared molded Torino glass shade with rippled exterior surface design overall, 21¹/₂in. high.
(Skinner Inc.) $13,200

Pairpoint scenic lamp, textured glass reverse painted featuring an antlered stag at lakeside, urn-form black metal base, 16in. high.
(Skinner Inc.) $1,870

Pairpoint Puffy Papillon and Roses lamp, mold blown glass shade with four reverse painted clusters of bright red blossoms and blue, yellow and orange butter-flies, 23in. high.
(Skinner) $4,500

Pairpoint Puffy Bride's Bouquet lamp, blown-out rose blossom dome reverse painted as white rose blossoms shaded with pink and yellow, 21in. high.
(Skinner) $8,000

QUEZAL

Quezal glass derives its name from the brightly colored Quezal bird of Central America. It was produced between 1901 and 1920 by Martin Bach Sr. at Brooklyn, New York with the avowed intention of imitating Tiffany's iridescent glass. A notable case is the twelve-light lily lamp, available in both Tiffany and Quezal versions.

Two Quezal gas light shades, both of opal glass in squat bulbed form, 5in. diam. (Robt. W. Skinner Inc.) $350

Quezal art glass shade on gilt lamp base, with four green and gold double hooked and pulled feather repeats, 8in. high. (Robt. W. Skinner Inc.) $800

A Quezal candle lamp, bronzed metal Art Nouveau standard with bell form gold iridescent glass shade signed on rim, 19¼in. high. (Robt. W. Skinner Inc.) $400

A Quezal desk lamp, with curved shaft adorned by a full bodied dragonfly, signed on rim, 17½in. high. (Robt. W. Skinner Inc.) $1,800

Rare Quezal twelve light lily lamp, gold iridescent ribbed blossom-form shades on slender stems arising from bronze leaf-pad base, 20in. high. (Skinner) $5,000

Early 20th century Tiffany bronze bridge lamp, New York, with a Quezal shade, 54½in. high. $5,000

A Quezal iridescent glass and bronze table lamp, decorated externally with green and silver-blue iridescent feathering, 64cm. high. (Phillips) $3,000

ROYCROFT

The Roycroft Craft Community was established in East Aurora NY in 1895 by Elbert Hubbard, following a visit to England in 1894, when he was much influenced by the Arts & Crafts Movement. A copper workshop was opened in 1908, and here many copper lamps were produced, their simplicity of form showing a distinct Art & Crafts influence. Shades, sometimes produced elsewhere by, eg. Steuben, also reflect the stark simplicity of the Arts & Crafts ideal.

STEUBEN

The Steuben Glass Works were founded in 1903 in Corning, New York by Frederick Carder (1864–1963). Here he produced Aurene, his own version of the Peachblow glass originally produced by the New England Glass Co. in imitation of Chinese peachblow porcelain. Fine iridescent glass was also produced and lamps were made in both of these materials. In 1918 the firm merged with the Corning glass works. Steuben glass is still made today.

A Roycroft copper lamp with Steuben gold iridescent glass shade, circa 1910, 16in. high. $5,000

Roycroft hammered copper and mica lamp, E. Aurora, N.Y., circa 1910, no. 903, 14¾in. high. (Robt. W. Skinner Inc.) $3,000

A Steuben Cintra sculptured lamp, of clear frosted glass with pink, blue, white and occasional yellow granules, 21in. high. (Robt. W. Skinner Inc.) $900

Steuben gold iridescent glass shade on Roycroft base, circa 1910, 10in. diameter. $2,500

Bronze table lamp with green swirl glass and calcite shade, probably Steuben, circa 1910, 14in. high. (Robt. W. Skinner Inc.) $1,000

Rare Steuben plum jade acid cut back lamp with gold aurene shades, mounted in gilt metal fittings, 13in. high. (Robt. W. Skinner Inc.) $1,300

A desk lamp with Steuben Aurene shade, bronzed metal standard, mirror luster at top, 13½in. high. (Robt. W. Skinner Inc.) $650

LAMPS
TIFFANY

Art glass and lamps really come together in Louis Comfort Tiffany (1848–1933) and his favrile iridescent glass shades and designs set the standard to which all other manufacturers aspired. One of his typical designs was a cast bronze stem in the shape of a stylized plant, and a shade of multicolored opaque favrile glass, set in irregular lozenges in a bronze mounting of overall tree or flower form.

Tiffany turtleback desk lamp, adjustable textured gold doré bronze cylinder lamp in the graduate pattern, 11¼ in. long. (Skinner Inc.) $2,750

Tiffany spider web lamp with bronze baluster base. $150,000

A Tiffany leaded glass lamp shade on Grueby pottery base, early 20th century, with dome shaped shade in acorn pattern, artist initialed A. L. for Annie Lingley, 17¾ in. high. (Robt. W. Skinner Inc.) $20,000

A Louis Comfort Tiffany bronze leaded glass and favrile glass two-light table lamp, 56cm. high. (Christie's) $8,500

Tiffany bronze and favrile lotus bell lamp, mottled green and white glass segments arranged in bell form geometric progression, signed "Tiffany Studios New York", 21in. high. $26,550

Tiffany bronze and turtleback glass table lamp, nineteen iridescent green tiles bordered above and below by mottled green square and rectangular favrile glass segments, 24in. high.
(Skinner Inc.) $23,000

Tiffany Studios Nautilus' gilt bronze table lamp inset with mother-of-pearl studs, 33.5cm. high. $6,000

Tiffany bronze and favrile glass dragonfly lamp, on conical shade with seven turquoise blue, opal and red-winged dragonflies arranged on leaded glass segments, 22in. high. (Skinner Inc.) $16,500

Tiffany bronze and favrile large linenfold lamp, twelve-sided angular gilt bronze lamp shade with amber fabrique glass panels, 24½in. high. $12,100

Spider web leaded glass, mosaic and bronze table lamp by Tiffany. $150,000

Tiffany bronze and favrile crocus lamp, green and gold amber glass segments arranged in four repeating elements of spring blossoms, 21½in. high. $9,000

Tiffany bronze and favrile apple blossom lamp, domed shade of transparent green segmented background for yellow-centered pink and white blossoms on brown apple tree branches, 22½in. high. $11,000

A Tiffany Studios stained glass dragonfly lamp/pendant, 25.5cm. wide, chain for suspension. (Phillips) $1,000

Tiffany bronze and favrile blue dragonfly lamp, conical tuck-under shade of seven mesh-wing dragonflies with blue bodies and jewel eyes, 22½in. high. (Skinner) $22,000

Tiffany bronze ten-light lily lamp, slender decumbent stem shade holders above lily pad stepped platform base with broad leaves, buds and vines, 16½in. high. (Robt. W. Skinner Inc.) $15,000

Tiffany style glass and bronze dragonfly table lamp, the conical shade composed of seven radiating dragonflies with opalescent purple-pink bodies, height overall 16in. (Butterfield & Butterfield) $2,000

One of a pair of Tiffany Studios three-light, lily-gold favrile glass and bronze table lamps, 33.2cm. high. (Christie's) $9,000

TIFFANY

A Tiffany three-light table
lamp, shade 40.6cm. diam.,
61.5cm. high. (Christie's)
$15,000

A Tiffany Studio lamp with
green-blue Favrile glass
molded as a scarab, N.Y.,
circa 1902, 8½in. high.
(Robt. W. Skinner Inc.)
$3,750

A Tiffany Studios bronze
and glass filigree table lamp,
42.5cm. high. (Christie's)
$5,000

Tiffany bronze lamp with
crocus shade, with three prong
shade holder and six footed
bulbous platform base, 22½in.
high, shade diam. 16in. (Robt.
W. Skinner Inc.) $20,000

A Tiffany Studios favrile
glass and bronze ten-light
lily lamp, 19½in. high.
(Woolley & Wall $9,500

A Tiffany bronze lamp with
spider and web shade, of mottled muted gray-green colored
rectangular panels divided into
six segments, 19in. high. (Robt.
W. Skinner Inc.) $20,000

Early 20th century Tiffany
bronze table lamp with
leaded shade, 22in. high.
(Robt. W. Skinner Inc.)
$3,500

A Tiffany Studios enameled
copper electric lamp base,
circa 1900, 15in. high. (Robt.
W. Skinner Inc.) $4,500

A Tiffany three-light table
lamp, the bronze base bun-
shaped on four ball feet,
41cm. diam. of shade,
63.5cm. high. (Christie's)
$15,000

Lead Favrile glass and bronze
table lamp, by Tiffany Studios,
circa 1910, 25¼in. high. $15,000

Early Tiffany blown-out bronze
and favrile Tyler lamp, shaped
dome shade of leaded glass
segments arranged as twelve
green swirling swags, 24in. high.
(Skinner Inc.) $44,000

A Tiffany Studios 'Dragonfly'
leaded glass and gilt bronze
table lamp, 46.7cm. high.
(Christie's) $35,000

Early 20th century Tiffany
blue iridescent candle
lamp, signed, 1924, New
York, 12¼in. high. (Robt.
W. Skinner Inc.) $1,500

A Tiffany Studios table lamp,
on four-pronged spider ring
attached to matching insert,
17in. high. (Robt. W. Skinner
Inc.) $2,500

A Tiffany Studios gilt bronze
and glass table lamp, stamped
Tiffany Studios New York
590, 48cm. high.(Christie's)
                        $3,500

A Tiffany Studios 'Pansy'
leaded glass and bronze table
lamp, 54cm. high. (Christie's)
                    $10,000

Tiffany bronze and favrile glass
three-light lily lamp, tripartite
upright stems hold gold
iridescent blossom shades, 13in.
high.
(Skinner Inc.) $2,600

An important and rare Tiffany
Studios leaded glass table lamp,
the shallow domed shade edged
with the bodies of bats, 48cm.
high. (Phillips) $100,000

A Federal mahogany
miniature chest of
drawers, 1790-1810,
14½in. wide. $1,500

Antique American lift-top
miniature blanket chest in pine,
14½ x 8in.
(Eldred's) $633

A 19th century painted
miniature ladder-back armchair, American. $400

An American, 18th century,
miniature Queen Anne maple
and pine slant-front desk,
with a cherrywood mirror,
the desk 11in. high.
(Christie's) $5,500

Late 19th century miniature
Chippendale walnut slant-
front desk, American, 7¼in.
high. (Christie's) $2,500

A 19th century, American,
miniature classical maple
fiddleback chair, 10¾in.
high, 8¼in. wide. (Christie's)
                         $900

A miniature Federal secretary, America, circa 1830,
13½in. wide. $4,000

A classical miniature carved
mahogany chest-of-drawers,
New York, 1830–1840, on
carved lion's-paw feet, 23¾in.
wide.
(Christie's) $1,980

Miniature painted Chippendale
tall chest, made by Jabez Rice,
Massachusetts, early 19th
century, painted brown, 15⅜in.
high.
(Skinner Inc.) $8,800

An American, 19th century, miniature painted bannister-back armchair, 9½in. high. (Christie's) $800

Early 19th century miniature Federal mahogany tilt-top tea table, American, 9in. high. (Christie's) $1,500

Miniature paint decorated Windsor armchair, America, last half of 19th century, the black ground painted with floral decoration, 8¼in. high. (Skinner Inc.) $850

A 19th century miniature Federal mahogany picture mirror, American, 9½in. high. (Christie's) $2,000

An American, 19th century, miniature Federal mahogany four-post bedstead with canopy, 15½in. high. (Christie's) $500

A 19th century miniature, Empire mahogany and painted chest-of-drawers, American, 19½in. wide. $1,250

A miniature Chippendale mahogany desk and bookcase, Rhode Island, 1760-80, 16in. high. (Christie's) $3,200

Two 19th century miniature painted side chairs, American, 9¾in. and 8¼in. high. (Christie's) $900

An American late Federal mahogany miniature chest of drawers, 10in. wide. $1,750

A 19th century miniature green painted pine blanket chest, American, 9½in. high. (Christie's) $600

A miniature putty grained blanket box, American, circa 1825, 14in. long. (Robt. W. Skinner Inc.) $1,800

A painted miniature pine blanket chest, attributed to Joseph Long Lehn, Pennsylvania, circa 1890, decorated with floral decals and landscapes, 8½in. wide. (Christie's) $935

A miniature painted blanket box, signed Edward Cornell and dated December 24, 1809, 13½in. high. (Robt. W. Skinner Inc.) $2,600

Miniature 19th century tin mantel clock with fluted base, 5in. high. $500

19th century tin miniature fireplace and tongs, 4in. long. $125

19th century miniature painted tin piano and stool, with hinged keyboard cover, 3¼ x 3½in. $125

Miniature country Chippendale bureau, America, late 18th century, raised on a molded bracket base (refinished, minor repairs), 14in. high. (Skinner Inc.) $400

Bird's-eye maple cannon ball doll's bed, America, circa 1830, the turned base on ball posts, 8¾in. high. (Robt. W. Skinner Inc.) $500

A fine Federal inlaid maple and mahogany dressing mirror, Philadelphia, 1800-1810, on ogee bracket feet, 22½in. wide. (Christie's) $1,320

A Federal giltwood verre eglomisé mirror, probably Boston, 1810–1820, with broken molded cornice above a frieze with vines and berries flanked by flowerheads over an eglomisé panel depicting a naval hero, 21in. wide. (Christie's) $2,090

A rare Chippendale carved mahogany dressing mirror, Boston, 1765–1775, with molded and gilt frame between two canted double-bead molded supports, 16³/₈in. high. (Christie's) $6,050

Federal giltwood looking glass, America, first quarter 19th century, with eglomisé tablet of "Harmony", 46in. high. (Skinner Inc.) $3,300

A Gustav Stickley hall mirror, style no. 66, circa 1905-06, 28in. high, 36in. wide. (Skinner Inc.) $1,500

Federal giltwood looking glass, America, early 19th century, projecting molded cornice hung with spherules, 45in. high. (Skinner Inc.) $413

Painted Chippendale mirror, New England, mid 18th century, the shaped crest over molded   and incised frame, 19¾in. high. (Skinner Inc.) $6,000

Mirror with box base in green and amber glass, 23¹/₂in. high, 1940s. (Muir Hewitt) $100

Classical giltwood mirror, America, second quarter, 19th century, the projecting molded cornice hung with acorn spherules above a tablet, 55in. high. (Skinner Inc.) $3,575

A 19th century Federal gilt-wood girandole mirror, 54½in. high, 40in. wide. (Christie's) $7,700

Giltwood mirror, probably Philadelphia, circa 1830, half round colonnettes orna-mented with raised floral baskets, 32½ x 22in. (Skinner Inc.) $650

Federal mahogany veneered inlaid and parcel gilt looking glass, England/America, late 18th century, 57in. high. (Skinner Inc.) $27,500

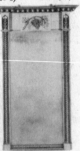

A classical giltwood mirror, probably Boston, 1805–1830, the broken molded cornice hung with acorns over a frieze centered by a fruiting grape vine flanked by ogee-arched niches, 67½in. high. (Christie's) $6,050

A Chippendale mahogany and giltwood mirror, labeled by James Musgrove, Philadelphia, circa 1780, the pierced and scrolled pediment centering a carved phoenix, 30in. high. (Christie's New York) $3,300

A classical carved giltwood verre églomisé mirror, New York, 1815–1825, the broken molded pediment above a verre églomisé panel depicting a tropical island and a ship, 47in. high. (Christie's) $1,650

A Federal giltwood and verre eglomisé mirror, Boston, Massachusetts, 1790–1810, a large rectangular verre eglomisé panel painted with a romantic landscape, 48½in. (Christie's) $3,850

A late Federal mahogany shaving mirror, William Fisk, Boston, Massachusetts, 1810–1825, swiveling between baluster and ring-turned supports with ball finials above a rectangular case, 24in high. (Christie's) $935

Labeled Federal giltwood and eglomisé mirror, Cermenati & Monfrino, Boston, circa 1806, tablet with naval engagement, 32¼ x 17in. (Skinner Inc.) $660

Chippendale mahogany looking glass, labeled Peter Grinnell & Son, Providence, Rhode Island, early 19th century, 39in. high. (Skinner Inc.) $550

Shop-O'-The Crafters mahogany wall mirror, Ohio, 1910, 27½in. high, 30½in. wide. (Robt. W. Skinner Inc.) $1,000

Art Deco dressing table mirror in wood and plaster, 14in. high. (Muir Hewitt) $100

A gilt pier mirror, probably American, 1815-1825, the broken rectangular cornice hung with acorn pendants, 58in. high. (Christie's New York) $2,200

A Federal carved giltwood convex mirror, American, early 19th century, with carved spreadwing eagle perched on a rocky plinth flanked by scrolled leafage above a cylindrical molded frame, 34in. high. (Christie's) $4,400

A painted and carved Federal courting mirror, painted in old red and black with yellow ochre, circa 1820, 12in. high. (Robt. W. Skinner Inc.) $4,750

Federal giltwood and eglomisé looking glass, America, early 19th century, 58¾in. high. (Skinner Inc.) $1,200

A table top mirror on shoe foot base, by Gustav Stickley, circa 1910, 21¼in. high. (Robt. W. Skinner Inc.) $850

Giltwood looking glass, America, second quarter 19th century, 52in. high. (Skinner Inc.) $1,500

A well presented radio controlled, electric powered model of the Mississippi Stern Wheel Steamer Creole Queen, built by R. Burgess, Mayfield, 15½ in. x 48in.
(Christie's) $750

An extremely fine and detailed builder's model of the steel schooner rigged single screw steam yacht Wakiva, built by Ramage & Ferguson Ltd. of Leith for W.E. Cox, Boston, Massachusetts, 19in. x 52in.
(Christie's) $60,000

Wood model of a coastal steamer, America, 20th century, (possibly the Fall River line), 33in. long.
(Skinner Inc.) $385

An early 20th century American steamship model, diorama scene in mahogany case, 48in. wide. $1,250

A contemporary mid 19th century model of the Paddle Steamer 'Atlanta', 18½ x 41in.
                                             $10,000

Shadow box with model of the 'Cumberland', America, late 19th century, of polychrome wood, paper and thread, 15½ in. x 26in.
(Skinner Inc.) $1,000

Painted wood model of the "Constitution", American Man-of-War, fully rigged, mounted in inlaid mahogany and glass case, 44½ in. wide.
(Skinner Inc.) $2,860

Wooden ship model of the New Bedford whaler 'Alice Mandell', well detailed, height 24in. (Eldred's) $1,870

The whaleship "Sunbeam", plank on beam construction using many fine hardwoods with mahogany hull, pearwood deck, and basswood masts, 67 x 23 x 52in. (Eldred's)   **$3,850**

Cased, carved and painted ship model, America, late 19th/early 20th century, polychrome model of the steam ship City New York, 35½in. wide. (Skinner Inc.)   **$1,400**

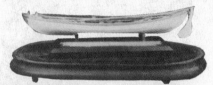

Painted wood model of a whaleboat, early 20th century, fitted with oars, harpoons, lances, tubs, lines, etc., mounted on stand, 23in. long. (Skinner Inc.)   **$715**

Painted wood model of a whaling boat, America, late 19th/early 20th century, mounted on a wooden base within a glass dome, 15½in. long. (Skinner Inc.)   **$770**

Painted wood canoe, "Old Town, Maine", early 20th century, the painted and stencil decorated wooden canoe with two caned seats, the body with stenciled line decoration, 47½in. long. (Butterfield & Butterfield)   **$12,100**

Shadow box with half-model of the three-masted ship "Lolo", signed *E. Ellard*, America, late 19th/early 20th century, with painted background, 27¾in. wide. (Skinner Inc.)   **$880**

Shadowbox with model of the brig "Alice", America, early 20th century, polychrome wood, with finely detailed painted back drop, 27¼in. wide. (Skinner Inc.)   **$880**

A finely engineered model of
an early 19th century four
column single cylinder beam
pumping engine originally
designed by D. E. Alban,
9½ x 9in. $1,250

Large monoplane model, made
by Charles R. Witteman, Staten
Island, New York, circa 1912,
62in. long, wingspan 78in.
                            $2,000

Wood and brass silo by G. Elias
& Bro., Buffalo, NY, circa 1900,
the varnished model of cylinder
shape with removable cone top,
25½in. high.
(Butterfield & Butterfield)
                            $2,475

A rare late nineteenth live
steam, spirit fired, stationary
steam set, with brass pot
boiler and fretwork firebox,
8½in. high, possibly American.
(Christie's) $288

Painted and metal brass
'braker' electric car, American,
circa 1896, the black painted
working model with a spindle
backseat, 10in. long.
(Butterfield & Butterfield)
                            $2,475

Painted brass and steel high
wheel bicycle (Penny Farthing),
American, late 19th/early 20th
century, the red painted
working model with handlebar
grips above a curved frame with
seat, 14in. high.
(Butterfield & Butterfield)
                            $3,850

Early 20th century American
wooden gabled roof doll's
house with glass windows,
24¾in. high. $550

An early single vertical
cylinder open crank gas
engine, probably Amer-
ican, 24 x 9in. $500

American diorama of an early
19th century hallway, circa
1950, fitted with dolls and
furniture, 19½in. wide. $400

Modern type money boxes began to appear in Europe in the 17th century and in the 18th, Staffordshire pottery money banks in the form of cottages were popular. 19th century Prattware examples also fetch good sums.

It was the 19th century that saw the manufacture of money boxes designed especially for children. Understandably, these had to be of a tougher material than pottery, and the first were of cast iron. Often, these were in the shape of animal or human heads, open mouthed to receive the coins, or of figures and buildings with slits in the top.

In comparison with the United States or even Europe, British versions were fairly unimaginative. Few mechanical versions were produced (though find one by John Harper & Co. and it could be worth a considerable amount).

It is however American money boxes which fetch the highest prices today. During the last 30 years of the 19th century such firms as Shepard Hardware and J & E Stevens of Cromwell, CT produced cast iron banks in such forms as acrobats, bucking broncos, and Punch & Judy. Most were mechanical, some operated simply by the weight of the coin, while others had a lever or catch action. The Jolly Nigger was a favorite example, and when a coin was placed on the tongue the eyes would roll. This 'Sambo' type was copied in the UK, though usually as a 'still bank' with no mechanical action.

There have been many more modern replicas of Sambo and his female counterpart Dinah, some of which have been aged to increase their value.

'Bad Accident' cast iron mechanical bank, J. & E. Stevens, Co., 1891-1911, 10.3/8in. long. $1,750

American cast iron money bank, 'Hall's Lilliput Bank'. (Phillips) $600

American made Oliver Hardy money bank, circa 1950. $40

A 'Jolly Nigger' mechanical money bank, in the form of a negro wearing a top hat, 21.5cm. high. (Phillips) $150

'World's Fair' cast iron mechanical bank, J. & E. Stevens, Co., pat. 1893, 8¼in. long. $1,500

'Tammany Bank', a cast iron mechanical bank, the seated gentleman with articulated right arm, 5¾in. high, by J. and E. Stevens Co., circa 1875. $300

American late 19th century Paddy and the Pig cast·iron mechanical bank, 8in. high. $1,500

Late 19th century American cast-iron leap frog mechanical bank, by Shepard Hardware Co., 7½in. wide. $1,000

Late 19th century American cast-iron 'Santa Claus' mechanical bank, 6in. high. $1,500

Pussycat chromium cast money bank, with key, circa 1935. (Auction Team Koeln) $50

Stevens cast-iron Indian and Bear mechanical bank, Conn., circa 1875, 10.9/16in. long. $2,000

'Stollwerck Bros. Post Savings-Bank', modeled as a chocolate dispenser, circa 1911, 6½in. high. $500

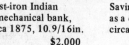

A mechanical bank, girl skipping rope by J. & E. Stevens, designed by James H. Bowen, 8in. high. (Christie's) $25,000

Late 19th century cast iron 'Speaking Dog' mechanical bank, by J. & E. Stevens Co., 7¼in. long. $2,000

Stump Speaker, a cast iron mechanical moneybox, with movable right arm and unusual counterbalanced talking mouth, pat. June 8 1886, 25cm. high. (Christie's S. Ken) $1,750

A cast iron 'Eagle and Eaglets' mechanical bank, by J. & E. Stevens, patented 1883, 6¾in. long. **$800**

'Chief Big Moon' cast iron mechanical bank, J. & E. Stevens, Co., pat. 1899, 10in. long. **$2,000**

Organ and Monkey mechanical bank, patented 1882, 7¼in. high. **$700**

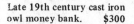

Late 19th century cast iron owl money bank. **$300**

'Trick Dog', a mechanical cast-iron moneybox, by J. & E. Stevens, circa 1888, 8¾ x 3in. **$1,000**

Jolly Nigger bank, with movable right arm, in original paintwork, by Shepard Hardware Co., Buffalo, N.Y., circa 1883, 7in. high. (Christie's S. Ken) **$400**

Plated clockwork Bulldog Savings Bank by Ives Blakeslee & Co. 18cm. high. (Auktionsverket, Stockholm) **$1,250**

Wooden Jug savings bank, with key, circa 1920. (Auction Team Koeln) **$40**

A mechanical cast iron money box, as a football player with articulated right leg, causing the player to shoot a coin into a goal and ring a bell, circa 1890, 10½in. long. **$1,750**

A J & E Stevens painted cast iron 'Creedmoor Bank', designed by James Bowen, marksman firing at target, 6½in. high. (Christie's S. Ken) $450

An amusing savings bank in the form of a typewriter. (Auction Team Koeln) $50

Late 19th century American reclining 'Chinaman' cast-iron mechanical bank, 8in. long. $3,000

An unusual tin 'Combination Safe' money box. $75

A cast iron novelty bank, by J. & E. Stevens Co., the building with front door opening to reveal a cashier, American, late 19th century. $750

Late 19th century American cast-iron 'Punch & Judy' mechanical bank, by Shepard Hardware Co., 7½in. high. $1,500

A cast iron money bank of a golly, 15.5cm. high. $250

'Bull Dog Bank' cast iron mechanical bank, J. & E. Stevens, Co., pat. 1880, 7½in. high. $1,250

Late 19th century American cast-iron 'Trick Pony' mechanical bank, by Shepard Hardware Co., 7in. wide. $1,250

A mechanical bank, a horse race, with flanged base, by J. & E. Stevens, designed by John D. Hall, 8in. high. (Christie's) $12,500

A cast iron two frogs mechanical bank, American, late 19th century, 8½in. long. $1,350

Late 19th century cast-iron Hall's Excelsior bank, American, 5¼in. high. $800

A 20th century Kenton cast iron flatiron building bank, America, 8¼in. high. $500

A cast iron 'Always Did 'Spise a Mule' money bank, American, circa 1897, by J. Stevens & Co., 10in. long. $2,000

Late 19th century American 'Uncle Sam' mechanical bank, by Shepard Hardware Co., 11½in. high. $700

Late 19th century cast iron clown mechanical bank, 9½in. high. $1,250

Lion and Monkeys cast iron mechanical bank, Kyser & Rex Co., Pat. 1883, 10in. long. $900

A 20th century English cast-iron 'Dinah' mechanical bank, by John Harper & Co. Ltd., 6½in. high. $300

1907 Buick "F" Touring, chassis no: 16313, two cylinders, 2.6 litre, right hand drive, driven by a single chain with two forward gears and one reverse.
(Christie's) $17,671

1962 Chevrolet Corvette convertible roadster, Reg. No. SSU778, V8 engine, overhead valve, 327cu. in. (5,360cc), 250bhp, recently totally restored, the body removed, the chassis overhauled and the car repainted in white. (Christie's London) $40,898

1930 Cadillac V-16 Madam X Imperial Landaulette, coachwork by Fleetwood. Body no. 3, Cadillac Style no. 4108 C, engine; 45 degree V-16; 3in. 76.2mm. bore; 4in. 101.6mm, stroke; 452.6cu. in. 7,412 c.c.
(Christie's New York) $522,500

1964 A.C. Cobra 289 two-seater sports, coachwork by A.C. Cars, Thames Ditton, engine; Ford V8 cylinder 4,727 c.c.
(Christie's New York) $225,500

1971 Cadillac Eldorado convertible, engine: V-8 cylinder, cast iron block, bore and stroke 4.30in. x 4.30in., 8200cc, overhead valve, pushrod actuated, compression ratio 9:1, 365bhp at 4400rpm, transmission, Turbo Hydra-matic longitudinally mounted with transfer case, suspension: front, independent via torsion bar and A-arms.
(Christie's) $10,580

1937 Packard 'Super Eight' town car, coachwork by Brewster & Company, New York, color, silver and maroon coachwork with black leather top, salmon cloth and black leather interior, engine; eight-cylinder in-line, L-head, two side valves per cylinder, cast-iron block, detachable alloy cylinder heads, 5240 c.c. (320 cu. in.), bore and stroke 80mm. x 127mm., compression ratio 6.5:1, 135 b.h.p. at 3200 r.p.m., single coil ignition, Detroit Lubricator carburettor.
(Christie's) $65,445

1902 Thomas Runabout, engine; water-cooled, single cylinder, 106.3 cu. in. (1,743 c.c.)), bore and stroke 121mm. x 152mm., transmission; three-speed, brakes; two wheels at the rear, single chain drive.
(Christie's) $24,200

1926 Lincoln Sport Roadster Model L–151, coachwork by Locke & Co., engine; V.8 side-valve, cast-iron block and cylinder heads, 357.8 cu. in. displacement (5,865.5 c.c.), wheelbase; 12ft. 0in., price when new $4,500, left-hand drive.
(Christie's)   **$77,000**

1939 Packard Six (1700) Station Wagon (Woody), coachwork by J.T. Cantrell, chassis No. 1700–2192, engine No. B–18672A, color; black coachwork with wooden sectioned bodywork, engine; side-cylinder in-line cast-iron monobloc, six valve, L-head, 245 cu. in., wheel base 10ft. 2in., front track 4ft. 11¼in., rear track 5ft., left-hand drive.
(Christie's)   **$35,200**

1931 Ford Model A roadster, color, black coachwork with brown interior trim, engine; four-cylinder in-line, water-cooled, cast-iron block, detachable cylinder head, side valves, 3300 c.c., bore and stroke 98.0mm. x 107mm., compression ratio 4.2:1, 40 b.h.p. at 2300 r.p.m., Ford positive feed carburettor, electric start.
(Christie's)   **$23,757**

1957 Ford Thunderbird Convertible, engine: V8, overhead valve, 5,800cc, 300bhp, power steering; gearbox: automatic; brakes: four wheel hydraulic; left hand drive. (Christie's London)   **$27,791**

A 1950 Buick 50L Super Sedan, chassis no. 15892395, with V8 124 H.P engine, excellent condition.
(Finarte)   **$14,229**

A 1965 Ford Mustang Convertible 289, chassis no. 8TO1C146048 with 8 cylinder, 289 brake hp engine, automatic gearbox and contemporary radio-stereo 8.
(Finarte)   **$20,454**

1969 Eagle (Santa-Ana) Indy single-seat race car, chassis no. 702, Manufacturer: All American Racers Inc, Santa Ana, California, color: dark blue with sponsor graphics as driven by Dan Gurney.
(Christie's New York)   **$143,000**

A rare pewter pint infusion pot, probably by Robert Palethorp, Jr., Philadelphia, 1817-1821, the scroll handle with three piercings, 13cm. high. (Christie's) $176

A pewter porringer, New England, late 18th/early 19th century, with a crown handle, unmarked, 13cm. diam. (Christie's) $286

Pewter coffee pot, Roswell Gleason (active 1822–1871), Dorchester, Massachusetts, mid 19th century, 11in. high. (Skinner Inc.) $250

Pewter coffee pot, Josiah Danforth, Middletown, Connecticut, early 19th century, 11in. high. (Skinner Inc.) $1,100

Three American pewter coffeepots, Josiah Danforth, Middletown, Connecticut, Boardman and Co., New York, R. Dunham, Portland, Maine, 19th century. (Butterfield & Butterfield) $1,760

A fine pewter quart tankard, by John Will, New York, 1752-1774, with a double-domed cover, 18.1cm. high, overall. (Christie's) $16,500

A pewter plate, by William Kirby, New York, 1760-1793, with single reed brim and a hammered booge, 9in. diam. (Christie's) $935

Large pewter flagon, by Samuel Danforth, Hartford, Connecticut, circa 1800, the domed molded cover over cylindrical body, 12in. high. (Robt. W. Skinner Inc.) $500

A pewter basin, by William Danforth, Middletown, Connecticut, 1792-1820, with a single reed brim, 20cm. diam. (Christie's New York) $935

368

PEWTER

Pewter flagon, Roswell Gleason, Dorchester, Massachusetts, mid 19th century, 10in. high. (Skinner Inc.) $450

A fine and rare pewter teapot by Peter Young, New York, 1775-1785, or Albany, 1785-1795, the domed cover with a beaded edge, 7¼in. high. (Christie's) $30,800

A pewter plate, "Love" Touch, Philadelphia, 1750-1800, with single reed brim, 21.3cm. diam. (Christie's) $286

One of three pewter fluid lamps, 19th century, two with acorn front, one with strap handle, marked *Curtis, New York*, the largest lamp 9¾in. high. (Christie's) (Three) $385

Pair of American pewter teapots, William Calder, Providence, Rhode Island, early 19th century, 9½in. high. (Butterfield & Butterfield) $550

A rare pewter funnel, by Frederick Bassett, New York or Hartford, 1761-1800, marked with Laughlin touch 465 (bruises), 6½in. long. (Christie's) $1,980

A Federal pewter pitcher, Boardman and Hart, New York, fl. 1828–1877, with flaring lip and peaked applied handle, 7¾in. high. (Christie's) $990

A pewter basin by William Will, Philadelphia, 1764-1798, with molded everted rim, marked in the center with Laughlin touch 542, 16.2cm. (Christie's) $3,190

A pewter pint mug, by William Will, Philadelphia, 1764-1798, the scroll handle with a bud terminal, 4½in. high. (Christie's) $8,250

A pitcher of baluster form, by Daniel Curtiss, 1822-40, marked with Laughlin touch 523, 7¾in. high. $900

A teapot of pyriform, by Luther or Thomas D. Boardman, circa 1840, 7¼in. high. $700

A vase-shaped pitcher, by George Richardson, 1828-45, marked with Jacobs touch 237, 7in. high. $425

A flagon with stepped domed lid, by Boardman & Co., N.Y., 1825-27, marked 'XX' and Laughlin touch 431, 12½in. high. $3,250

A tapering cylindrical mug, by Henry Will, N.Y., 1761-76, marked with Laughlin touch 491, 6¼in. high. $2,000

A small covered pitcher, by Simpson & Benham, N.Y., 1845-47, 6¼in. high. $350

A small pitcher, by Boardman & Hart, N.Y., 1830-50, marked with Laughlin touch 437, 4in. high. $350

A plate, by Frederick Bassett, N.Y., 1761-80 and 1785-99, marked with Montgomery touch, 8.3/8in. diam. $250

A cylindrical tankard, by F. Bassett, N.Y., marked on interior with Laughlin touch 468, 7in. high. $10,000

A covered sugar bowl, by Hiram Yale & Co., 1822-31, 6in. high. $475

Late 18th century porringer with dolphin handle, New London or Hartford, 5½in. diam. $1,500

A teapot, by Wm. Will, Phila., 1764-98, marked on inside with Laughlin touches 538 and 539, 6¼in. high. $25,000

A beaker, by Boardman & Hart, N.Y., 1828-53, 3.1/8in. high. $150

A tapering cylindrical mug, by Frederick Bassett, N.Y., 1761-80, marked with Montgomery touch, 4½in. high. $1,250

A flagon with a domed lid and scrolling thumbpiece, by Boardman & Co., N.Y., 1825-27, marked with Montgomery touch, 11.1/8in. high. $750

A covered pitcher of baluster form, by Thos. D. and S. Boardman, 1830-50, marked with Laughlin touch 435, 10in. high. $450

A circular pewter salt, attributed to Wm. Will, Phila., 1764-98, 2¼in. high. $800

A tankard, by Thos. D. & Sherman Boardman, marked with Laughlin touch 428, 8in. high. $6,500

A covered sugar bowl, by G. Richardson, Rhode Island, 1830-45, 5in. high. $2,750

A ship's hanging fluid lamp, by H. Yale and S. Curtis, N.Y., 1858-67, marked with Montgomery touch, 5in. high. $1,000

Early 19th century pewter pint mug, maker's mark T.D. & S.B., America, 4½in. high. $1,000

A beaker with two incised mid-bands on a single beaded base, by T. Boardman & Co., N.Y., 1822-25, marked with Laughlin touch 425, 3in. high. $250

A mug with double scroll handle, by Boardman & Hart, N.Y., 1827-50, 4½in. high. $750

A beaker, by Rufus Dunham, 1837-60, marked with Montgomery touch, 3.3/8in. high. $150

A tapering cylindrical tankard, by Wm. J. Ellsworth, N.Y., 1767-98, 9½in. high. $4,000

A circular plate, by Thos. Danforth II or III, marked with Montgomery touch, 9½in. diam. $1,250

A tankard with S scroll handle, by Parks Boyd, Phila., 1795-1819, marked with Laughlin touch 546, 7½in. high. $2,750

A tapering cylindrical pewter cann by Wm. Will, Phila., 1764-98, 5,7/8in. high. $4,000

An oval shaped teapot with a domed oval cover, American, 1790-1810, 7½in. high. $800

A Britannia flagon by Boardman & Co., N.Y., 1825-27, 12¼in. high. $1,250

A lighthouse coffee pot, by Israel Trask, Mass., 1813-56, 12¼in. high. $800

Pair of mid 19th century candlesticks, American, 9¾in. high, together with a modern pair, 7in. high. $450

A tapering, cylindrical flagon, by Boardman & Co., N.Y., 1825-27, marked 'X' and a Laughlin touch 431, 8in. high. $2,500

A cylindrical flagon, by Boardman & Co., N.Y., 1825-27, marked with Montgomery touch, 12½in. high. $3,000

A circular salt, the rim and footrim with a beaded molding, attributed to Wm. Will, Phila., 1764-98, 2¼in. high. $800

A coffee pot of shaped baluster form, by Luther Boardman, Mass., 1834-37, 11in. high. $350

A coffee pot of pyriform shape, by Roswell Gleason, Mass., 1821-71, 10¾in. high. $150

A globular teapot, by Chas. Yale, Conn., 1817-35, 8in. high. $225

A porringer with everted brim and curved sides, probably by R. Lee, 1795-1816, 4½in. diam. $325

A footed, vase-shaped pitcher, by Hiram Yale & Co., 1822-31, 13½in. high. $700

A mug on molded flaring base with double scroll handle, by T. Boardman & Co., N.Y., 1822-25, marked with Laughlin touch 432, 4½in. high. $700

A lighthouse coffee pot, by G. Richardson, Boston, 1818-28, 10½in. high. $450

Late 18th/early 19th century beaker, American, 3in. high. $150

A pewter basin, marked on the interior with two eagle touches and the 'Richmond Warranted' touch, by Thos. Danforth, Virginia, circa 1807-12, 11.7/8in. diam. $3,500

A ship's hanging lamp, by Yale & Curtis, N.Y., 1858-67, 7.7/8in. high. $750

A globular shaped teapot with a domed lid, by Roswell Gleason, Mass., 1830-40, with Jacobs touch 147, 7½in. high. $200

A porringer, by Thos. D. and S. Boardman, CT., 1810-30, the handle marked with Laughlin touch 428, 4in. diam. $425

Early 19th century pewter gimbal lamp, America, 6in. high. $600

A lighthouse coffee pot, by Wm. Calder, Rhode Island, 1817-56, marked with Laughlin touch 350, 11¾in. high. $350

A coffee pot of baluster form, by Leonard, Reed & Barton, Mass., 1835-40, 12¾in. high. $450

A pewter flagon with a domed lid, by Boardman & Co., N.Y., circa 1825-30, 12.1/8in. high. $2,500

Late 18th century porringer, with beaded brim and Penn. tab handle, 5.3/8in. diam. $175

A pewter circular plate, marked on base with 'Love' touch, Laughlin 868, Phila., circa 1750-1800, 8½in. diam. $400

A circular porringer, by S. Hamlin, marked with Laughlin touch 337, 5.5/8in. diam. $700

Late 18th century porringer, New England, 4½in. diam. $350

A globular shaped teapot, by Israel Trask, Mass., circa 1813-56, 7½in. high. $325

Pair of mid 19th century fluid lamps, each with a brass double wick holder, 6½in. high. $250

A circular pewter plate, Phila., marked on base with 'Love' touch, Laughlin 868, circa 1750-1800, 7¾in. diam. $350

A circular porringer with beaded brim and dolphin handle, by S. Danforth, marked with Laughlin touch 401, 5.5/8in. diam. $3,500

A circular pewter plate, by J. C. Heyne, P.A., circa 1756-80, marked with initial and Jacobs touch 169, 6.3/8in. diam. $7,000

A globular teapot, by Thomas D. and Sherman Boardman, marked with Laughlin touch 428, 7½in. high. $300

A circular plate, by F. Bassett, N.Y., 1761-80 and 1785-99, marked with Laughlin touches 467 and 464a, 9in. diam. $450

One of a set of mid 19th century American chalices, 8in. high. $700

Daguerreotype of a man holding a large iron worker's hammer, American, circa 1850. $400

Ralph Steiner, "Always- Camel AD", 1922, printed 1981, gelatin silver print, 3⅞ x 5in., signed. (Butterfield & Butterfield) $605

An early salt print of a young black boy, America, circa 1855, 12½ x 11in. $2,000

Ambrotype of a volunteer fireman, American, circa 1860, 1/6th plate image. $150

Daguerreotype showing a man holding a horse, American, circa 1850. $400

Tintype of a black nurse holding a white baby, America, 1866. $125

Outside daguerreotype ¼ plate image showing twenty-two school children and the school mistress, America, circa 1845. $750

Last photograph of Lincoln, 1865, copy enlargement 8 x 10in. $100

W. Eugene Smith, "Doctors", circa 1950, gelatin silver print, 13⅛ x 19¼in., photographer's name stamp in ink. (Butterfield & Butterfield) $550

Marion Post Wolcott, "Transportation for 'Hepcats', Louisville, KY", 1940, printed 1978, gelatin silver print, 6⁵/₈ x 9¹/₈in.
(Butterfield & Butterfield) $990

USA: Cleveland, Ohio-Cleveland baseball team, with crowd of onlookers and carriages beyond, 29 x 42cm. $979

USA: Cincinnati, Ohio, one of a fine four section panorama, looking north across the Ohio River, dated 1865, each 31 x 39cm., 152cm. long overall.(Phillips) Four $4,984

Weegee, Hands and Purse, circa 1940s, gelatin silver print, 13¹/₂ x 10³/₄in., the photographer's name stamp (three times) on verso.
(Butterfield & Butterfield) $715

William Klein — New York 1954 — Gelatin silver print, image size 13¾ x 9½in. photographer's signature and print date '1977'.
(Christie's) $881

Lou Stouman, '12 midnight, Times Square, N.Y.C.', 1940, printed later, gelatin silver print, 11⁵/₈ x 8⁵/₈in., signed in ink.
(Butterfield & Butterfield) $330

Walker Evans, 'Sharecropper, Hale County, Alabama', 1936, gelatin silver print, 9¹/₂ x 7⁵/₈in., framed.
(Butterfield & Butterfield) $2,475

Dorothea Lange, "Company housing for cotton workers near Corcorn, California", 1940s, gelatin silver print, 7⁶/₈ x 9⁶/₈in.
(Butterfield & Butterfield) $715

André Kertész, Snow street scene, New York, 1958, gelatin silver print, 6³/₄ x 4³/₄in., mounted as Christmas card on hand-made paper with untrimmed edges.
(Christie's) $1,278

PHOTOGRAPHS

USA: Richmond, Virginia, view of main street during flood, with crowds of on-lookers, signed and dated in negative 'Rees & Co., Oct 1 1870', 27 x 34cm. (Phillips)
$3,026

Edward S. Curtis, 'Aphrodite, (Spirit of the Sea)', circa 1920, blue-toned gelatin silver print, 10¹/₂ x 13¹/₂ in., signed with the *Curtis LA* copyright insignia. (Butterfield & Butterfield)
$1,430

Imogen Cunningham, 'Magnolia blossom', 1925, printed 1930s, gelatin silver print, 7¹/₂ x 9³/₈ in., signed in pencil on the mount. (Butterfield & Butterfield)
$15,400

Barbara Morgan, "Martha Graham–Letter to the World", 1940, printed 1980, gelatin silver print, 10³/₈ x 13¹/₄in., signed. (Butterfield & Butterfield)
$660

Diane Arbus, 'A family one evening at a nudist camp', 1965, printed later by Neil Selkirk, gelatin silver print, 15 x 15in., dry mounted covering the signature in ink. (Butterfield & Butterfield)
$1,045

Weegee, 'New Year's Eve at Sammy's-on-the-Bowery', 1943, printed later, gelatin silver print, 8¹/₄ x 12⁵/₈in., *The Weegee Collection* blindstamp in the margin. (Butterfield & Butterfield)
$770

Philippe Halsman, "John Steinbeck", 1957, gelatin silver print, 19¹/₂ x 15³/₄in., signed and titled in pencil. (Butterfield & Butterfield)
$2,090

Imogen Cunningham, "Magnolia blossom", 1925, printed circa 1979, gelatin silver print, 10⁵/₈ x 13¹/₂in. (Butterfield & Butterfield)
$1,760

Margaret Bourke-White, "Frank Profitt, folk singer", 1940s, gelatin silver print, 13²/₈ x 9⁶/₈in., framed. (Butterfield & Butterfield)
$2,475

Lewis Hine, 2 photographs: "Baltimore cannery", and Four schoolboys, both circa 1910, gelatin silver prints, the first 4³/₄ x 6⁵/₈in.
(Butterfield & Butterfield)
$605

Ansel Adams, "Dogwood, Yosemite National Park, California", 1938, printed 1970s, gelatin silver print, 13¹/₂ x 9¹/₂in., signed in pencil on mount.
(Butterfield & Butterfield)
$3,850

Ralph Steiner, "American baroque", 1929, printed 1949, gelatin silver print, 7⁷/₈ x 9⁷/₈in., signed and dated in pencil on verso.
(Butterfield & Butterfield)
$1,760

Peter Stackpole, "Minsky's dressing room", 1937, printed later, gelatin silver print, 9³/₈ x 7³/₈in., signed in pencil.
(Butterfield & Butterfield)
$550

Philippe Halsman, "Nixon jumping in the White House", 1955, printed 1969, gelatin silver print, 14 x 11in., signed, titled, and dated in pencil.
(Butterfield & Butterfield)
$935

William Heick, "Woman on bus, Seattle", 1951, gelatin silver print, 9⁷/₈ x 8in., signed and dated in pencil on the mount.
(Butterfield & Butterfield)
$715

Arthur Dunn, 'Mark Twain and Family at Dollis Hill', 1900, carbon print, 6 x 8in., mounted on card.
(Christie's)
$256

Nicholas Nixon, "MDC Park, Brighton, Massachusetts", 1979, printed later, gelatin silver print, 7¹/₈ x 9⁵/₈in., signed.
(Butterfield & Butterfield)
$880

William Heick, "Hats, Seattle", 1952, gelatin silver print, 9¹/₂ x 12¹/₂in., signed and dated in pencil on the mount.
(Butterfield & Butterfield)
$605

PHOTOGRAPHS

Max Yavno, "Orson Wells", circa 1942, gelatin silver print, 7⁶/₈ x 9⁶/₈in., photographer's stamp in ink.
(Butterfield & Butterfield)

$1,100

Max Yavno, "Muscle Beach Los Angeles", 1949, printed later, gelatin silver print, 7⁷/₈ x 13³/₈in.
(Butterfield & Butterfield)

$4,400

Ansel Adams, "Frozen lake and cliffs, Sierra Nevada, Sequoia National Park", 1932, printed later, approximately 8 x 10in.
(Butterfield & Butterfield)

$12,100

Photographer unknown, Portrait of a black woman with a white child, ¹/₂ plate tintype, gilt preserver, leather case broken at hinges.
(Butterfield & Butterfield)

$385

Horst P. Horst, 'Lisa Fonssagrives, New York, 1940', printed 1980s, platinum-palladium print, image size 18³/₄ x 15in., signed in pencil in margin.
(Christie's)

$3,652

Robert Frank, 'San Francisco 1956', printed 1970s, gelatin silver print, 13¹/₄ x 9in., signed and titled in ink in margin, matted, framed.
(Christie's)

$1,210

Man Ray, Head of a woman, 1946, solarised gelatin silver print, 8 x 6¹/₄in., includes signature and date.
(Butterfield & Butterfield)

$2,750

Nicholas Nixon, "Yazoo City, Mississippi", 1979, printed later, gelatin silver print, 7¹/₈ x 9³/₄in., signed.
(Butterfield & Butterfield)

$935

Anne W. Brigman, 'Incantation', 1905, gelatin silver print, 11³/₈ x 6⁵/₈in., signed in ink on the image, titled in ink and annotated in pencil on verso.
(Butterfield & Butterfield)

$3,025

Framed colored lithograph, American, mid-19th century, *Washington Entering New York*, by Herline & Henzel, with original key, 28½ x 42in. (Eldred's) $715

Paul Revere (American, 1735–1807), *A View of the Obelisk erected under Liberty-Tree in Boston on the Rejoicings for the Repeal of the – Stamp-Act 1766*, signed in the plate *Paul Revere Sculp*, engraving on laid paper with fleur-de-lis watermark, plate size 10 x 13⅝in. (Skinner Inc.) $48,400

United States Centennial International Exhibition 1776-1876, certificate for one share, issued by the Centennial Board of Finance 1875, 24in. x 20in. (Phillips) $1,674

Harper's February poster, by Edward Penfield, circa 1900. (Skinner Inc.) $110

Franklin Square Lithographic Company, publishers, Bird's-eye View of the Great Suspension Bridge connecting the cities of New York and Brooklyn, lithograph printed in colors, published New York, 1883, 17½ x 35½in. (Christie's S. Ken) $574

Currier and Ives, Publishers (American, 19th century) after Arthur Fitzwilliam Tait (American, 1819–1905), "American hunting scene/An early start", 1863, image size 18¾ x 27⅝in. (Skinner Inc.) $3,850

Currier and Ives, Publishers, The American National Game of Base Ball, Grand Match for the Championship at the Elysian Fields, Hoboken, N.J., lithograph with hand-coloring, 1866, on wove paper, 19¾ x 29¾in. (Christie's) $16,500

Masonic mark book, King Hiram Chapter of Greenwich Village and King Solomon's Chapter of Warren, Massachusetts, circa 1825, 8 x 6⁵/₈in.
(Skinner Inc.) $3,300

An illustrated booklet by Phinehas Post, Connecticut, late 18th century, depicting several illustrations including a bird, Eve, a mermaid, a man, and a skeleton, 4⁵/₈ x 3¹/₂in.
(Christie's) $3,300

"Camping Out, 'Some of the Right Sort'", 1856, (Conningham, 777). Lithograph with hand coloring on paper, image size 19 x 27¹/₄in.
(Skinner Inc.) $950

Currier and Ives, publishers, Life in the Woods, "Returning to Camp", by L. Maurer, lithograph with hand-coloring and touches of gum arabic, 1860, on wove paper, with margins, 18¹³/₁₆ x 27³/₄in.
(Christie's) $3,300

Charles H. Crosby & Co., Boston, lithographer, (American, 1819–1896), *Built by the Amoskeag Manufacturing Company*/early fire engines, identified in the matrix, chromolithograph on paper, sheet size 24 x 31⁷/₈in.
(Skinner Inc.) $4,675

The First Twelve Amendments to the Constitution of the United States, printed by Bennett Wheeler (1754–1806), Providence, Rhode Island, 1789, 15⁵/₈ x 12¹/₄in.
(Skinner Inc.) $7,700

"The Life of a Fireman, The Metropolitan System", 1866, image size 17¹/₄ x 26¹/₄in.
(Skinner Inc.) $1,300

J. C. Leyendecker, 'USA Bonds Third Liberty Loan Campaign Boy Scouts of America', double crown. (Onslow's) $350

'The Great Fire at Boston', published by
Currier & Ives, 1872, small folio. (Robt. W.
Skinner Inc.) $575

'Ethan Allen and Mate and Dexter', published
by Currier & Ives, 1867, large folio.
(Robt. W. Skinner Inc.) $1,200

'The Darktown Yacht Club — On The Winning
Tack', published by Currier & Ives, 1885, small
folio. (Robt. W. Skinner Inc.) $335

'The Celebrated Trotting Stallion George
Wilkes, Formerly 'Robert Fillingham'',
published by Currier & Ives, 1866, large
folio. (Robt. W. Skinner Inc.) $1,600

'The Celebrated Horse Lexington (5 years
old), by 'Boston' out of 'Alice Carneal'',
published by N. Currier, 1855, large folio.
(Robt. W. Skinner Inc.) $600

'Maple Sugaring', published by Currier &
Ives, 1872, small folio. (Robt. W. Skinner
Inc.) $650

'The Champion in Luck', published by Currier & Ives, 1882, small folio. (Robt. W. Skinner Inc.) $110

'The Accommodation Train', published by Currier & Ives, 1876, small folio. (Robt. W. Skinner Inc.) $350

'Notice To Smokers And Chewers', published by N. Currier, 1854, small folio. (Robt. W. Skinner Inc.) $900

'Rysdyk's Hambletonian', published by Currier & Ives, 1876, large folio. (Robt. W. Skinner Inc.) $1,800

'The Celebrated Horse Dexter, 'The King Of The World' Driven By Budd Doble'', published by Currier & Ives, 1867, large folio. (Robt. W. Skinner Inc.) $2,250

'The Trotting Mare Goldsmith Maid, Driven By Budd Doble', published by Currier & Ives, 1870, large folio. (Robt. W. Skinner Inc.) $1,350

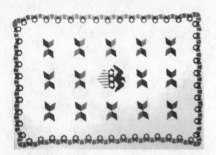

Pieced and appliquéd quilt, America, late 19th/early 20th century, red, white, navy blue and brown patches arranged in patriotic design, heightened with diamond, 89 x 66in.
(Skinner Inc.) **$850**

Crazy quilt, America, late 19th century, various velvet and silk patches, arranged in fan pattern and heightened with embroidery, 80 x 62in.
(Skinner Inc.) **$700**

Appliquéd quilt, America, 19th century, pattern of shaped medallions enclosed by a vine border worked in red and green printed cotton patches and heightened with compotes of flowers, 88 x 89in.
(Skinner Inc.) **$750**

Patchwork Amish coverlet, probably Pennsylvania or Ohio, early 20th century, fan pattern worked in cotton sateen in solid shades of purple, blue, green, pink, yellow, brown and black, 81 x 77in.
(Skinner Inc.) **$650**

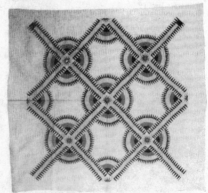

Pieced quilt, America, late 19th century, a "crazy star" pattern worked in various calico patches, heightened with diamond and parallel line quilting, 81 x 86in.
(Skinner Inc.) **$500**

A pieced and appliqued cotton quilted coverlet, American, circa 1870, worked in a New York Beauty pattern variation with five full circles quartered by intersecting sawtooth-edged bands, 84 x 74in.
(Christie's) **$550**

Album quilt, America, mid 19th century, floral, pictorial and geometric squares marked with various solid and printed cotton patches, 84 x 84in.
(Skinner Inc.)   **$2,800**

Strip quilt, early 19th century, comprised of bands of copper plate printed "British Naval Heroes", 86 x 91in.
(Skinner Inc.)   **$475**

Crazy quilt, America, late 19th century, various color satin and velvet patches embellished with floral, figural and geometric embroidery, 78 x 70in.
(Skinner Inc.)   **$400**

Pieced, appliquéd and embroidered silk and velvet crazy quilt, America, late 19th century, 70 x 70in.
(Skinner Inc.)   **$950**

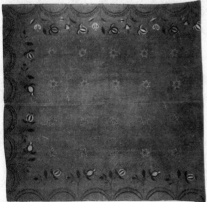

Embroidered wool coverlet, America, first half 19th century, the madder homespun ground embroidered with wool yarns in shades of blue, green, pink and yellow.
(Skinner Inc.)   **$1,200**

Appliquéd quilt, possibly Pennsylvania, with cross stitch inscription *Pieced by Grand Mother Statira Pease, Aged 82 Years May 8th 1856*, heightened with conforming floral and diamond quilting, 70 x 72in.
(Skinner Inc.)   **$700**

QUILTS

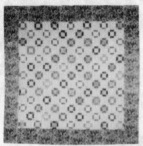

Glazed chintz quilt, America, early 19th century, light brown background with stylized floral bouquets, 120 x 104in. (Skinner Inc.) $600

Applique quilt, probably Pennsylvania, late 19th century, the red and green cotton patches arranged in patriotic motif with eagle, 74 x 72in. (Skinner Inc.) $3,000

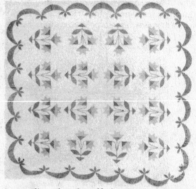

An appliqued cotton and quilted coverlet, American, circa 1850, worked in a modified Princess Feather pattern, the green and red feathers stitched in four pinwheels, centering a quilted pineapple, 88 x 88in. (Christie's New York) $4,620

An appliqued and stuffed cotton quilt, Pennsylvania, 1840-1850, worked in sixteen blocks of appliqued flowers alternating with nine blocks of trapunto tulips, 79½ x 78in. (Christie's New York) $3,850

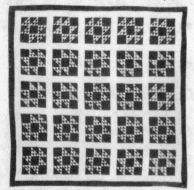

A pieced cotton quilted coverlet, Lincolnton County, Massachusetts, circa 1870, worked in 25 blocks of flying geese pattern with print fabrics on green ground framed in white sashing with green border, 82 x 82in. (Christie's New York) $990

An Amish pieced cotton and wool quilted coverlet, initialed J.F.K., Lancaster County, Pennsylvania, circa 1920, the diamond-in-the-square pattern with slate center diamond stitched in star and wreath framed in dusty pink with wide purple border, 82 x 82in. (Christie's New York) $2,860

Pieced album quilt, probably New Jersey, circa 1843, various calico and muslin patches arranged in the little sawtooth pattern, 96 x 96in. (Skinner Inc.) $1,500

An appliqued and quilted cotton coverlet, Hawaii, mid 19th century, worked with four enlarged floral and vine urns in blue fabric with white dots on a white ground, 78 x 80in. (Christie's New York) $5,500

An appliqued and pieced album quilt, Maryland, mid 19th century, centering a square reserve with a lemon tree, the inner border with 38 pictorial squares including tulips, roses, oak leaves, flower baskets, wreaths, birds and flags, 85 x 95in. (Christie's New York) $6,050

A pieced and appliqued cotton quilted coverlet, Hawaii, second half 19th century, centering a square reserve depicting the crest of the Hawaiian monarchy and inscribed *Kuu Hae*, above and *Aloha* below, 74 x 74in. (Christie's New York) $8,800

A Mennonite pieced cotton quilted coverlet, Lancaster County, Pennsylvania, circa 1880, worked in the Joseph's Coat of Many Colors pattern in a spectrum of bright fabrics with rope twist stitching, 82 x 86in. (Christie's New York) $6,050

A Mennonite pieced and appliqued cotton quilted coverlet, Lancaster County, circa 1880, worked in four blocks of Princess Star Feather in mustard and green fabric on red ground with floral baskets along the center, 72 x 80in. (Christie's New York) $2,860

Appliqued quilt, America, late 19th century, red cotton patches arranged in a 'Princess Feather' pattern, 96 x 98in. $1,250

Mid 19th century pieced and appliqued quilt, the calico patches arranged in 'conventional rose' pattern, 80 x 84in. $600

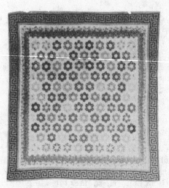

Mid 19th century crib quilt, the red, yellow and green calico patches arranged in the 'Star of Bethlehem' pattern, 28in. square. $550

Mid 19th century patchwork crib quilt, worked in mosaic pattern with various calicos, American, 42 x 44in. $2,000

An appliqued album quilt, cross stitch name in corner 'Miss Lydia Emeline Keller, 1867', American, 84 x 86in. $2,500

An Amish pieced cotton quilt, Lancaster County, Penn., circa 1900, with later embroidery JEB, 1920, 83½ x 85in. $500

Late 19th century applique quilt made up of green and red cotton prints on natural white ground fabric, 8ft.6in. x 6ft.9in. $3,000

An applique quilt composed of red and green calico patches on a white cotton field, America, circa 1845, 80 x 92in. $2,000

Mid 19th century patchwork and applique quilt, New England, 6ft.8in. x 6ft.5in. $2,000

A 19th century patchwork cotton quilt, with unusual tulip border motifs, America, 92 x 92in. $2,500

A 19th century cotton piecework quilt, American, with a center star motif, 90 x 91in. $2,000

An applique album quilt, New Jersey and Pennsylvania, 1853, 7ft.9in. x 8ft.7in. $5,000

Crazy quilt, America, early 20th century, comprised of various silk and velvet patches including printed tobacco silks depicting baseball players, 68 x 74in. (Skinner Inc.) $700

A Tree of Life variation quilt, composed of black and yellow sprigged cottons arranged as a series of trees, 74in. x 64in., American, late 19th century. (Christie's S. Ken) $650

A pieced and appliqued cotton quilted coverlet, American, mid 19th century, worked in red and green cotton with forty-two squares of various designs including floral motifs, 67 x 80in. (Christie's) $5,000

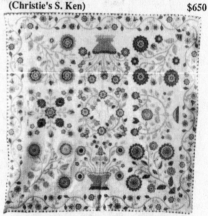

A pieced and appliqued cotton quilted coverlet, Mary Swartz, Shiloh, Ohio, 1853, the central floral medallion with appliqued tulips, posies and roses in yellow, red and green cotton, 80 x 78in. (Christie's) $5,000

A pieced and appliqued cotton quilted coverlet, Hawaii, 20th century, with four elaborate fern-like spokes radiating from the openwork center medallion, 80 x 90in. (Christie's) $1,100

A pieced and appliqued cotton quilted coverlet, North Carolina, circa 1850, worked in the Whigs defeated and rose pattern with red cotton and with green and yellow calico, 84 x 88½ in. (Christie's) $1,650

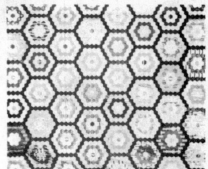

A pieced cotton quilted coverlet, Pennsylvania, 1860, with a central pieced blue calico square comprised of nine pieced fugitive yellow stars from which radiate vertical and horizontal blue calico bands with pieced yellow stars, 78 x 87in.
(Christie's) $1,600

A Grandmother's Flower Garden variation patchwork coverlet composed of various figured silks arranged in a series of hexagons, 76 x 88in., circa 1850.(Christie's S. Ken) $522

A patchwork cover top, composed of long hexagon patches of various figured silks, including tartan, 82in. square, with original templates intact, circa 1850s.
(Christie's S. Ken) $374

Pieced, appliqued and embroidered silk and velvet crazy quilt, initialed *L.A.S. 1885*, silk backing, 6ft. x 6ft. 1in.
(Skinner Inc.) $700

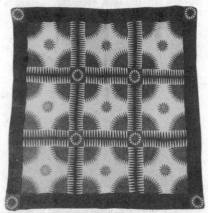

A pieced cotton quilted coverlet, American, late 19th century, worked in nine blocks of New York Beauty pattern embellished with star flower medallions, 88 x 88in.
(Christie's) $1,430

A framed patchwork quilt, composed of various floral printed patches arranged around a central panel, with the name *Eliza Westray, 1812* worked in blue silk, 86 x 92in.
(Christie's S. Ken) $903

A rare Amish or Mennonite pieced cotton quilted coverlet, Lancaster County, Pennsylvania, worked in the sawtooth diamond-in-the-square pattern with a central rose sawtooth diamond stitched *Martin M. Lichty 1879*, 84 x 86in.
(Christie's) $6,050

A pieced cotton quilted coverlet, American, circa 1890, the central Lone Star worked in yellow, red, black and blue calico on a blue calico ground with Princess Feather stitching surrounded by a red calico sawtooth border, 82 x 81in.
(Christie's) $770

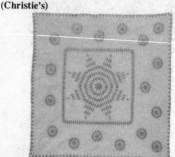

A pieced and appliqued stuffed and quilted cotton coverlet, American, mid-19th century, worked in brown calico on a white cotton ground centred by a Rising Star with floral trapunto corner blocks, 95 x 97in.
(Christie's) $2,200

An Amish pieced wool and cotton quilted coverlet, probably Ohio, dated *1914*, worked in twenty-four blocks of the Flying Geese pattern on a black ground, with an olive-green binding, 67 x 85½in.
(Christie's) $3,300

An Amish pieced and appliqued quilted cotton coverlet, probably Ohio, circa 1920, worked in red and white in twenty blocks of Hole in the Barn Door pattern variation alternating with blocks of scrolling Princess Feather leaves, 89 x 72in.
(Christie's) $1,650

A pieced and appliqued quilted cotton coverlet, American, mid-19th century, worked in eleven blocks of Mariner's Compass pattern with green, blue, orange, and red calico centered by halved Mariner's Compass blocks and quartered corner blocks of similar design, 84 x 95in.
(Christie's) $2,420

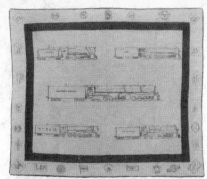

An embroidered cotton pictorial quilt, American, circa 1930, worked in red thread on a white ground framed by a wide red rectangular inner border, depicting numerous train engines and cars, 82 x 68in.
(Christie's) $2,090

A pieced and appliqued quilted cotton coverlet, American, mid-19th century, centered by a scrolling bud and floral medallion of green, red, and yellow calico surrounded by a continuous scrolling floral and bud vine, 89 x 92in.
(Christie's) $4,400

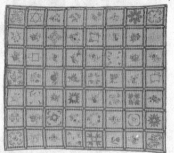

A pieced and appliqued cotton quilt top, Maryland, circa 1854, worked in fifty-six blocks of chintz and calico on a white ground with red sashing and depicting various designs including broderie perse floral bouquets, 94 x 81in.
(Christie's) $1,760

An Amish quilted wool coverlet, initialed A.S., probably Lancaster County, Pennsylvania, circa 1925, worked in the Diamond in the Square pattern with green and red wool on a diamond-stitched blue ground, 76$^{1}/_{2}$ x 78in.
(Christie's) $2,640

An Amish quilted wool and wool crepe coverlet, probably Lancaster County, Pennsylvania, circa 1940, worked in the Diamond in the Square design, the maroon diamond with Star, Princess Feather and Grape quilting on a jade diamond-stitched square, 75 x 74in.
(Christie's) $2,200

A pieced and appliqued cotton quilted coverlet, American, late 19th century, worked in green, red and yellow cotton on a white ground with six blocks of the New York Beauty pattern surrounded by echo stitching centered by rosettes, 76 x 90in.
(Christie's) $880

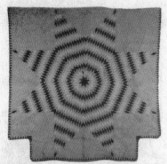

Pieced quilt, America, late 19th/early 20th century, worked in red, green, yellow and pink printed cotton patches arranged in the "Star of Bethlehem" pattern, 74 x 85in. (Skinner Inc.) **$330**

An Amish cotton quilted coverlet, Midwestern, circa 1930, worked in the flower basket pattern with lilac baskets on a black diamond-stitched ground, 77 x 84in. (Christie's) **$1,045**

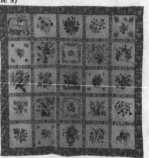

A pieced and appliqued cotton quilted coverlet, probably New York, circa 1860, worked in the Bethlehem Star pattern with green and red calico on a white diamond-stitched ground, 96 x 96in. (Christie's) **$2,200**

A pieced and appliqued friendship quilt, South Carolina, circa 1850, the broderie perse quilt composed of twenty-five blocks separated by chintz sashing, the blocks of various designs including many floral motifs, a stag, a classical female equestrian, and Zachary Taylor, 93 x 91in. (Christie's) **$4,400**

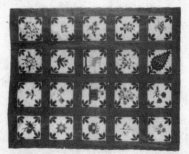

A pieced and appliqued cotton quilted coverlet, American, circa 1840, the central star worked in a variety of cotton prints of green, red, blue, brown and purple shades surrounded by spandrels of chintz trophies and wreaths, 99 x 100in. (Christie's) **$4,620**

A pieced and appliqued cotton album quilt top, New England, circa 1850, worked in twenty squares of various designs including a red brick house, a deer, crossed flags, an anchor, patriotic shields, and numerous fruit and floral motifs, 72 x 88in. (Christie's) **$2,860**

A pieced silk coverlet, American, late 19th century, worked in the pineapple pattern with a variety of prints including plaid, polka dot, stripe, and floral, 60 x 62in.
(Christie's) $1,430

Unusual pieced and appliqued sunburst quilt, America, 19th century, each of the twenty squares with layers of appliqued triangular yellow, red and green cotton patches, 88 x 71in.
(Skinner Inc.) $523

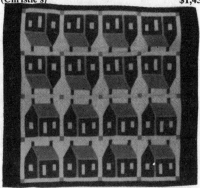

A pieced and appliqued cotton quilted coverlet, American, early 20th century, worked in the schoolhouse pattern with blue, red, orange, and green cotton on a white ground surrounded by a wide blue border, 75 x 80in.
(Christie's) $2,970

An International Order of Oddfellows pieced and appliqued cotton quilted coverlet, American, circa 1865, worked in nine squares of a heart-and-hand design on a diamond-stitched white ground, 82 x 83in.
(Christie's) $1,430

An Amish cotton and wool quilted coverlet, American, circa 1930, worked in the grandmother's dream pattern with twelve blocks in violet, blue, burgundy, and black, 68 x 86in.
(Christie's) $2,860

Pieced quilt, America, late 19th/early 20th century, worked in yellow, red and white cotton patches arranged in the "Star of Bethlehem" pattern, 75 x 78in.
(Skinner Inc.) $715

A patchwork quilt, Penn., signed and dated
in ink on the back, 'Phebeann H. Salem's(?)
Presented by her Mother 1848', 8ft.11in. x 9ft.
$3,000

A 19th century patchwork coverlet,
'Log Cabin', with 'turkey' red squares,
80 x 72in. $600

Early 20th century American pieced
and quilted coverlet with sixteen blazing stars, 97 x 95in.   £1,250

American 19th century cotton applique quilt, 88 x 86in. $2,500

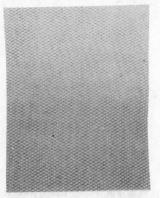

A 19th century pieced and quilted cotton
coverlet, American, 87½in. long, 71½in. wide.
$1,750

Mid 19th century appliqued quilt, the field
divided into squares with a variation of the
'Rose of Sharon' pattern, 92 x 104in. $800

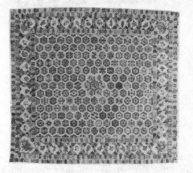

A wool bed rug, worked with a darning stitch in a tree-of-life pattern on a natural wool foundation, dated 1773, 84 x 85in. $15,000

An early 19th century patchwork coverlet in plain and colored printed glazed cotton, circa 1830, 2.70 x 2.24m. $1,500

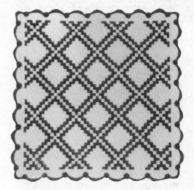

A pieced and quilted coverlet with blazing star pattern, circa 1920, 72 x 67in. $1,250

American 19th century polished cotton pieced quilt, pieced in the 'Irish chain' pattern, 80 x 80in. $2,500

Mid 19th century American pieced and appliqued quilted coverlet, 88 x 87in. $1,000

Mid 19th century applique and stuffed cotton quilt, American, 77½in. long, 74in. wide. $2,000

A fine pieced and appliqued cotton quilted coverlet, Palama Mission, Hawaii, 1899, centering a square reserve depicting the crest of the Hawaiian monarchy and inscribed "Ku'u Hae Aloha" surrounded by four Hawaiian flags and a yellow binding, 84 x 88in. (Christie's) $44,000

An Amish pieced cotton quilted coverlet, Lancaster County, Pennsylvania, 1920-1940, worked in the Sunshine-and-Shadow pattern, with a spectrum of green, purple and pink blocks, surrounded by a wide slate blue border, 84 x 88in. (Christie's) $3,850

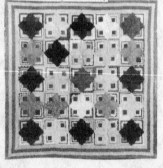

A Mennonite pieced wool quilted coverlet, Lancaster County, Pennsylvania, 1900-1925, worked in 100 blocks of Log Cabin pattern, each centering a green square surrounded by a quadruple border of alternating green and orange bands, 96 x 96in. (Christie's) $2,200

An appliqued and stuffed cotton coverlet, by Mary Clapper, Boonesboro, Maryland, 1830-1850, with three concentric rings of star-filled hexagons in the Grandmother's Garden pattern, alternating with elaborately quilted bands of flower baskets, 104 x 96in.(Christie's) $3,520

An appliqued cotton quilted coverlet, American, 1820-1830, centering a broderie perse floral urn with two square printed borders enclosing a zigzag printed border, surrounded by a border of appliqued eight-pointed stars in red, yellow and blue, 92 x 92in. (Christie's) $5,500

A fine stenciled cotton quilted coverlet, Vermont 1835-1840, with fifteen blocks stenciled with an eight pointed star in red, green and blue alternating with quilted blocks of white, 82 x 84in. (Christie's) $8,800

An Amish pieced cotton quilted coverlet, Kalona, Iowa, 1921, worked in thirteen blocks of Star pattern with slate blue, maize and black fabrics and diamond and floral branch stitching, 74 x 80in. (Christie's) **$4,950**

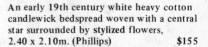

An early 19th century white heavy cotton candlewick bedspread woven with a central star surrounded by stylized flowers, 2.40 x 2.10m. (Phillips) **$155**

A fine embroidered navy wool coverlet, by Esther Williams, Connecticut River Valley, 1820-1830, the top embroidered "Esther Williams, Aged 69" and centering an embroidered eight pointed star enclosing fanciful flowers in each segment and with blossoms springing from each point surrounded by a light blue trailing vine with elaborate flowerheads, 99 x 106in. (Christie's) **$11,000**

A four-color wool and cotton Jacquard coverlet, Daniel Snyder, Hanover Township, Pennsylvania, 1839, worked in blue, red, green and white threads with a compass and thistle design surrounded by Bird of Paradise and Tree of Life border, 76 x 92in. (Christie's) **$2,420**

An Amish pieced wool quilted coverlet, Lancaster County, Pennsylvania, 1900-1925, worked in the Bars pattern with alternating panels of spruce green and russet, 72 x 80in. (Christie's) **$4,620**

An appliqued cotton quilted coverlet, American, 1815-1825, centering a broderie perse floral bouquet surrounded by similar applied reserves with grapevine stitching surrounded by running shell stitching and two printed borders 98 x 98in. (Christie's) **$3,520**

A pieced wool quilted coverlet, Lancaster County, Pennsylvania, 1900-1910, worked in the Bars pattern in alternating light and dark brown surrounded by a red inner border with purple corners and grape and oak leaf stitching, 75 x 75in. (Christie's) $8,250

An Amish pieced wool quilted coverlet, Lancaster County, Pennsylvania, circa 1920, worked in the Diamond-in-the-Square pattern with mulberry and slate fabrics framed in deep pink and with a mulberry border and slate blue binding, 76 x 76in. (Christie's) $10,450

A pieced and embroidered silk and velvet coverlet, Lexington, Kentucky, 1880-1900, the contained Crazy Quilt pattern worked in various jewel-tone velvet fabrics and herringbone embroidery stitches with four center blocks of eight-point stars enclosed by five concentric borders, 89 x 89in. (Christie's) $8,250

A pieced and embroidered wool coverlet, by Mary T. H. Willard, Evanston, Illinois, 1889, worked in a Crazy Quilt pattern in three vertical panels, each with polychrome fabrics embroidered with floral motifs and sentimental cross-stitch inscriptions of Biblical quotations, 67 x 85in.(Christie's) $12,100

An Amish pieced cotton quilted coverlet, Midwestern, 1900-1925, worked in thirty blocks of Jacob's Ladder pattern with deep blue, purple, black, gray and brown fabrics, 76 x 89in. (Christie's) $2,090

A pieced silk quilted coverlet, probably Philadelphia, 1880-1900, centering a Rising Star in reds, green, white, purple and blue on a gray ground, 80 x 80in. (Christie's) $8,800

An Amish pieced cotton quilted coverlet, probably Indiana, circa 1930, the sixteen blocks each in the Broken Star pattern in blue, pink, purple and green on a black ground, 86 x 86in. (Christie's) $2,640

A pieced and embroidered silk and velvet quilted coverlet, American, 1880-1890, with 169 blocks, worked in the Log Cabin pattern. (Christie's) $4,400

A Mennonite pieced cotton quilted coverlet, made by Fanny Snyder of Manheim, Pennsylvania, circa 1890, in the Joseph's-Coat-of-Many-Colors pattern, worked in the spectrum of primary colors, with fine feather and diaper stitching, 75 x 80in. (Christie's) $5,280

An appliqued cotton quilted coverlet, American, 1840-1860, worked in eight blocks of Oak Leaf variation interspersed with twelve blocks of assorted appliqued designs, including hearts and hands and birds in trees, each in red, green, yellow and pink calicos on natural ground, 68 x 86in. (Christie's) $1,980

An appliqued quilted cotton coverlet, probably New York, 1820-1830, centering a square reserve with red calico sawtooth border and enclosing a diamond reserve with red and yellow calico sawtooth border with a brown broderie perse floral spray, 105 x 105in. (Christie's) $3,080

An Amish pieced cotton quilted coverlet, Midwestern, 1900-1925, with sixteen blocks of Birds in Flight variation within a nine patch pattern worked in deep-tone fabrics, alternating with blocks of slate blue fabric, 72 x 72in. (Christie's) $9,350

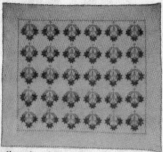

A white-on-white stuffed and quilted cotton coverlet, American, dated 1810, centered by a trapunto floral vase surrounded by a continuous scrolling trapunto princess feather vine design, 77 x 90in.
(Christie's) $3,850

An appliqued and trapunto quilted coverlet, Maryland, circa 1850, worked in the Carolina Lily pattern on a white ground with repeating stuffed pineapples and leaves framed by a pieced sawtooth inner border, 83 x 95in.
(Christie's) $1,000

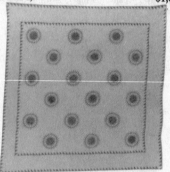

A pieced and appliqued cotton quilted coverlet, Pennsylvania, 1910, worked on a grid with thirty blocks of four repeating designs, the profiles of Abraham Lincoln and of George Washington alternating with a patriotic shield and a top hat, 76 x 86in.
(Christie's) $850

A pieced appliqued and trapunto quilted cotton coverlet, American, 19th century, worked in a mariner's compass pattern with eighteen squares of appliqued red-printed mariner's compass alternating with eighteen squares of trapunto scrolling wreath, 88¼ x 90in. (Christie's) $3,520

Pieced linsey-woolsey quilt, America, late 18th/ early 19th century, worked in lavender and yellow diamond patches, heightened with basket weave quilting, 101 x 95in.
(Skinner Inc.) $495

Pieced and appliquéd quilt, America, second half 19th century, "basket of flowers" pattern worked in printed navy blue patches, 80 x 82in.
(Skinner Inc.) $900

An Amish pieced cotton quilted coverlet, Midwestern, 1900-1925, worked in the Ocean Waves pattern with royal blue, slate green, brown, tan and mulberry fabric, 75 x 75in. (Christie's) **$3,520**

A fine white-on-white stuffed cotton quilt, signed Mary Young, August 23, 1821, centering a large Federal urn with floral swags and on a patterned pedestal surrounded by be-ribboned sheaves of wheat and an inner border of meandering vines, 100 x 100in. (Christie's) **$13,200**

An unusual appliqued and embroidered cotton pictorial quilted coverlet, by Jennie C. Trein, Nazareth, Pennsylvania, 1932, centering a scene depicting a family Sunday picnic with gathering guests, a house in the background, boats in the water, and the family graveyard surrounded by an inner border with "Sunbonnet Sue" figures, 84 x 82in. (Christie's) **$41,800**

An Amish pieced wool quilted coverlet, Lancaster County, Pennsylvania, circa 1900, worked in the Diamond-in-the-Square pattern, the cranberry diamond stitched with an 8-point star enclosed by a feathered wreath, on a turquoise ground framed in deep pink, 78 x 78in. (Christie's) **$7,150**

A Mennonite pieced wool quilted coverlet, Cumberland County, Pennsylvania, circa 1900, worked in the Barn Raising pattern, each block centering a red square with maroon inner border, 90 x 90in. (Christie's) **$2,640**

An Amish pieced and embroidered quilted wool coverlet monogrammed "K.F.", Lancaster County, Pennsylvania, dated 1922, worked in 16 blocks of contained Crazy Quilt pattern, 82 x 82in. (Christie's) **$8,800**

A cotton and wool Jacquard coverlet, New York State, 1816, the field of double rose and flower medallions. $750

An Amish patchwork quilt, Pennsylvania, early 20th century, in shades of red, green, blue, purple and black arranged in "Sunshine and Shadow" pattern, 83 x 85in. $1,750

A patchwork cover of log cabin design worked with brightly colored pieces of mainly floral printed cottons and worsted, 2.1m. x 2.04m. $600

A pieced and quilted cotton coverlet, American, late 19th century, worked in Triple Irish Chain pattern, 82 x 84in. $1,200

Patchwork quilt, America, 19th century, the red, green and yellow cotton patches arranged in the 'New York Beauty' pattern, 90 x 90in. $1,750

Pieced Star of Bethlehem quilt, New England, circa 1850, 90 x 92in. $1,250

An appliqued and stuffed cotton coverlet,
American, late 19th century, worked in
Basket of Flowers pattern, 80 x 86in.
$3,500

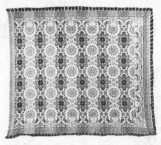

A wool and cotton Jacquard coverlet by
S. B. Musselman, Milford, Bucks County,
Pennsylvania, 1840, fringed on three sides
(minor staining), 102 x 82in. $3,250

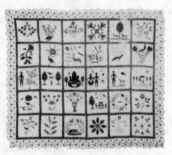

An applique quilt signed and dated 'Sarah
Ann Wilson - 1854', consisting of thirty
appliqued squares of floral and animal
design, 7ft.1in. x 8ft.4in. $35,000

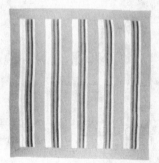

An Amish pieced and quilted cotton coverlet, probably Pennsylvania, early 20th century, of Joseph's Coat of Many Colors pattern, 89 x 89in. $1,750

An appliqued and quilted cotton coverlet,
Pennsylvania, late 19th/early 20th century,
with four spreadwing eagles centering a sunburst design, 67 x 72in. $500

A Mennonite pierced cotton quilt, Lancaster
County, Pennsylvania, late 19th/early 20th
century, a variant of the "Rainbow" pattern,
84 x 88in. $2,000

A piece of paper inscribed to a fan and signed *Love, love, love, love, love, love, love, love, love, love? Jimi Hendrix.*
(Christie's S. Ken) $1,264

A tooled leather guitar strap decorated with artist's name *Bill Haley* and a floral pattern, 49in. long, used by Haley in the late 1970s.
(Christie's) $817

An illustrated souvenir programme for The Jacksons tour, February 1979, the center page signed by Randy, Tito, Jackie, Marlon and Michael Jackson.
(Christie's) $241

An autograph letter signed to a fan by Jimi Hendrix [n.d. but 1967], written prior to a performance, *I wish I could see you in the flesh – I mean in person.*
(Christie's S. Ken) $2,738

An extremely rare drawing by Michael Jackson in blue ball point pen entitled 'Your Girlfriend' and signed, 18 x 11.5cm. (Phillips) $1,870

Stevie Wonder, a presentation 'Gold' disc, *Presented to Stevie Wonder to recognise the sale, in the United Kingdom, of more than £250,000 worth of the album 'Songs in the Key of Life' 1976.*
(Christie's S. Ken) $2,528

Eric Broadbelt, 'Jimi Hendrix', watercolor heightened with white, initialed and dated 'EB '67', signed and inscribed, 11¾ x 9in. (Christie's) $464

A pair of slate-gray suede shoes fastening at the side with a brass clip with maker's name *Thom McAn*, worn by Buddy Holly during the late 1950s.
(Christie's) $774

An American one sheet poster for Labyrinth, Tri-Star Pictures, 1986, signed and inscribed *Michael – Thank you, Jim Henson* and *For Michael with very best wishes, Bowie '91*, framed, 38½ x 26¾in.
(Christie's) $370

Led Zeppelin, a set of eight concert tickets for a show at the Chicago Stadium on Wednesday November 12th 1980. (Phillips) $481

Michael Jackson's gray and blue denim hat decorated with an elaborate pattern of colored sequins and mirror-work, inscribed *Mike* in pencil inside the brim. (Christie's S. Ken) $800

An album cover 'Born In The U.S.A.', Columbia, 1984, signed in black felt pen, with a red printed cotton scarf signed 'Bruce Springsteen' in black felt pen. (Christie's) $408

A presentation Gold disc *The Everly Bros. Greatest Hits*, above a plaque inscribed *Presented to Barnaby Records to commemorate the sale of more than 500,000 copies.* (Christie's S. Ken) $1,075

Buddy Holly, The Lubbock High School 'Westerner' yearbook 1953, signed by Buddy Holly on his photograph. (Phillips) $5,160

A rare autographed souvenir concert program, circa 1958, signed on the reverse by Buddy Holly. (Christie's S. Ken) $1,524

Bob Dylan, an album cover *The Times They Are A-Changin'*, 1963, signed on the front by Bob Dylan in black felt pen. (Christie's) $486

A pair of Michael Jackson's white lace-up dance shoes, each signed twice in blue ink. (Phillips) $7,106

Prince presentation R.I.A.A. platinum record for '1999', framed and glazed, 53x43cm. (Phillips) $1,032

Jimi Hendrix and the Experience, a page from an autograph book signed and inscribed *Be good in whatever you do, Jimi Hendrix, Love Mitch, Noel Redding and Gerry (road manager)*.
(Christie's)   **$1,271**

A Coral Records promotional postcard, 1958, signed by Buddy Holly, Joe Mauldin and Jerry Allison, 5³/₄ x 3¹/₂in.
(Christie's)   **$1,214**

A machine print publicity photograph of The Doors, signed by Ray Manzarek, Robby Krieger, John Densmore, and inscribed *Cheers J. Morrison*, 6³/₄ x 7¹/₂in. (Christie's S. Ken)
$896

Michael Jackson, a rhinestone stage glove of white cotton stockinette encrusted with sparkling hand-sewn imitation diamonds, with *Western Costume Co. Hollywood* woven label, printed with artist's name *Michael Jackson*.
(Christie's)   **$30,855**

A black felt trilby signed and inscribed on underside of brim *All My Love Michael Jackson* and stamped with artist's name in gilt lettering on inside band.
(Christie's)   **$1,619**

An excellent handwritten letter from Jimi Hendrix to a member of the Universal Autograph Collector's Club, written in red biro, circa 1967. (Phillips)
$2,992

A piece of paper signed and inscribed *J Morrison cheers THE DOORS*, in common mount with a portrait photograph of the subject, framed.
(Christie's)   **$1,271**

An autograph letter signed, from Fats Domino to a fan *Dear David, to be honest with you I don't perticulary* (sic) *care for Rap* (?) *music*, 11¹/₂ x 8¹/₂in.
(Christie's)   **$648**

Janis Joplin, a pair of portrait photographs by Jim Marshall, 1968, printed in 1988 taken in subject's dressing room backstage at the Winterland Ballroom, San Francisco.
(Christie's)   **$581**

A page from an autograph book signed by Buddy Holly, Jerry Allison and Joe Mauldin, and inscribed in a separate hand 'Tues. March 4th 1958, Sheffield City Hall'. (Christie's) $1,301

A Michael Jackson Phonograph, made by Vanity Fair, 1984, with instruction leaflet, in original box, 11 x 12½in. (Christie's) $142

An album cover, Andy Warhol, signed by subject in black felt pen, 12 x 12in. (Christie's S. Ken) $1,159

A presentation 'Gold' disc, inscribed 'Presented to The Jacksons to commemorate the sale of more than 500,000 copies of the Epic Records album and cassette "Victory". (Christie's) $1,487

Jimi Hendrix, a black felt hat trimmed with an American Indian style band of leather and metal decorated with circular panels, worn by Hendrix on stage, circa 1963. (Christie's) $9,108

A rare single-sided acetate for *Black Star, 20th Century Fox Film Corp.* white label with typescript details giving title of song by *Elivis Presley And Orchestra*, 78 r.p.m. (Christie's) $4,655

A polychrome tour poster for 'Jimi Hendrix Experience, presented by Lippmann and Rau', 47 x 33in.(Christie's) $464

A self-published, limited edition book An American Prayer, 1970, signed on the title page *J. Morrison*, 20 unnumbered leaves, original boards, titled in gilt. (Christie's) $3,086

A presentation 'Gold' disc, Morrison Hotel, *Presented to The Doors To Commemorate The SaleOf More Than One Million Dollars Worth.* (Christie's S. Ken) $2,528

A rare autographed souvenir concert program, 1958, signed on the reverse by Buddy Holly, Jerry Allison and Joe Mauldin. (Christie's S. Ken) $1,972

The Blues Brothers, an album cover, Briefcase Full of Blues, 1978, signed and inscribed *Dan Akroyd and Stay Cool, John Belushi.* (Christie's S. Ken) $1,159

A mirrored heart shaped 'bracelet', 3½ x 5in., signed and inscribed 'Love God P '88 x', reputedly worn by Prince on his recent 'Love Sexy '88' tour. (Christie's) $304

A Michael Jackson presentation Platinum disc *Bad* mounted above a plaque bearing the R.I.A.A. Certified Sales Award and inscribed *Presented to Epic Records to commemorate the sale of more than 1,000,000 copies.* (Christie's S. Ken) $1,793

An illustrated souvenir concert program, New Victoria Theatre, 24th August, 1976, signed on the cover *Luck, Fats Domino.* (Christie's S. Ken) $590

A page from an autograph book signed and inscribed *Stay Groovy Jimi Hendrix*, 3½ x 4¾in., in common mount with a half length publicity photograph, circa 1968. (Christie's S. Ken) $537

Jimi Hendrix, a silk screen print poster in gouache and gilt, 50 x 38in. (Christie's S. Ken) $548

An album cover, Born To Run, signed on the front by Bruce Springsteen, Clarence Clemons, Max Weinberg, Danny Federici, Garry Tallent, Roy Bittan and Nils Lofgren. (Christie's S. Ken) $590

Two pages from an autograph book, one signed by Jimi Hendrix and Mitch Mitchell, the other by Noel Redding. (Christie's) $836

A rare page of handwritten lyrics, Cars Hiss By My Window – a song on The Doors' last album, L.A. Woman, 1971, on yellow lined paper, inscribed at head of page *J.M./Doors*. (Christie's S. Ken) $5,477

Jimi Hendrix's 'Disc and Music Echo — Valentine Pop Poll' award for 1969, where he was named 'best guitarist in the world'. (Phillips) $3,784

Four pieces of paper signed individually by Jim Morrison, John Densmore, Robby Krieger and Ray Manzarek, in common mount with a machine print photograph of the Doors, 22 x 27^{1}/$_{2}$in. (Christie's) $1,720

Four previously unpublished photographs of Jimi Hendrix by photographer Graham Howe, taken at The Round House, Chalk Farm, London, in February 1967. (Christie's S. Ken) $986

Rare handwritten and type-script lyrics by Bob Dylan, circa 1966, comprising four verses from *Obviously Five Believers*, 1966, three verses handwritten in black biro with alterations and deletions, one verse typescript, on a piece of paper 8.58 x 14.94cm. (Christie's S. Ken) $2,689

Jim Morrison, a piece of paper signed and inscribed *Cheers Morrison*, in common mount with a half-length machine-print photograph. (Christie's S. Ken) $2,949

Chubby Checker, signed and inscribed vintage 8" x 10", full length in classic 'twist' pose, slight corner creasing. (T. Vennett-Smith) £30

An album cover *Prince – Love Sexy* 1988, signed and inscribed *Love God, P. '88*, additionally signed by seven members of the band. (Christie's S. Ken) $573

Prince — a presentation 'Gold' disc, 'When doves cry', the single mounted above a plaque, 16¾ x 12¾in., framed and glazed. (Christie's) $2,619

Jimi Hendrix, a signed, typed lyric sheet for 'Are You Experienced', mounted with a reduction of the U.S. 'Are You Experienced' LP sleeve. (Phillips) $860

Madonna presentation R.I.A.A. platinum record for 'Like a Virgin', 'presented to Warner Bros. Records to commemorate the sale of more than 1,000,000 copies'. (Phillips) $1,032

Bill Haley and the Comets, a good signed 8 x 10in. black and white publicity photograph, circa 1955/6.(Phillips) $481

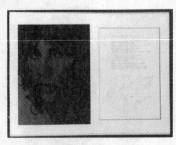

The Doors, a signed typed lyric sheet 'Break on Through', the lyrics typed on a sheet of note paper, 22 x 15cm., signed. (Phillips) $1,032

A full-size Spanish classical acoustic guitar, with ebony fretboard, spruce top signed and inscribed *To Simon, Best Wishes, Bob Dylan, 10.12.86.* (Christie's) $1,180

A piece of paper inscribed to a fan, annotated with a psychedelic doodle and signed *Love & Kisses to you FOREVER, Jimi Hendrix EXPERIENCE.* (Christie's) $884

An album cover *The Times They Are A-Changin'* Columbia Records, 1964, signed by Bob Dylan in blue felt pen, 12 x 12in. (Christie's S. Ken) $681

A presentation 'Gold' disc, *Presented to The Jackson Five to commemorate the sale of more than 500,000 copies of the Motown Records album, "Dancing Machine".* (Christie's S. Ken) $948

A signed, typed lyric sheet for the song 'Little Wing', signed beneath 'Love Jimi Hendrix', in black ballpoint pen, 31.5 x 42cm. (Phillips) $860

The earliest rocking horses had a boat shaped structure, consisting of two parallel semicircular panels held vertically by a small wooden seat between them.

By the late 17th century horses with free standing legs on a panel attached to bow-shaped rockers had become popular. These were now accoutred with saddles and bridles and had a prancing rather than galloping stance. Gallopers came in around a century later, beautifully and realistically carved. Dapple gray was the favoured shade. Earlier gallopers tended to be narrow, with irregular spots and steep bow rockers. Later, however, they became broader with more regular dapples and shallower rockers.

It was probably for safety reasons that the trestle base was developed in the 1880s. Legs were now attached to a pair of boards which swung on metal brackets mounted at the ends of a trestle base.

The first commercial makers of rocking horses were probably those who made fairground gallopers, wooden saddle trees etc.

The points to look for when buying an old rocking horse are a well-carved, lively head, original paintwork and trappings, and a luxuriant mane and tail of real horsehair.

A carved and painted rocking horse with hair mane and tail, America, circa 1880, 52in. long. **$1,750**

A large dappled rocking horse, on metal hinged rockers, 51½in. high. **$1,250**

A carved and painted rocking horse with horsehair mane and tail, glass eyes and leather bridle and saddle, America, circa 1880, 72in. long. **$4,000**

Hide covered rocking horse, attributed to Whitney Reed Corporation, Leominster, Massachusetts, 19th century, covered with dapple-brown hide, 43in. high. (Skinner Inc.) **$6,000**

Painted rocking horse, America, late 19th century, painted white with dapple gray spots having applied horse hair tail, 54½in. high. (Skinner Inc.) **$3,000**

Small carousel stander, mounted as a rocking horse, circa 1900. 27in. high, 29in. long. (Robt. W. Skinner. Inc.) **$1,750**

Painted wooden hobby horse, New England, early 19th century, painted dapple gray with green saddle and heart-shaped supports, 51in. wide. (Skinner Inc.) $1,300

415

Yarn sewn rug, New England, mid-19th century, worked with clipped cotton and wool yarns, 31 x 50in. (Skinner Inc.) $600

A large pictorial cotton hooked rug, American, late 19th/early 20th century, in two registers; the upper depicting a farm scene with a barn, 97 x 129in. (Christie's) $2,860

A large hooked cotton rug, American, late 19th/early 20th century, the central floral medallion worked in pinks, blues, greens and browns on a cream ground, 146½ x 106in. (Christie's) $6,050

Art Deco room size rug, mid 20th century, field comprised of panels in hues of brown accented by bands of muted turquoise, 10ft. 5in. long. (Skinner Inc.) $400

Pictorial hooked rug, America, dated '1934', worked in colorful yarns depicting the cruise ship 'Morro Castle', 30in. x 35in. (Skinner Inc.) $550

Gustav Stickley India hemp carpet, 1910, honeycomb pattern, brown on neutral ground, 11ft.8in. x 9ft.2in. (Skinner Inc.) $3,500

Grenfell hooked mat, Grenfell Labrador Industries, Newfoundland and Labrador, early 20th century, 39¼ x 26in. (Skinner Inc.) $700

One of two India Drugget scatter rugs, designed by Gustav Stickley, circa 1910, 38in. wide. (Robt. W. Skinner Inc.) $900

A hooked rug, the beige field centering a brown spotted dog, dated 1892, America, 27in. wide, 53in. long. (Robt. W. Skinner Inc.) $275

A pictorial hooked cotton rug, American, late 19th/early 20th century, with central oval depicting a three masted ship, 30 x 43¼in. (Christie's) $550

Pictorial hooked rug, America, early 20th century, bearing the inscription *Old Shep*, 27 x 34in. (Skinner Inc.) $900

Pictorial hooked rug, 20th century, an American ship at sea, worked in shades of blue, purple, red, yellow, green and tan, 37 x 58in. (Skinner Inc.) $450

Large hooked rug, America, early 20th century, patterned in the manner of an Oriental rug, 103 x 90in. (Skinner Inc.) $8,500

Grenfell hooked mat, Grenfell Industries, Newfoundland or Labrador, 20th century, 13ft. 14in. x 11ft. 8in. (Skinner Inc.) $550

Hooked rug, America, 20th century, patterned in the manner of a prayer rug, 40 x 46in. (Skinner Inc.) $385

Drugget flatweave area rug, 20th century, orange and black zig-zag pattern, 5ft.9in. x 3ft.2in. (Skinner Inc.) $400

A 19th century rectangular hooked rug, American, 2ft. 7in. x 5ft.2in. (Robt. W. Skinner Inc.) $1,100

Gustav Stickley drugget rug, circa 1910, honeycomb pattern and Greek key border, 7ft.11in. x 5ft.1in. (Skinner Inc.) $1,500

SAMPLERS

Needlework family record *Fanny Marks record and sampler wrought at the age of 15, 1825*, Keene area, New Hampshire, 24¼ x 16¼in.
(Skinner Inc.) $2,475

Needlework sampler, *Mary L. Montagu, A.D. 1828 AE 11 yrs.*, worked in silk threads in shades of black, green, blue and tan, 18¾ x 13¾in.
(Skinner Inc.) $300

Needlework sampler *Rebecca Justice Aged 11 Years*, circa 1835, worked in silk threads, on linen ground, in original frame.
(Skinner Inc.) $9,625

Needlework sampler, *Anna Brynbergs work done in the Eleventh Year of Her Age 1795*, Philadelphia, Pennsylvania, worked in silk threads in shades of blue, green, yellow, peach, cream and black, 15¼ x 17½in.
(Skinner Inc.) $5,500

A silk-on-silk needlework sampler, American, late 18th/early 19th century, depicting an alphabetic sequence above the poetic verse *While I am blest with Youthful bloom/I will adore the sacred lamb/If God inspires my heart with grace/And lets me see his shining face*, 12½ x 8½in.
(Christie's) $2,860

Needlework sampler by Mary Ann Hartshorne, American, early 19th century, executed in polychrome silk threads on a linen ground, 16½in. high.
(Butterfield & Butterfield) $1,045

Needlework sampler, *Wrought by Adaline Libby Aged 16 1827*, probably New Hampshire, worked with silk threads, 20 x 21in.
(Skinner Inc.) $825

Boston 'Adam & Eve' sampler by Lydia Hart, May the 28, 1744, 9 x 11½in. $40,000

Needlework sampler, *Rachel McClure, New York, 1760*, worked with silk threads in shades of blue, green, yellow and brown, 16 x 14in.
(Skinner Inc.) $4,500

Needlework sampler, *Wrought by Caroline Darling Marlborough August 1819 aged 11 years*, 17¼ x 13½in. (Skinner Inc.) $3,850

Needlework sampler *Wrought by Elizabeth Bigelow, Marlborough, Aged 11 Yeaf*, worked in silk threads in shades of green, pink, bittersweet, yellow and black on linen, 10 x 9½in. (Skinner Inc.) $1,045

A sampler 'Wrought by Harriot Wethrell May Aged 10 years, Plymouth Massachusetts, June 10th 1830', 16¼ x 16½in. $3,500

A needlework silk-on-linen sampler by Desire E. Demmen, Scituate, Massachusetts, 1804, worked in polychrome silk threads on a linen ground, the upper register depicting an alphabetic sequence, 19¼in. high, 15½in. wide. (Christie's) $6,600

Framed antique American sampler, verse reads, *This Sampler Is To Let You Know how Kind My Mother Was To Me She Learned Me To Read And Write And In Me Tok Great Delight*, signed Elisabeth Laughlin, aged 14, 1841, 17 x 17½in. (Eldred's) $468

Needlework sampler, inscribed *Mary Sheles work'd this in 1791* a variety of spot motifs worked in green, yellow, and brown silk, 14 x 10in. (Skinner Inc.) $412

Needlework sampler, *Sally Goss*, probably Pennsylvania, rows of alphabets above inscription and verse over a panel of flowering trees, 11½ x 15¾in. (Skinner Inc.) $1,750

Rare needlework sampler, worked by Sally Johnson Age 12, Newburyport, Massachusetts, 1799, one of a small and important group of samplers worked in Newburyport from 1799–1806, 19 x 27in. (Skinner Inc.) $33,000

A needlework sampler "Betsy Davis's sampler wrought at eight years of age, Providence October 22 1794", Balch School, Providence, Rhode Island, 11¾ x 8in. (Robt. W. Skinner Inc.) $2,000

An American needle-work sampler by Maria Alligood, 1802, 26¼ x 21¼in. $4,500

A needlework sampler, "Apphia Amanda Young's sampler wrought in the twelfth year of her age July 22 A.D. 1833", probably New Hampshire, 17in. wide. (Robt. W. Skinner Inc.) $1,350

Needlework sampler, 'Sally Butman her work in the 11th year of her age, 1801', Marble-head, Mass., 10.3/8 x 12½in. $25,000

Needlework sampler, worked by *"Sarah Elizabeth Wright, Aged 18 Years"*, Massachusetts, dated *"1821"*, 15¾ x 17in. (Skinner Inc.) $1,250

A needlework sampler made by Sarah Johnson, Newport, Rhode Island, 1769, 9 x 16in. $30,000

A needlework sampler by Susanna H. White, Marblehead, dated 1806, 14½ x 19in. $25,000

Needlework sampler, Boston area, second half 18th century, rows of alphabet and numbers over scenic panel with Adam and Eve, 11½in. high. (Skinner Inc.) $10,000

Early 19th century needle-work sampler, 'Phebe L. Slessor work aged 11 years', New England, 16 x 16in. $1,750

Early 19th century Adam and Eve sampler by Eliz. Tredick, New Hampshire or Southern Maine, 11 x 16in. $3,500

Needlework sampler, worked by *Elisabeth Lyon, aged 14 years 1791 New Haven,* Connecticut, 17¾ x 20¾ in. (Skinner Inc.) $5,000

Needlework sampler *Betsey Sergent's Sampler,* Stockbridge, Massachusetts, dated *September 28, 1788,* (faded) 12 x 7¾ in. (Skinner Inc.) $1,750

Early 19th century unfinished Shaker needlework sampler on natural linen, 8½ x 10¼ in. $1,250

A needlework sampler, Joanna Maxwell, Warren, Rhode Island, dated 1793, made by Joanna Maxwell, born May the 8 A D 1782 at Warren and further inscribed Wrought at Warren, September the 12 A D 1793. (Robt. W. Skinner Inc.) $40,000

A fine and rare needlework sampler, by Alice Mather, Norwich, Connecticut, 1774, 13¾ x 11½ in. (Christie's New York) $49,500

Needlework memorial sampler, Sarah Jane Campbell, America, 19th century, the upper panel depicting a woman mourning beside a tomb, 21½ x 17¼ in. (Skinner Inc.) $1,350

Needlework sampler marked 'Wrought by Sally Alden June 14 1811', Mass., 16 x 21 in. $7,000

Framed needlework pictorial verse sampler, by Eliza. A. Machett, New York, March 22, 1828, 16½ x 16 in. $1,100

An American needlework sampler, signed Jane Littlefield, circa 1810, worked in silk threads on a dark green canvas, 24 in. high, 15½ in. wide. $8,000

Needlework sampler, worked by *"Ruthy Long Poor born Oct. 28 1801, Aged 13"*, Newburyport, Massachusetts, 1814, 11¼ x 8¾in. (Skinner Inc.) $850

Needlework sampler, *Chloe E. Trask's work wrought in the year 18...*, probably Massachusetts, worked in silk threads, 15¾ x 16½in. (Skinner Inc.) $700

Needlework sampler "Polley Woodbery her sampler A 14 1787 Essex, Massachusetts', 10½ x 8in. (Robt. W. Skinner Inc.) $800

Needlework sampler, *Wrought by Eunice Goodridge Aet 16 yrs. Fitchburg 1825,* Massachusetts (fading, staining), 20½ x 16½in. (Skinner Inc.) $750

Needlework sampler, *Betsy Patten born September 1802, aged 11 A.D. 1812 Mary Cummings instructress,* Westford, Massachusetts, 17 x 17in. (Skinner Inc.) $500

Needlework sampler, *Orpha Starkwather 1804,* possibly Virginia or South Carolina, framed, 15½ x 18in. (sight), (minor discoloration). (Skinner Inc.) $2,000

Needlework family record, *Wrought by Sarah E. Foster Aged 11 years Roxbury, Dec. 24th 1830,* Massachusetts (good condition), 19½ x 16¼in. (Skinner Inc.) $1,750

A needlework sampler by Martha Evans, English or American, dated 1848, worked in poly-chrome wool yarns on an ivory silk ground, 23½ x 27½in. $1,000

A Georgian needlework sampler by Maria Coster, in the tenth year of her age, 1819, 1ft.5in. x 1ft.1in. $1,750

SCRIMSHAW

Polychrome engraved whale's tooth, 19th century, engraved with a woman and child enclosed by a leafy reserve, heightened with red and black ink, 4¹/₂in. high. (Skinner Inc.) $495

Pair of engraved polychrome whale teeth, 19th century, each engraved with ship at sea, enclosed by swag border, 6in. high. (Skinner Inc.) $1,100

Most unusual scrimshaw whale's tooth, 19th century, with cameo carving of a French naval seaman on one side, engraved *Donald McLaughton Mar 4, 1886* on the other, 5¹/₂in. long. (Eldred's) $715

Engraved whale's tooth, 19th century, engraved with a figure of a mother and child and *Lieut. Lovell*, 7in. high. (Skinner Inc.) $2,200

Pair of engraved whale's teeth, early 19th century, the first engraved with a cutting-in scene, the second also with a whaling scene, 7in. high. (Skinner Inc.) $1,320

Engraved whale's tooth, 19th century, deeply engraved with the figure of Liberty, a panoply of American flags and other patriotic devices, 4¹/₂in. high. (Skinner Inc.) $770

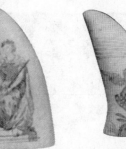

Scrimshaw Sperm whale's tooth, 19th century, decorated with the portrait of John Paul Jones on one side; a three-masted ship on the other, 4³/₄in. long. (Eldred's) $248

Pair of engraved whale's teeth, late 19th century, engraved with Liberty and Justice, Liberty heightened with red, 4³/₄in. high. (Skinner Inc.) $880

Engraved polychrome whale tooth, 19th century, engraved with American flags surmounting a spread eagle perched on a shaped foliate base, 5¹/₂in. long. (Skinner Inc.) $770

The Michigan Central Railroad 1881 $5,000
bond issued to W.H. VANDERBILT and
signed by C. VANDERBILT as Vice President.
(Phillips) $736

Philadelphia and Lancaster Turnpike Road
1795, One share, the earliest known U.S.
certificate with a vignette, black print on
vellum, hand signed by W. Bingham.
(Phillips) $404

Hukuang Railways 1911, £20 bond, issued
by American banks. Although 141 bonds outstanding out of 150 x £20 bonds issued, very
few seen in reasonable condition, one of the
rarest Chinese/American bonds. (Phillips
London) $1,580

State of Mississippi 1833, bond No.
F1247 for $1,000 with coupons, printed at
The Natchez Courier Office, signed by the
Governor, A. M. Scott, dated 1831. (Phillips
London) $395

The North American Land Company, 1795,
two shares. Handsigned by Robt. Morris, a
signatory of the Declaration of Independence.
(Phillips) $518

The Mobile & Alabama Grand Trunk
Railroad Co. 1874, large attractive $1,000
bond with five vignettes.
(Phillips) $843

American Express Company 1865, 1 x $500 share, signed, by Wells as president, Fargo as secretary and Holland as treasurer. (Phillips London) $537

Missouri, Kansas & Texas Railway Co., 1880, 100 x $100 shares, signed by Jay Gould as president. (Phillips London) $268

Union Gold Mining Company 1834, bearer certificate for 5 x $100 shares. Incorporated as a Chartered Company in January 1834, by an Act of the Legislature of Virginia, United States of North America. Corporate Seal of the Company at Philadelphia. (Phillips) $539

The Pere Marquette Transportation Co. 1897. One $1,000 Bond. 200 bonds issued for the payment in construction of the car ferry steamboat called "The Pere Marquette". (Phillips) $214

Venezuela, The Orinoco Steam Navigation Co. of New York 1851-7, $1,000 share. Chartered by the State of New York. The company had exclusive right to navigate the Orinoco and Apure Rivers by steam for 18 years (9 examples). (Phillips London) $258

USA — The Cuba Company, 1903, 4 x $50,000 shares, issued to and endorsed by E. H. Harriman on reverse. (Phillips) $265

SILHOUETTES

A silhouette of a young woman in original gold leaf frame, America, circa 1830, image 7¼ x 5in. (Robt. W. Skinner Inc.) $2,600

A silhouette of Friends of Charles Dickins, dated New York 1841, cut-out on card, 9½in. wide. $1,000

American school, 19th century silhouette portrait of a Masonic gentleman, with Masonic devices and the initials *J.W.*, 4¼ x 6⅝in. (Skinner Inc.) $750

American School, 19th century, Four silhouettes, Three Children and a Lady, unsigned, each cut-out and enhanced with watercolor, 2¾ x 3 7/8in. $550

Pair of watercolor silhouettes, America, circa 1830, 4¼ x 3¼in. $1,250

American School, 19th century, silhouette family portrait, 12 x 19in. wide, in gilt wood frame. (Skinner Inc.) $750

A lady, in profile to dexter, painted on plaster, circa 1795, oval 4in. $350

A free-cut silhouette of a family by Auguste T. Edouart, Providence, Rhode Island, dated 1840, 16¼in. wide. $2,000

426

BASKETS

Sterling silver handled basket by Watson Company made for Bailey Banks & Biddle, pierced edge, four feet, 10½in. long, 13.8 troy oz. (Eldred's) **$440**

A cake basket, American, circa 1895, with a pierced bail handle and four scroll feet, marked *Sterling* and *Tiffany & Co*, 9in. high, 33oz. (Christie's New York) **$2,200**

A silver cake basket, maker's mark of R&W Wilson, Philadelphia, circa 1830, with die-rolled Greek-key borders, 12in. diameter, 38 oz. (Christie's) **$1,100**

BEAKERS

A rare silver beaker by Samuel Kirk, Baltimore, circa 1840, deeply repousse and chased with buildings surrounded by flowers and trees, 3½in. high, 4½oz. **$1,750**

One of a pair of cylindrical beakers with an applied molded strap handle, Boston, 1790-1810, 3.1/8in. high, overall, 8oz. **$750**

A beaker, by William A. Williams, Alexandria, Virginia or Washington, D.C., early 19th century, with reeded rim and footrim, marked, 8cm. high, 4oz. (Christie's New York) **$1,650**

One of a pair of silver beakers, by John Taylor and H. Hinsdale, N.Y., 1804-30, 3½in. high, 9oz. **$850**

An ivory and silver cigar holder on six flattened ball feet, by Tiffany & Co., N.Y., 1881, 6½in. high. (Christie's) **£3,694**

A tall beaker by John Burt Lyng, New York, 1760-1780, with a flaring rim, engraved with a ruffle border, 4½in. high, 5oz. (Christie's New York) **$7,150**

BOWLS

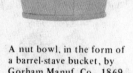

A nut bowl, in the form of a barrel-stave bucket, by Gorham Manuf. Co., 1869, 2¼in. high, 4¾in. wide, 3oz. **$650**

A Monteith bowl, by Samuel Kirk & Son, Baltimore, 1880-90, 5½in. high, 9½in. diam., 25oz. **$1,750**

A bowl, circular with flaring rim, by Josiah Austin, Boston, circa 1750-70, 3in. high, 5¾in. diam., 6oz. (Christie's) **$14,300**

A silver footed bowl, maker's mark of Samuel Williamson, Philadelphia, 1795–1810, on a flaring pedestal base over a square foot, 6⅝in. diameter, 15 oz. 10 dwt. (Christie's) **$2,200**

A silver covered sugar bowl, maker's mark of Tiffany & Co., New York, 1870–1875, the lobed body repoussé with scrolls and stylized foliage, 10¾in. high, 22 oz. (Christie's) **$2,200**

A silver punch bowl, maker's mark of Redlich & Co., New York, circa 1900, the openwork rims with trailing vine and flowerhead decoration, 10½in. diameter, 56 oz. 10 dwt. (Christie's) **$2,860**

Sterling silver centerpiece bowl by A. Stone & Company, maker's mark *G*, for Herman Glendenning (active, 1920–37), 30.4 troy oz. (Eldred's) **$1,540**

A silver gilt bowl, by Gorham Manuf. Co., Providence, 1884. 3¾in. high, 6oz. **$1,500**

A yachting trophy punch bowl, by Gorham Manuf. Co., 1884, the interior gilt, 9¼in. high, 18¼in. wide, 117oz. (Christie's) **$41,800**

BOWLS

Sterling silver centerpiece bowl, circa 1896–1903, by Mauser Manufacturing Company, applied and pierced floral decoration, 14in. diameter, 64 troy oz. (Eldred's) $3,080

A shaped circular bowl with two S-scroll twisted wire handles, by B. Schaats, N.Y., circa 1690-1700, 5.3/8in. diam., 6oz. (Christie's) $35,200

A centerpiece bowl with a scalloped rim, the sides fluted, by Simeon Coley, N.Y., circa 1768, 8.7/8in. diam., 21oz. 10dwt. (Christie's) $28,600

Kirk repoussé silver monteith, Baltimore, 1846–61, chased floral decoration, removable goblet holder with 1852 inscription, 10³/₄in. diameter, approximately 46 troy oz. (Skinner Inc.) $2,700

Coin silver sugar bowl. Christof Christian Küchler for Hyde & Goodrich, (1816-1866), New Orleans, c. 1850, 6¹/₄in. high. (Skinner Inc.) $3,300

Stieff Sterling Repousse Punchbowl, Baltimore, heavily chased with roses and assorted flowers, 12in. diam, approximately 75 troy oz. (Skinner Inc) $8,500

Rare Sterling silver bowl, circa 1930, by William Waldo Dodge, Jr. of Ashville, NC, hand hammered body, 10in. diameter, 20 troy oz. (Eldred's) $935

A covered silver sugar bowl, by Edmund Milne, Phila., circa 1785, 7¼in. high, 11oz. (Christie's) $4,500

A silver Martele centerpiece bowl, maker's mark of Gorham Mfg. Co., Providence, circa 1905, the undulating rim repoussé with strawberries, leaves and flowerheads, 15¹/₄in. long, 58 oz. 10 dwt. (Christie's) $10,340

BOWLS

A sterling silver bowl, by Arthur Stone, 1910-37, 5.3/8in. diam., 7 troy oz. (Robt. W. Skinner Inc.) $1,400

A footed fruit bowl by Whiting Manufacturing Company, North Attleboro or Newark, circa 1885, on a spreading cylindrical foot with a serpentine border, 4³/₄in. high, 21 oz. 10 dwt. (Christie's) $9,000

An inlaid silver Indian-style bowl, by Tiffany & Co., for the Columbian Exposition, circa 1893, 6¼in. high, 56oz. 10dwt. (Christie's) $125,000

A centerpiece bowl marked 'Milton A. Fuller, Inc. New York/Palm Beach', circa 1900, on four lion's-paw feet, 14in diam, 68 oz. (Christie's) $4,180

A sugar bowl, the cover with a green stone finial, by Tiffany & Co., N.Y., 1877-91, 3¼in. high, gross weight 13oz. (Christie's) $14,000

Hand hammered sterling silver bowl, R. Wallace & Sons Mfg. Co., Wallingford, Connecticut, with applied rim and four plaques of Austrian style geometric motifs, 4⁵/₈in. diameter. (Skinner Inc.) $100

Frederick Smith repoussé sterling fruit bowl, Denver, circa 1889, round with scalloped rim, 15 troy ozs. (Skinner Inc.) $400

Gorham sterling and crystal centerpiece, circa 1900, on a spreading circular base chased with roses, 14in. diam., approx. 27 troy oz. (Skinner Inc.) $2,100

A fine silver bowl, maker's mark of Whiting Mfg. Co., circa 1890, the sides elaborately repoussé and chased with clam, oyster and mussel shells amid seaweed on a matted ground, 10⁵/₈in. diameter, 32 oz. 10 dwt. (Christie's) $13,200

Kalo sterling silver bowl with attached underliner, Chicago, circa 1915, squat bulbous form, approximately 15 troy oz. (Skinner Inc.) $500

A shaped rectangular center-piece bowl, by Tiffany & Co., 1878-91, 4½in. high, 18.3/8in. wide, 8½in. deep, 67oz.10dwt. (Christie's) $18,000

Fine Sterling silver centerpiece bowl marked *Tiffany & Co.*, applied spiral shell bosses, twelve-lobed rim, probably circa 1873–91, 10in. diameter. (Eldred's) $5,170

BOWLS

A copper and silver applied bowl, by Gorham Manuf. Co., Providence, 1883, 3¼in. high. (Christie's) $2,000

A Gorham Sterling and mixed metal punchbowl and ladle. (Skinner Inc.) $18,700

Repousse sterling silver fruit bowl, by S. Kirk & Son Co., Maryland, circa 1890, 12½in. diam., 42 troy oz. $1,750

A presentation punch bowl, by Tiffany & Co., N.Y., 1890-91, 9in. high, 15¾in. diam., 101oz. (Christie's) $24,200

Sterling silver infant bowl and undertray by Gorham, with applied design of four children, date mark, 1903, bowl diameter, 5in.   (Eldred's) $1,760

A rare silver barber basin, maker's mark of William Moulton IV, Newburyport, circa 1815, 10¼in. diameter, 24 oz. 10 dwt. (Christie's) $5,500

A punch bowl by Herbert A. Taylor for Stone Associates, Gardner, Massachusetts, 1908-1937, the sides partly fluted, marked, 39cm. diam., 106oz. (Christie's New York) $9,350

A centerpiece bowl, by Gorham Manuf. Co., 1880, 3.1/8in. high, 7½in. diam., 11oz.10dwt. (Christie's) $750

A fine silver and glass punch bowl by Gorham, Providence, 1893, with a flaring scalloped brim repoussé and chased with grapes and mixed fruit, 16¼in. diam, 352 oz. (Christie's) $24,200

A trophy bowl for the New York Yacht Club, by Tiffany & Co., circa 1884, 15½in. diam., 97oz. 10dwt. $25,000

Fine Sterling silver punch bowl by Old Newbury Crafters, engraved monograms and dates, 16¼in. diameter, 107 troy oz. (Eldred's) $1,100

A circular silver bowl by Herbert Taylor, Massa., circa 1925, 9.7/8in. diam., 24oz. 10dwt. $1,250

CASTERS

A rare and important silver sugar caster, maker's mark of Jacobus van der Spiegel, New York, 1690–1708, the domed cover pierced with fleurs-de-lys and florettes and varied shapes including hearts and scrolls, 8¼in. high, 16oz.
(Christie's) $121,000

A caster, marked *HM*, probably New York, circa 1700, the domed and pierced cover with bayonet mounts and a turned finial, 3½in. high, 3oz.
(Christie's New York) $4,400

Sterling muffinier by Tiffany & Co., New York, New York, circa 1891–1902, raised on four ball supports, 6³/₈in. high, 6oz. 18 dwts.
(Butterfield & Butterfield) $605

A caster, the domed pierced cover with pinecone finial, by Zachariah Brigden, Boston, 1770-85, 5¼in. high, 3oz.
                                    $2,750

Silver pepper box, by Thomas Coverly, Newburyport, Massachusetts, circa 1760, with knob finial and domed cover above the straight sided octagonal body, 3 troy oz. (Robt. W. Skinner Inc.) $4,800

A caster of baluster form, by John Edwards, Boston, circa 1745, 5½in. high., 3oz.
                                    $4,000

CHOCOLATE POTS

A silver baluster shaped chocolate pot, by Samuel Kirk & Son Co., Baltimore, 1903-07, 10¼in. high, gross wt. 25oz. $1,750

Late 19th century copper and silver chocolate pot, 9¼in. high. $3,500

A sterling silver Martele chocolate pot, by Gorham Mfg. Co., circa 1900, 11½in. high, 23 troy oz. $4,000

432

COFFEE POTS

Antique American empire silver coffee pot, circa 1800–1830, raised petal decoration, wooden handle, ball feet, 11½in. high, 32 troy oz. (Eldred's) $440

A double pyriform coffee pot, by C. Wiltberger, Phila., circa 1785-90, 14¼in. high, gross wt. 51oz. (Christie's) $16,500

A silver coffee biggin, stand and lamp, maker's mark of Gale & Willis, New York, 1859, the body with elaborate foliate decoration, 11¼in. high, 43 oz. (Christie's) $1,650

A black coffee pot by Gorham, Providence, 1888, with a narrow curving spout and handle with insulators, 9½in. high, 14 oz. 10 dwt. $1,000

A parcel-gilt coffee pot and sugar bowl by Tiffany & Company, New York, 1892–1902, coffee pot 8¾in. high; bowl 4in. diam. $3,750

A rare silver coffee biggin, maker's mark of Garrett Eoff, New York, circa 1820, with a scroll spout chased with acanthus and a carved wood handle, 9½in. high, 32 oz. 10 dwt. (Christie's) $3,080

A coffee pot by Samuel Kirk & Son Co., Baltimore, 1903–1907, with a domed cover, curving spout and handle with insulators, 9¼in. high, 23 oz. $1,750

A silver Martele coffee pot by Gorham Manufacturing Company, Providence, 1899, of baluster form, 10¼in. high, 32oz. $4,000

A coffee pot by Dominick & Haff, New York, 1881, with a domed cover, a pointed finial scrolling handle and a narrow spout, 10¾in. high, 23 oz. 10 dwt. $2,500

A cream pitcher, urn-shaped, by Isaac Woodcock, Maryland, circa 1790-1810, 6¾in. high, 5oz. $3,500

A cream pitcher, by Albert Coles, N.Y., circa 1869, 6¼in. high, 6oz. $500

A covered cream pitcher, by Chas. Moore and J. Ferguson, Phila., circa 1801-05, 8¼in. high, 8oz. $2,500

A cream jug by Ephraim Brasher, New York, 1775-1785, with a beaded rim and a twisted scroll handle, 5¼in. high, 4oz. $2,500

Silver milk pitcher, maker's mark Hayden & Gregg, 1846-52, 6.5/8in. high, approx. 14 troy oz. $1,000

A milk pot on three scroll legs with pad feet, by T. Stoutenburgh, N.Y., circa 1735, 4¾in. high, 7oz.10dwt. $5,000

A double pyriform cream pitcher, by Cary Dunn, Newark, circa 1780-90, 5¾in. high, 7oz. 10dwt. $3,500

A silver cream jug, maker's mark of John Myers, Philadelphia, 1790–1804, helmet-shaped, with a molded strap handle, on a flaring pedestal base with a square foot, 7¹/₈in. high, 5 oz. 10 dwt. (Christie's) $2,640

A cream pitcher, pyriform, by Philip Syng, Jnr., Phila., 1750-80, 4in. high, 3oz. $7,500

434

A cream pitcher, marked 'ID', probably Phila., 1790-1810, 6¾in. high, 5oz.
$1,500

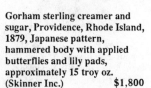

Gorham sterling creamer and sugar, Providence, Rhode Island, 1879, Japanese pattern, hammered body with applied butterflies and lily pads, approximately 15 troy oz. (Skinner Inc.)
$1,800

A silver pyriform cream pitcher, by Samuel Minott, Boston, circa 1750-60, 4¼in. high, 3oz.
$2,500

A silver cream jug, maker's mark of John Baptiste Dumoutet, Philadelphia, circa 1800, helmet-shaped, the spreading circular foot on square pedestal base, 7³/₈in. high, 5 oz. 10 dwt. (Christie's)
$1,760

Sterling Arts and Crafts style cream pitcher and open sugar bowl by Whiting Mfg. Co., Providence, Rhode Island, 1913, 8oz. 14 dwts. (Butterfield & Butterfield)
$302

A silver cream jug, maker's mark of Daniel Van Voorhis, New York, circa 1795, with cast double-scroll handle, on a pedestal foot, 5¹/₂in. high, 4 oz. 10 dwt. (Christie's)
$2,200

A silver cream jug of inverted pyriform with a scroll handle, by Wm. Hollingshead, Phila., circa 1760/80, 5in. high, 4oz.
$4,000

Late 18th century silver creamer, maker's mark INR, Phila., 4½in. high, 4 troy oz.
$600

A cream pitcher with a scalloped rim and scroll handle, by Z. Brigden, Boston, 1770-85, 4.7/8in. high, 3oz.
$2,500

Gorham Martelé sterling presentation loving cup, Rhode Island, circa 1902, 11in. high, approximately 92 troy oz. (Skinner Inc.) **$7,000**

Theodore B. Starr Sterling repoussé loving cup, 10¼in. high, approximately 82 troy oz. (Skinner Inc.) **$4,675**

A rare spout cup by William S. Nichols, Newport, Rhode Island, circa 18921, with a tubular side spout, a molded strap handle, and a reeded circular footrim, 2⅜in. high, 3 oz. (Christie's) **$1,650**

Sterling silver loving cup by Gorham, applied leaf and vine design, gold washed interior, 9⅜in. high, 21.4 troy oz. (Eldred's) **$495**

Pair of Sterling silver loving cups by Gorham, applied grapevine and Indian chief's head design, 8in. high, 39 troy oz. (Eldred's) **$2,310**

A loving cup, by Gorham, Providence, circa 1905, with an applied grapevine border and three sinuous handles, 19¼in. high, 107oz. (Christie's New York) **$10,000**

A trophy loving cup by Tiffany & Co., New York, circa 1889, with a serpentine brim and three curving handles formed as anchors, 9in. high, 57 oz. 10 dwt. (Christie's) **$3,000**

A spout cup, by Edward Winslow, Boston, circa 1710-20, 3¼in. high, 4oz. (Christie's) **$19,800**

A presentation loving cup, by Dominick & Haff, Newark, for J. E. Caldwell & Co., 1895, in original mahogany box, 11½in. high, 82oz. **$10,000**

DISHES

A Joel F. Hewes sterling silver hand-raised, footed candy dish, circa 1908, 6in. diam., approx. 10 troy oz. **$500**

A silver chafing dish, by A. Hartwell, Mass., bowl 6in. diam., 27oz.10dwt. **$1,500**

A tureen with domed cover, by Black, Starr & Frost, New York, circa 1900, 9½in. high, 14in. wide overall, 73oz.10dwt. **$3,750**

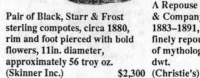

A sterling silver Martele oval centrepiece, by Gorham Mfg. Co., dated 1881 to 1906, 38 troy oz., 12¾in. long. **$3,000**

Pair of Black, Starr & Frost sterling compotes, circa 1880, rim and foot pierced with bold flowers, 11in. diameter, approximately 56 troy oz. (Skinner Inc.) **$2,300**

A Repouse Compote by Tiffany & Company, New York, 1883–1891, the sides formed of a finely repoussé and chased band of mythological figures, 33 oz. 10 dwt. (Christie's) **$5,500**

Mid 19th century Kirk repousse sterling covered vegetable dish of oval form, Maryland, approx. 100 troy oz. **$3,000**

One of a pair of silver covered vegetable dishes, by Tiffany & Co., N.Y., 1947-55, 5in. high, 11in. wide, 92oz.10dwt. **$3,000**

An enameled sterling silver and glass jam dish and spoon, by Mary P. Winlock, 4.5/8in. diam., approx. 5 troy oz. **$650**

A silver vegetable dish, maker's mark of Gorham Mfg. Co., Providence, circa 1870, with two stag-head handles, the domed cover with fawn finial, 13³/₄in. wide, 44 oz. 10 dwt. (Christie's) $2,640

Reed & Barton sterling chafing dish, early 20th century, on cabriole legs with paw feet, 10¹/₂in. high, approximately 81¹/₂ troy oz. (Skinner Inc.) $1,400

A rare Indian style silver mounted glass canoe form butter dish, by Shreve & Co., San Francisco, circa 1890, marked, 11cm. high, 24.78cm. long. (Christie's New York) $2,420

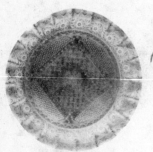

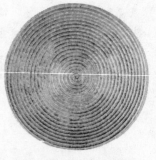

A plated dish by James W. Tufts, Boston, last quarter 19th century, with a flaring lobed brim, the entire surface chased with stylized foliate and geometric borders, 11³/₈in. diam. (Christie's) $275

A parcel-gilt silver compôte, maker's mark of Gorham Mfg. Co., Providence, 1870, one end forming a handle, elaborately clad with an entwined foliate frosted grape vine and applied gilt fox, 12¹/₂in. long, 39 oz. (Christie's) $3,520

A silver gilt basketweave dish, by Tiffany & Co., New York, circa 1890, in the form of an Indian basket, 5³/₄in. diam., 5oz. (Christie's New York) $1,320

A silver covered vegetable dish, maker's mark of Gorham MFG, Co., Providence, 1916, with foliate scroll side handles, length over handles 12¹/₂in., 36 oz. 10 dwt. (Christie's) $1,650

A medallion butter dish by Gorham, Providence, circa 1865, repoussé and chased with a band of cartouches, scrolls, and foliage, 5in. high, 16 oz. (Christie's) $1,250

A covered entree dish with a figural finial, by Samuel Kirk & Son, Baltimore, 1880-1890, the domed cover surmounted by a figure of a grazing deer, marked, 6³/₄in. high, 52oz. (Christie's New York) $5,280

DISHES

A silver butter dish, maker's mark of Gorham Mfg. Co., Providence, circa 1860, with two bifurcated foliate scroll side handles, 9¼in. wide, 14 oz. 10 dwt.
(Christie's) $715

Silver chafing dish, Jacob Hurd, Boston, circa 1745, pierced bowl with everted rim and removable pierced grate raised on three moulded scrolled supports, 16¾ troy oz.
(Skinner Inc.) $22,000

A covered entree dish, by Samuel Kirk & Son Co., Baltimore, 1896-1925, the cover and bowl repousse and chased with flowers and scrolls, 23cm. diam., 35oz. (Christie's New York) $3,520

'English Sterling' centerpiece, New York, circa 1870, the boat form bowl on a narrow waisted stem over a multi stepped expanding base, 8³⁄₄in. high, 42oz.
(Butterfield & Butterfield) $770

A parcel-gilt silver olive dish and tongs, maker's mark of Gorham Mfg. Co., Providence, 1887, formed as a cured olive with stem, 5³⁄₄in. long, 5 oz. 10 dwt.
(Christie's) $1,320

A parcel-gilt silver covered butter dish, maker's mark of Tiffany & Co., New York, 1881–1891, the spot-hammered surface applied with silver-gilt leaves and thistles, 5⁷⁄₈in. diameter, 15 oz. 10 dwt.
(Christie's) $2,860

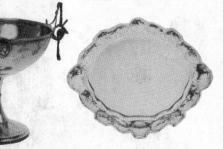

A silver butter dish and cover, maker's mark of Bigelow, Kennard & Co., Boston, circa 1880, in the Persian taste, elaborately repoussé with foliate scrolls and fluting, 8in. wide, 16¹⁄₂ oz.
(Christie's) $880

Coin silver compote by Goodnow & Jenks, Boston, cameo reliefs at rim, classical style handle, conical foot with Greek key motif, 8¹⁄₂in. high, 14 troy oz.
(Eldred's) $468

A silver Martele meat dish, maker's mark of Gorham Mfg. Co., Providence, circa 1905, the rim repoussé with flowers and leaves, the center engraved with a monogram, 20¹⁄₂in. long, 66 oz.
(Christie's) $6,600

EWERS & JUGS

A silver ewer by Edwin Stebbins & Company, New York, 1850-1856, with a scroll handle cast in the form of a branch, 15in. high, 30oz. $1,500

A 19th century American cordial or water jug of baluster form, maker's mark of Jones, Ball & Poor, Boston, circa 1845, 28cm. high, 30oz. $1,500

A ewer, by John Kitts, Louisville, 1838-76, 12¼in. high, 17oz. $2,850

A tall ewer, by William Forbes for Ball, Tompkins & Black, New York, 1839-1851, with a flaring cylindrical neck, 18¼in. high, 49oz. (Christie's New York) $2,860

A pair of silver presentation ewers, maker's mark of Forbes & Son, New York, circa 1836, with elaborate foliate scroll handles, 11¾in. high, 78 oz. (Christie's) $6,600

A vase-shaped silver ewer, by Thos. Fletcher, Phila., circa 1838, 13¼in. high, 39oz. $1,500

One of a pair of inverted, pyriform ewers, by F. Marquand, New York, 1826-39, 14½in. high, 38oz. 10dwt. $3,000

A 19th century American 'ivy chased' jug, by Tiffany & Co., circa 1870, 23cm. high, 27.5oz. (Phillips)   £2,100

A silver vase shaped ewer, by Jones, Ball & Poor, Boston, circa 1846, 16¼in. high, 41oz. $1,300

EWERS & JUGS

An American ovoid wine ewer, by Samuel Kirk, Baltimore, circa 1830, 16¼in. high, 48oz. $3,250

A large Tiffany and Co. japanesque jug, the copper baluster body applied with three Sterling silver fish, stamped *Tiffany and Co.*, 21.5cm. high over frog.
(Spencer's) $18,205

Silver ewer, Crosby, Morse & Foss, Boston, circa 1850, 14in. high, approximately 32 troy oz.
(Skinner Inc.) $750

An American ovoid wine ewer, the body chased over-all in the Chinese style, by S. Kirk, Baltimore, circa 1830, 16½in. high, 48oz.
$2,750

A silver covered hot-milk jug, maker's mark of Tiffany & Co., New York, 1891–1902, the spot-hammered surface etched with foliage and thistles, 7in. high, 20 oz. 10 dwt.
(Christie's) $3,300

A vase-shaped ewer, by Wm. Forbes for Ball, Black & Co., N.Y., 1851-circa 1860, 16½in. high, 46oz. $1,250

A presentation ewer, by Baldwin Gardiner, N.Y., circa 1835, 13½in. high, 45oz. 10dwt. $1,250

An American Aesthetic Movement white metal hot water jug, the oviform body extravagantly applied with pine-needles, 7in. high.
(Christie's S. Ken) $1,000

Silver ewer, Robert and William Wilson (active 1825–1846), Philadelphia, baluster form with foliate and acanthus decoration, 45 troy oz.
(Skinner Inc.) $1,400

FLATWARE

Kirk Sterling flatware service, 1880-90, repoussé pattern, 104 pieces, monogrammed, approximately 93 troy oz. weighable silver. (Skinner Inc.) **$1,430**

Part of a 140-piece mixed metal flatware service, by Tiffany & Co., 1880-85, dinner fork, 8.1/8in. long, ladel 13in. long, 201oz. 10dwt. excluding knives. (Christie's) **$100,000**

A parcel gilt fish slice and fork, American, circa 1885, each engraved with two intertwined carp, 11½in. long, 8oz. (Christie's New York) **$605**

A silver fish slice, maker's mark of James Conning, Mobile, Alabama, 1842–1862, engraved with a fish amid foliate scroll decoration, 11¾in. long, 5 oz. (Christie's) **$1,760**

A rare punch ladle, attributed to John Hastier, New York, 1725-1750, the circular bowl with a heart shaped join and an everted rim, marked (minor repair at handle join), 13½in. long. 3oz. (Christie's New York) **$1,870**

A pair of grape shears, by Tiffany & Co., circa 1880-85, of shaped scissor-form, 8in. long, 5oz. (Christie's) **$5,000**

Part of a 24-piece set of parcel gilt dessert knives and forks, by Tiffany & Co., circa 1880-85, knives 8¼in. long, 48oz.10dwt. (Christie's) **$6,000**

Three of seven parcel gilt condiment servers, by Tiffany & Co., circa 1880-85, serving spoon 9½in. long, sauce ladles each approx. 7in. long, 13oz. (Christie's) **$7,500**

FLATWARE

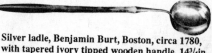

A silver ladle, maker's mark of Joseph Anthony, Philadelphia, 1785–1810, with downturned rounded-end handle, 10in. long, 3 oz.
(Christie's)   **$1,320**

Silver ladle, Benjamin Burt, Boston, circa 1780, with tapered ivory tipped wooden handle, 14³/₄in. long.
(Skinner Inc.)   **$715**

A pair of parcel-gilt silver fish servers, maker's mark of Gorham Mfg. Co., circa 1880, the ivory handles carved with swirling flutes, 12in. long.
(Christie's)   **$1,320**

A rare silver soup ladle, maker's mark of William & George Richardson, Richmond, Virginia, circa 1782–1795, with a downturned pointed-oval handle, 12¹/₄in. high, 4 oz. 10 dwt.
(Christie's)   **$1,870**

A rare pair of large silver ragout spoons made for Moses Michael Hays, maker's mark of Paul Revere, Boston, 1786, 12in. long, 8oz.
(Christie's)   **$46,200**

A pair of engraved fish servers by Albert Coles, New York, circa 1850-1855, the slice with a scrolled blade elaborately engraved with scrolls and foliage, 12in. long, 8oz.
(Christie's)   **$550**

Baltimore sterling rose pattern flatware service of 161 pieces, approximately 174 troy oz. weighable silver.
(Skinner Inc.)   **$3,700**

Part of a 146-piece flatware service, by Tiffany & Co., New York, 1878-1900, in the original fitted oak box, 230oz. excluding knives.
(Christie's)   **$9,000**

GOBLETS

An American silver wine goblet, by Samuel Kirk, Baltimore, circa 1840, 6.1/8in. high, and a beaker 4½in. high, 118oz.10dwt. **$1,200**

An American silver wine goblet, a footed beaker and a cann, the first by Robert & Wm. Wilson, Phila., the second by W. W. Hannah, Hudson, New York, the third circa 1850. **$850**

American silver goblet with chased decoration, cast vintage design base, unmarked, 8in. high, 11.2 troy oz. (Eldred's) **$303**

A presentation goblet; American, possibly Savannah, circa 1857, 7½in. high, 9oz.10dwt. **$1,750**

Coin silver goblet and a cup with handles and salt cellar, third quarter 19th century, by Peter L. Krider, Philadelphia, circa 1850–1860, 15oz. 14 dwts. (Butterfield & Butterfield) **$440**

A gilt-lined goblet on a beaded rim foot, the bowl engraved with an armorial and crest, possibly American circa 1860, 6in., 10.75oz. (Christie's S. Ken.) **$254**

Fine antique American coin silver goblet, mid-19th century, with chased hunting decoration, marked *Pure Coin*, Boston, 8in. high, 11 troy oz. (Eldred's) **$715**

Assembled and matching silver three piece presentation water set, pitcher marked *Vanderslice & Co., San Francisco, Cal.*; goblets unmarked, dated *1866*, 44oz. 2 dwts. (Butterfield & Butterfield) **$2,200**

One of two American silver wine goblets, by C. Bard & Son, one 5¾in. high, the other 6¼in. high, 9oz.10dwt. **$750**

INKSTANDS

SILVER

A silver inkwell, maker's mark of Shiebler & Co., New York, circa 1900, elaborately repoussé with scrolls and rocaille, the fitted silver-mounted glass bottles with fluted swirls, 10in. long, 19 oz. 10 dwt. (Christie's) $3,080

A martele inkstand, by Gorham, Providence, circa 1905, the stand repousse and chased with serpentine ribs and flowers, marked *Martele. 9584*, 10¼in. wide, 9oz. (Christie's New York) $2,200

A commemorative inkstand by Tuttle Silversmiths, Boston, 1945-1949, marked with pine tree shilling mark and *HT1*, for President Truman's first term, 8in. high, 35oz. (Christie's New York) $1,430

JARS

Mount Washington Crown Milano covered jar, blue background melon ribbed bowl with gold enhanced floral decoration, 6³/₄in. high. (Skinner Inc.) $330

A silver and mixed-metal ginger jar, maker's mark of Whiting Mfg. Co., circa 1885, the matted surface applied with a copper fish and with silver and copper foliage, 5¹/₂in. high, 10 oz. 10 dwt. (Christie's) $1,980

Cut glass and silver jar, brilliant hobstar and oval cut, with rose decorated flared silver rim, 9in. diameter. (Skinner Inc.) $750

Sterling ginger jar by Howard & Co., New York, New York, 1885, the body and lid allover chased and embossed with scrolling foliage and various flowers, 6in. high, 10oz. (Butterfield & Butterfield) $522

An unusual silver and enamel powder jar, maker's mark of Gorham Mfg. Co., Providence, circa 1895, repoussé with foliate and drapery swags below a laurel band, 4¹/₂in. diameter, 6 oz. 10 dwt. (Christie's) $1,210

Mount Washington Crown Milano biscuit jar, with shaded gold-amber color handpainted with leafy brown and green stalks, 7¹/₂in. high. (Skinner Inc.) $550

445

MISCELLANEOUS

A mixed-metal mustard pot and spoon by Dominick & Haff, New York, 1880, with a circular low-domed hinged cover with a ball finial, 2½in. high, gross weight 4oz. 10 dwt. $2,200

Sterling Smith Corona typewriter by Gorham Mfg. Co., Providence, Rhode Island, 1930, 10¾in. wide.
(Butterfield & Butterfield) $8,800

A medallion silver and gold belt buckle by Schiebler, New York, circa 1885, comprised of one oval and one rounded rectangular medallion, 3in. long, 2⅛in. high, 1 oz. 10 dwt.
(Christie's) $1,760

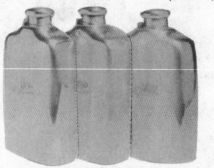

Mauser Co. Sterling Bottle Carrier, New York, c. 1900, in the form of a wine bottle with repousse vine decoration, 11½in. high, approximately 27.5 troy oz. $1,750

A set of three Tiffany & Co. spirit flasks, the flattened rectangular bodies with screwed hinged covers, 20.6cm. high. $2,500

A silver book-mark made for the Columbian Exposition of 1893, maker's mark of Tiffany & Co., 11½in. long, 8 oz.
(Christie's) $1,760

A silver presentation flask by Gorham Mfg. Co., 1888, 7¾in. high, 19oz. 10dwt. $2,500

A Tiffany & Co unusual late 19th century American Aesthetic Movement parcel gilt chamberstick, with in-curved sides, circa 1880, 11ozs. $10,500

Sterling silver cocktail shaker by Shreve, Crump & Low, hammered Art Deco style, San Francisco, circa 1910, 10¼in. high, 12.6 troy oz.
(Eldred's) $1,210

A cigar lighter by Gorham, Providence, 1881, in the neo-Grecque taste, the top dished, in a petal pattern, 4³/₈in. long, 4 oz. (Christie's) **$440**

A mixed metal mustard pot by Dominick & Haff, New York, 1880, the surface engraved in an all over blossom pattern, 6.04cm. high, gross weight 3oz. **$1,000**

A tazza with two scrolling strapwork handles, by Tiffany & Co., 1870-75, 6½in. high, 12.5/8in. wide, overall, 23oz.10dwt.**$1,750**

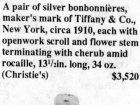

A silver tea caddy, maker's mark of Tiffany & Co., New York, 1879–1891, the shoulder and slip on cap chased with scrolls, 8¹/₈in. high, 9 oz. (Christie's) **$1,320**

A pair of silver bonbonnières, maker's mark of Tiffany & Co., New York, circa 1910, each with openwork scroll and flower stem terminating with cherub amid rocaille, 13¹/₂in. long, 34 oz. (Christie's) **$3,520**

An amusing flask, by Tiffany & Co., New York, 1891-1902 decorated with etched scenes of brownies frolicking and quarreling and avoiding mosquitoes, marked, 7¾in. high, 15oz. (Christie's New York) **$8,250**

A silver punch strainer, maker's mark of John David, Jr., Philadelphia, circa 1785, with pierced scrollwork handle engraved with initials *TSC* on front, 4¹/₂in. high, 1 oz. (Christie's) **$8,250**

A silver flask by Whiting Manufacturing Company, circa 1885, the front repousse and chased with a seahorse, 6in. long, 7½oz. **$3,000**

American Aesthetic movement Sterling tea caddy by Kennard & Jenks, Boston, Massachusetts, circa 1880, engraved in the Japanese taste on the four sides and lid, 5in. high, 12 oz. 6 dwts. (Butterfield & Butterfield) **$5,500**

MISCELLANEOUS

Plated lady's dressing table mirror with easel back, late 19th century, with wire easel back, 13½in. high.
(Butterfield & Butterfield) $495

Silver five-bottle caster frame with scrolled legs, leaf-form feet, turned handle with bright-cut engraving, possible American, 10¼in. high, 36.6 troy oz.
(Eldred's) $220

A silver tea caddy, maker's mark of Tiffany & Co., New York, 1891–1902, elaborately repoussé with flowers on a matted ground, 4½in. high, 7 oz. 10 dwt.
(Christie's) $935

A silver figural bell, maker's mark of Tiffany & Co., New York, circa 1875, the handle formed as a classical maiden, marked 5½in. high, 6 oz. 10 dwt.
(Christie's) $1,045

A fine silver and enamel desk set, maker's mark of Tiffany & Co., New York, circa 1886, decorated with polychrome enamel in the Islamic taste, in original fitted leather box dated 1886.
(Christie's) $6,600

A silver and mixed-metal pepper mill, maker's mark of Tiffany & Co., New York, circa 1889, inlaid with niello and copper tear drops and flowers, with bud finial, 3¾in. high, 5 oz.
(Christie's) $2,200

A figural cigar stand, Tiffany & Company, New York, 1865–1870, supported by three cast fully-modeled putti, on a shaped plinth base, 8³⁄₈in. high, 29 oz. 10 dwt.
(Christie's) $1,980

A silver tumbler cup, maker's mark of Andrew Billing, Preston, Connecticut, Poughkeepsie area, 1775–1808, engraved with script monogram JWK within circular bright-cut reserve, 2¹⁄₈in. high, 1 oz. 10 dwt.
(Christie's) $1,430

Silver six bottle revolving caster stand fitted with six glass castors by W.K. Vanderslice & Co., San Francisco, California, circa 1875, 14½in. high, 52oz.
(Butterfield & Butterfield)
$2,09⬤

A medallion mug by Gorham, Providence, circa 1865, with a squared handle and beaded borders, applied with two medallions, 3in. high, 4 oz. (Christie's) $440

Antique American .900 fine silver mug by Wood & Hughes of New York City, chased and applied decoration, gilt interior, dated 1872, 3³/₄in. high, 6 troy oz. (Eldred's) $363

Silver mug, George Hanners, Boston, circa 1740, tapering cylindrical form with molded mid-band and base band, scroll handle, 10 troy oz. (Skinner Inc.) $5,500

A silver mug, maker's mark of Tiffany & Co., New York, 1875–1891, baluster form on spreading rim foot, elaborately repoussé with flowers, 6in. high, 18 oz. (Christie's) $2,200

A mug by William B. Durgin Co., Concord, New Hampshire, circa 1880, with a curved handle, the spot-hammered surface repoussé and finely-chased, 3⁵/₈in. high, 7 oz. (Christie's) $1,100

A silver cann, maker's mark of William Homes, Sr., Boston, circa 1750, the S-scroll handle with molded drop and bud terminal, 5¹/₄in. high, 10 oz. 10 dwt. (Christie's) $1,320

A cann, by Joseph Richardson, Sr., Philadelphia, 1744-1784, with a molded rim and a molded circular foot, 5¼in. high, 11oz. (Christie's New York) $2,200

A silver applied enameled copper mug, by Gorham Manuf. Co., Providence, 1881, 6½in. high. $1,760

A rare silver cann, maker's mark of John Bayley, Philadelphia, 1760–1770, the double scroll handle with acanthus-leaf grip, on molded circular foot, 5in. high, 13 oz. 10 dwt. (Christie's) $3,080

PITCHERS

Dominick and Haff Sterling pitcher, late 19th century, chased vintage decoration, retailed by Bigelow Kennard and Company, 13¾in. high, 44 troy oz.
(Skinner Inc.) $1,320

Fine Sterling silver and cut and engraved crystal pitcher by Gorham, ornate leaf and berry decoration, 14½in. high.
(Eldred's) $1,980

A silver water pitcher, maker's mark of S. Kirk & Son., Baltimore, 1846–1861, elaborately repoussé with architectural landscapes amid flowers and foliage, 12in. high, 30 oz. 10 dwt.
(Christie's) $1,540

American Arts and Crafts hand beaten silver pitcher by LeBolt, Chicago, Illinois, circa 1915–1920, applied with cypher monogram on the side, 8¼in. high, 22oz. 6dwts.
(Butterfield & Butterfield)
                    $1,540

A fine silver and mixed-metal pitcher, maker's mark of Gorham Mfg. Co., Providence, 1880, the spot-hammered surface applied with a brass turkey, bamboo leaves, and a bronze fruit-tree branch, 7¾in. high, 30 oz.
(Christie's) $9,900

American silver octagonal pitcher by Whiting Mfg. Co., Providence, Rhode Island, 1921, on four cushion feet, hollow harp handle, 6¾in. high, 21oz. 8dwts.
(Butterfield & Butterfield)
                    $440

A pitcher, by A. E. Warner, Balitmore, circa 1810, the neck and base with reeded banding, the front engraved with armorials, 8¼in. high, 32oz. (Christie's New York)
                    $8,800

A pitcher, by William Gale for Tiffany & Company, New York, 1856-1859, the neck and foot with repousse acanthus leaf borders, marked, 11½in. high, 29oz. (Christie's New York) $2,090

A silver water pitcher, maker's mark of Arthur J. Stone, Gardner, Massachusetts, 1908–1937, the body repoussé and chased with irises, 10¾in. high, 33 oz. 10 dwt.
(Christie's) $3,300

PITCHERS

A silver-mounted 'craquelle' glass ice pitcher, maker's mark of Gorham Mfg. Co., Providence, circa 1880, with glass rope-twist handle and silver collar, 12¼in. high. (Christie's) $1,870

A silver water pitcher, maker's mark of John W. Forbes, New York, circa 1830, with foliate scroll handle and gadrooned rim, 12in. high, 31 oz. 10 dwt. (Christie's) $1,540

A silver water pitcher, maker's mark of S. Kirk & Sons, Co., Baltimore, 1903–1907, eleborately repoussé with architectural landscapes amid flowers and foliage, 12in. high, 43 oz. (Christie's) $3,300

A silver water pitcher, maker's mark of Whiting Mfg. & Co., circa 1885, elaborately repoussé with flowers on a matted ground, 7⅛in. high, 23 oz. 10 dwt. (Christie's) $1,870

A fine silver and mixed-metal pitcher, maker's mark of Tiffany & Co., New York, circa 1880, the spot-hammered sides and handle applied with a dragonfly and butterflies amid a trailing vine of gold and copper, 7¾in. high, 26 oz. 10 dwt. (Christie's) $28,600

A vase-shaped pitcher, in the Japanese taste, by Gorham Manuf. Co., Providence, 1885, 9in. high, 40oz.10dwt. (Christie's) $9,000

A presentation pitcher, by Newell Harding & Co., Boston, circa 1854, with a cast rustic handle and a cast grapevine spout, marked, 13in. high, 39oz. (Christie's New York) $1,650

American silver hand wrought water pitcher by Herbert Taylor for Arthur Stone, Gardner, Massachusetts, circa 1935, with mild harp thumbrest, helmet brim spout, 40oz. 4dwts. (Butterfield & Butterfield) $1,320

A silver water pitcher, maker's mark of Krider & Co., Philadelphia, circa 1851, elaborately repoussé with flowers enclosing a presentation inscription, with foliate scroll handle, 11in. high, 29 oz. 10 dwt. (Christie's) $990

451

Early 20th century Arthur Stone sterling silver water pitcher, Gardner, Mass., 9in. high, 31 troy oz. $2,250

A silver covered water pitcher by S. Kirk & Son Co., Baltimore, circa 1920, the flat hinged cover with a pierced thumbpiece, 9in. high, overall, 52oz. $4,250

A pitcher of baluster form, by Samuel Kirk, Baltimore, assay marks for 1824, 8¼in. high, 25oz.10dwt. $2,200

A pitcher of baluster form, with a curved spout and S-scroll handle, by Jones, Ball & Poor, Boston, circa 1852, 11¼in. high, 29oz. $1,250

A pitcher, by Tiffany & Co., New York, 1869-1891, the cast handle in the form of stylized leafage above classical mask handle join, marked, 22cm. high, 36oz. (Christie's New York) £2,213

A pitcher, by Haddock, Lincoln & Foss, Boston, circa 1855, with a rustic handle and a leaf form spout, marked (bruises), 9¾in. high, 33oz. $1,000

An urn-shaped pitcher, by Charters, Cann & Dunn, N.Y., circa 1850, 8½in. high, 12oz. $325

A water pitcher, American, circa 1815, with a squared handle and a broadly reeded body, unmarked, 8¼in. high, 26oz. $1,200

A sterling silver repousse water pitcher, marked S. Kirk & Son, Baltimore, 1846-61, 11.1/8in. high, 32 troy oz. $1,250

PITCHERS

A pitcher, by Edwin Stebbins, New York, 1828-1835, the foliate scroll handle with a cast helmet thumbpiece, marked, 13¾in. high, 45oz. $1,100

A pitcher, by Adolf Himmel, New Orleans, circa 1854-61, 11in. high, 25oz. $1,850

Silver overlay pitcher, with applied handle, decorated with silver rim and border panels centering cut floral designs, 10in. high.
(Skinner Inc.) $600

A plated pitcher, by Meriden Britannia Co., circa 1885, the entire surface spot hammered, the sides repousse and chased with a dragonfly, waterlilies and flowers, marked, 26cm. high. (Christie's New York) $1,100

A silver water pitcher, attributed to Dominick & Haff, New York, circa 1880, with an everted brim and a scroll handle, marked Sterling on base, 6¾in. high. (Christie's) $2,000

A vase-shaped pitcher, American, with unidentified eagle touch mark, circa 1825-35, 12in. high, 35oz. $1,600

A pitcher of baluster form with an open handle, by Gorham Manuf. Co., 1897, 8¾in. high, gross weight 31oz. (Christie's) $2,750

Kirk repoussé silver covered pitcher, Baltimore, 1846–61, recumbent deer finial, chased floral and village landscape decoration, 9in. high, aproximately 33 troy oz. (Skinner Inc.) $1,800

Tiffany sterling silver water pitcher of circular bulbous form, circa 1880, 8¾in. high, approx. 30 troy oz. $1,500

PLATES

A set of twelve silver dinner plates, maker's mark of Howard & Co., New York, dated *1907*, the center engraved with a coat-of-arms and crest, 10in. diameter, 292 oz. (Christie's) $6,600

One of a set of twelve plates, by Gorham Manuf. Co., 1907, 10¼in. diam., 204oz. $6,000

Set of Twelve Schofield Co. Sterling Dinner Plates, Baltimore, 20th century, in the Baltimore Rose pattern, 10½in. diam, approximately 242 troy oz. (Skinner Inc) $8,000

One of a set of twelve plates, by Redlich & Co., New York, circa 1900, 9¾in. diam., 160oz. $6,000

A parcel-gilt silver wheat-pattern serving plate and cake knife, maker's mark of Gorham Mfg. Co., Providence, 1871, the rim applied and chased with gilt wheat sheaves amid foliage, 10¼in. diameter, 22 oz. 10 dwt. (Christie's) $2,860

Twelve American Sterling service plates by International Silver Co., Meriden, Connecticut, Trianon, 10½in. diameter, 234oz. (Butterfield & Butterfield) $3,850

PORRINGERS

A silver porringer, maker's mark of Benjamin Burt, Boston, 1760–1800, with a pierced keyhole handle engraved *WMc to FH*, 8in. high, 7 oz. (Christie's) $1,760

A porringer by John Hancock, Boston, circa 1750–1765, with a pierced keyhole handle, 8¼in. long, 8 oz. (Christie's) $2,420

A silver porringer, by Benjamin Burt, Boston, 1750-1800, with a pierced keyhole handle, 5¼in. diam. 8oz. (Christie's) $1,980

PORRINGERS

A Gorham sterling silver porringer of circular form with two side mounted 'C' scroll handles, 4½in. diam., 7 troy oz. $450

Late 18th century Boston-style silver porringer, 5in. diam., 8 troy oz. $800

A Kirk sterling silver porringer with reticulated handle, 4¼in. diam., 8 troy oz. $700

A porringer by William Simpkins, Boston, 1730–1770, with a pierced keyhole handle engraved with block initials, 8in. long, 7 oz. 10 dwt. (Christie's) $1,980

Silver porringer by Thomas Dane, Boston, Massachusetts, circa 1760, with slightly domed base and bombé sides, cast pierced 'keyhole' handle, 7½in. long, 6oz. 2 dwts. (Butterfield & Butterfield) $1,210

A porringer by Jonathan Otis, Newport, circa 1750–1765, with a pierced keyhole handle engraved 'S. Coggeshall', 8in. long, 8 oz. 10 dwt. (Christie's) $2,860

A circular silver porringer, by Daniel Russell, Rhode Island, circa 1740-71, 7¾in. long, overall, 8oz. $2,500

A silver porringer by Thomas Edwards, Boston, circa 1750, with a pierced keyhole handle engraved with script initials, 5¼in. diam. 9½oz. with cover. (Christie's) $3,080

Silver porringer, Samuel Casey maker, South Kingston, Rhode Island, mid-18th century, 5in. diam., approx. 8 troy oz. (Skinner Inc.) $3,250

SALTS

One of a pair of silver octagonal salts, by Wm. Forbes for Ball, Tomkins & Black, N.Y., 1839-51, 2½in. high, 7oz. $850

One of a pair of oval salts, by Bigelow Bros. & Kennard, Boston, circa 1860, 2¾in. high, 4½in. long, 7oz. $450

A rare trencher salt, maker's mark of Richard Conyers, Boston, circa 1700, with gadrooned rim and foot rim, 2⅛in. high, 1 oz. 10 dwt. (Christie's) $18,700

A fine and rare pair of silver salt cellars, maker's mark of Simeon Coley, New York, 1767–1769, on four scroll feet with scallop-shell knees and stepped pad feet, 3¼in. wide, 6 oz. (Christie's) $3,080

A pair of knife rests and open salts, by Tiffany & Co., 1878-91. $1,750

A set of four salts by Daniel Fueter, New York, 1786-1806, on a spreading oval stem on a rectangular foot, 5.4cm. high, 12½oz. (Christie's) $3,520

A pair of salts by Tiffany & Co., New York, 1870–1875, with a die-rolled guilloche border and three cast ram's-head feet, 3in. diam, 4 oz. (Christie's) $770

A salt cellar by Gorham, Providence, 1872, with a bail handle attached to angular handles, on four flaring cylindrical raking legs, 3in. high, 2 oz. $660

Two of a set of four 18th century Americal oval salts on pedestal bases, by Lewis Fueter, N.Y., circa 1785, 13.75oz. $3,000

SAUCE BOATS

A sauceboat, oval, with a scalloped rim and double scroll handle, by John Coburn, Boston, circa 1750, 8½in. long, 14oz. (Christie's) $18,700

A pap boat, by William Thompson, New York, 1809-1845, oval, with an everted rim, a curving spout and a scroll handle, 16cm. long, 3oz. (Christie's New York) $440

Kirk Repousse sterling sauce boat, Baltimore, 1903-07, chased floral design, 8⅝in. long, approximately 9 troy oz. (Skinner Inc.) $400

SUGAR URNS

A sugar urn, by Joseph Richardson, Jr., Philadelphia, circa 1790-1810, the cover and foot with beaded borders, marked, 9½in. high, 17oz. (Christie's New York) $2,860

A sugar urn, by Christian Wiltberger, Philadelphia, 1793-1817, with a conical cover, urn finial, and a flaring cylindrical stem on a square foot, marked, 9¾in. high, 12oz. (Christie's New York) $1,320

Silver covered sugar urn, Philadelphia, 1790–1800, on square pedestal base, beaded border, bright cut with festoons and shields, 9in. high, 9¾ troy oz. (Skinner Inc.) $825

Silver gilt urn, by Howard & Co., New York, circa 1900, 14in. high, 45 troy oz. $2,000

A fine sugar urn by Robert Swan, Philadelphia, circa 1800, with a pierced gallery at the rim, a conical cover with an urn finial, 11in. high, 16¼oz. $4,250

Silver sugar urn, by Joseph Lownes, Phila., 1758-1820, 10in. high. $2,000

TANKARDS

Silver tankard, Benjamin Hurd, maker, 1739-1781, Boston, Massachusetts, circa 1760, 9in. high, approximately 30 troy oz. (Skinner Inc.)
$2,300

Silver tankard, Nicholas Roosevelt, New York, circa 1740, with molded base band, scrolled thumbpiece with oval shield terminal, 7in. high, 39 troy oz. (Skinner Inc.)
$880

A silver tankard, maker's mark of Josiah Austin, Charleston and Boston, Massachusetts, circa 1765, with a scroll handle applied with a molded drop, $8^{5}/8$in. high, 28 oz. 10 dwt. (Christie's)
$8,800

A trophy tankard by Tiffany & Co., New York, circa 1890, with a low circular cover and scrolled handle, $10^{1}/4$in. high, 47 oz.
$4,400

A repousse tankard, by Tiffany & Co., N.Y. finished March 10, 1893, for the World's Columbian Exposition, Chicago, 1893, 10in. high, 52oz. 10dwt.
$28,600

A tankard, the domed lid with a pineapple finial, by Wm. Hollingshead, Phila., 1760-85, $10^{1}/2$in. high.
$3,250

An antique American silver tankard by Thomas Fletcher and Sidney Gardiner of Boston and Philadelphia, circa 1812, $10^{1}/2$in. high, 43.6 troy oz. (Selkirk's)
$9,250

A silver tankard, maker's mark of John Hastier, New York, circa 1740, with a flat-domed cover and a corkscrew thumbpiece, 7in. high, 29 oz. 10 dwt. (Christie's)
$15,400

A rare silver tankard, maker's mark of Eleazer Baker, Ashford, Connecticut, circa 1785, with an applied midband and a molded circular base, 8in. high, 29 oz. 10 dwt. (Christie's)
$37,400

A kettle on stand and a teapot, by Tiffany & Co., New York, 1876-1891, each globular, kettle 13in. high, gross weight 85oz.   **$1,870**

A tea kettle on stand, retailed by Starr and Marcus, N.Y., circa 1910, 14½in. high, 53oz. 10dwt.   **$1,750**

Late 19th century rococo Revival hallmarked silver kettle on stand, by Tiffany & Co., 10¼in. high, approx. 24 troy oz.   **$850**

A silver kettle on stand, maker's mark of *Gorham Mfg. Co., Providence, 1885–1895*, the sides elaborately repoussé and chased with flowers on a matted ground, 12in. high, gross weight 66oz.
(Christie's)   **$1,430**

Dominick and Haff sterling kettle and lamp stand, circa 1880, the hammered globular body decorated in the Japanese taste, 11½in. high, approximately 37 troy oz. (Skinner Inc.)   **$4,600**

American style silver hot water kettle on stand, marked *Old Friend*, 20th century, similar to Gorham's Plymouth, possibly Chinese, the kettle with swing handle over urn form body, 11³/₄in. high, 60oz. 10dwts.
(Butterfield & Butterfield) **$880**

A pyriform kettle on stand, by Grosjean & Woodward for Tiffany & Co., 1854-65, 11.5/8in. high, 30oz.   **$1,250**

A fine tea kettle and stand by Tiffany & Co., New York, 1881–1891, in the Japanese taste, 12³/₄in. high, 467 oz.   **$12,100**

Late 19th century sterling silver hot water kettle on stand, by Dominick & Haff, New York, 11½in. high.   **$1,000**

TEAPOTS

A compressed pyriform teapot by Otto Paul de Parisien, New York, 1763-85, 6 5/8in. high, 18oz.10dwt. $6,000

A silver teapot, oval, with a domed hinged lid, by F. Marquand, Georgia, 1820/26, 9½in. high, gross weight 33oz. $850

A silver teapot with an S-shaped spout, by Samuel Williamson, Phila., 1794/1813, 7¾in. high, gross weight 28oz. $1,350

A silver repousse teapot, probably Boston, circa 1835, 9½in. high, approx. 39 troy oz. $600

A teapot by William Ball, Baltimore, 1790–1800, with a conical cover, and a carved wood handle, 11½ in. high, gross weight 28oz.
(Christie's) $9,350

An urn-shaped teapot with a domed cover, by Bailey & Co., Phila., circa 1848-65, 10¾in. high, gross weight 37oz. $1,250

Silver teapot, 18th century, pear form with median molding, double scrolled ebony handle, 7¾in. high, 24 troy oz.
(Skinner Inc.) $1,980

Silver teapot, Joseph Lownes, Philadelphia, circa 1800, engraved with foliate monogram on circular pedestal foot with square base, 11in. high, 26 troy oz.
(Skinner Inc.) $2,310

Silver teapot, Fletcher and Gardner, Philadelphia, circa 1810, applied mid band of grapevine on a pedestal base, 8½in. high, 28 troy oz.
(Skinner Inc.) $715

TEAPOTS

A teapot, by Joseph Richardson, Sr., Philadelphia, 1745-1765, the spout with a scallop shell and drop, with later wood finial, 8½in. long, overall, gross weight 16oz. (Christie's New York) $9,350

A fine teapot by John Hurt, Boston, 1735–1745, the flat circular cover with a bell-shaped finial, 5in. high, 9¼in. long overall, 16 oz. (Christie's) $7,700

A teapot by Tiffany & Co., New York, circa 1877-80, in the Japanese taste, 5in. high, 19oz. $5,000

A rare teapot, New York, circa 1740–1760, the domed hinged cover with gadrooning and a turned finial, 8¼in. high, 24 oz. 10 dwt. (Christie's) $16,500

A teapot, urn-shaped, the conical cover with a pineapple finial, by Charles Westphal, Phila., circa 1790-1800, 11in. high, gross weight 25oz. $10,000

A teapot, pyriform, with a high domed cover, marked 'HM', N.Y., 1715-25, 5¾in. high, gross weight 16oz. 10dwt. $41,800

A square teapot, the hinged cover with a green stone finial, by Tiffany & Co., N.Y., 1877-91, 5in. high, gross weight 15oz. (Christie's) $16,500

A pyriform teapot with a domed hinged cover, by Peter Van Dyck, N.Y., circa 1720-35, 7¾in. high, 25oz. (Christie's) $93,500

A teapot on stand after Paul Revere by George C. Gebelein, Boston, circa 1930, with a straight spout, a hinged domed oval cover, and a carved wood handle, 11¼in. wide, gross weight 28oz. (Christie's) $2,090

TEA & COFFEE SETS

Whiting repoussé sterling five-piece tea and coffee service, mid 19th century, floral decoration, approximately 85 troy oz. (Skinner Inc.)   **$2,640**

Dominick and Haff sterling five-piece coffee set, retailed by Shreve, Crump & Low Co., early 20th century, chased scroll and floral decoration, approximately 91 troy oz. (Skinner Inc.)   **$1,980**

A five-piece tea service and tray, by Tiffany & Co., New York, circa 1881, comprising a coffee pot, a covered sugar bowl, a cream pitcher, a waste bowl and a large two-handled tray, coffee pot 8½ in. high, tray 27¼ in. long, gross weight 306 oz. (Christie's)   **$41,800**

A five-piece tea service, by Joseph Lownes, Phila., circa 1815, teapot 7 in. high, gross weight 115 oz.   **$6,000**

TEA & COFFEE SETS

A six piece tea service, by Ball, Tompkins & Black, New York, 1839-1851, the scrolled handles with insulating rings, the domed lids with floral finials, each marked, kettle 14½in. high, gross weight 177oz. $5,000

A six-piece tea service and tray, by Gorham Manufacturing Co., comprising a kettle on stand, a coffee pot, a teapot, a covered sugar bowl, a cream pitcher, a waste bowl and a large two-handled tray, kettle 13in. high, tray 31¼in. long, gross weight 374oz. $16,500 (Christie's)

A five-piece tea and coffee service, by George B. Sharp for Bailey & Co., Phila., circa 1848-50, comprising a kettle on stand, a coffee pot, a teapot, a covered cream pitcher and a covered sugar bowl, coffee pot 15¼in. high, 231oz.10dwt. (Christie's) $19,800

TEA & COFFEE SETS

Tiffany sterling three piece tête à tête, circa 1864, pear form, pineapple finial, chased ivy decoration, together with a pair of small Whiting sugar tongs, approximately 28 troy oz. (Skinner Inc.) **$2,640**

Three-piece silver tea set, John Vernon, New York, circa 1800–10, each of bulbous oval form engraved with herringbone border and shields, 44 troy oz. (Skinner Inc.) **$2,860**

An American 19th century four-piece tapering molded circular medallion tea service, Ball, Black and Co., circa. 1880, height of teapot 6in., 32.25oz. **$1,000**

Dominick & Haff three-piece sterling tea set, chased with Renaissance-style panels with swags, floral bouquets and laurel wreath borders, approximately 44 troy oz. (Skinner Inc) **$1,300**

A six-piece silver 'Renaissance' tea service and tray, all pieces except tray 1904–1905, designed by Paulding Farnham, the body elaborately repoussé and chased with female and male therms amid fruit and flowers, gross weight 498 oz. 10 dwt. (Christie's) **$44,000**

Three-piece silver partial teaset, America, 1870's, coffee pot 12in. high, approx. 78 troy oz. **$1,000**

TEA & COFFEE SETS

Silver tea and coffee service, Edward Lownes, Philadelphia, with applied bands of rococo decoration, with three pinwheel devices between marks, 146 troy oz.
(Skinner Inc.) $3,850

Three-piece Sterling silver tea set, circa 1854–55, made by the John C. Moore Company for Tiffany, Young & Ellis, chased floral decoration, 26.6 troy oz.
(Eldred's) $1,760

A three-piece tea service, by Tiffany & Co., N.Y., teapot 9in. high, gross weight 71oz.
$2,000

A three-piece tea service, by John Targee, N.Y., circa 1810-14, teapot 9in. high, gross weight 61oz. $2,750

Towle sterling seven-piece tea and coffee service, water kettle and stand, tea and coffee pots, creamer, sugar, waste bowl and sterling tray, approximately 270 troy oz.
(Skinner Inc.) $4,400

Part of a five-piece tea and coffee service, by Tiffany & Co., N.Y., 1907-47, coffee pot 9¼in. high, gross weight 125oz. $2,750

A six-piece part tea and coffee service, by various makers for Ball, Black
& Co., N.Y., circa 1851, coffee pot 11¼in. high, gross weight 162oz. $3,500

A five-piece tea and coffee service with a tray, by Heer-Schofield Co.,
Baltimore, circa 1905/28, tray 28½in. long, coffee pot 11in. high,
gross weight 229oz. $8,000

A six-piece tea and coffee service, by Bigelow, Kennard & Co., Boston, circa 1901, kettle
12in. high, gross weight 168oz.
$4,500

TEA & COFFEE SETS

A three-piece tea service with a pair of teacups and saucers, by Gorham Mfg. Co., Providence, 1880, teapot 4½in. high, gross weight 24oz.

$2,750

An eight-piece tea and coffee service and tray, by Tiffany & Co., N.Y., circa 1860/70, Etruscan pattern, coffee pot 11¾in. high, tray 34in. long, gross weight 397oz.10dwt. $25,000

A six-piece tea and coffee service, the wooden handles squared and reeded, by Fletcher & Gardiner, Phila., 1813/14, coffee pot 10in. high, gross weight 194oz. $15,000

TRAYS & SALVERS

Tiffany sterling silver butler's tray, rectangular, stylized foliate border, 21in. wide.
$15,000

Coin silver tray, Newel Harding & Co., Boston, circa 1855, engraved with the arms of the Bates family, 21in. wide, 103 troy oz.
(Skinner Inc.) $4,400

A fine silver chrysanthemum-pattern tea tray, maker's mark of Tiffany & Co., New York, 1902–1907, with cast chrysanthemum border, 29in. long, 270 oz. 10 dwt.
(Christie's) $22,000

An inlaid waiter with an everted brim, on four cast feet, by Tiffany & Co., 1878-91, 9½in. diam., gross weight 10oz. $19,800

Tiffany sterling and mixed metal salver, circa 1880, decorated in the Japanese taste with a dragonfly and maple branch on a hammered ground, 11¾in. wide, approximately 19 troy oz.
(Skinner Inc.) $13,000

A fine silver and mixed-metal salver, maker's mark of Tiffany & Co., New York, circa 1880, the spot-hammered surface inlaid with three butterflies of copper, gold, platinum, and brass, 11in. diameter, 26 oz. 10 dwt.
(Christie's) $13,200

A waiter, by Gorham, Providence, 1881, the surface engraved with swallows and cattails, above a raised and chased folded damask napkin, marked, 6in. diam., 5oz. $1,750

Mixed metal salver in the Persian taste by Tiffany & Co., New York, New York, circa 1880, of shaped octagonal form, 12in. wide, 26oz. 14 dwts.
(Butterfield & Butterfield) $9,350

A small salver, square, with cusped corners and a molded rim, by Jacob Hurd, Boston, circa 1740-50, 5¾in. square, 5oz. $10,000

TRAYS & SALVERS

Tiffany & Co. Sterling Tray, New York, early 20th century, 20in. long., approximately 74 troy oz. $2,000

A silver smoking tray, by Tiffany & Company, New York, circa 1900, the hammer faceted tray with three rectangular wells for cigars and cigarettes, 10¼in. wide, 30oz. $1,750

An oval silver salver, by Wm. Forbes for Ball, Tompkins & Black, N.Y., 1839/51. 13in. long, 24oz.10dwt. $750

A silver tazza on circular foot, by Gorham Mfg. Co., bearing the mark of Kennard & Jenks, Boston, circa 1880, 10½in. diam., 19oz. (Christie's) $13,200

A Tiffany sterling silver sealing wax set, N.Y., circa 1891-1902, 8½in. sq., wt. approx. 20 troy oz. $1,000

A silver tray, by Howard & Co., N.Y., circa 1900, 18¼in. diam., 78oz.10dwt. $2,000

A silver salver on four cast foliate lion's paw feet, by Obadiah Rich, Boston, circa 1835, 14in. diam., 47oz. $800

One of a pair of silver bread trays with open foliate handles, by S. Kirk & Son Co., Baltimore, 1903-07, 14¼in. long, 44oz. $2,000

A sterling silver strapwork tray, signed Shreve & Co. San Francisco Sterling, circa 1918. 12½in. diam., 26 troy oz. $850

TUREENS

A fine silver tureen and cover by Tiffany & Co flanked either side with scroll handles, 12½in. high, 68oz.10dwt. **$6,000**

A covered tureen, by Samuel Kirk & Son, Baltimore, 1880-1890, the low domed cover with a pineapple finial, marked, 10in. high, 57oz. **$2,250**

A silver covered tureen, maker's mark of Tiffany & Co., New York, 1875–1891, the foot and lower body repoussé with spiral flutes, 11in. wide, 41 oz. (Christie's) **$3,850**

One of a pair of silver sauce tureens, maker's mark of Edward Lownes, Philadelphia, circa 1825, the sides applied with cast vintage decoration and two cast handles, 48 oz. (Christie's) (Two) **$17,600**

A covered soup tureen, with domed oval lid, by Bailey & Kitchen, Phila., 1833-46, 15½in. high, 16in. wide, 127oz. **$4,250**

'Japanese Movement' Sterling soup tureen with cover and associated ladle by Tiffany & Co., New York, New York, circa 1881, 13in. wide, together with a Tiffany & Co. soup ladle. (Butterfield & Butterfield) **$13,200**

A covered soup tureen by William Gale, Jr., New York; retailed by Ford & Tupper, circa 1860, with a cast steer finial above repoussé and chased grass, 11¾in. high, 90 oz. (Christie's) **$8,250**

S. Kirk and Son repoussé silver covered tureen, circa 1885, round with pineapple finial, 10½in. high, approximately 49 troy oz. (Skinner Inc.) **$4,290**

A silver covered sauce tureen, maker's mark of Gorham Mfg. Co., Providence, 1868, the angular handles surmounted by alligators and terminating in a flowerhead and ribbon, 7¼in. wide, 15 oz. 10 dwt. (Christie's) **$3,080**

URNS

Tiffany sterling coffee urn on stand, 1938–47, tapering fluted body cast with basketweave and Renaissance motifs, 15in. high, approximately 90½ oz. $7,500

A silver plated Art Nouveau covered urn, circa 1900, 16¼in. high. $300

A tea urn, by Eoff & Shepherd for Ball, Black & Co., N.Y., 1839-51, 18in. high, 15in. wide, 112oz.10dwt. $4,000

A rare silver tea urn by Stephen Richard, New York, circa 1812, with a domed rectangular cover, a knop finial, a curved spigot and two cylindrical open handles, 14¾in. high, 104oz. (Christie's) $38,500

A rare tea urn, attributed to Edward and Samuel S. Rockwell, New York, circa 1825, on a shaped square base with four lion's paw feet, the spigot in the form of a dolphin, 16in. high, 139oz. (Christie's New York) $5,500

A silver tea urn, New York, circa 1810; maker's mark indistinct, probably those of John and Peter Targee, with a domed cover, ball finial, two ring handles, faceted spout, and flaring stem with square base, 15¾in. high, 68 oz. (Christie's) $4,180

A tea urn, by Gorham, Providence, 1890-1910, the conical cover with an ivory urn finial, marked, 17½in. high, gross weight 94oz. $2,250

A plated tea urn, by Gorham, Providence, 2nd half 19th century, on four angular supports each surmounted by a figure of a seated Chinese man, marked, 14¾in. high. $2,000

A coffee urn, with a conical cover, by Samuel Kirk & Son, Baltimore, probably 1846-61, 16½in. high, 56oz.10dwt. $4,000

VASES

Black, Starr and Frost sterling vase, New York, early 20th century, with an overall chased flowering clematis vine, 14³/₄in. high, approximately 44 troy oz. (Skinner Inc.) $3,000

A pierced vase by Tiffany & Co., New York, 1902–1907, with fluted sides, scalloped rim, scrolling handles and a repoussé foliate base, 11¹/₂in. high, 51 oz. 10 dwt. (Christie's) $5,000

A fine silver-mounted ivory vase, maker's mark of *Tiffany & Co., New York 1889–1891*, 17³/₄in. high. (Christie's) $24,200

A Vase by Tiffany & Company, New York, 1892, with two cast handles, each in the form of two swan's heads with elongated necks, 13¹/₄in. high, 30 oz. (Christie's) $5,000

Important Sterling silver trophy, 19th century, by Tiffany, cast handles in the form of angels holding children, either side with applied full, two-dimensional figures of women in diaphanous clothing, 24.8 troy oz. (Eldred's) $3,300

A fine silver, enamel and stone-set "Viking" vase, maker's mark of Tiffany & Co., New York, circa 1901, designed by Paulding Farnham, the shoulder applied with stylized masks, 12in. high, 30 oz. (Christie's) $22,000

A bud vase, the body inlaid in copper and niello with butterflies and cherry blossoms, by Tiffany & Co., 1872-91, 5in. high, 3oz.10dwt. (Christie's) $3,750

An enameled vase by Gorham, Providence, 1897, with a flaring square rim and foot, the front and back cast with a pond and lilypads, 7³/₄in. high, 16 oz. (Christie's) $2,750

A trophy vase by Whiting Manufacturing Co., New York, 1887, with a flaring scalloped rim, the sides etched with mermaids riding seahorses, 15¹/₂in. high, 37 oz. 10 dwt. (Christie's) $6,000

VASES

A silver enameled bud base, by Tiffany & Co., N.Y., circa 1893, 5.3/8in. high, 5oz.10dwt. (Christie's) $1,750

Gorham Sterling vase, circa 1878, repoussé decoration, chased stag's head handles, 9½in. high, approximately 19 troy oz.
(Skinner Inc.) $715

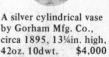

A silver cylindrical vase by Gorham Mfg. Co., circa 1895, 13¼in. high, 42oz. 10dwt. $4,000

A silver vase, maker's mark of Gorham Mfg. Co., Providence, circa 1910, applied with acanthus leaves and acanthus and geometric strapwork, 12³/₄in. high, 52 oz.
(Christie's) $3,850

Pair of silver vases by Gorham Manufacturing Co., marked 'Martele', 14½in. high, 69oz. 10dwt. $10,000

A rare presentation vase by W. K. Vanderslice, San Francisco, circa 1876, with a flaring rim and two scrolling handles enclosing pierced and chased oak leaves and acorns, 11⁵/₈in. high, 31 oz. 10 dwt.
(Christie's) $3,410

A vase by Towle, Newburyport, circa 1910, with a molded circular rim and footrim, 9⁵/₈in. high, 30 oz.
(Christie's) $1,250

A cut glass and silver vase by Gorham, Providence; glass by Hawkes, circa 1912, 15in. high. (Christie's) $2,250

An ovoid vase, by Tiffany & Co., N.Y., 1878-90, 6.5/8in. high, 14oz. (Christie's)
$8,500

473

VASES

A late 19th/early 20th century Arts & Crafts sterling silver vase, America, 22 troy oz.
$500

A vase of flaring cylindrical shape, by Tiffany & Co., 1903-07, 12¾in. high, 50oz. $2,000

An urn-shaped vase with two cast mask handles, by Shreve, Stanwood & Co., Boston, 1860-69, 13in. high, 24oz. $1,000

An urn-shaped vase, by Ball, Black & Co., N.Y., 1851-76, 9½in. high, 6oz.10dwt. $800

A rare elephant tusk humidor by Tiffany & Company, New York, the body formed by an oval shaped section of an elephant's tusk, repousse and chased in stylized floral motifs in the Indian taste, 10½in. high.
$10,450

A silver double vase on stand, by The Sweetser Co., New York, circa 1900-15, the stand of copper, 11½in. high, gross wt. of vase 20oz.10dwt. $2,000

WINE COOLERS

American Sterling Arts and Crafts wine cooler by Shreve & Co., San Francisco, California, circa 1909–1922, with pair bracket handles at sides, overall peened finish, 8½in. high, 45oz. 12dwts.
(Butterfield & Butterfield)
$2,475

Sterling silver two-handled champagne cooler by Shreve, Crump & Low, chased medial band, 10¾in. high, 36.8 troy oz. (Eldred's) $853

Art Nouveau Sterling wine cooler by Mauser Mfg. Co., New York, circa 1900–1910, with outwardly tapering sides rising to an irregular pierced lip applied with grape clusters and leaves, 10in. high, 72oz. 9 dwts.
(Butterfield & Butterfield)
$2,000

STOVES

Mid 19th century cast-iron stove, by Warnich & Liebrandt, Philadelphia, 26in. wide. $1,500

A 19th century Shaker iron stove, Canterbury, 17in. high. $1,000

Cast iron Franklin stove, America, 19th century, marked *Wilson & Co., Patent,* 56in. high. (Skinner Inc.) $1,500

An American Heating No. 14 luminous stove with smoke circulation and warming compartment, 1900. $1,500

Gas stove with side tap rail with six brass lever taps for three ring burners, two grill burners and the oven, circa 1905. $750

An American Heating No. 44 decorative luminous stove, with smoke circulation system and warming compartment, 1890. $1,250

Art Nouveau style pedestal table boiling burners, circa 1905. $200

Shaker iron stove, probably Harvard, Massachusetts, circa 1800, the lift lid above a base with canted corners on cabriole legs, ending in wrought penny feet, 26in. high. (Skinner Inc.) $4,675

The American Heating No. 12 light oven with glimmer glass to all sides and urn finial, 143cm. high, circa 1900. (Auction Team Koeln) $1,750

475

President Chester A. Arthur's Parade flag, red wool field of several sections, American, circa 1883, 69 x 45in. $1,650

A fine and rare pictorial needlework single pocketbook, probably Rhode Island, third quarter 18th century, worked in wool tent stitch, 5in. high. (Christie's) $18,700

Thirteen Star American flag, circa 1810, 28 x 45in. (Robt. W. Skinner Inc.) $450

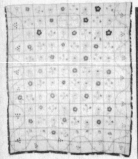

Embroidered blanket, *Lucretia Brush Busti, 1831,* probably New York, each square of white and blue checked wool, 6ft.4in. x 7ft.4in. (Skinner Inc.) $3,000

Mid 18th century Boston School needlework picture of a shepherdess and piper in a landscape, 19 x 14in. $90,000

Needlework and watercolor picture, America, early 19th century, depicting a young lady seated under a tree, 5½in. (Skinner Inc.) $600

An 1812 Chippewa flag, made by the British to present to Indian War Chiefs, 21 x 34in., together with letters. $6,000

America, late 18th century, man's homespun cotton double breasted tailcoat. (Skinner Inc.) $660

A needlework picture worked in polychrome silk threads on a natural ground, by Lois Burnham, Mass., 1775, 15¾ x 22in. (Christie's) $2,420

Gentleman's dress waistcoat, late 18th century, satin weave silk embroidered with silk and metallic threads and heightened with spangles. (Skinner Inc.) $605

Muhammad Ali World Championship autographed fight trunks, worn during the Ali vs. George Foreman Championship bout in Zaire on October 31, 1974. (Christie's N. York) $13,200

Needlework picture, worked by a Mehitable Goddard, Sutton and Worcester, Massachusetts, circa 1770, inscribed with the initial *MM* and *The 24 chapter of Genesis*, 14¹/₂ x 10¹/₂in. (Skinner Inc.) $7,000

A needlework single pocketbook, signed Ann Pitman, Rhode Island, and dated 1793, worked in Queen's stitch, 4¼in. high. (Christie's) $440

Needlework picture, 'Mary Anne Rowe's Work, Reading, 1834', Penn., silk yarns on canvas, 18 x 22½in. (Robt. W. Skinner Inc.) $15,000

Embroidered friendship bed cover, Massachusetts, late 19th/ early 20th century, square muslin patches embroidered with various motifs, 65 x 76in. (Skinner Inc.) $412

A silk-on-linen needlework picture, signed *Martha D. Ball*, American, early 19th century, worked in polychrome silk threads on a linen ground with a house surmounted by a flag on a hillock, 14¹/₄ x 12¹/₈in. (Christie's) $2,090

Pair of child's western chaps, circa 1920, label reads, *A.J. Williamson, Casper, Wyo.* (Eldred's) $220

Knitted appeal to President Andrew Johnson, Washington Insane Asylum, February, 1868, worked with yarns in brown, red, gray blue and natural wool, 20 x 28in. (Skinner Inc.) $1,100

TIN

Large presentation tin and wood foot warmer, America, early 19th century, heavy wooden frame with turned corner posts, 9in. high. (Skinner Inc.) $1,700

Painted and decorated tin coffee pot, America, 19th century, hinged domed lid above flaring conical form, 8½in. high. (Skinner Inc.) $1,300

Painted and decorated tin document box, America, early 19th century, asphaltum ground decorated with yellow swags, 8in. wide. (Skinner Inc.) $300

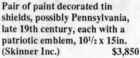

Punchwork decorated tin coffee pot, Pennsylvania, early 19th century, with potted tulip design, hinged lid with brass finial, 11in. high. (Skinner Inc.) $1,400

Pair of paint decorated tin shields, possibly Pennsylvania, late 19th century, each with a patriotic emblem, 10½ x 15in. (Skinner Inc.) $3,850

A painted toleware coffee pot, attributed to Louis Zeitz, Pennsylvania, early 19th century, the stepped dome lid with brass finial, 12in. high. (Christie's) $2,090

'White Rock' advertising tip tray, copy reads 'White Rock, The World's Best Table Water.' $125

Painted Tin Trade sign, America, 19th century, painted ochre and green (paint loss), 8in. high. (Skinner Inc.) $1,100

Painted and decorated tin coffee pot, America, 19th century, of flaring conical form with straight spout and strap handle, 21.3cm. high. (Skinner Inc.) $800

Painted tin panel, Pennsylvania, circa 1870, depicting an American eagle with outspread wings grasping a banner inscribed *Rainbow Fire Company*, 9½ x 13½in. (Skinner Inc.) $1,500

Pair of tin whale oil chamber lamps, America, 19th century, 11in. high. (Skinner Inc.) $375

Painted and decorated tin bread tray, America, 19th century, shallow rectangular form with bowed ends, 13in. long. (Skinner Inc.) $800

Painted and decorated tin coffee pot, America, first half 19th century, with polychrome floral roundels and yellow stylized leaves, 10½in. high. (Skinner Inc.) $1,000

Rare pair of painted and decorated tin wall sconces, New England, circa 1830, each with crimped circular crest, 13½in. high. (Skinner Inc.) $1,800

Late 19th century American Toleware painted and stenciled chocolate pot, 8½in. high. (Christie's) $1,100

Painted and decorated tin tray, 19th century, stenciled and free hand decoration in green, yellow, red and brown, 65.7 x 48.3cm. (Skinner Inc.) $950

A painted and decorated toleware document box, probably Massachusetts, early 19th century, 9¾in. wide. (Christie's) $495

Painted and decorated tin bread tray, America, 19th century, having flowerheads and buds in red, green, and yellow, 12¾in. long. (Skinner Inc.) $650

Painted and decorated baby carriage, America, 19th/20th century, painted light green and heightened with red and black pinstriping. $325

A Keystone aerial ladder truck, finished in red and having twin side ladders and bell on the hood, the sides having partial decals, 30in. long. (Butterfield & Butterfield) $660

A number "7" American national pedal car, circa 1910, of tin, wood and brass, finished predominately in red with cream and green rectangular striping, 42in. long. (Christie's) $9,900

A rare 'laughing Roosevelt teddy bear', with dark golden mohair plush, glass eyes, jointed arms and legs, by Columbia Teddy Bears Manufacturers, circa 1907, 23in. high. $850

A fine Landau baby carriage, circa 1870, by S. H. Kimball, Boston, Mass, featuring a turned push bar, 40in. long. $4,500

'The Juba Dancers', carved and stained wood mechanical toy, by Ives, U.S.A., circa 1874, 10in. high. $750

Marx tin wind-up Moon Mullins and Kayo Handcar, America, 1920's, 5½in. high. $600

Tootsietoy Greyhound Bus (U.S.A.), diecast, circa 1940. $100

Max lithographed tin Amos and Andy, N.Y., 1930, 11½in. high. $800

Six-piece carved wooden leopard, by Schoenhut of Philadelphia, 7in. $300

An extremely rare boxed "Buck Rogers" set of six figures, circa 1935, made by Britains Ltd. exclusively for the John Dille (USA) Company, all approximately 2¼in. tall. (Christie's) $3,740

A large Ohio pressed steel roadster finished in red and black with gray and red wheels, 18½in. long. (Butterfield & Butterfield) $523

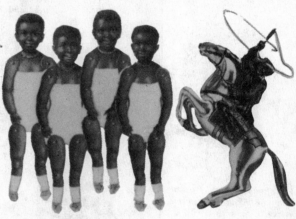

A beechwood child's perambulator, with gilt metal fittings, painted dark green, upholstered in American cloth, 52in. long, circa 1880. $800

Set of four articulated paper dolls, circa 1890, each 9in. high. $100

Marx, clockwork Hi-Yo-The Lone Ranger, boxed. $200

Painted and decorated baby carriage, America, late 19th century, ground painted white and heightened with blue and yellow, 56in. long. (Skinner Inc.) $550

All Metal Toy Co. (U.S.A.), tinplate coach, 1940's. $75

Nomura, friction The Great Swanee River Paddle Steamer, colorfully lithographed with deck details and passengers, 27cm. $150

'Popeye the Sailor', No. 268, a printed and painted tinplate toy of the cartoon sailor in a rowing boat, 14in. long, by the Hoge Mfg. Co., Inc., USA., circa 1935. $3,500

Painted composition cat squeak toy, America, late 19th century, painted white with orange and black markings seated on a bellows base, 7³/₄in. high. (Skinner Inc.) $1,250

A 'Hillclimber' ship with four lifeboats and twin stacks, the boat finished in light gray with stylized green waves around base, 12¹/₂in. long. (Butterfield & Butterfield)

$330

The famous George Brown tinplate "Charles" hose reel, circa 1875, finished with beautiful hand-painted decorative scroll work, probably the rarest early American tin toy known to exist, 23in. long. (Christie's) $231,000

'Last in Space Robot', 1970 American, plastic battery operated robot. $200

A Lincoln pedal car, circa 1935, finished in lime green with fenders/running boards, features include chrome plate steering wheel, 45in. long. (Christie's) $8,800

American composition character automaton, circa 1880, 21in. high. $800

'Sparkling Rocket Fighter Ship', a printed and painted tinplate rocket fighter, by Marx, American, 1950's, 12in. long. (Christie's) $400

Carved and painted dancing toy, probably America, 19th century, in the form of a black man wearing a black vest, 11½in. high. (Skinner Inc.) $1,750

An Arnold lithographed tinplate clockwork motorcycle, with civilian rider, luggage rack and sparkling-flint headlamp, late 1930's, 7½in. long. (Christie's) **$522**

A golden plush-covered musical teddy bear, playing Sonny Boy by Al Jolson, 20in. high, circa 1930. **$1,500**

Painted wood model of a milk wagon, New England, early 20th century, each side decorated with seal of *H.P. Hood & Sons Dairy Products*, 22in. wide. (Skinner Inc.) **$2,090**

Lithographed tin Toonerville Trolley, New York, 1922, 6½in. high. **$1,000**

A lithographed stand-up American policeman dressed in blue and white uniform, a lever behind enables the figure to raise and lower his arms, 21cm. (Phillips) **$200**

American wooden doll's house by the Bliss Toy Co., Rhode Island, circa 1900, 18 x 12 x 9in. **$1,000**

American carved wooden five-piece goose, with two-part articulated head and throat, by Schoenhut of Philadelphia. **$500**

A brass 'Canary songster' photographer's birdie in maker's original box by the Risden Mfg. Co., Naugatuck, U.S.A. (Christie's S. Ken) **$1,000**

Late 19th century Connecticut clockwork dancing black couple, 10½in. high. **$5,000**

A three tier Williams No. 2 American type bar machine with 'grasshopper' mechanism, 1897. (Auction Team Koeln) $706

An unusual Burnett American typewriter with slanting type basket and streamlined shape, one of only four models known, 1907. (Auction Team Koeln) $8,988

A very early American Granville Automatic fender machine with two carriage return handles, by Mossberg & Granville Mfg. Co., Providence, Rhode Island, USA, 1896. (Auction Team Koeln) $2,499

An early American Remington No. 2 upstrike machine with special carriage return lever, *WH Jayne patent applied for,* 1879. (Auction Team Koeln) $513

An Odell No. 4 decorative American dial typewriter, nickel badly rubbed, 1889. (Auction Team Koeln) $963

A rare Daugherty American type bar machine, low serial no. 1871, 1890. (Auction Team Koeln) $1,798

A rare Buckner Lino-Typewriter keyboard machine for typesetters, adapted for Smith Premier 1 Model for practice purposes, circa 1896. (Auction Team Koeln) $1,798

A Columbia No. 2 very early typewriter, invented by New York clockmaker Charles Spiro, with large type wheel for large and small lettering, in fine mahogany case, 1884. (Auction Team Koeln) $4,173

A robust American Densmore No. 4 upstrike typewriter without cylinder turning buttons, 1902. (Auction Team Koeln) $481

American Standard Folding portable typewriter with fold over case, 1907. (Auction Team Koeln) $417

A rare Morris index typewriter, American, circa 1885. (Auction Team Koeln) $21,854

A very rare Crown American type wheel machine with controls by Byron A. Brooks, New York, 1894. (Auction Team Koeln) $15,407

A Rem-Sho Bronze American understrike typewriter with shift and copper colored housing, 1896. (Auction Team Koeln) $1,540

A Commercial Visible 'wasp waist' type bar machine with reverse hammer strike, in original wooden box, 1898. (Auction Team Koeln) $3,531

A Salter Improved No.5 typewriter, No. 2164, with gilt transfers and wood baseboard (bright parts corroded). (Christie's S. Ken) $4,330

The Fox No 23, decorative American front strike machine, 1906. (Auction Team Koeln) $328

A Columbia Bar-lock No. 11, American full keyboard typewriter with decorative type basket, two keys missing, 1900. (Auction Team Koeln) $245

A rare Bar-Lock Model 1b typewriter by Columbia Type Writer Co New York with highly ornate cast iron type basket. (Auction Team Koeln) $5,395

Cast zinc and molded copper weathervane, H. Howard & Co., West Bridgewater, Massachusetts, 1854-1867. 34in. long. (Skinner Inc.) $8,000

A zinc weather vane formed as a figure of a running fox, 28½in. wide. (Christie's) $440

A painted sheet iron small weathervane in the form of an Indian, American, late 19th/early 20th century, with feather headdress, traces of original paint, 15½in. high overall. (Christie's New York) $2,420

Molded copper weathervane, America, 19th century, flattened full bodied figure of 'Colonel Patchen', with an applied cast zinc head, 26½in. long. (Skinner Inc.) $1,700

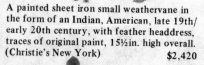

A gilt copper weather vane with fleur-de-lys finial, pierced with a winged dragon, 21in. high.(Christie's) $616

Molded copper weathervane, America, 19th century, the full bodied American eagle with outspread wings and a tilted head, wing span 24in. (Skinner Inc.) $500

Molded copper weathervane, possibly Cushing & White, Waltham, Massachusetts, 19th century, full bodied jockey astride a full bodied running horse, 26¼in. long. (Skinner Inc.) $2,400

A molded and gilded copper horse weathervane, by J. Howard & Co., Bridgewater, Massachusetts, third quarter 19th century, modeled in the form of a full bodied walking horse. (Christie's New York) $6,050

A 19th century running horse and hoop weathervane, America, 30in. long. $6,000

Molded copper weathervane, New England, 19th century, full bodied figure of a codfish with molded scales, 36in. long. (Skinner Inc.) $5,500

A cast molded and gilt pig weathervane, American, 19th century, the standing pig with applied ears and cast zinc curlique tail, 16in. high, 26in. long. (Christie's New York) $8,800

A 19th century iron weather vane formed as an Indian on horseback, 36½in. wide. $492

Sheet iron weathervane, America, 19th century, silhouette of a prancing horse, supported with iron bracing (bullet holes), 34in. long. (Skinner Inc.) $800

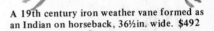

Molded copper weathervane, attributed to Harris & Co., Boston, 19th century, the flattened full bodied figure of a stag leaping over a flower covered log (regilt), 32½in. long. (Skinner Inc.) $10,000

Molded copper weathervane, attributed to Harris & Co., Boston, 19th century, flattened full bodied figure of a trotting horse pulling a sulky with a jockey, 33in. long. (Skinner Inc.) $800

A molded and gilt trotting horse weathervane, New England, 19th century, the fully extended trotting horse with cast zinc head, 42in. long, 21½in. high. (Christie's New York) $6,600

Copper and lead painted repoussé running horse, American, 19th century, the full-bodied figure painted yellow over old gilt, 42in. long. (Butterfield & Butterfield) $1,100

Copper airplane weather vane, 20th century, 25in. long. (Skinner Inc.) $770

Fine antique American horse weather vane, in copper and zinc, no pole, 26in. long. (Eldred's) $1,210

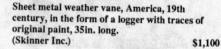

Sheet metal weather vane, America, 19th century, in the form of a logger with traces of original paint, 35in. long. (Skinner Inc.) $1,100

A cast zinc weathervane, possibly A.L. Jewell & Company, Waltham, Massachusetts, circa 1850–1867, in the form of a running centaur with bow and arrow and serrated tail, 27in. high, 33in. long. (Christie's) $2,090

Molded copper black hawk weather vane, America, 19th century, bole surface with traces of gilt, 25in. long. (Skinner Inc.) $2,530

Molded gilt copper Gabriel weather vane, attributed to Cushing & White, Waltham, Massachusetts, late 19th century, 30½in. long. (Skinner Inc.) $1,760

Molded copper weather vane, Cushing and White, Waltham, Massachusetts, second half 19th century, full-bodied figure of Dexter, fine verdigris surface, 43½in. long. (Skinner Inc.) $4,250

American molded and painted copper rooster weathervane, 19th century, with cut copper comb, crop and tail, the rooster with repoussé body painted green, yellow, brown and white, 32in. wide. (Butterfield & Butterfield) $5,225

A molded and gilded copper and zinc weathervane, attributed to J. Howard and Company, Bridgewater, Massachusetts, circa 1850–1868, the farmhouse form with uplifted ears above a modeled head and mane over a full body with raised right foreleg, 27in. high. (Christie's) $5,500

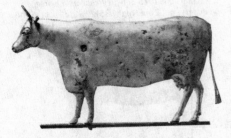

A gilded and molded copper cow weathervane, American, circa 1875, the standing cow with upswept horns and lifted ears above a modeled face, 27⅝in. long. (Christie's) $3,800

Molded copper rooster weather vane, America, 19th century, verdigris surface with traces of gilt, 20in. high. (Skinner Inc.) $1,870

A molded copper 'North Wind' weathervane, in the form of a cherub's head blowing stylized air, 23in. high, 56½in. long. $25,000

Copper car weathervane, Prides Crossing, Mass., circa 1914, 3ft.8in. long. $8,000

Late 19th century 'Racing Horse and Jockey' weathervane, U.S., 17in. long. Skinner Inc.) $5,000

A molded copper weathervane in the form of a running horse, by Harris & Co., Boston, circa 1878, 20in. high, 26in. wide. $2,000

'Mayflower' silhouette weathervane, attributed to E. G. Washburne & Co., N.Y., circa 1920, 36in. long. $3,000

An American 19th century cast iron horse weathervane, 26in. high, 35in. wide. $16,500

'Foxhound' weathervane, L. W. Cushing & Sons, Waltham, Mass., circa 1883, with traces of gold leaf and weathered verdigris surface, 27in. long. $12,500

A hollow gilt copper and cast iron weathervane in the form of a bull, American, 1885-1890, bull 39in. long, 23in. high. $4,000

A locomotive and tender copper weathervane, America, circa 1882, 61in. long. (Robt. W. Skinner Inc.) $185,000

A gilded centaur weathervane, probably A. L. Jewell & Co., Waltham, Mass., circa 1860, 30¼in. high, 40in. long. (Robt. W. Skinner Inc.) $130,000

Late 19th century trotting horse weathervane, made by J. Howard & Co., 40in. long. $12,000

A moulded copper stag weathervane, attributed to J. Harris & Co., Boston, circa 1879, 30½in. high. $28,000

'Flying Horse' weathervane, A. L. Jewell & Co., Waltham, Mass., circa 1870, 35½in. long. $7,000

Cast iron and sheet iron cock weathervane, U.S., circa 1860, 22in. high. $3,000

'Colonel Patchen' full bodied copper running horse weathervane, America, late 19th century, 40½in. long. $1,750

Late 19th century ewe weathervane, molded sheet copper body and tail with cast metal head, 29in. wide, 18in. high, America. $1,500

Molded copper and zinc weather vane, stamped *A L Jewell & Co Waltham, Mass* 1852–1861, in the form of Ethan Allen, (bullet holes, imperfections), 42in. long.
(Skinner Inc.) $4,400

A molded copper weathervane, American, late 19th/early 20th century, modeled in the form of a shooting star continuing to a serrated and fluted banner mounted on a spire, 41in. long.
(Christie's) $7,150

American molded and patinated zinc trotting horse weathervane, late 19th/early 20th century, with flowing mane and tail, 39in. high.
(Butterfield & Butterfield) $1,210

A silhouette sheet iron weathervane, American, 19th century, depicting a horse with cut ears, full tail, and raised foreleg and a standing groom holding his reins, 28³⁄₄in. long.
(Christie's) $1,870

A molded copper weathervane, American, late 19th century, modeled in the form of a full-bodied running horse with rippled mane and outstretched tail, 30¹⁄₄in. long.
(Christie's) $3,000

Gold leafed molded copper trade sign in the form of a horse, America, in the half round, 60in. long.
(Skinner Inc.) $4,675

Molded copper weather vane, New England, late 19th century, in the form of Smuggler, fine verdigris surface, traces of bolle, 24 x 41in. (Skinner Inc.) **$2,640**

Carved and painted trumpeting angel weathervane, America, 19th century, the figure of a woman with trumpet painted white, black, pink and blue-green, 33¼in. wide. (Skinner Inc.) **$2,200**

Molded copper and zinc cow weather vane, attributed to Cushing and White, Waltham, Massachusetts, late 19th century, verdigris surface, 27½in. long. (Skinner Inc.) **$2,640**

Molded copper stag weather vane, attributed to Harris & Co., Boston, 19th century, with fine verdigris surface, (bullet holes), 31in. long. (Skinner Inc.) **$4,675**

A gilded and molded copper weathervane, American, late 19th century, the Angel Gabriel form with spreadwings rising above the figure attired in a loose shift blowing a horn and on raised foot balanced upon a ring-turned sphere, 39in. high. (Christie's) **$148,500**

A molded copper and zinc weathervane, American, late 19th century, cast in the form of a copper running horse with windswept mane ridden by a cast zinc jockey mounted on an iron rod, 33¼in. long. (Christie's) **$9,350**

Sheet copper weathervane, America, late 19th century, silhouette of a cannon, 24in. wide. $1,000

Mid 19th century cut out sheet iron banner weathervane, Lafayette, Rhode Island, 50in. long. $2,750

Mid 19th century American copper cow weathervane, possibly from the Howard Co., 15½in. high. $1,250

Copper bull weathervane, America, late 19th century, full-bodied figure standing bull, 18½in. high. $1,000

Cast iron horse weathervane, Rochester, New Hampshire, late 19th century, full bodied figure of a prancing horse, 36in. wide. $11,000

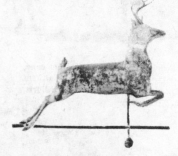

Mid 19th century molded copper and zinc leaping stag weathervane, New England, 27in. high, 30in. long. $5,500

A large late 19th century sheet iron horse weathervane, America, 30in. long. $750

A 19th century molded copper and zinc trotting horse weathervane, America, 23¼in. high, 34in. long. $3,400

Rare fire hose wagon weathervane, Mass., last quarter 19th century, full-bodied figure of copper horse pulling copper and iron hose wagon.　　　　　$55,000

Early 20th century copper train weathervane, America, 60in. long, 12½in. high.　　$11,000

Sheet iron train weathervane, America, late 19th/early 20th century, silhouette of Locomotive and tender on railroad track, 22in. long.　　　　　$1,000

19th century American fine moulded copper peacock weathervane, 20in. high.　　　　　$5,000

Full bodied copper rooster weathervane, by I. W. Cushing & Sons, Mass., 1883, 26in. high.　$4,000

A trumpeting angel silhouette weathervane, constructed of sheet iron, supported by wrought-iron strapping, New England, circa 1800, 59in. long.　　　　　$40,000

Mid 19th century copper telescope weathervane, New England, 62in. high, 49in. long.　　　　　$4,500

Late 19th century copper horse and trainer weathervane, America, traces of gold leaf under yellow **ocher** paint, 29in. long.　　　　　$4,000

A molded copper gorse-and- sulky weathervane, American, circa 1875, the hatted rider with crop and reins in hand atop the sulky, 30½in. long.
(Christie's) $11,000

A gilded and molded copper peacock weathervane, attributed to A.L. Jewell and Company, Waltham, Massachusetts, active 1852-1867, the lifted head above a slender neck over a shaped body.
(Christie's) $16,000

A fine and rare molded and gilt copper. weathervane attributed to A.L. Jewell & Co., Waltham, Massachusetts, circa 1870, the galloping shell-bodied centaur, with drawn bow and arrow and shaped head and beard, 39in. long.
(Christie's) $33,000

A molded copper and cast zinc horse weathervane, A.L. Jewell and Co., Waltham, Massachusetts, 1850–1867, with cast head and applied ears above a molded body, 17in. long.
(Christie's) $4,950

Fine small index horse weather vane, J. Howard & Co., Bridgewater, Massachusetts, third quarter 19th century, 18in. high.
(Skinner Inc.) $4,000

A painted copper weather vane, depicting a running fox, 31in. long.
(Christie's) $244

A molded copper gilt bull weathervane.
attributed to L.W. Cushing and Sons,
Waltham, Massachusetts, circa 1875, with
applied horns and cut ears, 29½in. long.
(Christie's) $6,050

Molded gilt copper and zinc weather vane,
America, late 19th century, in the figure of the
horse 'Colonel Patchen', 30in. long.
(Skinner Inc.) $1,100

An extremely rare and important molded
copper and zinc horse-and-rider weathervane,
J. Howard and Company, West Bridgewater,
Massachusetts, circa 1860, 76½in. high,
36½in. wide.
(Christie's) $104,500

Copper weathervane, America, 20th century,
in the form of a sailboat with directionals,
26½in. wide.
(Skinner Inc.) $400

A large molded and gilt copper cow
weathervane, American, late 19th century,
with horns rising above copper ears and large
molded eyes, 36in. long.
(Christie's) $3,850

Large copper cow weathervane, America, late
19th century, 28in. high.
(Skinner Inc.) $500

A molded copper cow weathervane, probably Cushing & White, Waltham, Massachusetts, late 19th century, flattened full bodied figure of standing cow, 25in. long. (Robt. W. Skinner Inc.) $3,250

A copper and zinc horse and sulky weathervane, attributed to W. A. Snow, Boston, Massachusetts, late 19th century, 37in. wide. (Robt. W. Skinner Inc.) $8,000

A cast iron prancing horse weathervane, Rochester Iron Works, third quarter 19th century, the prancing horse with raised foreleg and wavy sheet metal tail, 27¾ x 36¼in. (Christie's) $4,950

A fine and rare molded and gilt copper weathervane, American, 19th century, modeled in the form of a centaur, 40in. long. $71,500

Cast zinc and copper weathervane, by J. Howard & Company, West Bridgewater, Massachusetts, circa 1875, 24¾in. wide. (Robt. W. Skinner Inc.) $3,000

A painted zinc horse weathervane, America, 19th century, flattened, full bodied figure of standing horse, with applied ears and glass eyes, approx. 29in. long. (Robt. W. Skinner Inc.) $2,700

A cast iron horse weathervane, American, 19th century, of a full bodied figure of a horse with raised foreleg, 35in. wide. (Christie's) $8,250

A molded copper trotting horse weathervane, America, 19th century, flattened full bodied figure of Black Hawk, 16in. high. (Robt. W. Skinner Inc.) $3,100

Large molded zinc and copper horse weathervane, America, 19th century, flattened full bodied figure of 'Colonel Patchen' (bullet holes). (Robt. W. Skinner Inc.)
$3,000

A copper and zinc cow weathervane, America, late 19th century, the full bodied copper figure of standing cow, 43in. long. (Robt. W. Skinner Inc.)
$1,800

Sheet copper weathervane, America, 19th century, the finial in the form of a sunflower molded in the full round, above a square banneret, 37in. wide (Robt. W Skinner Inc.)
$550

A molded sheet iron weathervane, American, late 18th/early 19th century, molded in the form of a swell bodied rooster, 54.3cm. high. (Christie's)
$132

A copper and zinc horse weathervane, attributed to A. L. Jewell & Co., Waltham, Massachusetts, 19th century, 29in. long. (Robt. W. Skinner Inc.)
$4,000

A molded and gilt copper weathervane, American, molded as a standing rooster with a sheet iron tail on a feathered arrow, 25in. high, 32in. long. (Christie's)
$1,210

Moulded gilt copper weathervane, America, 19th century, figure of an eagle with outspread wings perched above a sphere, 19in. high. (Robt. W. Skinner Inc.)
$2,600

A copper and zinc banneret weathervane, America, 19th century, surmounted by cast lightning bolt and ball finial, regilded, 72in. high, 66in. wide. (Robt. W. Skinner Inc.)
$1,600

Carved and painted eagle and shield, attributed to John H. Bellamy, Kittery Point, Maine, late 19th century, 55in. wide. (Skinner Inc.) $5,000

Probably 19th century carved and stained maple figure of an eagle, American, 34½in. high. (Christie's) $8,250

Large burl bowl, New England, 19th century, of deep circular form, 12¼in. diam. (Skinner Inc.) $850

Late 19th century painted wooden sled, America, 48½in. long, 12in. wide. (Robt. W. Skinner Inc.) $1,600

Two large carved and painted articulated dancing dolls, American, early 20th century, 43½in., 41in. high respectively. (Christie's) $2,000

A carved and painted pine parrot by William Schimmel, Cumberland Valley, Pennsylvania, 1865-1890, painted yellow, green, red and black, 10¼in. high. (Christie's New York) $7,700

A 19th century American carved wood butter stamp, depicting a standing pig on grass, and a cylindrical cover, top 5¾in. diam. (Christie's) $264

A rare carved and painted pine weathervane in the form of a spotted hen, New England, 1850-1860, 16½in. high. (Christie's) $24,200

A carved and painted cane, possibly the Balley Carver, Mount Pleasant, Berks County, Pennsylvania, carved as two faces, 38in. long. (Christie's) $660

WOOD

Mid 19th century painted wooden splint basket, probably Pennsylvania, 11 in. wide, 7½ in. high, 8 in. deep. $1,000

A 19th century American carved wooden rooster, 12½ in. high. $1,750

Late 18th century carved burl bowl, with carrying handles, America, 22½ in. diam. (Robt. W. Skinner Inc.) $1,600

A carved and painted wood figure, American, 19th century, in the form of a man wearing a tailcoat, 31 cm. high. (Christie's New York) $660

A stylized figure of a carved wooden horse, America, 23 in. high, 23 in. long. $1,500

A 19th century carved and polychrome allegorical figure, America, 52 in. high. (Robt. W. Skinner Inc.) $5,500

A carved and painted pine rooster by William Schimmel, Cumberland Valley, Pennsylvania, 1865-1890, painted yellow with carved red comb, 3¾ in. long. (Christie's)
$4,400

A carved walnut cakeboard, stamped *J. L. Watkins, N.Y.*, circa 1850, centering a mounted soldier enclosed by a foliate medallion, 10¾ x 10¾ in. (Christie's New York)
$825

A carved root cane, possibly the Balley Carver, Mount Pleasant, Berks County, Pennsylvania, carved as a dog's head, 35¼ in. long. (Christie's)
$352

Carved and painted eagle, New England, late 19th century, painted yellow and green, 36in. wide.
(Skinner Inc.) $880

A carved maple cane, possibly by John Simmons, Virginville, Berks Co., Pennsylvania, 19th century, carved as a steer's head, 36in. long. (Christie's)
                    $264

A carved mahogany wood figure, American, 20th century, in the form of a mermaid with fish-scale details, 42in. long.
(Christie's) $2,500

Carved polychrome wooden cigar store figure, America, circa 1900, of a seated man carved in the full round, 52in. high. (Skinner Inc.) $900

Walnut pastry mold, S. Y. Watkins, New York, first half of 19th century, carved with an American eagle, 10¾ x 11¼in. (Skinner Inc.)
                    $1,300

Carved and painted eagle, America, early 20th century, the stylized figure painted in naturalistic color, 13¾in. high.
(Skinner Inc.) $1,300

Shaker turned bowl with mustard wash, probably Harvard, Massachusetts, late 19th century, 9in. diameter.
(Skinner Inc.) $8,250

Carved and painted mermaid tavern sign, America, 19th century, 22in. long.
(Skinner Inc.) $3,190

Late 18th century carved hard pine spoon rack with chip carved decoration, New Jersey, 21in. high. $2,250

A gilded, painted, and carved pine eagle attributed to John Bellamy, Portsmouth, New Hampshire, mid/late 19th century, 43½in. wide.
(Christie's) $39,600

A 20th century American carved and painted full length wooden figure of a black man, 35in. high.
$2,500

Carved and painted American eagle, circa 1900, attributed to John Hales Bellamy (1836–1914), Kittery Point, Maine, wings heightened with gilt, 73in. wide.
(Skinner Inc.) $8,250

Automated wood and brass horse and sulky with driver, America, first half 20th century, the carved and painted driver, articulated horse with leather tack, 24in. long.
(Skinner Inc.) $3,500

Snowflake stand attributed to John Scholl (1827–1916), Germania, Pennsylvania, 1907–1916, painted in white and gold with a spoked snowflake-shaped wheel, 68in. high.
(Christie's) $8,800

Carved and painted figure of Uncle Sam on horseback, America, late 19th/early 20th century, 19in. high.
(Skinner Inc.) $4,400

Early 19th century pine staved tankard, probably New England, 11¾in. high. $450

Early 20th century primitive carved eagle, American, the body carved from a single block of pine, 21in. long.
(Robt. W. Skinner Inc.) $375

Carved and painted tavern figure of King Gambrinis, America, 19th century, 26½in. high.
(Skinner Inc.) $2,860

Carved and painted horse and sulky with driver, early 20th century, mounted above a shaped wooden stand (imperfections), 11¾in. long. (Skinner Inc.) $2,000

Carved gilt and painted wall plaque, attributed to John Haley Bellamy (1836–1914), Kittery Point, Maine, 28in. long. (Skinner Inc.) $2,800

Painted sunburst fixed slat louvred blind, New England, early 19th century, bearing the inscription *Mrs Mary Stone dec'd AEt. 26*, 23½in. wide. (Skinner Inc.) $2,100

Mid 19th century child's wooden velocipede, probably New York State, 31in. long. $450

A carved and painted tobacconist's trade figure, America, circa 1875, in the form of a standing Indian maiden with plumed headdress, long articulated hair and a fringed robe, 68¼in. high. (Christie's) $8,800

Miniature painted wooden pail, possibly Shaker, 19th century, with green and brown sponge decoration, 4½in. high. (Skinner Inc.) $650

Carved wooden panel, by Adelaine Alton Smith, Boston, 1909, mahogany relief carved grape clusters and vines, signed, 24in. high. (Skinner Inc.) $660

Shaker maple dipper, 19th century, 6in. diameter. (Skinner Inc.) $500

Carved and painted parrot, probably Pennsylvania, late 19th/early 20th century, on a turned wooden base, 8¾in. high. (Robt. W. Skinner Inc.) $1,300

Paint and gilt decorated sled, America, late 19th century, painted blue and gilt inscribed *Elaine* at sides, 23¹/₂in. long. (Skinner Inc.) $935

Miniature carved and painted squirrel, America, early 20th century, 3¹/₂in. high. (Skinner Inc.) $225

Mid 19th century burl wood bowl, circular, with a molded rim, American, 24in. diam. $2,250

Firkin, 19th century, in pine, stamped *C. Wilder & Son, So. Hingham, Mass*, 10in. high. (Eldred's) $110

A 20th century carved wooden tobacconist figure, America, overall height 77½in. (Robt. W. Skinner Inc.) $2,500

Wood and wire birdcage, America, late 19th/early 20th century, in the form of a two storey building (imperfections), 25 x 25in. (Skinner Inc.) $550

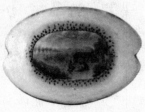

American School, late 19th century, carved and painted watermelon frame and genre scene, signed *R.S.P. 98*, 21 x 14¹/₂in. (Skinner Inc.) $1,540

Late 19th century carved and painted wooden boxer figure, America, 18in. high. $2,500

Late 19th century Folk Art painted and carved mechanized wooden model of five bearded men at work, America, base 18½in. long. $1,500

INDEX

INDEX